ELI GINZBERG

HYMAN BERMAN

The American Worker
in the Twentieth Century

A HISTORY THROUGH
AUTOBIOGRAPHIES

THE FREE PRESS OF GLENCOE

COLLIER-MACMILLAN LIMITED, LONDON

Second printing March 1964

For information, address:

The Free Press of Glencoe
A Division of The Macmillan Company,
The Crowell-Collier Publishing Company
60 Fifth Avenue, New York 11

DESIGNED BY JOAN LAWS

Library of Congress Catalog Card Number: 63-10649

Collier-Macmillan Canada, Ltd.,
Toronto, Ontario

To John A. Krout

Preface

THE Conservation of Human Resources Project at Columbia University has been carrying on basic research investigations into the multiple aspects of work and workers since 1950. As part of its initial design, the Conservation Project committed itself to pursue historical studies about the transformation of work in twentieth-century United States. In 1953 the Project published a monograph on *European Impressions of the American Worker,* and in 1959 it published *Women and Work in America,* both written by Robert W. Smuts.

Late in 1959, Mr. Smuts, under the general supervision of Dr. Henry David and myself, began the systematic collection of firsthand materials about the working and living conditions of the American wage earner during the past seven decades. When he left the staff a year later, Mr. Smuts had assembled some of the materials included in Chapter IV.

Dr. Hyman Berman joined the staff at that time and played a major role in developing the life history materials for most of Chapter IV and for Chapters VII and X as well as in helping to edit them for publication.

The life history material out of which this book has been constructed was garnered largely from four sources: personal accounts written by workers and published in periodicals or books, most of them obscure and out of print; testimony given by workers before federal and state legislative and administrative bodies; recorded materials in the depositories of oral history projects; and unpublished interviews with workers collected in the course of scientific investigations.

Most of the life histories in Chapter X—as well as some in Chapter VII—represent interviews that were made available by colleagues whose generous contributions are recorded explicitly in the Acknowledgments.

Several limitations and restrictions have helped to shape this volume. Major emphasis has been placed on the industrial wage earner. No attempt was made to exploit important manuscript collections, which itself would have been a major undertaking. The rich veins contained in novels were not mined. In two instances we sought interview materials underlying earlier major sociological investigations into work but found that they had been destroyed.

We explored in our search for usable materials many other sources, such as union archives, company files, printed materials in state historical societies, likely governmental sources. While some yielded interesting items, none survived the final selection. This helps to explain why certain important groups of industrial workers are not included.

Ruth Szold Ginzberg made a significant contribution to the preparation of the final manuscript by helping to reduce the initial selections, which totaled almost one million words, without sacrificing unique materials.

Eli Ginzberg, Director
Conservation of Human Resources

COLUMBIA UNIVERSITY
MARCH 1963

Acknowledgments

The scope of this volume was broadened by the willingness of publishers to grant permission for reprinting the following selections:

American Labor Education Service for "From North to South," from *I Am a Woman Worker*, edited by Andria Taylor Hourwich and Gladys L. Palmer, Affiliated Schools for Workers, 1936, pp. 17 ff.

American Management Association for "Assembly Line Worker," "Men and Machines" by Robert H. Guest, *Personnel*, May, 1955.

Institute of Industrial Relations, University of California, Berkeley, for the following three oral history interviews: "San Francisco Drayman," *Teamster Life in San Francisco Before World War I*, as told by William J. Conboy to Corinne L. Gilb, Spring, 1957; "The Milk Driver," *The Dairy Industry and the Milk Drivers Union in the San Francisco East Bay*, Woodie E. Daniels as told to Corinne L. Gilb and Jeffrey Cohelan, December 2, 1957; "Grocery Clerk," *The Early Days of Grocery Clerk Unionism*, Claude H. Jinkerson as told to Corinne L. Gilb and D. F. Silvin, February 25, 1958.

General Motors Corporation for "G.M. Draftsman," *My Job and Why I Like It*, 1948, pp. 71 ff.

Harcourt, Brace & World, Inc. and the author, for "Tirebuilders in Akron" and "On the Street," both from *Industrial Valley*, Ruth McKenney, 1939, pp. 93 ff. and 49 ff.

Harper and Row, Publishers, for "Giant Steel Worker," *From Many Lands*, Louis Adamic, 1940, pp. 147 ff.; "Skilled Foundrymen," *Steeltown*, Charles

R. Walker, 1950, pp. 230 ff.; "A Bomber an Hour," *Willow Run, A Study of Industrialization and Cultural Inadequacy,* Lowell Julliard Carr and James Edson Stermer, 1952, pp. 135 ff.

Holt, Rinehart and Winston for "Teamsters' Strike," *American City,* Charles Rumford Walker, 1937, Chs. VII and VIII. Copyright 1937 by Charles Rumford Walker.

University of North Carolina Press for the following selections from *These Are Our Lives,* W.P.A., 1939: "Lace Curtains," pp. 4 ff.; "Farm and Factory," pp. 224 ff.; "A Day at Kate B's House," pp. 135 ff.; "Grease Monkey to Knitter," pp. 166 ff.; "I'd Rather Die," pp. 236 ff.; "The Lord Will Take Care of You," pp. 231 ff.

Efforts were also made to secure permission to use "Child Workers," *Child Workers in America* by Katherine DuPre Lumpkin and Dorothy Wolff Douglas, McBride, 1937, pp. 4 ff.; "Alteration Painter," *Unvarnished,* Philip Zausner, Brotherhood, New York, 1941, pp. 28 ff.

The following colleagues and research institutions generously made available to us unpublished interviews: Robert J. Havighurst, University of Chicago—life histories #35, 36, 37, 38, 44, 45, 46, 76, 87, 88, 92, 93; Theodore V. Purcell, Loyola University—life histories #81, 82, 83, 86; Survey Research Center, University of Michigan—life histories #72, 73, 74, 80, 90, 91; William F. Whyte, Cornell University—life history #75; Richard C. Wilcock and Gladys L. Palmer, Institute of Industrial Relations, University of Illinois— life history #89.

Acknowledgment is also gratefully made to the following individuals whose assistance proved very helpful at different stages of the project:

Margaret F. Brickett, Librarian, U.S. Department of Labor, Washington, D.C.
Eleanor Coit, American Labor Education Service, New York City
Melville Dalton, Professor of Anthropology and Sociology, University of California, Los Angeles
Margaret S. Gordon, Associate Director, Institute of Industrial Relations, University of California, Berkeley
Walter J. Heacock, Director, Hagley Museum, Wilmington, Delaware
Gwendolyn Lloyd, Institute of Industrial Relations, University of California, Berkeley
Dorothy Kuhn Oko, Labor Education Specialist, New York Public Library
Vern K. Proctor, Employee Programs Section, General Motors Corporation
Stanley Seashore, Survey Research Center, University of Michigan, Ann Arbor
Donald F. Shaughnessy, Oral History Research Office, Columbia University
Louis M. Starr, Director, Oral History Research Office, Columbia University
David Sullivan, General President, Building Service Employees' International Union
Louis Waldman, Esq.

In preparing the final manuscript for press the authors were aided by Joan Shapiro, Lydia F. Augustson, and Patricia Farley.

Contents

Part Three

Part Four

Part Five

* For complete list of Life Histories, see Index of Cases.

Part
ONE

I

The Autobiography
of the American Worker

CONSIDERING the amount of time that men and women spend at work and the extent to which the conditions under which they work and the wages they receive shape their lives, we know surprisingly little about the world of work. Our best insights come from great novelists who fashion tales of significance out of the actions and reactions of people, ordinary and extraordinary.

But the insights of the novelist are not a substitute for hard historical fact or for the evaluative studies of social scientists. Yet, in the main, scholars have eschewed large-scale investigations into the role of work in contemporary society, perhaps because such inquiries are made so complex through the continuing and rapid changes in the conditions governing the ways in which people earn their livelihood and spend their leisure time.

The focus of this present study is on the wage earners—the men and women who do most of the world's work. There is no shortage of books concerned with the work and lives of statesmen and politicians, generals and admirals, business executives and labor leaders, even scientists and scholars. The successful have long been attracted to autobiography and have long served as subjects for biography. The records that are preserved from one generation to the next are limited

3

almost exclusively to the work of leaders. Hence, much of history is the history of the successes and failures of those who held positions of power and influence.

But a dull silence prevails when it comes to the work and lives of working men and women, those who grow the food we eat, mine the coal we burn, cut and stitch the clothing we wear, transport the goods we produce, type the letters we write, carry the mail we send, clean the hotel rooms we sleep in—and engage in the myriad other tasks essential in the manufacture, transportation, and merchandising of the goods and services that together constitute the work of a modern industrialized society.

These wage earners not only account for the vast majority of the population but they provide the heredity, the environment, and the developmental experiences for a high proportion of those who, in the next generation, will rise to positions of leadership and authority. So the true history of a nation can never be known unless we know about the work and lives of the laboring population—for they are the broad base on which all material achievement rests; they are the progenitors of a significant proportion of the talented minority who tomorrow will provide new meaning and direction for the nation; and finally the quality of the lives of these working men and women are the primary measure of the success of a democratic society.

But it is not easy to find materials that detail over a long period of time the working lives and experiences of large numbers of wage earners. We confront a major difficulty. Most of what is written is destroyed because the information seems unimportant. The facts of the ordinary lives of ordinary people—at what time they started to work, the conditions in the shop, how much time they had for lunch, what they ate, at what hour they quit, what they did after work, the conditions of their home, the number of wage earners in the family, how their present circumstances compare with what they had known in their youth, their aspirations for their children—these and many more facts, figures, and formulations, which surely were put down at least periodically on paper, did not appear worthy of preservation. So the letters, the notebooks, even the occasional diaries, as well as the fugitive magazines and newspapers that paid particular attention to the lives of working men, were likely to be lost to later generations. Few considered them worth preserving, for they spoke primarily of the struggles of ordinary men and women with the ordinary problems of life.

If we were to attempt merely the assemblage of materials without reference to their range and representativeness the yield would be quite different. For instance, a few industries such as coal mining and textiles have frequently been the center of economic difficulties, social concern, and political investigation, with the result that libraries contain a very sizable body of information about the men, women, and children who worked in the mine or at the loom. But this very richness is a trap if the student wants to learn about the conditions of the American working man in general rather than about the coal miner or textile worker in particular. In a democratic society which was slow in developing a public conscience in matters economic and social, the industries that present special problems are the ones most likely to attract and hold widespread attention. Hence the legislative inquiries, state and federal, with their volumes of testimony, are heavily biased in the direction of the pathological.

If we set out to tell the story of the most deprived and depressed sectors of the laboring population heavy reliance on such materials would be justified. But if the objective is to convey a more balanced picture of the entire wage-earning group, great care must be exercised not to rely too much on such pathological materials. A major task which confronted us was to search for a wide range of materials that would reflect conditions in widely disparate industries and regions. Even today the gulf between a skilled transportation worker in the Northwest and a migrant worker in the South or Southwest is immense. Early in the century the differences between North and South, rural and urban, white and Negro, man and woman, native-born and immigrant, skilled and unskilled were even greater.

The achievement of representativeness has been a major goal of the present study. A conscious effort has been made to include materials about workers from every important sector—agriculture, mining, heavy manufacturing, light manufacturing, transportation, merchandising, the service trades. Moreover, care has been taken to include different types of workers in terms of social and ethnic background, education and skill, and the area of the country in which they live. A major effort has been made to capture the range and variety of conditions prevailing in the American economy and society during the past seventy years.

As early as 1890 there were skilled workers who earned enough to be able to save as much as or more than they spent to keep their families well-fed, well-housed, and well-clothed; while at the same time there were unskilled laborers in the new mill towns of the Southeast who were in all respects, except in the eyes of the law, chattels of the owner, beholden to him for everything—their jobs, their homes, their food, their school, their church. One hundred years after the adoption of the Constitution they had few, if any, of the basic rights detailed therein. And these mill hands were not the only group of workers excluded, at least temporarily, from full participation in the good things of life that made the United States the dream of so many of the world's downtrodden and impoverished. Others, equally miserable, were found among the immigrants in the urban North and among the Negro population, which occupied the lowest rung in American society.

Today, the extremes found among the groups of the laboring population have been narrowed, but wide differences continue to exist between those at the top and at the bottom of the occupational ladder. It is not at all unusual for the family of a skilled worker in the North or West whose wife is also employed to earn $8000 or $9000 annually or even more; whereas a farm family in the Southeast may consider itself lucky to clear $2500 annually, even after allowance is made for the value of the food which they themselves grow and consume. The persistence of these substantial differentials in earnings, which are paralleled by differentials in living conditions, access to public services, and even political freedom, result in markedly different patterns of work and life among various subgroups of the American wage-earning population at the beginning of the 1960's.

This is a book about wage earners written by wage earners. The decision to limit the basic materials to firsthand accounts about how workers work, live and think represented the key commitment around which the project was constructed. While a great novelist is able to identify with the deeper springs of action and thought of his principal characters, even though his experience and theirs have little in common, there are few great novelists. Many students of social and economic life tend to see others in their own image. Their judgments about the work and life of the laboring population are likely to be projections, sometimes not even thinly disguised, of their own responses and reactions to specific conditions. Hence, much of the secondhand literature about the wage earner, written by men and women who have never held a routine laboring job, who do not know the rural or the urban slum, who have no real appreciation of the values and goals of the people who live close to the margin of poverty—this secondary literature is not a reliable guide.

This volume represents an effort to develop such a guide; in this book the American workers tell their own stories. In fact the book could well be entitled "The Autobiography of the American Worker," for such is its aim and objective. The interpretative chapters have been developed for the purpose of providing a setting for the life history collection. It is the personal accounts of the working men and women that form the core of this book.

It is our hope, in fact our expectation, that a great many different individuals with different interests will have an interest in the auto-biographical materials of the American worker. Not only the historian and the social scientist but also such diverse groups as politicians, ministers, writers, and philosophers will find meat here for their theories and criticisms. There remains the interested citizen—employer or employee—the fulcrum of a progressive democracy. His ability to pull his full weight as a member of the body politic is very much a function of his knowledge, his understanding, and his concern. These vivid life histories of the American worker during the past seven decades provide him with an opportunity to broaden and deepen his knowledge of an important segment of the nation's life and experience, knowledge that will provide a firmer foundation for charting its future.

II

The Historian,
the Social Scientist,
and the Worker

PARADOX prevails in scholarship as in life. If logic governed the actions of scholars, one would expect that many students would devote their talents to appraising the role of work in structuring the lives of people and communities. For it would be hard to find any phenomenon in contemporary life that exercises a more compulsive influence on the way in which men use their energies and in turn determines the rewards which they receive.

But—here is the paradox—this is not the case. While historians and social scientists for many decades have been concerned with studying selective aspects of work in an industrial society, their interests in these matters have not been focused on the worker himself. Before venturing an explanation for this strange phenomenon we will set out schematically, but necessarily briefly, the major thrust of such investigations as have been pursued. In order to keep such an account from becoming unwieldy, it will be restricted to the American scene, to this century, and it will be keyed primarily to representative studies concerned with the industrial worker.

8

The Historian and the Worker

All systems of classification are of limited value in that they inevitably result in the compression of much that is different into the same category. Yet no significant advance in understanding is possible unless a small risk is run in favor of a greater gain. Without classification it is necessary to cope with the full range of diversity, and that is usually beyond the power of even a very skillful analyst. Therefore, in full awareness of the dangers of over-generalization, we will attempt to classify the work of contemporary American historians in order to identify the place of labor history within this structure.

The vast majority of academic historians have always been concerned primarily with problems that lie within the broad field of political, military, and diplomatic history. The spate of new publications engendered by the centennial of the Civil War provides one index of their interest. The review of publishers' lists in the years preceding the centennial is confirmatory, as is a study of the course offerings in colleges and universities.

In addition American historians have long been interested in settlement and expansion. Many studies have been made about the Colonial period and considerable attention has been directed to the frontier and other specific regions, particularly the South.

More recently American historians have become increasingly concerned with the intellectual and social developments that helped to shape, and in turn were shaped by, the duality of our experience. The people who crossed the Atlantic brought much with them. Their tradition and attitudes affected the society into which they were absorbed. And the unusual hardships and unusual opportunities to which they were exposed left their mark on these new Americans.

Early in this century Charles Beard helped to focus attention on still another dimension of American experience by beginning his fundamental reassessments of the role of economic forces in our national development. For reasons that are not easy to understand, the study of economic history never attracted many students. In a nation so preoccupied with making goods and making money, one might have anticipated that the economic approach would quickly have found favor. But this did not happen. Part of the explanation may lie in the difficulties of gathering and evaluating the historical materials out of which our economic development can alone be reconstructed. Part may lie in the nature of graduate instruction. In graduate schools, the historians kept away from the economists and as a consequence they failed to acquire until very recently a body of theory and a collection of tools that could prove helpful to them. Again, part of the explanation may lie in the disinclination of most historians to approach the arena of class conflict.

Some years before Charles Beard began publishing his incisive reinterpretations of American history, Edwin R. A. Seligman, McVicker Professor of Political Economy at Columbia University and a highly respected member of the academic community, published his *Economic Interpretation of History,* in which he set out in a nonpolemical manner the essentials of Karl Marx's pioneering contribution to the study of history. Seligman's effort provided a cloak of respectability for others who might be inclined to pursue investigations into the economic realm, but most scholars continued to give problems of economic conflict a wide berth. There might be glory but not advancement or security for the scholar who dealt with issues of economic power and exploitation. These were the days, it should be recalled, when trustees of private and public institutions felt very strongly that faculty members should not present issues in any way that might give aid and comfort to radicals who were seeking to restrict and restrain the power and prerogatives of property.

Although Beard's influence was great, economic history never developed into a broad stream, and certainly it never became a mighty river. There were many excellent monographs about one or another facet of our economic development, but few broad studies.

In recent years business history, which has focused increasingly on studies of entrepreneurship, attracted investigators. But many become involved in writing company histories, and this is a type of undertaking that often inhibits the full use of the historian's critical capacities. There are some studies of scope and depth but not many.

Another strand was represented by textbook writers. They did their best to consolidate the new approach of considering the development of the nation largely in terms of its economic growth and transformation. But textbook writers are inevitably restricted to work that has gone before. Moreover they are limited in the interpretations which they can advance, for if these prove too new or too extreme, their central objective of seeing their books accepted in a large number of institutions will fail.

Economic history, then, had a modest development until its recent quickening. The cognate field of labor history—of primary interest in relation to this volume—has also had a modest record.

There are first and foremost the pioneering studies of John R. Commons and his disciples, particularly Selig Perlman and Philip Taft, who together with other collaborators produced many basic volumes dealing with the development of trade unionism and with organized labor's efforts to accomplish important social and economic objectives through political action.

There are Norman Ware's two comprehensive volumes on the industrial worker in the nineteenth century. There are a limited number of incisive historical studies of particular unions or of particular episodes in the struggle of labor for recognition and power, such as Henry David's *The History of the Haymarket Affair*. There are also a few studies dealing with immigrant workers and their trade union activities. Once again, there are a series of textbooks; but once again what these writers were able to accomplish was largely limited, restricted to what had previously been produced. Reference must also be made to the earlier and later work emanating from Johns Hopkins under the leadership of George E. Barnett and Jacob Hollander and including William Leiserson and Lloyd Ulman. The central concern of this school has been with the structure and functioning of the trade union as an institution.

Another field of work is the studies that deal with unions beyond the pale of respectability, such as Paul Brissenden's *Industrial Workers of the World;* David Saposs' *Left-Wing Unionism;* and Theodore Draper's comprehensive study of American Communism.

In a comprehensive inventory much more would have to be noted; the aim of this cursory review is simply to indicate that labor history in the United States has been first and foremost the history of the institutions of organized labor—the individual union, the American Federation of Labor, and more recently the Congress of Industrial Organizations. Secondly, it has been in part a byproduct of studies whose primary focus has been on political action and the vagaries of particular trade union activities in relation to such action. The field is now expanding. Two pieces of evidence are the large-scale project at Harvard University under John Dunlop, which has already resulted in several basic volumes, and the recent establishment of a magazine entitled "Labor History." But these signs of growth must not be exaggerated. Labor history does not now form, nor is it likely to form in the foreseeable future, an important segment of the total effort devoted to historical research.

Putting to one side for now a consideration of the weight of labor history, let us note that almost all work to date has been concentrated in and around the institutions—above all the trade union—that the working man created to advance his special claims. It would be hard to point to a single instance where he, the working man, has preempted the center of the stage. Irving Bernstein in his recent volume on *The Lean Years* did his best to shift the focus from the labor institutions to workers but a serious dearth of accessible materials made his effort only partially successful. Prior to Bernstein, it is questionable whether any historian was ever attracted to the idea of giving the stage to the individual worker.

The question as to why historians, one and all, eschewed this approach can be answered in terms of inadequate materials. But this answer is too simple. We know that historians are frequently able— if not immediately, then slowly and after a careful search—to find the materials they need to tell the story they consider worth telling. The story of the industrial worker in the United States spans a period of a century or less. It is the most recent period in our history and therefore it is the one most likely to yield materials.

There must be more to the story. One dominant theme in American historical research has been the unique role of the entrepreneur in our economic development. In contrast to Europe, the United States was built by the labor of the independent farmer, the independent craftsman, the independent businessman. We now know that at the apex of its development even the antebellum South had only a small number of slave owners, and a still smaller number of large plantation owners. The actual and the ideal type for several centuries of American economic development was the man who independently owned and managed his farm, his shop, or his business. Of course there were men who owned no property and who therefore had to hire themselves out to others. But the historian had little reason to pay particular attention to them for they were neither very numerous nor very powerful.

This original preoccupation with the role of leadership within the private enterprise system probably goes a long way to explain the historians' continuing lack of interest in the problems of the industrial working population even after it became much more numerous and significant as the industrial sector of the economy underwent very rapid expansion around the turn of this century.

Next, it is likely that the fact that so many of the new industrial work force were foreigners, or the children of foreigners, helped to perpetuate the historian's neglect. For foreigners were not Americans, they were Americans in transition, and as such their problems, difficulties, aspirations, and disappointments were relatively unimportant. They were not yet in the mainstream of American life. They would sooner or later join the mainstream and when that happened they would no longer have special characteristics.

A third explanation for the historian's lack of interest in the industrial wage earner is associated with his opinion that ownership was centrally important and that time would see the immigrant become fully assimilated. There was much evidence available, as there still is, that a man of capacity and determination can rise out of the class into which he was born and through his own efforts acquire property, status, and power. Historians shared with others a strong belief in social and economic mobility: People of ability are able to pull themselves up by their own bootstraps.

Since the ablest members of the laboring group could be expected to rise out of it and join the middle class or even the upper class, those who remained wage earners must be individuals of lesser capacity and motivation. The historian, therefore, who devoted his efforts to ferreting out the more potent levers of national progress, saw no reason to devote particular attention to wage earners.

One more explanation can be added for this neglect. Open society or no, most historians were not the sons of workers. Therefore they had little sympathetic understanding of the mainsprings of the actions which gave meaning and direction to the lives of working people. There is a wide barrier between the working man and the university scholar, a barrier that goes beyond a difference in background and experience, significant as these are. Throughout all of American history the working man has been interested, in Gompers' words, in "getting more." And while he has not usually been interested in fashioning revolutionary or even radical political instruments for this purpose he has been willing and able to use a wide assortment of devices, many of his own creation, to unsettle the status quo so as to increase his own rewards and power.

Basic therefore to the neglect of the industrial worker by the historian has been an implicit conflict of values. The student of the past is likely to be drawn to the study of those aspects of life and thought for which he feels an affinity. He is most likely to eschew that which is alien to him or to which he is hostile.

And so, if our speculations are not too far afield, it is no longer surprising that the industrial worker has escaped the interest and concern of the historian. But the fact that this is so makes it much more difficult for all of us to understand our own past, present, and future—in which the industrial worker has played, is playing, and will undoubtedly continue to play a role of major significance.

The Social Scientist and the Worker

It could be argued that it is not sensible or realistic to distinguish sharply between historians and social scientists with regard to the inquiry at hand. The distinction is more a matter of convenience than of conviction. The two groups have much in common; in fact, many labor historians, such as Commons and Ware, considered themselves, and have been considered by others, to be economists or sociologists. Moreover, many economists, as we shall soon see, have followed primarily an historical approach in evaluating changes in the conditions of the working population. Nevertheless, while considerable overlap exists between the work of the historians and that of social scientists, their respective approaches can be distinguished.

The Economists

American social science has long favored empirical studies, which helps to explain the early interest of Paul Douglas and Leo Wolman, among others, in developing statistical data concerning trends in wages, hours, and trade union membership. In recent years, this line of investigation has been broadened to include a wider range of considerations, for instance, the study of trends in occupational distribution, employment, and unemployment.

Once scholars begin to collect figures there is a tendency for them to broaden and deepen their efforts in order to improve the reliability and comprehensiveness of the data. The source data, especially for the more distant past which in the case of labor statistics usually means prior to World War I, are relatively sparse and unreliable. The student who seeks to build his analysis on a base of solid figures usually faces another difficulty: to establish comparability between data gathered in different time periods under different methods.

Since good data are better than poor data, students reared in an environment that places stress on scientific methodology are frequently drawn into efforts to improve the series with which they are working. Frequently this task of improving the statistical data becomes all-absorbing so that little time or effort remains for the assessment of other bodies of information that might prove illuminating. Moreover, the relevance of further refinements and improvements is not always clear. It may be a matter of little moment whether the original data understated daily earnings of American workers in the first decade of this century by a few cents, for there is so much else that cannot be pinned down: the extent of seasonal and cyclical unemployment; hours of overtime employment; how many workers held only part-time jobs; changes in the cost of living; number of wage earners in the family; and much else that is relevant to a deeper understanding of the sums earned and the standard of living maintained by the working population in decades past.

Another important cut-in point that empirically minded economists, such as Gladys Palmer and Margaret Gordon, have followed in more recent years has been the study of the labor market with regard to how particular regions or industries secure their manpower. Their interest stems in large measure from a concern with the role of labor mobility in economic development. It has long been believed that one of the major strengths of the American economy has been the willingness of its labor to move to wherever jobs are available. There is considerable justification for this assumption since the West and Southwest could never have grown at the rate they did in recent decades had they not been able to draw large numbers of workers from the East, the Middle West, and the South.

A second concern of students of the labor market was to learn more about the ways in which people hear about jobs, apply for them, and are screened; and also to discover the frequency with which they change jobs, employers, and locations. In all of these inquiries, the economists, such as Lloyd Reynolds, Charles Myers, and Richard Lester, seek to learn what is actually happening in the labor market. Often, they attempt to check on the simplified assumptions of the theorists, for example, the old contention of Adam Smith that people do not respond to the market in the same way as commodities. These students of the labor market have sought to bring the theories and the facts into closer alignment.

By far the largest group of labor economists have been concerned with studying the institutions of collective bargaining and the ways in which these institutions function. Some have focused on the individual union in its attempts to enhance the wages and working conditions of its members. These investigators usually develop their materials against a background of the changes that are under way in industrial technology, market conditions, and the larger socio-economic framework. Theirs is a special type of labor-industry analysis, with primary focus on the union and its members. The work of Lubin, Slichter, Jensen, Rees, Seidman, and Barbash come quickly to mind; there are many others who fit into this category.

At a somewhat higher level of generalization are the studies, made primarily after the onset of the New Deal, that have sought to appraise the changing fortunes of organized labor as a whole in a world characterized by depression, war, and relatively full employment.

In recent years there has been a plethora of studies devoted to one particular aspect of this more general development—whether or not, and the extent to which, the power of organized labor can be held responsible for the upward push of the price level. As one might expect, the conclusions of even the most elaborate of these analyses have been inconclusive, for economic theory alone is inadequate to such a subtle task.

The passage of the Wagner Act in 1935 represented a major structural shift in the political, legal, and administrative framework within which collective bargaining is ensconced. Since then there has been additional Federal legislation such as the Taft-Hartley and Landrum-Griffin Acts. There has also been considerable state legislation. With legislation has come a marked expansion in the elaboration of governmental administrative machinery concerned with the interpretation and implementation of the new legislation. Small wonder, therefore, that this area has been a focus of considerable research. It lies at the very heart of the daily operations of the trade union movement.

Still another approach that has found favor among the academic students of labor in recent decades has been comparative study of trade unionism in various industrialized countries, exemplified by the work of Walter Galenson and Maurice Neufeld. These have inquired into such problems as whether a particular trade union movement relies primarily on collective bargaining or on governmental action for achieving the claims of its membership; whether there is a national wage bargain or whether wage setting is highly decentralized; whether the trade unions place heavy stress on ideological and political indoctrination. These studies have indicated that it is very difficult to generalize across national boundaries. Where they exist in strength trade unions are so much an integral part of each nation's history that they must be evaluated largely in terms of the specific social and economic development of the people and the country of which they are a part.

Despite the substantial variety of approaches employed by economists in recent decades in the study of labor, one generalization of moment to the present inquiry can be ventured. The economists have focused their attention on various institutions characteristic of the contemporary economy and political structure that help to determine the demand and supply of labor, the conditions under which people work, and the wages and fringe benefits which they receive. But they seldom, if ever, directed their attention to the individual men and women who work. In this regard they resembled their colleagues in history who sought to generalize about the working population by considering the major drift of events without inquiry into the actions of individuals who brought the drift about. Nor did they consider the reactions of the drift on the individual men and women who comprise the working population which in turn comprises such a large segment of the total population.

Sociologists and the Worker

Just as the distinction between labor economists and labor historians is difficult to make and maintain, so it is with whatever distinctions are ventured between sociologists and their confreres in history and economics. To demonstrate: Early in this century two men who were members of economics faculties, Thorstein Veblen and Carleton Parker, wrote *The Instinct of Workmanship* and *The Casual Laborer.* The former is a broad treatment of the compulsive influence of the role of work on the structure and functioning of society; the latter is a specific analysis of the interplay between men on the periphery of society and the jobs that are open to them, most of which are seasonal, poorly paid, and performed under arduous conditions. Both these works are largely sociological. But the point at issue is not to classify these authors or their works but to indicate the blurring of the lines that exists between what has already been reviewed and that which follows.

The early years of this century saw substantial interest manifested by sociologists in many facets of the work and life of the American laboring population. The heart of their concern had three aspects— immigration, industrialization, urbanization—and the three were closely related. It is likely, although detailed evidence must still be developed, that at the turn of this century the capacity of the American economy to absorb ever larger numbers of people was entering a new phase. There developed among many sectors of the population an opposition to the continuing heavy immigration. Much of this came from groups of workers who feared that their wages and working conditions would be adversely affected if the inflow were not reduced, but many others, farmers, businessmen, and professionals, were concerned less with economic considerations and more with the prospective quality of American life and culture.

Many sociologists feared for the welfare of the nation if the immigrant stream were not controlled. These were E. A. Ross, Henry Pratt Fairchild, Madison Grant, and many others. The Immigration Commission of the early 1900's employed Jeremiah W. Laucks and William J. Jenks as their principal investigators. There was a surprising unanimity among these sociologists. One and all, they emphasized the great difficulties facing the United States in assimilating the newer immigrants from southern and eastern Europe in contrast to the ease of absorbing the earlier immigrants from western and northern Europe. They collected statistics to prove the existence of widespread pathology among these recent immigrant groups—criminality, insanity, poverty. Some had even more extreme views. They were certain that the newer immigrants were of basically poorer stock and an admixture of them with the superior stock represented by the native population could lead only to a long-term deterioration in the American of tomorrow. But it was not long before the shallowness of their analyses was revealed by, among others, Isaac A. Hourwich in his incisive studies. But where there is a will there is a way to have false doctrines gain acceptance. The disquietude of the public at large was constantly mounting. Though Taft and Wilson vetoed various bills, it is significant that Congress passed legislation repeatedly aimed at restricting the influx of new immigrants.

The sociologists were also concerned about other aspects of contemporary trends. These were the decades when the independent farmer was being pushed away from the center of the economy to make way for the new industrial empires with their hordes of hired laborers. The United States had long adhered to the tradition that the fulcrum of its economic progress and political freedom was the independent man who was master of his property and of himself. It was this tradition that was buffeted by the rapid expansion of industry, for the employees of the new factories had neither property nor freedom. America was being rapidly transformed, and many of the sociologists who studied the transformation were deeply concerned. The negatives of industry were easy to observe: The destruction of the countryside; the widening gap between owners and workers; the corruption of politicians; the disregard for human rights—and much else that mocked the American dream with its promise of material well-being and political and social freedom for all.

The growth of the city slum was a further source of concern to the sociologists. They knew that only social disorder could result from herding large numbers into a small area where they had to live on top of each other in bad housing, with little or no play space for children, with few supportive institutions to help them over personal emergencies such as loss of a job, loss of a spouse, or other traumatic experiences. Moreover, the fact that so many of the inhabitants of slum areas were recent immigrants presented a basic threat to a progressive society. Many of the new arrivals continued to speak a foreign tongue, follow foreign practices and, most damaging of all, looked forward to the time when they would have accumulated enough money to return to their native country. Here was assuredly an indigestible nut.

And so the early sociologists centered their work on problems of population and social pathology. In this they came closer than either the historians or the economists to studying the problems of laboring men and women. Their assumptions may not always have been valid; their data were frequently selective; they could not foresee the potential for progress in the new industrialization and they had no way of knowing about the changes that World War I would bring in its wake. But much of their work was focused on real people with real problems.

The two decades following the end of World War I saw a marked expansion in the scope and depth of sociological studies of the adjustment of the working population. The range of inquiries was substantial; many studies included the analysis of a region, ethnic groups, income classes, or the working population's response to crisis, such as unemployment.

Sociologists at the University of North Carolina, especially Howard W. Odum and Rupert B. Vance, were responsible for large-scale and penetrating studies of the ways in which the laboring man in the Southeast, white or Negro, had been affected by and in turn helped to shape the substantial transformations under way in a region where industrialization had a late start, and where its development had moved forward only in certain industries rather than across a broad base.

Florian Znaniecki and William I. Thomas in *The Polish Peasant in Europe and America* succeeded in capturing what had eluded most of their predecessors—the tension and turmoil inherent in the adjustments made by Eastern Europeans who had to shape a new life for themselves in twentieth-century United States. They made excellent use of the life histories of a representative group of these immigrants as the basic documents for social-psychological evaluation.

The Lynds, in *Middletown* and its sequel *Middletown in Transition*, established a new type of sociological inquiry. These studies, though not centered exclusively on the working population, inevitably devoted much attention to it in their effort to set out the structure and functioning of a modern American community. The Lynds included, among their primary objectives, an effort to make explicit the range of parallels and differences among representative groups in the community, using as their instrument of differentiation the dimension of power as reflected in economic well-being, which in turn was so greatly dependent on occupational status.

Somewhat later, W. Lloyd Warner and his collaborators extended and modified the approach of the Lynds in their five-volume study of Yankee City by centering their attention on social class and social status rather than on occupational role and income. Warner recognized that these two dimensions of life, the social and the economic, were not independent of each other and the Yankee City study includes an entire volume devoted to a strike.

The overwhelming impact of the Great Depression of the 1930's stimulated a series of studies about what prolonged unemployment does to people. Among the most important of these was E. Wight Bakke's two major volumes describing what transpired in the New Haven area. Robert C. Angell of Michigan sought to trace the impact of the depression on family structure and family life, and similar studies, though not as broadly conceived, were carried on by other investigators.

The late 'thirties also saw important studies of the economic position of minority groups. Especially notable was Horace R. Cayton and Sinclair Drake's penetrating analysis of the problems faced by the migrant Negro population which had moved to Chicago. In the early 1940's Gunnar Myrdal completed his comprehensive study of the Negro: *The American Dilemma*. An economist by training, Myrdal assembled a staff composed primarily of sociologists; many of the basic studies out of which he built his synthesis were developed by sociologists who analyzed the several institutions in American life that set the framework within which Negroes are raised, work, and live. Since the overwhelming majority of the Negro population was at the bottom of the economic ladder, *The American Dilemma* was concerned primarily with a segment of the working population which consisted mainly of unskilled workers.

Since the end of World War II sociologists have continued to study selected facets of the lives of American workers, but for the most part their concern has been more restricted and specialized than between the two World Wars. Robert J. Havighurst and his colleagues at the University of Chicago have studied various aspects of value formation and life planning among children from working-class families, with particular reference to these children's access to educational opportunity. They have also explored problem areas at the other end of the spectrum—the retirement and withdrawal of older persons from the labor force.

While much contemporary empirical research has had relatively narrow focus, the last decade or two has also seen some broad ideological inquiries into various aspects of the role of the working population in contemporary society. Seymour M. Lipset and Reinhard

Bendix at Berkeley have concerned themselves with classic questions of social mobility, the distribution of power, and political and administrative structures and their functioning. Many of these approaches have also interested other sociologists, such as David Riesman, David Bell, and C. Wright Mills.

Scientific research is always two-way: new instruments are applied to old problems; and new problems are studied with existing instruments. During the last few decades there has been a substantial expansion in survey and polling techniques. These new methods of inquiry consequently have recently been applied to studying the attitudes and behavior of different social and economic classes, including the wage-earning group. Among the more interesting explorations along these lines has been the work carried on by various research centers.

Stimulated by the work of Kurt Lewin, there has been during the last years a rapid development in the study of small groups. This approach was adapted to the story of the trade union local by, among others, Leonard R. Sayles and George Strauss. Advances in psychiatric knowledge, as well as in psychology, have also left their mark on labor studies. Arthur W. Kornhauser, for instance, has devoted particular attention to the study of labor conflict by applying new knowledge about emotional forces to analyses of individual and group behavior.

It would be possible to identify the work of a great many other sociologists and social psychologists who have contributed meaningfully to a deepened understanding of the working population. For instance there are studies of disadvantaged groups other than the Negro—in particular, studies of the Spanish-speaking population and of farm migrants. The woman worker has evoked many investigations. There is a considerable literature on families that are not self-supporting. Careful investigations have been made about particular occupational groups. Since the aim of this review, however, has been to indicate the range and type of studies that have been undertaken by sociologists rather than to prepare a comprehensive inventory, there is no need for further elaboration. The major axes have been identified.

Human Relations Specialists

Closely related but still distinct from the sociologists are the human relations specialists who might also be identified as industrial psychologists or industrial sociologists. They represent a tradition that spans a half century, and which began with the work of Frederick W. Taylor in the first decade of the twentieth century. Taylor, L. M. Gilbreth, C. E. Bedeaux and other imaginative consulting engineers came to realize that the productivity of American industry depended not only on improved machinery but on improved methods of putting machines and men together into an efficient system. They began to look at the factory as a laboratory in which the behavior of workers could be influenced by management policy—by changes in the physical conditions under which work was carried out, the quality of their supervision, and the reward and punishment structure.

The next major advance ascribable to these specialists was the pioneering work of Elton Mayo and his collaborators on the Hawthorne studies. Mayo saw the factory as a human organization, in which the physical forces—machinery, raw materials, gauges, and control systems—were of secondary importance. It was Mayo's contention, which he supported with imaginative empirical investigations, that the central challenge to management is to understand the psychological forces, individual and group, that determine the behavior of the work force. He contended that new understanding of these forces held the key to better morale and consequently higher productivity.

Mayo gained many converts among personnel managers and the last two decades have seen a vast proliferation of studies that have been based on his assumptions. While later investigators, such as the members of the Michigan Survey Research Center under the leadership of Rensis Likert, became aware that some of the simple relationships between morale and productivity which had been postulated by Mayo could not be substantiated, they nevertheless followed his broad approach of seeking to manipulate the psychological environment in order to raise worker productivity.

Shortly thereafter other human relations specialists, such as William F. Whyte at Cornell and Theodore V. Purcell at Loyola, considerably broadened the frames of their inquiry by making room in their investigations for the totality of the forces in the worker's environment not only on the job but also off the job. They stressed that workers were people with aspirations, conflicts, and needs and that their behavior with respect to their work could be properly appreciated only within a structure that was sufficiently broad to accommodate all relevant factors.

Still another type of inquiry that falls within the rubric of human relations is exemplified by such investigators as Burleigh Gardner, formerly of the University of Chicago, and William E. Henry who is still there, who have sought to illuminate various aspects of workers' behavior through the adaptation of personality theory. This brings them very close to the large number of psychologists who have found a berth in industrial personnel divisions where they have applied and modified the tools of their discipline so as to improve the processes of selection, assignment, and evaluation. Important as these efforts may be from the viewpoint of management they do not bear directly on the total life of the American worker and hence lie beyond the limits of this book.

Life Histories

The preceding review of the ways in which historians and social scientists have studied the American worker in the twentieth century points to one clear conclusion. They have not followed any unique or single method for delineating and evaluating the key factors that have helped to shape and give form to the work and lives of the laboring population. A second less obvious precipitant can also be distilled from this review. The scholars who have concerned themselves with the ways in which members of the working population prepare for work; the pattern of their experiences on the job; and the circumstances which determine their plane of living and give focus and direction to their thinking about the present and the future have made relatively little use of personal accounts of these matters. For the most part they have relied on secondary materials.

Yet there is much to commend an approach based on life histories and similar types of personal documents. The quality of a society is in large measure a reflection of the quality of the lives of its members; in a democratic society a key component is the quality of the lives of the great mass of the population.

Now it is very difficult indeed to probe beneath the objective manifestations of the world of work—the age at which young people begin to work, the number and types of jobs which they hold down, the wages which they earn, the length of the working week, and similar considerations—and to assess how the wage earner feels about himself, his family, and his future. Yet the student who seeks to understand what is happening to a society must explore these deeper levels of experience and meaning, for many of the crucial issues that he seeks to understand can be touched only at these levels.

There is a further reason for the historian and the social scientist to exploit the personal accounts of the work and lives of laboring men and women. The last seven decades have been marked by great orders of change that have deeply affected the working population. The composition of the labor force has been radically altered; the length of the work week has been dramatically shortened; the conditions under which work is carried out have been vastly improved with respect to both safety and cleanliness; the physical burden of working has been greatly reduced; the real income of the working population has been vastly expanded; and many other radical changes have taken place in the work and lives of the American worker.

While many scholars have succeeded in assembling and assessing the objective manifestations of these changes, the significance of these changes as perceived and responded to by the people most directly affected has been for the most part neglected.

This study of the life histories of the American worker will help fill these two important gaps. It will provide a basis for a deepened perspective of the lives of the working population, on and off the job, and it will provide an additional criterion for appraising the significance of the dynamic changes which have characterized the economy and society during the past several decades.

Many of the actions of men are determined by the exigencies of the moment, but the over-all quality of their lives is determined by long range considerations which involve the juxtaposition of expectations and reality. How a worker feels about his job, his wage, his standard of living, the prospects for his children depends as much, if not more, on his expectations as on the objective developments themselves. The unique contribution of the life history approach is the longitudinal axis it provides for the systematic study of the continuing interplay between the objective and the subjective, between reality and expectations. We hope the use of life histories for the study of the American worker in the twentieth century will prove itself.

Part
TWO

Part
TWO

III

The Turn of the Century

THERE are many ways of looking at human experience. One is through the eyes of the student who views the past from the vantage point of the present. Another is through the eyes of the participants, whose circumstances assume meaning and significance primarily in terms of their own past and their aspirations for the future. In an economy and society undergoing very rapid change, such as has characterized the United States in most decades, the prospect heightens for wide gaps to develop between the interpretations of students and the reality experienced by the participants. This is a particular danger in those areas where the changes have been greatest—as in the conditions under which people grow up, work, and live. Hence special care must be taken in an attempt to reconstruct for earlier periods the composition of the labor force, the nature of the economy, the conditions under which people worked, and the circumstances which shaped their pattern of living. Only thus will it be possible to penetrate beneath the surface and elicit something of the real quality of their lives as workers and citizens.

Population and Labor Force

By 1890 contemporary observers had noted that the frontier had vanished. The population of the United States was shifting rapidly from a primarily rural pattern to an urban society. But much had to happen before the full transformation to an industrial urbanized nation was achieved.

The dynamism of the period that we have designated as the turn of the century, which covered the years from the Depression of 1893 to the outbreak of World War I, is indicated by the sheer growth of the nation's population. The Census of 1890 revealed a total population of just under 63 million; the Census of 1910 totalled in excess of 92 million. Within these two decades, the total population increased by almost 50 per cent.

While most of the increase of about 30 million people represented an excess of births over deaths it is important to note that approximately 3.7 million immigrants entered the country in the decade 1891–1900, and an additional 8.8 million during the first decade of this century, or a total of about 12.5 million in the two decades.[1] While several million immigrants decided to leave the United States during these years, usually to return to their homeland, the vast majority elected to remain and contributed substantially to the rapid increase in population and the correspondingly rapid increase in the labor force.[2]

In 1890 the total labor force was approximately 22 million. As the new century was ushered in, it approached 27 million. And at the end of the first decade of this century it approximated 33 million. Thus the number of employed or employable persons had increased during these two decades by roughly 50 per cent.[3]

In the decade of most rapid immigration—1900 to 1910—when almost 9 million individuals from abroad arrived in the United States, less than 1 million were children under the age of fourteen. Since there were very few who immigrated who were too old to work and since many under the age of fourteen were able to find employment, the immigrant group contributed very substantially to swelling the labor force.[4]

In 1890 the vast majority of immigrants continued to come from northwestern Europe and Germany. By 1900 the pattern had shifted. The principal countries of origin were in central, eastern, and southern Europe, and these countries continued to be the major source of immigrants to the United States throughout all of the years up to the outbreak of World War I. A few figures underscore the magnitude of the shift. In 1890 about 445,000 emigrated to the United States from Europe. All but 160,000 came from England, Scandinavia, other north-western countries, and Germany. In 1910, total immigration from Europe was approximately 925,000. Of this number only about 200,000 came from northern or western Europe; the vast majority were from Austria, Hungary, Poland, Russia, and Italy.[5]

The occupational background of the immigrants was heavily weighted toward the lower end of the scale. Of a million immigrants who entered in one year toward the end of the first decade of this century, about four out of five reported that they had earned their living in their homeland as laborers, in farm or other unskilled employment, or as household servants. The remaining fifth had been, in descending order, craftsmen or operatives, managers or officials, clerical workers or professionals.[6]

Here was a large group of workers who, believing that they had little to lose and much to gain, were willing to pull up stakes, leave their homes, and cross an ocean in search of a new home and a new job. Having been accustomed at home to long hours, hard work, and little pay they were willing to continue the struggle in the New World. They looked forward, however, to the day when their efforts would be better rewarded and when they could enjoy more of the good things in life. Some expected their fortunes to shift immediately upon arrival. Most of this group were disappointed and many returned home. But the vast majority were willing to give the New World a chance to prove that it could be a good world.

In 1900, of a total population in the United States of 76 million, approximately 9 million, or 12 per cent, were Negro. About 8 million of the 9 million Negroes still lived in the South, where they accounted for more than 35 per cent of the total population. In contrast, in the Northeast the less than 400,000 Negroes accounted for less than 2 per cent of the total population; and the almost half million Negroes in the Northern Central states also accounted for less than 2 per cent of the total in that region. There were only 30,000 Negroes in the West out of a total population of over 4 million.[7] Located predominately in the South, the Negro was still living primarily on the land, seeking to make ends meet as a tenant farmer.

At the beginning of this century women accounted for less than one out of every five members of the labor force.[8] Of the women who worked, a much higher proportion were Negro than white, which was a reflection of tradition, poverty, and family structure. The heritage of slavery left the Negro woman as the responsible parent.

The majority of American women who were employed were young

girls from lower socio-economic groups who left school in their early teens and worked until they married, usually in their middle twenties. The others were for the most part widowed or had husbands who were unable or unwilling to support them. In 1890 only about one in six women who worked was married and living with her husband.[9]

Another aspect of the labor force at the turn of the century was the relatively large number of young people who held jobs. In 1890 the Census reported that about 1.5 million out of a total of about 23 million wage earners were between the ages of ten and fifteen, or roughly one in sixteen. There is no question that the figures are understated because many children who lived on the farm or in tenements worked at least part of the time but were not counted.[10]

Although, as noted earlier, agriculture had slipped by 1890 from a position where it accounted for more than half of the total employment, it still dominated the economy for it provided approximately 10 million out of 23 million jobs. Manufacturing, including the hand trades, the next largest sector, provided only about half as many jobs. Trade and finance provided employment for approximately 2 million persons. Transportation, construction, and domestic service each had a total of approximately 1.5 million gainful workers. Professional and governmental services, including education, accounted for about 1 million; and about 700,000 worked in mines, in forestry, or in fishing. Approximately another 700,000 were engaged in providing personal services other than those classified above.[11]

In the two decades between 1890 and 1910 the urban population increased from 27 million to 42 million, or by 55 per cent. During this same period the rural population increased from 41 to 50 million or by about 22 per cent. Since farm families tend to have considerably larger families than urban dwellers, these figures suggest what more detailed data confirm: at that time, many young adults, both men and women, left the farm for the city in search of a job, a spouse, and a better way of life. Labor in the industrial centers of the nation was drawn therefore not only from abroad where workers knew how to do a hard day's work under adverse conditions, but also from the farm. Large numbers of native-born young persons who likewise had been reared to a life of strenuous work were filtering into the city.

There is one additional aspect of the demographic structure of the United States at the turn of the century that warrants note. The 10 million foreign-born individuals living in this country were heavily concentrated in the industrial centers of the Northeast and North central states. Only about half a million had taken up residence in the South. In the Northeast the foreign born accounted for just under 25 per cent of the total population. But even these figures understate the heterogeneity of the culture in the United States at the turn of this century. It was truly a melting pot which provided an opportunity for a great many different groups to sink their roots and find employment, but continue nevertheless to follow the traditions and folkways they had brought with them.

To the 10 million who were foreign born must be added another 16 million who were of foreign-born or mixed parentage. Many of these were assimilated in the sense that their education, behavior, and outlook on life was indistinguishable from that of individuals with native-born parents. But many others had grown up and lived under European influences which were reflected in language, tradition, work, and social relations.

In 1900, the United States had a total population of 76 million. Of this number about 25 million lived in the South. Almost all of the 10 million foreign born and the 16 million of foreign and mixed parentage were included in the other 50 million. Thus only about one out of every two Americans outside of the South in 1900 was native born with native-born parents.[12]

The Employment Environment

The large numbers of immigrants who had left their homes and crossed the ocean to sink roots in the New World had done so in the belief that they would be able to find jobs, and that in time they would be able to better themselves and their children. For this they were willing to wrench themselves from their homes and loved ones and make the major efforts required to fit themselves into America's dynamic economy about which they had heard so much.

Many of those who immigrated toward the turn of the century arrived with little more than the clothes on their backs; the vast majority had no capital to tide them over a period of adjustment. They were under pressure to support themselves literally within a very few days after they arrived. In light of the crucial need of the immigrants for work it is not surprising that every significant fluctuation in the employment outlook in the United States was reflected, with about a year's lag, in the number of new arrivals. For instance the number of new immigrants in 1891 and again in 1892 totalled about 570,000. With the bad times initiated by the depression of 1893 persisting, the figure for 1895 dropped to about 260,000—considerably less than half of the total only four years earlier. This is but one piece of evidence, though very revealing, of the way in which economic fluctuations in this country affected the estimates of prospective immigrants of their chances of making a livelihood in the United States.

The years immediately following 1893 brought a great deal of hardship to the working man because jobs were scarce, wages were cut, and many had only short hours of work.[13] The magnitude of the distress brought on by the depression of 1893 is suggested by the estimate that at the low ebb of the cycle as many as three million workers, or approximately one out of every five nonagricultural workers, was without a job. The index of manufacturing production, which had reached a high point in 1892, dropped by about 15 per cent in the next two years and did not regain its former peak until about 1898.[14]

Among the more dramatic consequences of the depression were the "marches" on Washington of various "industrial armies," the best known of which was headed by Jacob S. Coxey. These groups wanted Congress to take the initiative to provide employment on highway and other public construction for those who were out of work.[15] This period also saw major labor turmoil which culminated in the Pullman strike which literally grew into a strike that involved all of the major railroads of the country and was finally broken only by the intervention of the federal government and the courts.[16]

One response to bad times has already been noted: the flow of immigrants slackened. Another was the return of many to their homeland. Undoubtedly many who suffered the hardships of unemployment and underemployment had previously questioned the wisdom of their relocating permanently in the United States. Bad times helped them resolve their indecision. Also included in the emigrating group were men who had made a success and were returning to their homeland where they could now look forward to a life of reasonable comfort and respect.

The depression also affected many who had moved into the city from nearby and more distant farm communities. Many among the recent arrivals had not yet firmly settled in the city and so they were able to pick themselves up and return home, at least temporarily, until the urban employment situation would again improve. The flow back to the farm of many recent migrants to the city undoubtedly helped reduce what might otherwise have been an impossible burden on local charity. As it was, many men, women, and children went hungry during the bad years following 1893.

The severe drop in production and employment during the middle 1890's must not obscure the dominant trend of the two decades which definitely broadened the industrial base and which was reflected in large-scale expansion in output and employment. In the ten years between 1897 and 1907 the index of manufacturing production almost doubled. If the year preceding the outbreak of World War I is compared with 1890, this index shows a gain of no less than 190 per cent. While much of this gain reflected large-scale capital investments, improvements in technology, and greater managerial skill, it depended in very considerable measure on large labor inputs.

Key to the worker's well-being is the availability of work. Next in importance is what he earns. He is also concerned with the number of hours that he must labor and the conditions under which he must work. Once the depression of the 1890's lifted, the direction of the economy was definitely favorable from the point of view of the worker. The first ten years of this century saw the creation of 900,000 additional jobs for laborers outside of agriculture; 700,000 more for service workers outside of private households; 1.7 million more for operatives and kindred workers. This expansion in jobs for laborers and semiskilled workers, amounting to 3.3 million, represented an increase of 40 per cent in a single decade.[17]

But the number of jobs available for the immigrant, the farm migrant, and the urban worker who had little to offer a prospective employer other than brawn was actually even larger. Many who had previously held these jobs were able to rise in the occupational scale and thus make room for others. At the same time that the absolute number of unskilled and semiskilled jobs was increasing rapidly, an even more rapid expansion occurred at the upper end of the occupational scale. For instance, in the first ten years of the century the number of professional, managerial, clerical, sales, and craftsmen jobs increased by 4.3 million, an expansion of about 53 per cent in a single decade.[18]

The two largest gains were experienced by clerical and kindred workers and by craftsmen—respectively 1.1 and 1.3 million. The first opened up many new opportunities for women as well as men, and the latter was the principal avenue for advancement for established industrial workers, many of them native born, who in the period of sustained expansion were able to move up the skill ladder.[19]

These years saw much antagonism between various groups of workers, between native-born and foreign-born as well as between groups composed of different ethnic and religious backgrounds. The only type of continuing conflict that was more or less avoided was between white and Negro, and that only because most Negroes remained in the South, largely on the farm. However the periodic use of Negroes as strikebreakers left deep scars. But the tension and conflicts among these different groups would have led to more explosions had it not been for the fact that such good opportunities existed for so many of the more firmly established employees to move up the skill and income ladders.

What about the other important determinants of the worker's adjustment to his work—his wages, hours of work, and the other conditions under which he is required to work? First of all it should be noted that the welfare of the working population will be affected not only by what they are paid per hour or per piece but also by the number of hours of employment that they are able to obtain during the course of the year. Beyond this, what they can buy with their wages depends on what is happening to the prices of the goods which they customarily use. In view of these many factors it is difficult to summarize trends in the real income of the working population, especially if we are to take note of the substantial differences in the circumstances of various groups.

Other factors must also be considered. Although most workers are paid as individuals they spend their income as members of a family unit. Consequently the family's position will be much affected by the number of wage earners there are. Some of the contribution of members of the family may be in kind. This was particularly true in earlier decades when the difference between one family and another was frequently a function of the housekeeping skills of the wives. If she were a skillful purchaser; if she were able to cook appetizing meals with inexpensive foods; if she were a skillful seamstress; if she were able to keep a vegetable garden and possibly even a cow and a few chickens—if she were able to do all this, and some energetic women did even more—then indeed her husband's and children's wages would be likely to go quite far. But if she were sickly, slovenly, or uninterested, she would spend much more money and would have much less to show for it.

We must also mention what now goes under the name of "fringe benefits." In former years this had its counterpart in the value of goods and services that many employers provided their workers without charge or at a nominal charge. The most important was housing. Many employers, especially in small villages, provided housing for their workers at no rent, or, more typically, at a rent below the market value of the housing. Fuel also was frequently provided at little or no cost. Depending on the location, the nature of the employment, the attitude of the employer, and the labor market, many other "benefits" were given to workers—for instance, gifts of food and clothing to domestic servants. This was typical in the upper-income families in the South.

These arrangements were not always a net benefit to the worker.

One need only recall the many mill towns where unscrupulous employers frequently established exorbitant prices on the goods handled by company stores; where they extended credit at usurious rates; and where whatever rent they charged was too high, for the shacks they offered their workers were unsuitable for human habitation.

All of these complexities make it difficult to assess working and living conditions at the turn of this century, when the economy was undergoing very rapid changes. But the major outlines can be presented.

In 1890, the average number of hours worked per week in manufacturing was 60, with the small unionized sector working about 54. Men in bituminous coal mining had a standard 60-hour week, while those in the building trades worked an average of about 51 hours and postal employees slightly less—48 hours.

Twenty years later saw some reduction in these hours but not much. There had been a decline of about 3½ hours in manufacturing shared by both the unionized and non-unionized sectors. The bituminous coal miners had made a significant gain in 1898 when their work week was reduced from 60 to under 53 hours, but in the next twelve years they were able to shave only one additional hour off the total.

The building trades made their gains in the few years following the recovery of the economy from the depression of 1893, particularly between 1898 and 1903 when their work week was reduced by about three hours. During the rest of the decade they were able to reduce their work week by only about one addition hour. There was no improvement whatever in the 48-hour week which the postal clerks had already achieved by 1890.

Average money earnings of manufacturing employees stood at the same figure in 1899 as it had in 1890—14.5 cents an hour; but the "real" value of the earnings was somewhat greater, for the consumer price index had dropped during this period by about 10 per cent. The next eleven years saw, however, a substantial rise in average money earnings from 14.5 to just under 20 cents an hour. But part of this gain was "eaten up" by increases in the prices for goods that workers had to pay. Nevertheless the real compensation of manufacturing employees calculated on an hourly basis improved over the two decades by approximately one-third. Most of this gain was achieved during the second decade.[20]

The single most important index of the well-being of the working population in a period when the price level is relatively stable is average annual earnings. In 1890 wage earners in manufacturing earned approximately $440 per annum. This was roughly $35 more than the amount earned by bituminous coal miners and about double

the earnings of farm laborers. Some groups of workers fared much better: clerical workers in manufacturing and railroading had annual
earnings of about $850, or close to double that of the average manu-
facturing employee. Workers in gas and utility industries did relatively well; their annual earnings approximated $690 or roughly 50
per cent more than manufacturing workers. Postal employees received
a little more than clerical workers, which made them the best paid of
any large group.[21]

During the next twenty years the annual earnings of wage earners
in manufacturing, which was $440 in 1890, increased to about $560
in 1910, more than 25 per cent. The earnings of clerical workers and
bituminous coal miners were increased by almost one-third. Postal
employees showed less of a gain than did manufacturing workers;
their earnings increased about 20 per cent. The earnings of gas and
electrical workers showed an actual decline; their earnings were about
10 per cent lower in 1910 than they had been in 1890.[22]

In appraising these figures it is important to bear in mind that the
general upward trend in annual earnings obtained in the face of some
decline in the number of hours worked. More significant is the fact
that individual workers who had been in the lower occupational
groupings in 1890 had succeeded in advancing into preferred sectors
of employment. Their gains of course were very substantial and reflected both the general upward shift in the wage level and the special
gains that they were able to make by adding to their skills.

Variations among different groups of workers during these two
decades were very substantial. There was a difference of about 300
per cent between the average for farm laborers and that for clerical
employees. The fact that the averages were so far apart suggests that
the total range was very much greater. There were children who
earned only 10 cents a day and steel workers who made up to $10 a
day![23]

The Larger Society

Among the important aspects of employment that are not directly
translatable into money is the frequency with which workers may be injured, may lose a limb or even their life as a result of industrial accidents. While accidents usually have a monetary consequence—loss of
wages and expenditures for medical care, their significance cannot be
gauged solely in dollar terms.

Although there are no reliable accident data that go back to the turn of the century except on a very limited basis, there is considerable evidence that attests to the fact that at that time employment was fraught with many serious risks and that, further, there was no ready protection for the worker in the event that he was injured on the job, even if the injury reflected negligence on the part of the employer. True, in such an event the injured working man could have recourse to the courts, but the remedy was more theoretical than practical for the working man usually knew little if anything about his rights, frequently had no savings with which to hire a lawyer, and even under the best of circumstances would face extraordinary difficulties in attempting to present proof that would hold up in a court of law.

The 1890's and the early 1900's witnessed the revulsion of large sections of society with the hazards and dangers to which many working people were exposed. Major disasters in mine, factory, and loft led to a considerable amount of protective legislation, including the beginnings of the all-important compulsory systems of workman's compensation, the first of which was passed by Maryland in 1902. However, major efforts at remedial legislation did not gain much momentum until near the end of the first decade of this century, and even then there were only a few states where a strong reform movement held sway, with Wisconsin and New York among the leaders. However many early efforts at constructive actions by legislatures were frequently put to naught by courts which in general refused to permit interference with the owners of property who until then were allowed to make any type of contract with people who sought to work for them.

Had reforms of the work place been forced to wait on shifts in political power and judicial interpretation, they would have been introduced very slowly indeed. Fortunately technological changes and advances in the art of management speeded many reforms. Employers found it to their advantage to establish clean and safe working environments with proper lighting and fresh air. And as their equipment became more expensive they became more aware that it could be properly operated and maintained only by workers who were encouraged to do their best and given the opportunity to do so. Hence many of the more egregious aspects of the new industrialism were transformed because of the self-interest of the industrialist as well as the promptings of the reformer.

A word about trade unions. As late as 1898 there were only a half million members in organized trade unions. Almost half of the union members were in two trades—transportation and building. During the next five years the total increased to just under two million, a gain of 300 per cent. This substantial growth largely reflected successful organizing in transportation and building trades and significant union successes in mining, heavy manufacturing, and in the food, liquor, and tobacco industries. Modest gains were also made in a great many other sectors.[24]

After its many faltering starts, Gompers had been able to put the American Federation of Labor on a path along which union progress might be slow but had a fair chance of becoming permanent. He set his sights on organizing the craftsmen and skilled workers; he stressed building locals from the ground up; and he assiduously avoided carrying more ideological baggage than was absolutely necessary to give some hegemony to the movement as a whole. But it was a tortuous struggle. Had it not been for the intervention of President Roosevelt in 1902 during the anthracite coal miners' strike the miners' organization might have gone under.

Every effort of labor to organize was met by strenuous opposition from the employer group who saw their prospects of power and profits in mortal jeopardy. The employers were convinced that, unless labor's aggression were met and contained, their own position would be permanently impaired. They consequently fought with all of the weapons under their control—economic pressure, blacklisting, labor spies, private armies, bribery, and all other instruments of private and political power that they could command or coerce. The success of their efforts can be read in the failure of the trade unions to make any appreciable gains in membership after 1903 until the end of the decade.[25]

Since about 10 million workers were employed in 1900 in sectors of the economy where unions had a toehold or prospects of gaining one, the fact that between 600,000 and 700,000 workers were involved in work stoppages during the first five years of the new century underscores the turbulence and turmoil that characterized the labor scene. While many of the strikes involved wages, many others were rooted in the struggle of the unions for recognition.[26]

In view of later gains in real earnings, in enhanced protection by government, in support in depth from their own organizations, in the heightened sensitivity of management and the public to human needs, the position of the American worker at the turn of the century has frequently been considered as very unsatisfactory. And as the following chapter makes clear many workers did live and work under appallingly poor conditions. What is worse, they had nothing to look forward to and there was little or no prospect for their children to escape from the grinding round of hard work, poverty, and despair. But as we shall see this was not true of the great majority. While there was much in their lives and work which they found unsatisfactory, their over-all view of their present circumstances and future prospects was favorable. For their point of reference was their own past, and most of them appreciated the fact that they were on the way up.

IV

Immigrants and
Migrants: Life Histories

Mill and Mine

1. GIANT STEEL WORKER

TO HIS multitudinous family, relatives, and friends, Anton Kmet
is Oché Toné—*oché* meaning "father" or "old man" in his native
Slovenian tongue, while Toné is the familiar abbreviation of his first
name. He is an old man, no doubt about that. . . .

His story, however, is not without significance, if that is the right
word to attach to anything pertaining to an old man who has never
been anything but a laborer. Perhaps I should say that parts of his
story are typical of many aged immigrants who have been in America
a long time without becoming citizens, and who are now dying at
an increasing rate—albeit Oché Toné is apt to live to be a hundred.
He wants to. . . .

At thirty, on landing at Castle Garden in New York Harbor, Toné
Kmet was what Slovenians call a *korenjak,* one who might be described as a "giant," or one constructed on a heroic scale. He was
six foot three and all bone, blood, muscle, and hide; strong and

straight as a pillar holding up the ceiling in a church, and not hard to look at otherwise.

From New York, Toné traveled in an immigrant train to Cleveland. The morning after he arrived there he joined the job-seeking crowd in the yard of the American Steel and Wire Company's mill on Fortieth Street. Taller by a head than almost anyone else on the scene, he was among the first hired that morning, and assigned to a German straw boss, who put him to work with two other laborers. The job consisted of putting great bundles and coils of wire from a platform into freight cars.

Mochan kot hrast—strong as an oak, Toné Kmet tossed the coils and bundles as though they were trifles. The straw boss noticed this immediately and called the boss, who called the assistant plant superintendent, who called the chief superintendent, who decided that with Toné around the other two workers had nothing to do, and, indeed, were in his way; so he ordered them taken off the job and left Toné alone to do the work of three men. This, Toné continued to do with the greatest of ease; in fact, he thought the job was somewhat of a sinecure, and soon he received a higher wage—12 cents an hour, while the other laborers were paid only 10.

He worked from ten to twelve hours daily, but not infrequently overtime stretched his workday to sixteen and occasionally even to eighteen hours. Sometimes his muscles creaked with fatigue when he took himself home, and he felt a little groggy, but thought he was doing all right, and America looked good to him. . . . Oché Toné likes to tell of those days:

"To get married and start a home was no great stunt then. Sometimes I got only $15 on payday, which came every two weeks, but that wasn't bad. You managed on $7 or $8 a week. If there was a lot of *obertaim* [overtime] and I brought home $18 or $20, that was something to let the neighbors know about.

"Believe it or not, for $35 we got everything we needed. . . . You could get a four-hundred-pound hog for $4; then there was enough meat and lard to last the winter and well into spring, if you did not have too large a family or too many boarders. If you went into a butcher shop and bought a few pounds of pork or beef, you got free of charge all the tripe and lungs you wanted to take along; the butcher was glad to get rid of such stuff. . . . And any time of day you could step into a saloon, buy a glass of beer for a nickel, and eat your fill off the free-lunch counter. *Ya-ya*, this was a wonderful *kontra* then. . . ."

For ten years Toné Kmet tossed the great bundles and coils of wire from the platform into the cars. Then he was promoted to a "better" job in the cooling department, where wire was treated in chemicals. The work here was much less strenuous and by now this, too, was all right with Toné Kmet. He had got to be forty and the heavy work on the platform had taken something out of him. Also, since the new job involved some responsibility, the pay was higher, "which didn't get me mad, either."

Like most peasant immigrants, in whom the property instinct was strong, Toné and Karolina Kmet aspired from the start to live in a dwelling of their own. To realize this on his laborer's wages was no easy matter, especially since a child was born to them on the average of every two years. But in 1907 they bought their first home, a small, cramped one-family house. Toné then acquired a couple of lots, mostly because everybody else he knew was plunging into real estate; and with Cleveland expanding at a great rate, he sold them in 1911 for three times the price he had paid for them. . . .

Karolina bore the eleven children, three boys and eight girls, during the first twenty years of their marriage. To say nothing of keeping up the payments on the house and lots, it was a problem to feed and clothe so large a family, for the cost of living, of course, did not stay at the 1893 level, when they married; yet all eleven children achieved adulthood and ten are still living and, in their various ways, doing as well as most Americans of the lower-middle or working class. . . .

Toné Kmet was always careful in the matter of his health. Even as a young man he ate and drank moderately and never ate anything warmed over. He avoided drafts. In 1910, at fifty, after a long cold which had "got into his bones" and forced him to go to bed for a couple of weeks, he became a bit of a hypochondriac. . . . He had half a notion then to quit working. In fact, he sent word to that effect to the mill. The bosses, who had known him for two decades, came to see him and told him not to be a fool. What was the big idea, anyhow? He had twenty years of service to his credit; in five more years he would be entitled to a pension. They raised his wages from 50 to 60 cents an hour, and he went back to work for another half-decade—chiefly because, on careful thought, he realized if he quit now the family might have the devil of a time making ends meet; the house was not quite paid for and the two children who had begun to work were not yet earning very much. . . .

And the idea of a pension check fascinated him. At moments in the past he had not quite believed he would ever get it. In the old country only government employees received pensions; people who were educated and seemed to amount to something, while he, Toné Kmet, here in America, was only a laborer. . . . In the past, he had at once believed and disbelieved he would receive it; now, sitting in the chair in the kitchen at fifty-five, he decided to retire in part also to test this pension plan. He would see whether or not this outfit called the United States Steel and Carnegie Pension Fund, of which the American Steel and Wire Company was a member, was a fiction or the real thing. . . .

One morning about a month after this, the postman brought a long, narrow envelope, and Anton Kmet opened it. There was a check. He looked at it a long time, studying it, feeling the crisp paper. There was the name of the United States Steel and Carnegie Pension Fund in heavy print; there was his name, ANTON KMET, typewritten in capital letters, all correct; there were a couple of signatures at the bottom; and there was the amount in figures and words: twenty-one dollars and forty cents. . . . And the check has been coming ever since; for twenty-five years now. Oché Toné looks for it every first of the month, or on the second if the first happens to be a Sunday or holiday; yet, in a way, it freshly surprises him every time he pulls it out of the envelope. . . .

"The whole thing is funny, if you come to think of it. Me getting a pension! It's a joke; but maybe only to me. So I want to live a long time yet. I enjoy it so. What are jokes for but to be enjoyed; and if I die, who would enjoy this one?"

2. LIFE IN HOMESTEAD

Some of the . . . means adopted to secure a home are illustrated in the story of a delightful Englishman, once a silk weaver but now an engineer in the mill, who lives in Munhall Hollow. The meaning of the word Homestead is all but forgotten by its people, but the story of this man's house-building shows much of the spirit of the old settlers. When he wished to build, he had very little money. Mr. Munhall, who was then living, gave him a note to a lumber firm, who sold him $200 worth of lumber on credit. He paid down $24 for the lease of a lot. Since he did part of the work, the labor cost on his three-room house was only about $40. As soon as these debts were paid, he incurred another for $200 in order to enlarge the kitchen and build a second bedroom over it; then he added a front porch and later a shed in the rear for a storehouse, with a chicken coop beside it. All this was done while there were three children at home, and on the income of an engineer, not over $3 a day. Now he and his wife, despite the disadvantage of not having a freehold in the land, take in their comfortable though simple home the pride of the creator as well as of the owner—a feeling rare in these days of huge tenements and "company houses," when men accept whatever can be had for the renting and when long shifts make it difficult for them to put the work of their hands into their homes if they would.

When the house is paid for, the family often takes a genuine pleasure in its improvement. Sometimes it is the addition of a bathroom; sometimes the repapering in the spring which the busy mother finds time to do; sometimes the building of a washhouse in the yard. To plan and carry out these improvements always means the development of a sense of family life and its common interests. . . .

To have a bathroom is a real ambition with the native white families, and some of those who live in the otherwise excellently equipped company houses mentioned the lack of one as a great drawback to their convenience. A number of families who owned their houses had themselves gone to the expense of putting in baths, while others proposed some day to do the same. . . .

The following bill of fare for four days is fairly typical of the English-speaking households. The head of the family in this instance earned about $3 a day.

MONDAY

Breakfast: Oatmeal and milk, eggs and bacon, bread, butter, jelly, coffee.
Dinner: Soup, bread, fruit.
Supper: Meat, beans, potatoes, fruit, red beets, pickles.

TUESDAY

Breakfast: Chocolate, eggs, bread, butter, and jelly.
Dinner: Spinach, potatoes, pickles, warmed-over meat, fruit, bread, butter.
Supper: Meat, sweet potatoes, carrots, beans, tomatoes, tea, bread, butter, and fruit.

WEDNESDAY

Breakfast: Eggs, corncakes, potatoes, coffee, rhubarb, bread, butter.
Dinner: Soup, bread, butter.
Supper: Lamb stew with dumplings, cucumber, eggplant, beans, corn, coffee, bread and butter, fruit.

THURSDAY

Breakfast: Eggs, fruit, eggplant, coffee, cakes.
Dinner: Soup, bread and butter, cakes, fruit.
Supper: Fish, potatoes, tomatoes, cucumbers, pie, tea.

Perhaps in the expenditure for food more than in any other there is a chance for women to display their skill, an asset which must be included in the family resources. Two households, undoubtedly extreme types, will serve to illustrate this point.

The first was a Scotch family of seven who had been in this country for about fifteen years. Besides the three younger children in school there were two sons at work, whose wages brought the family income up to $32 a week. The six-room house was none too large to make them all comfortable and enable them to have a pleasant sitting room. As I stepped into the kitchen one frosty morning, I was greeted by the odor of preserves which the wife was making ready to vary the monotony of dinners to be eaten from a "bucket." We fell to discussing methods of economy and she told me many of her thrifty ways; about the pig they would buy as soon as cold weather came, to provide salt pork and ham for the winter; the pickles and preserves she was putting up; the $50 she was saving to buy the winter's supply of dry groceries from the wholesaler's. That this thrift did not amount to parsimony was shown by the good gas range and washing machine in view, and by evidences of ample provision of food. By planning ahead, by extra labor, by wise buying, even luxuries were secured on a food expenditure of only 24 cents per person a day.

The other extreme was shown in the home of a poor, unintelligent woman who had gone to work at the age of eleven, and could neither read nor write. As enough to pay the rent was the only contribution to the family purse made by her husband, a ne'er-do-well, she herself was obliged, by washing and by taking a lodger, to provide money for food and clothes. This money, which averaged $4.40 a week, was very irregular, as the lodger was frequently out of work. With a wayward boy in school and a sickly baby at home, she had but little time and thought to give to housekeeping. Food was bought daily by the five and ten cents' worth—pork chops, cheap preserves at ten cents a jar, two quarts of potatoes, a loaf of bread, etc.—a pitiable record viewed either from the standpoint of the children's health or of the pocketbook. The least nutritious food was bought in the most expensive way, because of ignorance and of a small and uncertain income. The items of her expenditures (at 25 cents per day) were deficient in the elements which provide heat and energy to the body, and lacking in the foods which replace wornout cells. . . .

Let us consider . . . how the economic problem of life can be worked out on $1.65 a day.

With the single men the problem is of course a simple one. Many care little how they live so long as they live cheaply. One of the lodging houses which I visited during the depression consisted of two rooms one above the other, each measuring perhaps 12 by 20 feet. In the kitchen was the wife of the boarding boss getting dinner—some sort of hot apple cake and a stew of the cheapest cuts of meats. . . . A crowd of men were lounging cheerfully about, talking, smoking, and enjoying life, making the most of the leisure enforced by the shutdown in the mill. In the room above, double iron bedsteads were set close together and on them comfortables were neatly laid. In these two rooms, besides the "boarding boss," a stalwart Bulgarian, his wife and two babies, lived twenty men.

The average expense for each man was about $11 a month. In prosperous times these men make regularly $9.90, which may be increased when they work more than 10 hours a day, and on Sunday, to as high as $12 a week. It is obvious, therefore, that if the fixed expenditure of these single men is about $3 a week, a large margin remains over and above clothes either for saving or indulgence. They can thus send for wife and children, fulfill their duties to aged parents, live high according to their lights, or make provision for their own future.

While this program is an economical one, it by no means furnishes to this group of homeless foreigners a normal life. Though some expect to return and others to send for their families when they have made their fortunes, all for the time being are in a strange country with neither the pleasures nor the restraints of home life. As in all barracks life, drunkenness and immorality are common.

One morning I entered a two-room tenement. The kitchen, perhaps 15 by 12 feet, was steaming with vapor from a big washtub set on a chair in the middle of the room. The mother was trying to wash and at the same time to keep the older of her two babies from tumbling into the tub full of scalding water that was standing on the floor. On one side of the room was a huge puffy bed with one feather tick to sleep on and another for covering; near the window stood a sewing machine; in the corner, an organ—all these besides the inevitable cook stove upon which in the place of honor was simmering the evening's soup. Upstairs in the second room were one boarder and the man of the house asleep. Two more boarders were at work, but at night would be home to sleep in the bed from which the others would get up. Picture if you will what a week or a season means to a mother in such a home, the overwork, the brief respite from toil—to be increased afterward—when the babies come?

Again, take a family of six. The father, still only about thirty years old, had been here for over fifteen years. Out of his wages—about $3.50 a day at fairly skilled work in the mill—he was buying a small house with a garden. He was naturalized and the family stood as a fair type of our new citizens. They took no lodgers, but many limitations were imposed by such thrift.

They live in two rooms comfortably furnished, one a living room and the other a bed room. They have a sewing machine on which the mother does the sewing for her family.

They wear plain clothing. The woman does all her own mending with care. The father buys ready-made clothing. They have a change of clothing for Sundays, of a fairly good quality. They live principally on vegetable diet, not using much fruit. The man works hard and they are obliged to have good substantial food. . . . They belong to lodges so that their family may have benefits in case of a death, either father or mother.

The man goes when his lodge gives a dance, it being expected of every member to buy tickets. Neither he nor his wife ever attend theatres, on account of being kept at home with their family. The woman cannot remember having been to any of the parks or amusements of any kind.

It is by such thrift that some of the Slavs attain their ambition to own a home. An official in the foreign department of one bank said he knew of twenty-five Slavs who had purchased homes in 1907. . . . One family, for example, had bought an eight-room house on one of these busy streets. The four rear rooms they rented, but with evident regard for appearances lived themselves in the four that faced the front. With the aid of the rent from the rear tenement they had succeeded in freeing the house from the mortgage. The families more often, however, move further from the mill. One I knew bought a house on the hill with two porches and a big yard where they kept chickens. While they had only succeeded in paying $500 on the $1700 the place cost, now that a son was at work they hoped to be able to clear the debt. In the meantime they truly rejoiced in being on the hill above the smoke and away from the bustling courts.

3. LITHUANIAN MEAT PACKER

Soon after my arrival in this country, I knew that money was everything I needed. My money was almost gone and I thought that I would soon die unless I got a job, for this was not like home. Here money was everything and a man without money must die.

. . . One morning my friends woke me up at five o'clock and said, "Now, if you want life, liberty and happiness," they laughed, "you must push for yourself. You must get a job. Come with us." And we went to the yards. Men and women were walking in by thousands as far as we could see. We went to the doors of one big slaughter house. There was a crowd of about 200 men waiting there for a job. They looked hungry and kept watching the door. At last a special policeman came out and began pointing to men, one by one. Each one jumped forward. Twenty-three were taken. Then they all went inside and all the others turned their faces away and looked tired. I remember one boy sat down and cried, just next to me, on a pile of boards. Some policemen waved their clubs and we all walked on. I found some Lithuanians to talk with, who told me they had come every morning for three weeks. Soon we met other crowds coming away from other slaughter houses, and we all walked around and felt bad and tired and hungry.

That night I told my friends that I would not do this many days, but would go some place else. "Where?" they asked me, and I began to see then that I was in bad trouble, because I spoke no English. Then one man told me to give him $5 to give the special policeman. I did this and the next morning the policeman pointed me out, so I had a job. I have heard some big talk since then about my American freedom of contract, but I do not think I had much freedom in bargaining for this job with the Meat Trust. My job was in the cattle killing room. I pushed the blood along the gutter. Some people think these jobs make men bad. I do not think so. The men who do the killing are not as bad as the ladies with fine clothes who come every day to look at it, because they have to do it. The cattle do not suffer. They are knocked senseless with a big hammer and are dead before they wake up. This is done not to spare them pain, but because if they got hot and sweating with fear and pain the meat would not be so good. I soon saw that every job in the room was done like this— so as to save everything and make money. One Lithuanian, who worked with me, said, "They get all the blood out of these cattle and all the work out of us men." This was true, for we worked that first day from six in the morning till seven at night. The next day we worked from six in the morning till eight at night. The next day we had no work. So we had no good, regular hours. It was hot in the room that summer, and the hot blood made it worse.

I held this job six weeks and then I was turned off. I think some other man had paid for my job, or perhaps I was too slow. The foreman in that room wanted quick men to make the work rush, because he was paid more if the work was done cheaper and quicker. I saw now that every man was helping himself, always trying to get all the money he could. At that time I believed that all men in Chicago were grafters when they had to be. They only wanted to push themselves. Now, when I was idle I began to look about, and everywhere I saw sharp men beating out slow men like me. Even if we worked hard it did us no good. I had saved $13—$5 a week for six weeks makes $30, and take off $15 for six weeks' board and lodging and $2 for other things. I showed this to a Lithuanian, who had been here two years, and he laughed. "It will be taken from you," he said. He had saved a hundred dollars once and had begun to buy a house on the instalment plan, but something had happened that he did not know about and his landlord put him out and kept the hundred dollars. I found that many Lithuanians had been beaten this way. At home we never made a man sign contract papers. We only had him make the sign of a cross and promise he would do what he said. But this was no good in Chicago. So these sharp men were beating us.

I saw this, too, in the newspaper. I was beginning to learn English, and at night in the boarding house the men who did not play cards used to read the paper to us. The biggest word was "Graft" in red letters on the front page. Another word was "Trust." This paper kept putting these two words together. Then I began to see how every American man was trying to get money for himself. . . . I felt very bad and sorrowful in that month. I kept walking around with many other Lithuanians who had no job. Our money was going and we could find nothing to do. At night we got homesick for our fine green mountains. We read all the news about home in our Lithuanian Chicago newspaper, *The Katalikas*. It is a good paper and gives all the news. . . .

Those were bad days and nights. At last I had a chance to help myself. Summer was over and Election Day was coming. The Republican boss in our district, Jonidas, was a saloonkeeper. A friend took me there. Jonidas shook hands and treated me fine. He taught me to sign my name, and the next week I went with him to an office and signed some paper, and then I could vote. I voted as I was told, and then they got me back into the yards to work, because one big politician owns stock in one of those houses. Then I felt that I was getting in beside the game. I was in a combine like other sharp men. Even when work was slack I was all right, because they got me a job in the street cleaning department. . . . All of us were telling our friends to come soon. Soon they came—even thousands. The employers in the yard liked this, because those sharp foreman are inventing new machines and the work is easier to learn, and so these slow Lithuanians and even green girls can learn to do it, and then the Americans and Germans and Irish are put out and the employer saves money, because the Lithuanians work cheaper. This was why the

American labor unions began to organize us all just the same as they had organized the Bohemians and Poles before us.

Well, we were glad to be organized. We had learned that in Chicago every man must push himself always, and Jonidas had taught us how much better we could push ourselves by getting into a combine. Now, we saw that this union was the best combine for us, because it was the only combine that could say, "It is our business to raise your wages." . . .

One night that Irishman did not come and Jonidas saw his chance and took the chair. He talked very fine and we elected him President. We made him Treasurer, too. Down in the saloon he gave us free drinks and told us we must break away from the Irish grafters. The next week he made us strike, all by himself. We met twice a day in his saloon and spent all of our money on drinks and then the strike was over. I got out of this union after that. I had been working hard in the cattle killing room and I had a better job. I was called a cattle butcher now and I joined the Cattle Butchers' Union. This union is honest and it has done me a great deal of good.

It has raised my wages. The man who worked at my job before the union came was getting through the year an average of $9 a week. I am getting $11. In my first job I got $5 a week. The man who works there now gets $5.75.

It has given me more time to learn to read and speak and enjoy life like an American. I never work now from 6 A.M. to 9 P.M. and then be idle the next day. I work now from 7 A.M. to 5:30 P.M., and there are not so many idle days. The work is evened up.

With more time and more money I live much better and I am very happy. . . . So is my wife, Alexandria. She came a year ago and has learned to speak English already. . . . We have four nice rooms, which she keeps very clean, and she has flowers growing in boxes in the two front windows. We do not go much to church because the church seems to be too slow. But we belong to a Lithuanian society that gives two picnics in summer and two big balls in winter, where we have a fine time. I go one night a week to the Lithuanian Concertina Club. On Sundays we go on the trolley out into the country.

But we like to stay at home more now because we have a baby. When he grows up I will not send him to the Lithuanian Catholic school. They have only two bad rooms and two priests, who teach only in Lithuanian from prayer books. I will send him to the American school, which is very big and good. The teachers there are Americans and they belong to the Teachers' Labor Union, which has three thousand teachers and belongs to our Chicago Federation of Labor. I am sure that such teachers will give him a good chance.

Our union sent a committee to Springfield last year and they passed a law which prevents boys and girls below sixteen from working in the stockyards.

We are trying to make the employers pay on Saturday night in cash. Now they pay in checks and the men have to get money the same night to buy things for Sunday, and the saloons cash checks by thousands. You have to take one drink to have the check cashed. It is hard to take one drink.

The union is doing another good thing. It is combining all the nationalities. The night I joined the Cattle Butchers' Union I was led into the room by a Negro member. With me were Bohemians, Germans, and Poles, and Mike Donnelly, the President, is an Irishman. He spoke to us in English and then three interpreters told us what he said. We swore to be loyal to our union above everything else except the country, the city, and the State—to be faithful to each other—to protect the women workers—to do our best to understand the history of the labor movement, and to do all we could to help it on. Since then I have gone there every two weeks and I help the movement by being an interpreter for the other Lithuanians who come in. That is why I have learned to speak and write good English. The others do not need me long. They soon learn English, too, and when they have done that they are quickly becoming Americans.

But the best thing the union does is to make me feel more independent. I do not have to pay to get a job and I cannot be discharged unless I am no good. For almost the whole 30,000 men and women are organized now in some of our unions and they all are directed by our central council. No man knows what it means to be sure of his job unless he has been fired like I was once without any reason being given.

So this is why I joined the labor union. There are many better stories than mine, for my story is very common. There are thousands of immigrants like me. Over 300,000 immigrants have been organized in the last three years by the American Federation of Labor. The immigrants are glad to be organized if the leaders are as honest as Mike Donnelly is. You must get money to live well, and to get money you must combine. I cannot bargain alone with the Meat Trust. I tried it and it does not work.

4. ANTHRACITE MINER

Q. How long have you been connected officially with the miners' organization?—*A.* I have been connected officially with them since December, 1897.

Q. What were you engaged in prior to that time?—*A.* Prior to that time I was engaged in my occupation as a miner, and have been mining since that time.

Q. Of what nationality are you?—*A.* I am Welsh.

Q. At what time did you come to this country and how old were you?—*A.* I came to this country some time in the seventies when a very small child. I was born in December, 1867.

Q. Have you mined coal in the anthracite region during your whole career as a coal miner?—*A.* No; I mined coal in the State of Iowa; in fact, that was where I first entered the mines. I was then about twelve years old. In Iowa I mined coal . . . about six years. In the anthracite region I have been actively engaged as a miner and mine laborer for nine years. . . .

Q. What are we to understand by contract miners?—*A.* Those miners who mine coal by the car measure. At that time the miners of Jeanesville were compelled to buy their supplies of the company. The word "supplies" means powder, oil, cotton, and all things that may be needed to mine and produce coal. In July or August of 1897 . . . the mine foreman employed by the Lehigh Valley Coal Company at Jeanesville went through the mines with a list of all miners who bought their supplies of the company and a list of all those who did not. He called at my working place and asked my partner and myself where we bought our supplies. My partner told him we got them where we could buy them cheapest. The mine foreman told me that he had been instructed to tell us that unless we bought our supplies from that company's supply store we could take our tools out.

Q. Did you take your tools out?—*A.* We did not.

Q. Did they make the same discriminating charges or overcharges for provisions?—*A.* They do at many places. At that place there was no company store. . . .

Q. Did they charge exorbitant prices for supplies?—*A.* They did.

Q. Much larger than you could get in the village or town near there?—*A.* They charged $2.75 per keg for powder, when we could buy from individuals or persons running individual stores for $1.25 and $1.50 per keg all we wished of it; and those coal companies bought, and buy at this time, powder at 90 cents and $1 per keg, while they charge the miners $2.75 per keg for it.

Q. And charge for the other materials of which you spoke proportionately?—*A.* Yes. . . .

Q. Do the company stores prevail to any great extent through the anthracite region?—*A.* They do. As far as supplies are concerned, there is not a colliery in the anthracite region today at which they do not keep supplies for the miners—not one; and while the operators will say that the men are not compelled to deal with them, they will not employ them if they refuse. . . .

Q. Will you give to this commission the name of the company for whom you were working when this compulsory treatment was imposed upon you?—*A.* I think I did; the Lehigh Valley Coal Company. . . .

Q. How many kegs of powder usually will two men who are working together use in an ordinary month's work? I have spoken with men lately who stated that owing to the hard nature of the coal which they had to blast they have used as many as twelve kegs of powder in one month.—*A.* While that is above the average, I will say that six kegs of powder is a fair average. In 1897 there were over 1,272,000 kegs of powder used in the anthracite; or, in other words, at $1.50 per keg above what we could buy it at from individuals, we were overcharged $1,908,000 on powder alone.

Q. Anything to say on the subject of injunction?—*A.* The injunction in strikes . . . has a tendency to keep a man down to the low level he is at present, or, in other words, it gives the coal operators an undue advantage of the miners.

Q. What have you to say in regard to weekly, semimonthly, or monthly payments?—*A.* I wish to say that a law was passed in Pennsylvania stating that employees should be paid semimonthly "on demand." Those two words prevented the miner from receiving his wages semimonthly, because if he demands it there is no more work for him. . . . We are in favor, however, of a weekly payment; if we cannot get that, we would like by all means to receive our pay semimonthly. The reason for this is that the workmen could spend the small amount of money they earn to a better advantage; they could buy the necessities of life at a much cheaper rate than they can at the present time, for with the monthly payment the majority of miners use the book, and they as a rule charge more in those stores than at places where they deal strictly for cash. . . .

Q. Have any of your miners, either singly or collectively, demanded, in compliance with that law, the pay due them?—*A.* I have been told that they have, and have received it, but could not get employment at that colliery afterwards.

Q. What is your rule of mining in the anthracite region, by the ton or by the car, and the price?—*A.* . . . Company miners receive $1.08 for ten hours' work. Company laborers, or all other inside help working by the day, received $1.10, $1.44, and $1.64—three prices. . . . Other laborers outside, in and around the breaker, receive $1 to $1.20 per day. The majority of them receive $1. The old man who is not able to follow his occupation as a miner any more is sometimes given employment in the coal breakers. They receive generally 90 cents per day. Boys on the breakers at that place receive from 50 to 75 cents per day. The house rent—they live in company houses, nearly all of them—is $5 to $6 per month. A reduction in the house rent was granted on request of the miners in 1897, at the time of the strike. . . .

Q. What can a good practical miner make per day in mining by the car?—*A*. I have worked in places where I was fortunate to earn $2, probably, and sometimes $2.50, while I have worked in other places where I was not able to earn $1, and would work equally as hard, sometimes harder than I did when I was earning a larger amount. My earnings last year were $404 for about 240 working days.

Q. Will you explain to the commission what advantage it is to the miner to go to work when the colliery is idle—colliery not hoisting coal?—*A*. In the anthracite, at the present time, each colliery is allowed so many cars to fill for a week or a month by the company. The miner goes in the mines and works on idle days, and he is thus able to load a larger amount of coal than he could had he not worked this idle time. The company is able to fill their quota for that colliery in a much less time . . . by the miners working idle time . . . deprive all inside day help and all outside help of those extra two days; but that plan is carried on today in the anthracite to a great extent.

Q. Describe the dockage system.—*A*. The company have what they call a "docking boss" on every coal breaker. When the cars of coal are dumped he is at liberty to take one-quarter, one-half, three-quarters, and in many cases he takes the whole car from the miner, after the miner has mined it, and in some collieries in the anthracite today they dock on the average from ten to twelve cars out of every hundred. At the place where I was employed last, at Jeanesville, they never took less than a full car, and in my career there as a miner I was docked sometimes as high as two cars out of four. . . . For these two cars I would not receive one cent, although I had blasted that coal, had paid for my powder and other supplies, and had been put to a great deal of expense oftentimes to get that coal. . . .

Q. What was the cause of your being docked?—*A*. They claimed it was because there was too much slate, or at other times they would say there was bone in it. . . . I was docked full cars of coal while mining when I was positive and could have taken an affidavit there was not 25 pounds of impurity in any one car. . . .

Q. What becomes of the coal that you were docked?—*A*. It is put by the company into the same chute as the coal they pay for.

Q. They do not take any of this out?—*A*. They do not take any more out than they do out of cars paid for. It is all dumped in the same chute.

Statement of Comparative Selling Prices of Provisions at Company and
Cash Stores (Scrantonion, May 8, 1899)

Provisions	Company Store	Cash Store	Provisions	Company Store	Cash Store
Flour (1 barrel)	$8.50	$6.50	Cheese (1 pound)	$ .125	$ .10
Butter (1 pound)	.25	.19	Sugar (17 pounds)	1.00	—
Bacon (1 pound)	.10	.075	Sugar (20 pounds)	—	1.00
Eggs (1 dozen)	.25	.125	Raisins (1 pound)	.125	.05
Tomatoes (1 can)	.12	.085	Pickles (each)	.10	.03

Q. It is part of their system—selling the necessaries of life and working utensils to miners?—*A.* Yes; but they are kept in a separate place; those things are kept separate on a miner's check. One remarkable feature about some of the miners' checks is that when they would have 20, 30, or 40 cents left after paying the store bill the company would always manage to claim that much for blacksmithing, so that the miners would draw a blank. . . . Here we have one where the miner earns $24 and they manage to bring things out to the exact cent. I promised the miners their names would not be used. Some of them are very poor men; in fact, all are, and if they would be thrown out of employment they would not have car fare to go any place else. . . . They have a law on the statute books of Pennsylvania which says that they shall not run company stores in connection with collieries, but they appear to do this in defiance of the law. The law, however, has been declared unconstitutional; but they do at the present time, to a certain extent, compel the miners to deal in their stores. . . . The influence of organized labor on wages—at the time there was an organization in the anthracite better wages prevailed; the men had better terms and conditions of employment than at the present time. Where I worked last, Jeanesville, the conditions of emploment were much better after the men became organized than they were prior to that time. In fact, a person would scarcely think he was working for the same company or under the same foreman, the change was that great. . . .

The number of employees in the anthracite is fully as great today as ever were. There are more men in the anthracite than can find employment. There are a great many idle all the time, and it has a tendency to keep wages down below what they should be.

Q. Was not that surplus of labor brought about by the operators importing the foreign labor under contract?—*A.* It was. Prior to that time all men wishing work could find employment. The only way that I know to remedy this is to adopt the eight hour work day, if possible, to give employment to a greater number of men. I know of no other way to give work to the unemployed.

There are thousands of very young boys employed in the mines in the anthracite as door boys, and in the breakers. There are many employed who are compelled to work by reason of their fathers not being able to support the family and in other cases you will find many working who are the sons of widows, and who are compelled to work in order to help support the family. The law of Pennsylvania states that no one shall be employed in the mines under the age of fourteen years. I have no doubt but what many are employed under 14 years.

The effect of immigration on employment in the anthracite is this: It has reduced wages and has caused a surplus of labor which enables the operator to enforce conditions upon the miners and upon the workmen today which they could not enforce upon them did this surplus of labor not exist.

Q. Are the miners in that region—English-speaking and people speaking other languages—in favor of limiting the immigration?— A. The English-speaking people are. The foreign-speaking people I have not approached on that subject, for the reason that the majority of them are not far enough advanced to speak intelligently on that subject. While there are some, yet there is only a small percentage of them able to discuss that question intelligently.

Q. Are most of the English-speaking people in the anthracite region, to whom you refer as in opposition to immigration of foreign birth?— A. The majority of them are of foreign birth. A great number of them are of foreign birth, while there are thousands that are born of foreign parents.

Q. Yet they all unite on that one point.—A. That there should be some restriction on immigration.

Q. Is there any colored labor in the anthracite region?—A. There is not that I am aware of. I have never seen a colored man in the anthracite working in a mine.

Q. How is your public-school system?—A. Very good in all the schools in the anthracite that I have any knowledge of.

Q. Well adapted to the needs of the working people?—A. If any child is kept in the public school there until he has gone through their branches of study, he will have a very good education, and such that it will fit him for all ordinary purposes. . . . If it is possible to effect a thorough organization among them, I have no doubt but what those evils can be remedied, at least to a great extent. The local meetings take the place of a school; in other words, the men meet to educate each other as to our needs and to the proper way of adjusting differences and remedying evils. I have worked in the anthracite mines within the past year where I could not work a full day at any one time, the air was so impure; and the current of air was not sufficient to drive away the smoke, so that I would be compelled to leave my work at six or seven hours, and then would not be in a fit condition to walk home many times. . . .

Q. You have worked every day that you had an opportunity?—*A.* I did, and worked a great many days that the mine did not work.

I know the needs of the anthracite miners as perhaps few know them. I have seen within the last two years, in the winter time, children without shoes to put on their feet—could not go to school, could not go out of the house—and at the same time they have been refused a pair of shoes out of those very company stores that I have mentioned. I have known families in the past year to do without meat for a month at a time; that did not know what it was to have meat. And I have known cases where families did not have the bread to give their children on their rising from their beds in the morning.

5. MINER'S STORY

I am thirty-five years old, married, the father of four children, and have lived in the coal region all my life. Twenty-three of these years have been spent working in and around the mines. My father was a miner. He died ten years ago from "miners' asthma."

Three of my brothers are miners; none of us had any opportunities to acquire an education. We were sent to school (such a school as there was in those days) until we were about twelve years of age, and then we were put into the screen room of a breaker to pick slate. From there we went inside the mines as driver boys. As we grew stronger we were taken on as laborers, where we served until able to call ourselves miners. We were given work in the breasts and gangways. There were five of us boys. One lies in the cemetery—fifty tons of top rock dropped on him. He was killed three weeks after he got his job as a miner—a month before he was to be married.

In the fifteen years I have worked as a miner I have earned the average rate of wages any of us coal heavers get. Today I am little better off than when I started to do for myself. I have $100 on hand; I am not in debt; I hope to be able to weather the strike without going hungry.

I am only one of the hundreds you see on the street every day. The muscles on my arms are no harder, the callous on my palms no deeper than my neighbor's whose entire life has been spent in the coal region. By years I am only thirty-five. But look at the marks on my body; look at the lines of worriment on my forehead; see the gray hairs on my head and in my mustache; take my general appearance, and you'll think I'm ten years older.

You need not wonder why. Day in and day out, from Monday morning to Saturday evening, between the rising and the setting of the sun, I am in the underground workings of the coal mines. From the seams water trickles into the ditches along the gangways; if not water, it is the gas which hurls us to eternity and the props and timbers to a chaos.

Our daily life is not a pleasant one. When we put on our oil-soaked suit in the morning we can't guess all the dangers which threaten our lives. We walk sometimes miles to the place—to the man way or traveling way, or to the mouth of the shaft on top of the slope. And then we enter the darkened chambers of the mines. On our right and on our left we see the logs that keep up the top and support the sides which may crush us into shapeless masses, as they have done to many of our comrades.

We get old quickly. Powder, smoke, after-damp, bad air—all combine to bring furrows to our faces and asthma to our lungs.

I did not strike because I wanted to; I struck because I had to. A miner—the same as any other workman—must earn fair living wages, or he can't live. And it is not how much you get that counts. It is how much what you get will buy. I have gone through it all, and I think my case is a good sample.

I was married in 1890, when I was twenty-three years old—quite a bit above the age when we miner boys get into double harness. The woman I married is like myself. She was born beneath the shadow of a dirt bank; her chances for school weren't any better than mine; but she did have to learn how to keep house on a certain amount of money. After we paid the preacher for tying the knot we had just $185 in cash, good health and the good wishes of many friends to start us off.

Our cash was exhausted in buying furniture for housekeeping. In 1890 work was not so plentiful, and by the time our first baby came there was room for much doubt as to how we would pull out. Low wages, and not much over half time in those years, made us hustle. In 1890–91, from June to May, I earned $368.72. That represented eleven months' work, or an average of $33.52 per month. Our rent was $10 per month; store not less than $20. And then I had my oil suits and gum boots to pay for. The result was that after the first year and a half of our married life we were in debt. Not much, of course, and not as much as many of my neighbors, men of larger families, and some who made less money, or in whose case there had been sickness or accident or death. These are all things which a miner must provide for.

I have had fairly good work since I was married. I made the average of what we contract miners are paid; but, as I said before, I am not much better off than when I started.

In 1896 my wife was sick eleven weeks. The doctor came to my house almost every day. He charged me $20 for his services. There was medicine to buy. I paid the drug store $18 in that time. Her mother nursed her, and we kept a girl in the kitchen at $1.50 a week, which cost me $15 for ten weeks, beside the additional living expenses.

In 1897, just a year afterward, I had a severer trial. And mind, in those years we were only working about half time. But in the fall of that year one of my brothers struck a gas feeder. There was a terrible explosion. He was hurled downward in the breast and covered with the rush of coal and rock. I was working only three breasts away from him and for a moment was unable to realize what had occurred. Myself and a hundred others were soon at work, however, and in a short while we found him, horribly burned over his whole body, his laborer dead alongside of him.

He was my brother. He was single and had been boarding. He had no home of his own. I didn't want him taken to the hospital, so I directed the driver of the ambulance to take him to my house. Besides being burned, his right arm and left leg were broken, and he was hurt internally. The doctors—there were two at the house when we got there—said he would die. But he didn't. He is living and a miner today. But he lay in bed just fourteen weeks, and was unable to work for seven weeks after he got out of bed. He had no money when he was hurt except the amount represented by his pay. All of the expenses for doctors, medicine, extra help, and his living were borne by me, except $25, which another brother gave me. The last one had none to give. Poor work, low wages and a sickly woman for a wife had kept him scratching for his own family.

It is nonsense to say I was not compelled to keep him, that I could have sent him to a hospital or the almshouse. We are American citizens and we don't go to hospitals and poorhouses.

Let us look at things as they are today, or as they were before this strike commenced.

My last pay envelope shows my wages, after my laborer, powder oil, and other expenses were taken off, were $29.47; that was my earnings for two weeks, and that was extra good. The laborer for the same time got some $21. His wages are a trifle over $10 a week for six full days. Before the strike of 1900 he was paid in this region $1.70 per day, or $10.20 a week. If the 10 per cent raise had been given, as we expected, his wages would be $1.87 per day, or $11.22 per week, or an increase of $1.02 per week. But we all know that under the present system he doesn't get any eleven dollars.

Well, as I said, my wages were $29.47 for the two weeks, or at the rate of $58.94 per month. My rent is $10.50 per month. My coal costs me almost $4 per month. We burn a little over a ton a month on an average and it costs us over $3 per ton. Light does not cost so much; we use coal oil altogether.

When it comes down to groceries is where you get hit the hardest. Everybody knows the cost of living has been extremely high all winter. Butter has been 32, 36 and 38 cents a pound; eggs as high as 32 cents a dozen; ham, 12 and 16 cents a pound; potatoes away up to a dollar, and cabbage not less than a cent a pound. Fresh meat need not be counted. Flour and sugar did not advance, but they were about the only staples that didn't. Anyhow, my store bill for those two weeks was $11. That makes $22 per month. The butcher gets $6 per month. Add them all, and it costs me, just to live, $42.50. That leaves me $17 per month to keep my family in clothes, to pay my church dues, and to keep the industrial insurance going. My insurance alone costs me 55 cents a week, or $2.20 a month.

The coal president never allows his stable boss to cut the amount of fodder allotted to his mules. He insists on so many quarts of oats and corn to the meal and so much hay in the evening. The mule must be fed; the miner may be, if he works hard enough and earns money to buy the grub.

Company stores are of the time that has been. Their existence ended two years ago. But we've got a system growing up that threatens to be just as bad. Let me explain. Over a year ago I was given a breast to drive at one of our mines and was glad to get it. My wife took her cash and went around the different places to buy. When I went to the office for my first pay the "super" met me and asked me if I didn't know his wife's brother George kept a store. I answered "Yes," and wanted to know what that had to do with it.

"Nothing, only I thought I'd call your attention to it," he answered.

No more was said then. But the next day I got a quiet tip that my breast was to be abandoned. This set me thinking. I went to the boss and after a few words, told him my wife had found brother-in-law George's store and that she liked it much better than where she had bought before. I told him the other store didn't sell the right kind of silk waists, and their patent leather shoes were away back. Brother-in-law George had the right kind of stuff and, of course, we were willing to pay a few cents more to get just what we wanted.

That was sarcastic, but it's the cash that has the influence. I have had work at that colliery ever since. I know my living costs me from

10 to 15 per cent extra. But I kept my job, which meant a good deal.

Now you must take into consideration that I am a contract miner and that my earnings are more than the wages of three-fourths of the other fellows at the same colliery. It is not that I am a favorite with the boss. I just struck a good breast. Maybe next month my wages would be from two to six or seven dollars less.

In the days of Pardee, Coxe, Fagley, Fulton, Dewees, Paterson, Riley, Repplier, Graeber, and a hundred others, men were better paid than they have ever been since the centralization ideas of the late Franklin B. Gowen became fixed institutions in the anthracite counties. It may be true that in the days of the individual operation the cost per ton of mining coal was less than it is today. But it is not right that the entire increase in the cost of mining should be charged to the miner. That is what is being done. If you count the reductions made in wages.

We miners do not participate in the high prices of coal. The operators try to prove otherwise by juggling with figures, but their proving has struck a fault, and the drill shows no coal in that section. One-half of the price paid for a ton of coal in New York or Philadelphia goes into the profit pocket of the mine owner, either as a carrier or miner.

We all know that the price of coal has advanced in the past twenty years. We also know that wages are less, that the cost of living is higher. I remember the time, when I was a wee lad, my father used to get his coal for $1 per ton. Now I pay $3. In those days we lads used to go to the dirt banks and pick a load of coal, and it cost our parents only a half a dollar to get it hauled home. We dare not do that now. Then we did not need gum boots, safety lamps, or any such things as that; and for all of them we must now pay out of wages that have been reduced.

Our condition can be no worse; it might and must be better. The luxuries of the rich we do not ask; we do want butter for our bread and meat for our soup. We do not want silk and laces for our wives and daughters. But we want to earn enough to buy them a clean calico once in a while. Our boys are not expecting automobiles and membership cards in clubs of every city, but they want their fathers to earn enough to keep them at school until they have a reasonably fair education.

6. COLORADO MINER

Before I went to Cripple Creek I went to work in a chlorination mill in Florence, which is just thirty miles south of Cripple Creek, and found that I had arrived just in time to reap the benefit of a strike there, which the mill workers had won the day before. It seems that they had been working nine and ten hours a day for from $1.50 to $2 per day, and as one could not get board and room anywhere for less than $30 per month, it took just about all one could earn to live on, especially as the mill would shut down for at least two days every month and 2 per cent of the wages were deducted for hospital fees. The work in the mill is not so dangerous as disagreeable and unhealthy, as one is all the time in an atmosphere of sulphur dioxide, or chlorin, or dust, so that one cannot see an object two feet away; so it was no wonder to me that they struck. But $2 for eight hours of that kind of work is nothing great.

It was not long before the dust and gas began to act on me and I went to the mill surgeon about it. He told me I had better quit, but asked me not to tell the managers, for they always had a hard time to fill those places, and that no man could stand it long. So I quit and went to Cripple Creek.

The minimum wages for miners and men working around the mines at Cripple Creek was $3 per day. Men running machine drills got from $4 to $6 per day, according to the kind of place they had to work in—that is, whether the place was wet or dangerous. Machine men working in a wet shaft usually got about $6, and the helpers got from fifty cents to a dollar less than the machine men. Engineers received from $4 to $7 a day, depending on the place they worked in.

In all the mines around Cripple Creek the miners worked only eight hours a day, and on a good many mines the miners were allowed to go down in the mine, come out of the mine, eat dinner, and change clothes on the company's time. That means, that if the men begin to go down into the holes at 8 A.M., come out at 11:30 and eat dinner, go down again at noon, begin to come out sometimes as early as twenty minutes to four and change clothes, and at 4 P.M. they can go; so they do not all of them work eight hours, but oftentimes nearer seven hours. Of course, most of the mines worked the men the full eight hours.

The last mine in which I worked was a very safe mine compared with most of them, but the dangers do not seem so great to a practiced miner, who is used to climbing hundreds of feet on stulls or braces put about six feet apart, one above the other, and then walking the same distance on a couple of poles sometimes not larger than fence rails, where a misstep would mean a long drop. But to a novice all the dangers stand out doubly strong. . . .

The hospital discount is usually from one to two dollars a month, and merely gives one attendance if he is hurt. This is deducted from your check every month. On some mines it is compulsory to take this. This is not admitted by the managers, but the unions have watched it pretty carefully, and if a man does not pay hospital fees he does not stay very long at his job. The same thing is true of the mine insurance, which is from three to five dollars a month. This insurance is put up by some of the insurance companies, and, of course, as they do not have to have an agent to collect this money every month, it is supposed that the management gets a rake-off. But the worst of it is that if a man is hurt badly or disabled for life through the carelessness of the mine's managers, before he receives his insurance he had to sign a paper releasing the mine owners from all responsibility for the accident, and then he cannot collect damages in the courts. In this way the mine owners shield themselves against the consequences of their neglect of the legal precautions for the safety of the men. The managers say that they have this insurance as a help for the men, as some of them would not have a cent if they were killed and leave large families, but on some of the mines, even if a man had insurance in a good company and did not want to, or could not afford to, take out more, he has the mine insurance forced on him against his will, and at higher premium than he would have to pay to an independent company. In Cripple Creek there are no company stores, and the miners do not have to furnish their own powder when they work for wages.

While I was in Cripple Creek there was only one mine, the "Strong," which would not employ union men, and a number of them would employ nothing but union men, and every month the men would have to show their union card paid up; but at most of the mines it made no difference whether a man was union or non-union, just as long as his work was satisfactory.

Shortly after I went to Cripple Creek the union posted notices that all men working in mines would have to join the union by a certain date, or be called a scab, and the walking delegate came to me and told me if I did not join I could not work at the mines. If he had asked me to join I would probably have done it, but as it was I didn't join for a year, when a friend of mine presented the matter in a favorable light.

There were a few fights and deeds of violence after the date set for joining the union, but they subsided, and one seemed just as safe whether he was union or non-union. Up to the time I joined I was acquainted with a number of very nice men who belonged to the union, and most of the union men I met did not treat me any differently than they did members. I joined because I saw it would help me to keep in work and for protection in case of accident or sickness, for the union is just like any other secret order that way. They pay

$10 a week sick benefits, and hire three nurses at $3 per day of eight hours; so if one is alone and sick he is sure to be taken care of. There were a good many mines where they required union men, and as I was out of work a good deal I found out that it was easier to get work and keep work on those mines if I had a union card. . . .

The president and the secretary of the union I belonged to were both young men, who were leasing a mine and hiring men themselves and were making quite a stake, but they held on to the union; and when a strike was called they would not even ship their own ore, because it would go to a non-union mill, so they stopped work until they could get a union mill to treat their ore for them. This was the time when the strike was first started in sympathy with the mill men in Colorado Springs and Colorado City.

While I was in Cripple Creek about a dozen Austrians came up from the coal camps and were going to do cheap labor; so a bunch of men escorted them out of town and told them not to come back; but these men were not all union men, for even non-union men like to draw their three and three and a half dollars a day. . . .

The mining laws of Colorado are not enforced at all, and it is on account of this that so many lives are lost. The mine inspector very seldom goes to Cripple Creek, and when he does, he does not stay more than a few days, and, of course, cannot see one hundredth part of the mines. If he should make an inspection of a single one of the big mines it would take all the time he usually spends in the entire district.

For example, the mining laws of Colorado require a cage for every shaft over two hundred feet deep, and I do not know one hole two hundred feet deep that has a cage, and know of lots that are from four to six hundred that have nothing but a bucket. Things like these an inspector would not have to go down in a mine at all to find out.

Then, too, many of the mines have immense stopes with hardly a timber in them, and these places are known all over the camp, but the mine inspector seems never to find it out. In short, the mine inspection in Cripple Creek is nothing but a farce. . . .

The part of the mining that bothered me the most was the mine gas, owing to poor ventilation, and many times I have been carried out unconscious and not able to work for two or three days after. Several men died from effects of gas while I was in the district. But outside of getting a couple of toes smashed from falling rocks and a crack on the head from a bolt which fell about two hundred feet down the shaft and struck the door and glanced into the station, knocking me out for over a week, I got out of the district rather luckily.

I batched for the last year I was in Cripple Creek, as I found I could save a little money that way. The house I lived in was made of one thickness of boards, covered with corrugated iron—an oven in summer and an ice-box in winter. I had to get up early in the morning, eat my breakfast half cooked and half frozen, and then walk, or run, a mile and a half over the trail to the mine. A man changes every two weeks to another of the three eight-hour shifts into which the day is divided. After I got back to the shack and got cleaned up and my supper cooked and eaten, it was usually too late and I was too tired to do anything more than read the paper, or write a letter home or to the one who would soon make a home for me.

Young Men at Work

7. POTTERY WORKER

Q. You may give your name and your occupation.—*A.* John W. Morgan: I am a jiggerman.

Q. Employed at the present time in one of the Trenton potteries?—*A.* Yes.

Q. How long have you been here?—*A.* It is thirty-three years since I first came.

Q. Did you ever work abroad in this industry?—*A.* Yes; in England.

Q. Before we start on this I would like to have the witness explain the definition and origin of the word "jiggerman."—*A.* The potter that is termed a jiggerman makes plates, saucers, cups, and wash basins. Even when a machine is used, most of the work is really hand work. Before the introduction of machinery it took a boy in this country five years to learn the trade; in foreign countries, in England and Scotland, seven years.

Q. Is the trade as far advanced here as there, so far as the employment of facilities and the introduction of fine designs and methods are concerned?—*A.* Yes—as far as the facilities are concerned. We get labor much cheaper over there than we do here. Where we are compelled to pay $9 a week here, we could get the same work done over there for about $2.25.

Q. Does that wide difference run all through the industry there?—

A. Where we are compelled to hire help. For instance, my own expenses are $6 a day for my help before I can begin to earn anything myself.

We turn out a considerably greater number than they do. We go at a killing pace in this country.

Q. When you say "a killing pace," do you mean that the pace that you work at here impairs your strength and shortens your lives?—*A.* No, I don't know that it does. It seems to me we live on about the average of potters in other countries. But as the custom of the American citizens is to go ahead in everything, we do the same. Imitation counts for a great deal in this country. For instance, if one person gets a bicycle everybody else wants one. You go to work at seven o'clock in the morning Monday mornings, while in England and Scotland that would be about breakfast time. Then they quit somewhat earlier than we do. As a rule we keep at it ten hours a day except Saturday, and quit on Saturday at four.

Q. You can produce more goods in a day than they are in the habit of producing there?—*A.* Yes.

Q. But you claim you should be entitled to more earnings when you produce more goods?—*A.* Yes. We get a better price than the workman does over there for his goods. If we did not we would not be here.

Q. Many employers and many representatives of labor unions have testified that the American workman in any industry turns out a greater amount of finished product that the English worker will do, and they even go so far as to say that is true of the Englishman transplanted to this country: that there is something in the air or the living that induces him to turn out a greater product. I would like to ask you if it has been your observation that that is true, and if true, what do you think are the causes that bring it about?—*A.* It is true: the causes I do not know.

Q. Is it better living—better conditions under which the people work?—*A.* I will say we live somewhat better than they do in foreign countries. The opportunities present themselves. I do not think that even the child has the opportunity of living in foreign countries as he does here. He has everything in season, and he lives better. It is a necessity that he does or he could not keep this pace up. I have known men to come to this country and start to work, and found the pace so rapid that they have retired and gone back. The very experience of seeing us with our shirts off scared them into hysterics almost.

Q. How large a proportion of the men who come here become naturalized?—*A.* I claim that 98 per cent do.

Q. Do you think it is substantially true that they all do?—*A.* Yes.

They make up their minds to go back, some of them, but in all likelihood they turn up again and come back here. For instance, I came in 1868 and went back in 1871 with the determination of never coming to America any more.

I tried for two years and three months to adapt myself to the country of my birth, but I could not do so. It was a failure. I came back to America and have stayed here since, perfectly satisfied.

8. *ON A CATTLEBOAT*

Upon the prosecution of some agencies in New York City, the following facts were brought out: That although the shipping companies furnish transportation free, the agencies charge the men "passage fees" ranging from $5 to $25; that although prompt sailings are advertised, the men, even when engaged by the agency, often find after being sent to the port of sailing that they have to wait days or weeks, paying their board at a place near the dock meantime; that misinformed men are often stranded without means of return; that they are told the work is light and the food good, and that instead they find the hours long, the work heavy, and their food only what the regular cattlemen leave; that they are often inhumanly treated and have undesirable places in which to sleep; and that some agencies refuse to let the men carry their baggage to the steamers, but make them bring it to the agency and charge from 25 cents to $1 for taking it down. The following is a typical advertisement for men:

Just a few dollars will provide you at our office a fast voyage to your old country on the best passenger boats doing some light work. Brotherly treatment. Passage from seven to nine days. Boats leave every other day to Hamburg, Bremen, Rotterdam, and Antwerp. All expenses covered. Try and write to us.

Here is an example of the "brotherly treatment" and easy work, as experienced by the investigator:

There were five of us, and when we obtained our tickets we were taken to the office of a third agent where nine more men joined us, and then we were all taken to the Wall Street pier and there placed on a boat bound for Fall River. The agent gave to every one of us a ticket for this boat and a train ticket from Fall River to Boston. The boat started at half-past six. All of the fourteen men were sitting in one corner of the smoking room, and, as we did not get any berths to sleep in, we passed the whole night talking to each other. I found out that five Hungarians paid $12 each to one agent for their passage to Hamburg, but they had no order to any agent in Liverpool, neither did they have any tickets farther than Liverpool.

In Boston we were met by a man who took us and some more men who came direct from the train to another shipping agency which is rather a store than an office, upon which were signs reading "Shipping Agency" and "Cattlemen Wanted."

The agent told us that we should not leave the office even for a minute because he expected a telegram from the steamship company and then we must come to the boat at once. In a timetable I found out that no boat leaves that day and I did not mind the agent's order not to leave the place.

In the evening of the same day, the agent told us that the boat will leave early next morning, and to prevent our getting lost in town he recommended us to a lodging house next door to his house where we had to pay 25 cents each for the night. The agent's clerk, a young man by the name of "Jack," came up to us and told us that not all of our party, consisting of twenty-eight men, can go with the next boat, and those who do not wish to remain should pay him one dollar each and he will see to it that they leave next morning by this early boat. Some of the men agreed to this and handed him the dollars, but I did not.

About six o'oclock the next morning, October 17th, we were taken to the dock. Those who paid the one dollar to the clerk were not especially privileged as several of them were left behind.

We were shown to a cabin over the entrance of which was the inscription "Cattlemen's Cabin." It was a very small cabin with narrow passages between the berths. A table, which consisted of a board put on two poles, was fixed in the center of the room. The board of the table was lifted up, as it turns on hinges, and kept turned vertically all the time to allow more room to pass by, except during meals. Thirty-four "bunks" were fixed in around there and two cases of provisions. We placed our baggage in our berths. There were twenty-two men, eight of them Americans, the others Hebrews and Poles.

The boat started about 9 A.M. After we had arranged our baggage in our berths, every one of us expressed a strong wish to get something to eat. Four men entered our cabin and introduced themselves to us as our foremen. They were drunk and swore terribly and asked for whiskey and money. Half an hour later a supervisor came in and commanded us to go to work. Some of the men protested, asking for something to eat first, but the foremen drove us out of the cabin. Each foreman took five men to his section which consisted of more than two hundred cattle. Water pipes were drawn through the whole ship, but the openings were removed far from one another, and our work was to carry the filled buckets to our foreman who gave to each bull three buckets full of water. We worked till 1 P.M., when we got through with watering, and all dirty, tired, and hungry we came gladly back to the cabin hoping to get something to eat. A steward appeared and handed to us each a mug, a tin dish, a spoon, and a knife and fork. He also brought in two large dirty dishes and told us to go with him to the kitchen where we would get our dinner. Two of our men took up the dishes and went to the kitchen. A few minutes later they came back with full dishes. One dish contained some soup which looked like dirty dishwater; the other contained a brownish black hot mess. They also brought twenty loaves of bread. All the men threw themselves eagerly on the food and began to eat, but in a few minutes they all stopped, and I could hear them swear and curse over the soup. Every one cut off a piece of the browny black matter in the other dish, but ate none of it and neither could we eat the bread because it was raw and sour.

The only things we could eat were potatoes in dresses. About fifteen minutes after dinner we were called to work again. We worked for several hours in succession, lifting heavy bales of hay which were hoisted by a block on the upper deck. At four o'clock we came back to the cabin and some of our men went to the kitchen expecting to get something to eat, and they brought down a kettle of hot but not boiled water and some rotten biscuits. There was neither tea nor coffee, but we all drank the hot water eagerly as it was. We found out later that sugar and luxurious "jam" was also sent to us, but our foremen took it away for themselves. At five we were again at work which consisted in carrying and dividing hay for the cattle. We worked till eight, then we got our supper; again soup, what the men called "ash," and tea. No bread was given us.

After supper we had to work for two hours more. About half past ten we got straw mattresses, pillows, and blankets and went to bed. Every day regularly we worked about sixteen hours a day.

Our foreman would curse while instructing us what to do. Those of the cattlemen who understood them and fulfilled their commands were their favorites; those who did not understand them were tortured severely. Among those unfortunate ones were four Jews. One gave some money to his foreman before he started to work and was well treated the first day, but on the following day was put to the hardest work. Another did not understand English, so he was beaten for not acting in accordance with his orders, but this only happened the first few days, after which he knew what to do and tried his best to work earnestly so the foreman stopped beating him.

One fellow was somewhat idiotic. He did not understand his orders and would not do them right even when he was shown what to do. The foreman beat him terribly and he would sit down and cry. He worked at the opposite end of the ship from where I was working so I never saw him at work, but at night he would come to his berth which was next to mine, and cry for hours.

When we landed in Liverpool, we were met by agents who took us over to their offices. I gave them the envelope which the agent had given me. He opened it in my presence and found in it three dollars and a card. . . . He refused to give me a ticket to Hamburg, telling me that it costs $4.86, and he has no connection with the agent in New York. He gave the three dollars and the advice back after having made a statement in writing over his signature on the back of the advice.

9.   HOBOKEN SEAMAN

Twenty years ago, and probably at an earlier date still, the traveler bound for Europe on any of the ships, sailing from Hoboken, might have seen, had he been curious enough to look about him, a strange collection of men of all ages, sizes, and make-ups, huddled together nights in a musty cellar only a few steps from the North German Lloyd's docks. And, had he talked with this uncouth company, he would have learned much about the ways and means necessary to make big ships go and come an their ocean voyages.

Somewhat less than twenty years ago, say eighteen, a greasy paper sign was tacked to the door of the cellar for the benefit of those who might be looking for the dingy hole. It read: "Internashnul Bankrupp Klubb—Wellcome!" The words and lettering were the work of an Italian lad, who had a faculty for seeing the humor in things which made others cry and sigh. In years that have passed the sign has been blown away, and a barber to-day holds forth where the "Bankrupps" formerly lodged. The store above, a general furnishing establishment for emigrants and immigrants, has also given way to a saloon, I think, and the outfitting business of former days has developed, in the hands of the old proprietor's sons, into a general banking and exchange affair near-by around the corner. The old proprietor has long since been gathered unto his fathers, I have been told; but the boys possess much of his business acumen and money-getting propensities and are doing well, preferring, however, to handle the currencies of the various nations to selling tin pots, pans, mattresses, and shoddy clothing, as did the old man.

Their father was a Hebrew, who may or may not have had a very interesting history before I met him, but at the time of our acquaintance he looked so fat and comfortable and money was so plainly his friend and benefactor that he was a pretty prosaic representative of his race. I had heard about him in New York, after making unsuccessful attempts there and in Brooklyn to secure a berth as caretaker on a Europe-bound cattleship.

I finally heard of the corpulent Hebrew and the "Bankrupps" Club in Hoboken. A German sailor told me about the place, describing the cellar as a refuge for "gebusted" Europeans, who were prepared to work their way back to their old country homes as coal-passers. The sailor said that any one, European or not, was welcome at the club, provided he looked able to stand the trip. The Hebrew received two dollars from the steamship companies for every man he succeeded in shipping.

My first interview with this man, how he lorded it over me and how I answered him back—these things are as vivid to me today as they were years ago. "Du bist zu schwach" (you are too weak), he told me on hearing of my desire for a coal trimmer's berth. "Pig mens are necessary for dat vork," and his large Oriental eyes ran disdainfully over my shabby appearance.

"Never you mind how *schwach* I am," I assured him; "that's my look-out. See here! I'll give you two dollars besides what the company gives you, if you'll get me a berth."

Again the Oriental's eyes rolled, and closed. "Vell," the man returned at last, "you can sleep downstairs, but I t'ink you are *zu schwach.*"

The week spent "downstairs" is perhaps as memorable a week as any in my existence. Day after day went by, "Pig mens" by the dozen left the cellar to take their positions, great ships whistled and drew out into the mighty stream outward bound, my little store of dimes and nickels grew smaller and smaller—and I was still "downstairs," awaiting my chance (a hopeless one it seemed) with the other incapables that the ships' doctors had refused to pass. The Italian lad, with his sweet tenor voice and sunny temperament, helped to brighten the life in the daytime and early evening, but the dark hours of the night, full of the groans and sighs of the old men, trying for berths, were dismal enough. Nearly every nationality was represented in the cellar during the week I spent there, but Germans predominated. What tales of woe and distress these men had to tell!

They were all "gebusted," every one of them. A pawnbroker would probably not have given five dollars for the possessions of the entire crew.

"Amerika" was the delinquent in each reported case of failure—the men themselves were cock-sure that they were in no particular to blame for their defeat and bankruptcy. "I should never have come to this accursed land," was the claim of practically all of the inmates of the cellar, except the little Italian. He liked *Neuvo Yorko, malto una citt bellissima*—but he wanted to see his mother and *Itallia* once more. Then he was coming back to *Neuvo Yorko* to be mayor, perhaps, some day. The hope that is in Americans was also in him. He believed in it, in himself and in his mother; why should he not become a good American? Why not, indeed?

But those poor old men from Norway! Theirs was the saddest plight. "The boogs" (bugs), one said to me, an ancient creature with sunken eyes and temples, "they eat down all my farm—all. They come in a day. My mortgage money due. They take my crops—all I had. No! America no good for me. I go back see my daughter. Norway better." I wonder where the poor old soul is, if he be still on earth. Ship after ship went out, but there was no berth for his withered up body, and after each defeat, he fell back, sighing, in his corner of the cellar, a picture of disappointment and chagrin such as I never have seen elsewhere, nor care to gaze upon again.

Our beds were nothing but newspapers, some yellow, some half so, and others sedate enough, I make no doubt. We slept, however, quite oblivious of newspaper policies and editorials. Looking for our meals and wondering when our berths on the steamers would be ready constituted our day's work, and left us at night, too tired out to know or care much whether we were lying on feathers or iron. I have since had many a restful night in Hoboken, and to induce sleep, even with mosquitoes as bedfellows, nothing more has been necessary than to recall those newspaper nights in the Hebrew's underground refuge. I trust that he is resting well somewhere.

"Get up, *presto!* We're all going, *presto!*" It was five o'clock on a cool October morning, and my friend, the little Italian, was tugging away at my jacket. "Get up, *fratello,*" he persisted. "Mucha good news." The light was struggling in through the cobwebbed windows and doorway, and the Norwegian was wakefully sighing again. I sat up, rubbed my eyes, and stared wonderingly at the Italian.

"Where's your good news?" I yawned, and pulled on my jacket.

"Mucha—mucha," he went on. "Policeman, he dead. Eighteen firemen and passers put hatchet in his head right front here. Blood on the sidewalk. Firemen and passers are pinched. Ship—she call the *Elbe*

—she sail nine o'clock. The old Jew, he got to ship us. No time to look 'roun'. Mucha good news, what?"

10. SAN FRANCISCO DRAYMAN

I was born in Philadelphia on October 5, 1888, but came to San Francisco as a baby. Both of my parents were born in Ireland. . . . My father was a teamster. There were seven children in the family, four boys and three girls. . . . The boys all became teamsters. . . . I went to work at around age fourteen. . . .

Hours and Conditions. Hours of work were generally from sun up to sun down. It was practically a seven day a week job. Monday through Saturday was actually the work week, and on Sunday it would be necessary for us to go to the barn to feed and water the horses, clean the harness, and . . . curry the horses. Working conditions were all but pleasant in most cases. If we were late for a day, that would mean the loss of a day's employment and we would get an unruly team, an unpleasant order to pick up at the local docks, any obnoxious cargo. One I have particularly in mind is "green hides." This would be more repulsive on a hot summer day, due to the fact that these hides would be crawling with maggots and naturally quite odorous. What did the teamsters gripe about most? If they felt that others were being given favored assignments and it would seem to them that they were getting the more difficult tasks to perform, especially if it continued on more than one day. We had a foreman in those days whose job it was to see the work was properly done. Many of them were ambitious men who showed no consideration for the worker, but were more concerned with their own well-being and ambitions.

My duties were those of the average teamster picking up and delivering to and from the San Francisco docks. . . . The part of the work that I liked best was that, having toiled and perspired, I would proceed to the docks to discharge the load for export. In so doing it would take time for the papers to be cleared. . . . There would be such a line-up that it would possibly be an hour or two before your turn came to unload. In the meantime, this would give us a chance to have a beer at one of the many saloons located along the dock area. . . . This would be comparable to our "coffee-break" of today.

Most men worked steadily because they had to. They could not afford to lose a half day. Truthfully, . . . I was young, big, strong, and willing to do the task at hand. The few times I was out of work was caused by our labor differences with the employer wherein we had to strike.

Wages and Living Standards. Although our wages were not high by today's comparisons, the dollar of that day was worth one hundred cents. For instance . . . hamburger in those days could be purchased two pounds for twenty-five cents, and coffee was in the neighborhood of fifteen cents per pound. Sugar was twenty pounds for one dollar and butter was thirty cents per pound. The usual teamster's home was an ordinary, typical San Francisco flat with two bedrooms, kitchen, dining room, sitting room or "parlor." The rent was generally about $18 a month. As for entertainment, our desires were never too great. Once in a while we would attend the Bella Unions and other entertainment spots. . . . This only required ten cents, which included carfare and we would get a glass of beer and a free lunch, which was so common in that era.

Many of the teamsters were Irish. About 70 per cent were Californians, and the balance were from out of the city.

Did many of the teamsters hope to be able to own a team? If so, it certainly was never made known because of the great amount of money in those days it would take to purchase a team and wagon. A good team would cost in the neighborhood of $500 and the cost was practically prohibitive in those days.

Which teamsters had the most prestige? Basically, the general freight hauling teamster was considered the backbone of the teaming industry. The others would form little groups or cliques of their own.

The Arrival of Automotive Trucks. The automotive trucks replaced horse-driven vehicles about 1917. The average teamster by no stretch of the imagination welcomed the advent of the motor truck. . . .

There was a gradual orientation of the old-time teamster. Soon he became adept at the handling of the various motor trucks.

The team drivers certainly retained their higher prestige. For a few years . . . the arrival of the motor trucks . . . had a tendency to reduce the hours in the work week because there was no occasion to go to the barn on Sundays to take care of the horses as we previously did. The motor vehicle naturally required a mechanic for any repairs that might be necessary. The trucks being faster, we were able to handle more freight within a given period. For instance, where it would take a team to haul a load from San Francisco to San Mateo a whole day, trucks could make several trips to San Mateo in a day's time.

11. ALTERATION PAINTER

My trip on the then new liner *America* was uneventful. . . . Early one morning in . . . October, 1907 . . . we approached America. My attention was first attracted by what I now know to be the Whitehall Building. I shall never forget the depressed feeling the sight of that building gave me. The little black square dots so close to each other couldn't possibly be windows of spaces large enough for human beings. . . .

I had arrived just in time for the great crisis of 1907. I made my temporary home with my girl's uncle, a capmaker by trade, who received me in a very friendly and hospitable manner. He told me however, that my coming to America in such a crisis was ill-advised. . . .

He had been in America for quite a few years, had a shop of his own and, though working hard from dawn to dusk, he had a hard struggle to support a family of six. "The Uncle" was rated as almost a millionaire by my girl's folks on the other side.

Before I had been two days in this country, I began worrying about a job. Neither my host nor any of his friends or acquaintances knew anything about my work which was jewelry engraving, or how to connect with a job in my trade.

I went out hunting on my own, following the help-wanted ads in the *World* with the help of a pocket-size German-English Dictionary which I always carried with me. During my daily travels in search of work, I learned from everyone I contacted that there were hundreds of seekers for every available job. Shallow engraving on jewelry and silverware, being part of a luxury industry, was naturally more keenly affected by the crisis than other occupations. . . .

I began to realize that in order to fit in, if and when I should strike a job, I would have to start learning how to do things the American way. I continued hunting for a job, but like a blind man I was groping in the dark. I had been at it for many weeks before I struck the first job through an ad in the paper; one of Brooklyn's department stores was advertising for an engraver to work on a piece-work basis. I applied and got the job, but it lasted only the 3 weeks before Christmas.

From then on I was tramping the streets almost all winter without being able to land a day's work at anything. Toward spring I managed to pick up odd jobs such as polisher in a smoking-pipe factory, common laborer in a luggage shop, street vendor, newspaper peddler, window cleaner, and sundry other jobs. I was making no headway.

By sheer accident I met a neighbor of my brother-in-law, a boss house painter. After a short talk with me, he discovered that I had some knowledge of colors, pigments and paints and varnishes. . . .

Although I had no experience at practical house-painting, I did have a theoretical knowledge of the trade and knew how to talk like a painter. I was hired. My new boss had a paint store and shop on Avenue C and did most of his work on the lower East Side.

I had been ordered to come to the shop at six-thirty in the morning but I was there ahead of time. Several men were already in their red and green, paint-covered overalls which only at the shoulder straps revealed traces of the white duck they were made of.

I stood around waiting for orders while the men mixed paints and prepared for the day's work. Suddenly the boss's voice woke me as from a trance. "What're you standing around like a lummox? Why don't you take some stuff and follow the men?" I did not answer but took a ladder and carried it out into the street. . . . I kept on carrying the stuff into the street until the boss motioned one of the men to "take care" of me. This fellow showed me how to carry a ladder and a plank and a couple of pots in each hand besides.

I took my load and followed my partner, who was carrying a load no smaller than mine, for eight or nine blocks and then up three flights of stairs. At a distance of but a half a block I could hardly see my partner's body and head. All I saw was walking ladders and pots and cans.

We unloaded in the hallway, my partner knocked at the door and announced the painters were here. . . . The kitchen was so crowded there was hardly room to set up a ladder, but my partner seemed perfectly at home. With a swiftness and skill that took my breath away, he piled up the kitchen furniture, one on top of the other, and whatever else was in the way, pots, pans, shoes, clothing, food, he put under the table and proceeded to do the same in the bedroom. "Room-bedroom" was all the job consisted of. By this time I had got the idea and helped my partner get things out of the way. There wasn't much that I could do to help him except hand him whatever he called for. I marveled at the way my partner worked under such a handicap.

Long before twelve o'clock he had finished "painting" both rooms. The ceiling was white-washed a deep blue white, the walls were a shiny, grass green and the doors, casings, closets and windows were covered with a yet shinier dirty-red paint. The missus, her little four- or five-year-old boy and every article of furniture and clothing, bore samples of the three colors which my partner used.

Finished, my partner collected all our material and tools and on our way we went to another job. As we were hurrying to our next destination, the boss ran right into us. He stopped my partner long enough to tell him what a slow man he was and that it took him too long to do two lousy rooms.

Our next job was easy, three rooms that were vacant. Here I got my first chance to do actual painting. My partner started me painting the bedroom walls. I asked, "Aren't we going to white-wash the ceiling?" "Don't say white-wash, say calcimine." No sooner did he finish his lecture than he dipped his large brush into the whiting and blue which he called calcimine, sprinkled the floor with it, and with a meaningful grin turned to me and said, "You see! The ceiling is already done!" When I found out what that ceremonial sprinkling of the floor meant, I realized that I had received my first lesson in beating the speed-up system at its own game.

All the way down the line, "logical" reasons were offered for the kind of smearing that was being done for the East Side slum dwellers. The landlords claimed that most of their tenants moved out rather than pay rent. Most flats had to be painted four or five times a year, since no tenant wanted to move in on live cockroaches. The dead ones were not so objectionable.

The boss painter, who got as little as $1.25 for "painting" a room complete, claimed he had to get production in order to be able to pay wages. The worker who received from $1.50 to $2 for a nine- or ten-hour workday knew that he couldn't hold the job if he didn't produce four and five rooms a day complete. In most cases, particularly in cases of unoccupied rooms, there was hardly any difference between the appearance of the rooms before and after painting.

My first week as a "Columbus painter" (that is, a painter who had learned the trade in the U.S.) netted me one dollar in wages. The boss acted like a philanthropist when he handed me my pay. "When I was a greenhorn," he said to me, "I had to pay the boss for teaching me the trade and here you are learning the trade for nothing and getting paid in the bargain."

I worked all summer for this boss and learned a few tricks of the trade the hard way.

My wages were increased from time to time until I reached the munificent sum of $5 a week. By that time I was already producing as good a day's work as most other men, and while I still did not have the least idea about real house painting, yet at least so far as the boss's interests were concerned, he had a bargain in me. On the eve of the fall season, when East Side painters were going uptown, to work in the better houses, I asked the boss for a raise. He flatly refused and was quite irritated over my "ingratitude." I packed him in, and again went after the help-wanted ads.

Painters were in great demand and there was quite a selection of jobs available. I obtained employment in a small shop which was doing a fairly good class of residential work in the Flatbush section of Brooklyn. This employer was a more civilized person than my last one. His work was of a better and cleaner nature, and the homes in which the work was done were neat, well-ordered American homes.

Considering the then prevailing standards of wages and working conditions, I was getting along pretty nicely. My new employer, judging by my knowledge of various paint materials and my ability to mix colors with taste and accuracy, was under the impression that I was a painter from the old country. Whenever I failed to turn out a job to his complete satisfaction, I used the stock excuse that we didn't do it that way back home. However, before long, I adapted myself to his ways and style of doing work and we got along swell.

Thus my personal problems seemed nearer solution than ever before. Living modestly, I was able to put aside a few pennies to pay up my debts, chief among which was my girl's passage money to America. So the great day came when Salka and I got married and lived in a room with our relatives in Brooklyn.

Once a week or so, I used to go to New York to meet my new East Side acquaintances, some of whom were painters. From then on I heard a lot more about miserable conditions, low wages and inhumanly long hours.

Nominally, the eight-hour workday was universal. It had been established in the building industry, in all its branches, decades before, but without benefit to the unorganized painters. These slaves in white labored from dawn to dusk during the longest hours of a summer's day. There were no regular hours. It was the invariable habit of the bosses to blow in on the men just at quitting time and it was too bad for the painter who took his five o'clock quitting time seriously. "What are you, a union man?" the boss would yell irritatedly. "Afraid I'm gonna get rich on you?" It made no difference how much work the man had accomplished for the day. The boss always expected him to either "finish up" or "get things started, to make it easier for the next day."

But long hours were not the only curse in the alteration painter's life. His wages, often as little as $1.50 a day, were not enough to keep body and soul together even in the "good old days" of the big schooner of beer with the bowl of soup and bread and cheese and baloney into the bargain for one nickel.

Those that were married and had children lived "for themselves" in room-bedroom, that is, a kitchen and a black airless windowless hole called a bedroom. The single men were boarders with or without board. Their home often consisted of a corner in the kitchen and a broken down couch or sofa, the springs of which made circular imprints on the boarder's body so distinct that one was ashamed to go to a Turkish Bath. There was no sense in complaining for what could one expect for three or four dollars a month?

The East Side immigrant painter, particularly the Columbus product, knew nothing about the poisonous effects of his trade. When as a result of his hurried lunching with lead-covered hands he conveyed the poison into his bowels and got a sudden attack of lead-colic, he didn't know why he was in pain. Maybe it was the extra large piece of watermelon which he ate with bread for supper last night—maybe that had caused his bellyache.

12. KANSAS FARM HAND

On the completion of my junior year in the Burlington high school, I felt that I ought to get out and do some real work, work that should not only preserve me from further idleness, but bring some financial advantages besides; so I agreed to tend the twenty-five acres or so of corn on the farm of Napolean and Abigain Thornrich, for the consideration of $14 per month and keep. . . .

The first week or so of sociological life was a rather bitter experience, for besides being green to hard work, I was decidedly ill. . . . Whatever the cause, I had during those first days neither satisfactory rest nor appetite. I had only thirst and high ideals of the mission of the hired man. My employer was very kind and kept counselling me, "Take it easy, bub" . . . but I thought I had hired out to work and had to earn my salary, and so I resigned. Shortly afterward, I hired out again to my brother for the haying season. . . .

When my brother's hay was all in, the Thornrich farm was once more in need of a hand, so I hired out again, this time at the advanced wages of 75 cents a day, during the haying season. This advance was given me, first because I was now skilled labor, and secondly because of the theory that haying is harder than ordinary farm work—an economic fiction in this case, for quite the reverse was true. For, since I had to perform the whole round of haying duties myself, I had plenty of variety, and lighter work than that of the man who pitches on the load and on the stack all day. . . .

During my time, adult hired men got from $15 to $17 a month,

board, room, washing, and lodgings included. In some exceptional
cases, more was paid. At the present time wages are a little higher—
$17 to $20 a month. In other words, it takes the earnings of about
five days to buy a pair of top boots and overalls, while in my time
it took about a day longer. To earn a top buggy now requires the
savings of about four months, and to earn a suit of good clothes requires a full month longer. So counting in the expense of horse feed
—the hired man usually owns a horse—nearly a whole season's work
is needed to properly equip the farm laborer for the pleasures of the
winter literary society, singing school, and church socials. At the
present time some farmers furnish a small house and garden, with
privileges of pasture to a married man and his wife. Both board
themselves and do their own washing. Under such conditions, the
man receives from $20 to $25 per month. Since top buggy and other
society expenses are saved under these circumstances, this is probably
the most economical way to hire out.

From a consideration of the income of the hired man, we are . . .
led to . . . The Pleasures of the Hired Man.

Among these I will mention first the athletic pleasures. It seems
peculiar that the man who works hard with his muscles from about
five in the morning until half-past eight in the evening, with a short
nooning, of an hour perhaps, should, especially if he be a young
man, turn to athletics the first thing after the chores are done in the
evenings. Foot-races, jumping, turning pole, swimming, all are popular, especially if some neighbor lad comes over from the next farm
to join in. . . .

Among the pleasures not athletic are the summer ice-cream socials,
destined more for the glory and advancement of the church, however,
than for the pleasure of man. You ride six or eight miles of a dark
night after a hard day's work, your fatigue aggravated by the good
clothes you have to wear. Arriving at the schoolhouse, you are invited
to pay ten cents for a dish of watery ice cream and a square of cake,
served by some young woman whom you do not know and are afraid
of being introduced to. After the refreshments, if you are refreshed,
and the programme, if there is a programme, you drive home again,
to arrive, perhaps, a little before breakfast-time.

But the real, the substantial pleasure of the hired man's life, especially if he is hired by the day during the haying season, is the
rainy day. . . . When you meet your employer downstairs, your face
wears a look of gloom. "It's too bad, isn't it, to lose that hay we raked
up yesterday; but"—and how easy it is for your countenance to
lighten up again—"but this is a mighty fine thing for the corn."

For the present . . . I shall put my paragraph on the Religious Life of the Hired Man in with the social pleasures, though it must be admitted that the expedient is hardly a happy one. For, in the first place, it is necessary to put on a coat and vest for the church-going, and, since the same good suit does for both summer and winter, it is a costume hardly suitable for a hot summer day. You ride to the service seated on the front seat of the spring wagon with your employer, while the women folks of the family occupy the seat behind, the one with a back to it. And, while your seat may be cushioned, it seems far less comfortable than the hayrack, and the whole drive is in harmony with your stiff Sunday suit. . . .

The going home is rather pleasanter, for you have the immediate prospect of getting into some more comfortable clothes, and the more remote one of getting something to eat. The attendance at church and Sunday-school delays domestic operations somewhat, and the Sunday dinner is always late.

The parlor is open Sunday afternoons, and you may enter with the rest of the family and have your turn at the religious and the secular weekly. There may be callers to help entertain, and you get the temporary relaxation of turning the ice-cream freezer or of going out to the well to haul up the watermelon. Together with your employers, you rise into the higher social status of the day, a remark which brings me to . . . The Social Status of the Hired Man.

As children, we used to number the years on the farm by the "hands" we had employed, much as nations mark their calendars by their changes of kings. There was the year of Will Williams, the years of Owen Williams, the summer we hired Bill Jones, the interregnum which followed the turning off of Bob Peters, and so on. One of the marked characteristics of American farm life is its democracy, and this is well illustrated by the relations which exist between employer and hired man. Often the son of a neighboring farmer, the "hand" enjoys the same consideration as that received by a member of the family. He sits at the same table, and shares in the dishes as early and often as the other men of the family. He probably would be asked to join in the evening game of checkers or authors, if there were any evening between summer chores and bedtime. He has a voice in family debates regarding the election of a new schoolma'am, and his opinion is of weight in the discussion of current politics or the proper time for weaning calves. His joys are those of his employers and his sorrows their sorrows. . . .

13. AN ITALIAN BOOTBLACK

We were so long on the water that we began to think we should never get to America or that, perhaps, there was not any such place, but at last we saw land and came up to New York.

We were glad to get over without giving money, but I have heard since that we should have been paid for our work among the coal and that the young men who had sent us got money for it. We were all landed on an island and the bosses there said that Francisco and I must go back because we had not enough money, but a man named Bartolo came up and told them that we were brothers and he was our uncle and would take care of us. He brought two other men who swore that they knew us in Italy and that Bartolo might be my uncle. I had never seen any of them before, but even then Bartolo might be my uncle, so I did not say anything. The bosses of the island let us go out with Bartolo after he had made the oath.

We came to Brooklyn to a wooden house in Adams Street that was full of Italians from Naples. Bartolo had a room on the third floor and there were fifteen men in the room, all boarding with Bartolo. He did the cooking on a stove in the middle of the room and there were beds all around the sides, one bed above another. It was very hot in the room, but we were soon asleep, for we were very tired.

The next morning, early, Bartolo told us to go out and pick rags and get bottles. He gave us bags and hooks and showed us the ash barrels. On the streets where the fine houses are the people are very careless and put out good things, like mattresses and umbrellas, clothes, hats, and boots. We brought all these to Bartolo and he made them new again and sold them on the sidewalk; but mostly we brought rags and bones. The rags we had to wash in the back yard and then we hung them to dry on lines under the ceiling in our room. The bones we kept under the beds till Bartolo could find a man to buy them.

Most of the men in our room worked at digging the sewer. Bartolo got them the work and they paid him about one quarter of their wages. Then he charged them for board and he bought the clothes for them, too. So they got little money after all.

Bartolo was always saying that the rent of the room was so high that he could not make anything, but he was really making plenty. He was what they call a padrone and is now a very rich man. The men that were living with him had just come to the country and could not speak English. . . . Bartolo told us all that we must work for him and that if we did not the police would come and put us in prison.

He gave us very little money, and our clothes were some of those that were found on the street. Still we had enough to eat and we had meat quite often, which we never had in Italy. Bartolo got it from the butcher—the meat that he could not sell to the other people— but it was quite good meat. Bartolo cooked it in the pan while we all sat on our beds in the evening. Then he cut it into small bits and passed the pan around, saying:

"See what I do for you and yet you are not glad. I am too kind a man, that is why I am so poor."

We were with Bartolo nearly a year, but some of our countrymen who had been in the place a long time said that Bartolo had no right to us and we could get work for a dollar and a half a day, which, when you make it *lire* [reckoned in the Italian currency] is very much. So we went away one day to Newark and got work on the street. Bartolo came after us and made a great noise, but the boss said that if he did not go away soon the police would have him. Then he went, saying that there was no justice in this country.

We paid a man five dollars each for getting us the work and we were with that boss for six months. He was Irish, but a good man and he gave us our money every Saturday night. We lived much better than with Bartolo, and when the work was done we had nearly $200 saved. Plenty of the men spoke English and they taught us, and we taught them to read and write. That was at night, for we had a lamp in our room, and there were only five other men who lived in that room with us.

We got up at half-past five o'clock every morning and made coffee on the stove and had a breakfast of bread and cheese, onions, garlic, and red herrings. We went to work at seven o'clock and in the middle of the day we had soup and bread in a place where we got it for two cents a plate. In the evenings we had a good dinner with meat of some kind and potatoes. We got from the butcher the meat that other people would not buy because they said it was old, but they don't know what is good. We paid four or five cents a pound for it and it was the best, though I have heard of people paying sixteen cents a pound.

When the Newark boss told us that there was no more work Francisco and I talked about what we would do and we went back to Brooklyn to a saloon near Hamilton Ferry, where we got a job cleaning it out and slept in a little room upstairs. There was a boot-black named Michael on the corner and when I had time I helped him and learned the business. Francisco cooked the lunch in the saloon and he, too, worked for the bootblack and we were soon able to make the best polish.

Then we thought we would go into business and we got a basement on Hamilton avenue, near the Ferry, and put four chairs in it. We paid $75 for the chairs and all the other things. We had tables and looking glasses there and curtains. We took the papers that have the pictures in and made the place high toned. Outside we had a big sign that said:

THE BEST SHINE FOR TEN CENTS

Men that did not want to pay ten cents could get a good shine for five cents, but it was not an oil shine. We had two boys helping us and paid each of them fifty cents a day. The rent of the place was $20 a month, so the expenses were very great, but we made money from the beginning. We slept in the basement, but got our meals in the saloon till we could put a stove in our place, and then Francisco cooked for us all. That would not do though, because some of our customers said that they did not like to smell garlic and onions and red herrings. I thought that was strange, but we had to do what the customers said. So we got the woman who lived upstairs to give us our meals and paid her $1.50 a week each. She gave the boys soup in the middle of the day—five cents for two plates. . . .

We had said that when we saved $1000 each we would go back to Italy and buy a farm, but now that the time is coming we are so busy and making so much money that we think we will stay. We have opened another parlor near South Ferry, in New York. We have to pay $30 a month rent, but the business is very good. The boys in this place charge sixty cents a day because there is so much work.

At first we did not know much of this country, but by and by we learned. There are here plenty of Protestants who are heretics, but they have a religion, too. Many of the finest churches are Protestant, but they have no saints and no altars, which seems strange.

These people are without a king such as ours in Italy. It is what they call a Republic, as Garibaldi wanted, and every year in the fall the people vote. . . .

There are two kinds of people that vote here, Republicans and Democrats. I went to a Republican meeting and the man said that the Republicans want a Republic and the Democrats are against it. He said that Democrats are for a king whose name is Bryan and who is an Irishman. There are some good Irishmen, but many of them insult Italians. They call us Dagoes. So I will be a Republican.

I like this country now and I don't see why we should have a king.

Garibaldi didn't want a king and he was the greatest man that ever lived. . . .

There are plenty of rich Italians here, men who a few years ago had nothing and now have so much money that they could not count all their dollars in a week. The richest ones go away from the other Italians and live with the Americans.

We have joined a club and have much pleasure in the evenings. The club has rooms down in Sackett Street and we meet many people and are learning new things all the time. We were very ignorant when we came here, but now we have learned much.

On Sundays we get a horse and carriage from the grocer and go down to Coney Island. We go to the theatres often and other evenings we go to the houses of our friends and play cards.

I am nineteen years of age now and have $700 saved. Francisco is twenty-one and has about $900. We shall open some more parlors soon. I know an Italian who was a bootblack ten years ago and now bosses bootblacks all over the city, who has so much money that if it was turned into gold it would weigh more than himself. . . .

14.   LUMBERMAN

Speaking from personal experience in lumber camps, Raymond Robins says:

Let me present some details for your consideration. The lumber industry is one of the ancient trades. In the old days the logger was, in his rough, uncouth way, a splendid type of the pioneer. He went forth from his cabin to the forest to fell trees in the timber strip and returned at night to his home and family. It was from such conditions that the men and women came forth to lead the industry and government of the West. From such a home came Lincoln! What are the conditions today in the great lumber camps of the West and South? Let me describe one in which I worked. We slept in bunks four tiers deep, one rack on each side and two in the center of a big tent. When called for dinner, we washed our hands and faces, if the habit still lingered, at a trough of running water. Then, lined up in front of the hash tent, we waited for the bar to go down. In we rushed, each man grabbing whatever he could reach and then, covering his plate with his hands, looked about to see if he had missed anything. At night, we slept in our clothes minus coat and shoes. We did this because our clothes, wet with sweat, protected us from the other inhabitants of our bunks. One night the tent leaked just above my bunk, and I got up. A light was shining in the foreman's cabin. I went over and found him wrestling with some accounts. I told him I was some shark at figures myself and asked if I might help him. He consented, and after I had straightened out his muddle, we lighted our pipes and had a talk. Some men from the nearby settlement had been at the camp that day asking for work. We were short of hands, yet they were sent away. I asked this foreman why he did not hire these men. He said that the company preferred men like us that were shipped out from the city. Pressed for the reason, he said, laconically, "You fellows don't kick about the hours or the wages or the grub. When you get fired you leave camp. If you get killed, the company don't have to pay."

Every man but two that I talked with in that camp seemed to be interested in just three things: whiskey, women, and the gamblers' trance. They were all waiting to get a stake large enough to have a "good time" in the red-light district of Chicago, Seattle, or San Francisco.

15.   SIX MONTHS' WORK, NOT ONE PENNY

The 3rd October, 1912, I arrived with S. S. *Noordam* at Hoboken and had about $20 in my pocket. I stay in Hoboken two weeks looking for a position as office clerk not knowing that there were more jobs as that for me. I never heard in my country about dishwasher, janitor, and other positions as waiter and many others were not in my way because I never had any experience about them.

After my money was spent I left Hoboken and went as given in a newspaper to Park Row to an office where they sent men out in this State for farmers and the reason that the manager was a Dutchman found a good place in my heart that I could get some advice around there. He told me he had a job for $12 a month and I get it. Well I took it, he paid my fare to Erieville, about forty miles from Syracuse (N.Y.) and arrived following day at the farmer. After working for three weeks the farmer told me that that kind of work was nothing for me and that I had to go. He give me $2.13 being $9.00 minus $6.87 fare what he paid for me when I was send to him. The money being $2.13 was not enough to go back to New York and was the only way for me to go to Syracuse for 87 cents. In Syracuse, a small town, was no work at all. I stay there for three months and sleep in the station or walk outside in the snow and cold night. At last I work in a lunch-room as dishwasher for $5 a week, meals free.

In the same time a friend of me was working Morris Plains (N.J.) Hospital, and wrote me a letter that I must come to him because he could give me a position for $20 a month in the laundry. The reason that he was a countryman from me and friend in my town I listened to him and came two days later for $6.78 in Morris Plains. He had send me $6 for fare. In all the time being four months I had my trunk with clothes in Hoboken at a hotel, Hudson Street, for his keeping. I had to pay every months $1.25, so that I must pay him for four months $5. The manager heard that I was working, wrote me a letter that he would not be any longer responsible for my trunk and ordered me to take the trunk away and told me in two days. I was in Morris Plains just about one month and pay day was a few days later. There my clothes were from fine quality and I would not lose them. I must quit my job for to get money. I received about $18. I paid my friend his $6 and the hotel-keeper $5, for the train 78 cents— $11.78, so that when I was in New York I had $6 in my pocket. I took my trunk and took it with me to my room Hudson Street, where I was only one week, and till this day my trunk was left in that room and never saw her again. I went in the Bowery because people told me, it was in February, I could get if I had no money always something to eat down there, and from that time the miserable life was beginning. After a few weeks the Bowery Mission gave me a position as writer addresses in Barclay Street where I work one and one half months. They had no work more and I had to quit. I went to Hoboken one night and got a job as bartender in Hudson Street. I must work there eighteen hours a day for $5 a week. I get up 9 A.M. and has as my first duty to clean the bar and rooms what tooks about five or six hours and in the same time bartender. At 3 P.M. the manager comes down and then I am a waiter. But don't supposed that I could sit down for a rest. No if he could not find more work to do, then he ordered me to play the piano, and many times that I did that from 3 P.M. till 11 P.M. while he had told me that the afternoon was for me to take a walk. And when I was playing I had to keep music all the time; he only found that we had to take a rest in bed after 3 A.M. when I was finished. Once he did not understand me right and became so mad that, so he always did with his customers, took his police stick and would hit me. I found it the best way to beat it, and not asking for my money went out and to New York where I got a job as orderly in a hospital. There I work three weeks as orderly and after that the sister gives me a porter job what only tooks one week. After that the sister came in the morning and told me that she heard I wasn't a

Catholic and there I had money enough made I could look for another job. Before she hired me she told me that the salary was $12 a month. I went down the office with her and thinking to get $12 I received $4.50, and told me that it was all the money she got.

After that I was discusted and after paying $2 I was shipped to Venango about sixty miles from Buffalo to work as laborer at the railroad. There I came to the recovering that I had to do with a bunch of thieves. I work one and one half months and quit with $8.25 left. The commissary man where a man buy his stuff, so as meals, clothes, etc., was a big thief, and he steal from us Americans and other men all he could get. He steal the money before my face and as I told it him then I have to be very quiet because he did not care to kill me. From there I went for $2.90 to Cleveland, Ohio, and paid at an agency $2—that was all the money I had—for a job in West Virginia with a tie treating plant at $1.75 a day. I arrived and was surprised to hear that it was piece-work and there were no jobs for $1.75. I had to take it and work one month. I made about between 75 cents and a dollar a day and had to pay 60 cents for meals. I went after one month to the railroad who was laying a new track in the neighborhood. They took me as laborer and in the hope that there were no thieves there, started the laborer job again. But the railroad is worse as the New York roads. The commissary man was all right; sometime he took some dimes more but he did it not so often as his partner in Venango Erie railroad. Now was it the railroad who did not pay me $9 and I found it after three months' work better to go to New York when they lay us off and came first in Philadelphia bought clothes there and walk from Philadelphia without one penny in New York's Bowery after six months' work and all kind of experiences.

16.   JACK-OF-ALL-TRADES

In every instance of employment I always found it possible to save from my wages. . . .

In my early experience, I was never obliged to look long for work and never, as I recollect, over a single day without finding it; but that, however, was in country communities or relatively small towns. But when I entered Chicago, I was in the midst of a large industrial center and found that I was there simply one of the army of the unemployed: that the supply of labor was in excess of the demand by many thousands of men, and that the search for work there was under wholly different conditions. . . . Two weeks of effort to find employment proved fruitless, but when I did find employment as a hand truckman in a factory on the west side of Chicago, I received a wage of $1.50 a day. This represented a sum considerably above the means of subsistence. I got board in a tenement house immediately opposite the factory for $4.25 a week. The margin between the $4.25 and the $9 a week represented practically the possibility of saving, because my only expenses above my board were laundry and a few items of that kind, which were relatively unimportant. . . . With the possible exception of one or two cases, I never found employment which did not offer the means of improved position; however unpromising and restricted the opportunities, I found in every instance that there was a chance of working to an improved condition. As a hotel porter, working for $8 a month and often working for sixteen hours out of the twenty-four, I found the chance of securing a position as assistant gardener was open to me with a great improvement as to position and as to wages.

While working in the logging camp in Pennsylvania and knowing nothing of the nature of work in the woods, I was at a great disadvantage. But I had not been there long before I found that the boss of the camp, while an admirable manager of his business, was ignorant of anything outside the range of his work. The very fact that I could be of assistance to him in the matter of keeping his accounts immediately gave me a standing in the camp which I had not at all as a mere unskilled laborer, and put me in such a position with reference to the boss that he was more than willing to keep me at a very much improved wage over that which he paid me at the beginning, which was 75 cents a day and my keep. This acquaintance with elementary arithmetic would be within the range of any boy who had had a few years' teaching in public school.

In the factory on the West Side in Chicago men who entered the factory as unskilled laborers advanced to positions of advantage as soon as they showed any capacity for the piece-work system. . . .

I readily secured employment with a gang of men who were making roads on the exposition grounds, and there again noted the same care on the part of those who were in positions of responsibility and authority to discover any special capacity among the men whom they were employing. So. . . .

First, no man in this country who is willing to work and is willing to accept any form of honest employment, and is not bound down to any one locality, but is free to go out into the country and look for work, need long look fruitlessly for employment; and in the second place, every form of employment which I secured as an unskilled laborer practically opened the way to improved position. . . . But my observation with regard to the ease with which employment may be found does not apply at all in general, and does not apply at all with reference to particular cases.

When I was in Chicago in that congested labor market, I came to know numbers of individuals, some of them unskilled laborers, others who belonged to the skilled trades, but who were bound to the community by reason of family ties; their wives and children were there, and they were not free to go out into the country. A very large proportion of the working classes are in communities from which they are not at liberty to move with ease. . . .

The working class in the country lives and fares far better than any working class in any part of the world; in living with gangs of working men, even with unskilled working men, I lived for the most part in houses that were kept as mechanics' boarding houses. The houses themselves were good, the beds were good, and our food was uniformly good. It not infrequently happened that the woman who kept the mechanics' boarding house had previous to her marriage been out at service, and had in this way acquired some exceptional knowledge of cooking, and her cooking was excellent as a result. It was my common experience that we had meat three times a day. Indeed, working men seem to demand as their right that they should have meat three times a day. In the tenement house in Chicago we breakfasted at half past six in the morning, had a porridge, meat, a vegetable, we had all the coffee we wanted for breakfast, and excellent bread—all . . . very well prepared. For our midday meal at each man's place was a steaming bowl of soup. It was replaced with a plate containing a slice of roast of some sort, and two or three vegetables and an abundance of bread, and after that would come dessert, usually pie— or sometimes a pudding. In the evening, after our day's work was done, we had a simpler meal, some cold meat and a hot vegetable, with an abundance of bread, and we finished up with a fruit.

That is perhaps the most favorable instance; but it is fairly typical of the sort of living that I got as a laboring man; and the rate I was paying there was $4.25 a week.

Women Workers

17. SHIRT WORKER

The population of this small town is 3346. Of these, 1000 work in the knitting-mill, 200 more in a cutlery factory, and 300 in various flour, butter, barrel, planing mills, and salt blocks. Half the inhabitants are young hands. Not one in a hundred has a home in Perry; they have come from all western parts of the state to work. There are scarcely any children, few married couples and almost no old people. . . .

At the mill . . . all hummed to the collective activity of a throng, each working with all his force for a common end. Machines roared and pounded; a fine dust filled the air—a cloud of lint sent forth from the friction of thousands of busy hands in perpetual contact with the shapeless anonymous garments they were fashioning. There were, on their way between the cutting and the finishing rooms, 7000 dozen shirts. They were to pass by innumerable hands; they were to be held and touched by innumerable individuals; they were to be begun and finished by innumerable human beings with distinct tastes and likings, abilities and failings; and when the 7000 dozen shirts were complete they were to look alike, and they were to look as though made by a machine; they were to show no trace whatever of the men and the women who had made them. Here we were, 1000 souls hurrying from morning until night, working from seven until six, with as little personality as we could, with the effort to produce, through an action purely mechanical, results as nearly as possible identical one to the other, and all to the machine itself. . . .

At the threshold of the mill door my roommate and I encountered Mr. Norse. There was irony in the fates allotted us. She was eager to make money; I was indifferent. Mr. Norse felt her in his power; I felt him in mine. She was given a job at 25 cents a day and all she could make; I was offered the favorite work in the mill—shirt finishing, at 30 cents a day and all I could make; and when I shook my head to see how far I could exploit my indifference and said, "Thirty cents is too little," Mr. Norse's answer was: "Well, I suppose you, like the rest of us, are trying to earn a living. I will guarantee you 75 cents

a day for the first two weeks, and all you can make over it is yours."
My apprenticeship began under the guidance of an "old girl" who
had been five years in the mill. A dozen at a time the woolen shirts
were brought to us, complete all but the adding of the linen strips
in front where the buttons and buttonholes are stitched. The price
of this operation is paid for the dozen shirts 5, 5½, and 6 cents, according to the complexity of the finish. My instructress had done as
many as forty dozen in one day; she averaged $1.75 a day all the year
around. While she was teaching me the factory paid her at the rate of
10 cents an hour.

Above the incessant roar and burring din my comrades called gaily
to each other, gossiping, chatting, telling stories. What did they talk
about? Everything, except domestic cares. Most frequently dress and
men.

A phrase which I heard often repeated at the factory speaks by itself
for a condition: "She must be married, because she don't work." And
another phrase pronounced repeatedly by the younger girls: "I don't
have to work; my father gives me all the money I need, but not all the
money I *want*. I like to be independent and spend my money as I
please."

What are the conclusions to be drawn? The American-born girl is
an egoist. Her whole effort (and she makes and sustains one in the
life of mill drudgery) is for herself. She works for luxury until the day
when a proper husband presents himself. Then she stops working and
lets him toil for both, with the hope that the budget shall not be
diminished by increasing family demands.

In those cases where the woman continues to work after marriage,
she chooses invariably a kind of occupation which is inconsistent with
child-bearing. She returns to the mill with her husband. There were
a number of married couples at the knitting factory at Perry. They
boarded, like the rest of us. I never saw a baby nor heard of a baby
while I was in the town.

On Saturday night we drew our pay and got out at half past four.
This extra hour and a half was not given to us; we had saved it up by
beginning each day at fifteen minutes before seven. In reality we
worked ten and a quarter hours five days in the week in order to work
eight and a half on the sixth.

By five o'clock on Saturdays the village street was animated with
shoppers—the stores were crowded. At supper each girl had a collection of purchases to show: stockings, lace, fancy buckles, velvet rib-
bons, elaborate hairpins. Many of them, when their board was paid,
had less than a dollar left of the five or six it had taken them a week
to earn.

Lynn is made up of factories—great masses of ugliness, red brick, many-windowed buildings. The General Electric has a concern in this town, but the industry is chiefly the making of shoes. The shoe trade in our country is one of the highest-paying manufactures, and in it there are more women employed than in any other trade. Lynn's population is 70,000; of these 10,000 work in shoe shops.

Now hatless, shirt-waisted, I was ready to labor amongst the 200 bond-women around me.

On my left the seat was vacant; on my right Maggie McGowan smiled at me, although, poor thing, she had small cause to welcome the green hand who demanded her time and patience. She was to "learn me pressin'," and she did.

As raw edges, at first defying my clumsiness, fell to fascinating rounds, as the awl creased the leather into the fluting folds, as the hammer mashed the gummed seam down, I enjoyed the process; it was kindergarten and feminine toil combined, not too hard; but it was only the beginning!

The next morning I applied at another factory, again one of the largest in Lynn. The sign read: "Cleaner Wanted!"

"Cleaner" sounded easy to learn.

I did not even know, as I do now, that "cleaning" is the filthiest job the trade possesses. It is in bad repute and difficult to secure a woman to do the unpleasant work.

Two high desks, like old-time school desks, rose in the workshop's center. Behind one of these I stood, whilst the foreman in front of me instructed my ignorance. . . . In an hour's time I did one-third as well as my companion. I cleaned a case in an hour, whilst she cleaned three.

"Bobby" was not talkative or communicative simply because she had nothing to say. Over and over again she repeated the one single question to me during the time I worked by her side: "Do you like your job?" and although I varied my replies as well as I could with the not too exhausting topic she offered, I could not induce her to converse. She took no interest in my work, being absorbed in her own.

The place was so close and foul-smelling that eating was an ordeal. If I had not been so famished, it would have been impossible for me to swallow a mouthful. I bought soup and beans, and ate, in spite of the inconveniences, ravenously, and paid for my dinner 15 cents. Most of my neighbors took one course, stew or soup. I rose half-satisfied, dizzy from the fumes and the bad air. . . .

In Lynn, unless she boards at home, a girl's living costs her at best $3.75 a week. If she be of the average ($8) her month's earnings are $32. Reduce this by general expenses and living and her surplus is $16, to earn which she has toiled 224 hours. You will recall that there are, out of the 22,000 operatives in Massachusetts, 5000 who make under $5 a week. I leave the reader to compute from this the luxuries and possible pleasures consistent with this income.

19. PICKLE PROCESSOR

I have become with desperate reality a factory girl, alone, inexperienced, friendless. I am making $4.20 a week and spending $3 of this for board alone, and I dread not being strong enough to keep my job. I climb endless stairs, am given a white cap and an apron, and my life as a factory girl begins.

The factory has been built contemporaneously with reforms and sanitary inspection. There are clean, well-aired rooms, hot and cold water with which to wash, places to put one's hat and coat, an obligatory uniform for regular employees, hygienic and moral advantages of all kinds, ample space for work without crowding.

Side by side in rows of tens or twenties we stand before our tables waiting for the seven o'clock whistle to blow. In their white caps and blue frocks and aprons, the girls in my department, like any unfamiliar class, all look alike.

One hour passes, two, three hours; then the twelve o'clock whistle blows. Up to that time the room has been one big dynamo, each girl a part of it. With the first moan of the noon signal the dynamo comes to life. It is hungry; it has friends and favorites—news to tell. We herd down to a big dining-room and take our places, five hundred of us in all. The newspaper bundles are unfolded. The menu varies little: bread and jam, cake and pickles, occasionally a sausage, a bit of cheese or a piece of stringy cold meat. In ten minutes the repast is over. The dynamo has been fed; there are twenty minutes of leisure spent in dancing, singing, resting, and conversing chiefly about young men and "sociables."

At twelve-thirty sharp the whistle draws back the life it has given. I return to my job. My shoulders are beginning to ache. My hands are stiff, my thumbs almost blistered. The enthusiasm I had felt is giving way to a numbing weariness. I look at my companions now in amazement. How can they keep on so steadily, so swiftly? Cases are emptied and refilled; bottles are labeled, stamped and rolled away; jars are washed, wiped, and loaded, and still there are more cases, more jars, more bottles. Oh! The monotony of it, the never-ending supply of work to be begun and finished, begun and finished, begun and finished!

I sweep and set to rights, limping, lurching along. At last the whistle blows! In a swarm we report; we put on our things and get away into the cool night air. I have stood ten hours; I have fitted 1300 corks; I have hauled and loaded 4000 jars of pickles. My pay is 70 cents.

There is no variety in my morning's work. Next to me is a bright, pretty girl, jamming chopped pickles into bottles.

"How long have you been here?" I ask, attracted by her capable appearance. She does her work easily and well.

"About five months."

"How much do you make?"

"From 90 cents to $1.05. I'm doing piece-work," she explains. "I get seven-eighths of a cent for every dozen bottles I fill. I have to fill eight dozen to make seven cents. Downstairs in the corking-room you can make as high as $1.15 to $1.20. They won't let you make any more than that. Me and them two girls over there are the only ones in this room doing piece-work. I was here three weeks as a day-worker."

"Do you live at home?" I ask.

"Yes; I don't have to work. I don't pay no board. My father and my brothers supports me and my mother. But," and her eyes twinkle, "I couldn't have the clothes I do if I didn't work."

"Do you spend your money all on yourself?"

"Yes."

I am amazed at the cheerfulness of my companions. They complain of fatigue, of cold, but never at any time is there a suggestion of ill-humor. Their suppressed animal spirits reassert themselves when the forewoman's back is turned. Companionship is the great stimulus.

20.   THE LAST BOX WAS DONE

The order on which we worked was, like most of the others on the floor that day, for late-afternoon delivery. Our ruching-boxes had to be finished that day, even though it took every moment till six or even seven o'clock. Saturday being what is termed a "short-day," one had to work with might and main in order to leave at half-past four. . . . Therefore we did not stop to eat, but snatched bites of cake and sandwich as hunger dictated and convenience permitted, all the while pasting and labeling and taping our boxes. Nor were we the only toilers obliged to forgo the hard-earned half-hour of rest.

The awakening thunder of the machinery burst gratefully on our ears. It meant that the last half of the weary day had begun.

Every girl limped now as she crossed the floor with her towering burden, and the procession back and forth between machines and tables began all over again. Lifting and carrying and shoving: cornering and taping and lacing—it seemed as though the afternoon would never wear to an end.

Blind and dizzy with fatigue, I peered down the long, dusty aisles of boxes toward the clock. It was only two. Every effort, human and mechanical, all over the great factory, was now strained almost to the breaking point.

The head foreman rushed through the aisles and bawled to us to "hustle for all we were worth," as customers were all demanding their goods.

"My God! ain't we hustling?" angrily shouted Rosie Sweeny, a pretty girl at the next table, who supplied most of the profanity for our end of the room. "God Almighty! how I hate Easter and Christmas-time! Oh, my legs is 'most breaking," and with that the overwrought girl burst into a passionate tirade against everybody, the foreman included, and all the while she never ceased to work. There were not many girls in the factory like Rosie.

By four o'clock the last box was done. Machines became mute, wheels were stilled, and the long black belts sagged into limp folds. Every girl seized a broom or a scrub-pail, and hilarity reigned supreme while we swept and scrubbed for the next half-hour, Angelina and her chorus singing all the while endless stanzas of the "Fatal Wedding."

Henrietta sent me for a fresh pail of water, which I got from the faucet in the toilet-room; and as I filled my bucket I made a mental inventory of my fellow-toilers' wardrobes. Hanging from rows of nails on all sides were their street garments—a collection of covert-cloth jackets, light tan automobile coats, black silk box-coats trimmed in white lace, raglans, and every other style of fashionable wrap that might be cheaply imitated. Sandwiched among the street garments were the trained skirts and evening bodices of the "Moonlight Maids" of the night before, and which were to be again disported at some other pleasure-club festivity that Easter evening, now drawing near.

I hurried back with my bucket of water, hoping in my heart that the pleasure their wearers got out of this finery might be as great as the day's work which earned it was long and hard.

21.   *THE STAR ROSE-MAKER*

It would seem that all the world's wife and daughters were to wear nothing but poppies that season. But ours was only a small portion of Rosenfeld's output. Violets, geraniums, forget-me-nots, lilies-of-the-valley, apple-blossoms, daisies, and roses of a score of varieties were coming to life in this big garden in greater multitudes even than our common poppies. Forty girls worked on roses alone. The rose-makers are the swells of the trade. They are the best paid, the most independent, and always in competitive demand during the flower season. Any one can learn with patience how to make other kinds of flowers; but the rose-maker is born, and the thoroughly experienced rose-maker is an artist. Her work has a distinction, a touch, a "feel," as she calls it, which none but the artist can give.

The star rose-maker of the shop, next to the forewoman (who was reputed the finest in America), was about twenty-five. Her hair was fluffy and brown, and her eyes big and dark blue. She was of Irish birth, and had been in America about fourteen years. One day I stopped at her chair and asked how long it took her to learn.

"I'm still learning," she replied, without looking up from the tea-rose in her fingers. "It was seven years before I considered myself first-class; and though I'm at it now thirteen, I don't consider I know it all yet." She worked rapidly, flecking the delicate salmon-colored petals with her glue-finger, and pasting them daintily around the fast-growing rose. I watched her pinch and press and crease each frail petal with her hot iron instruments, and when she had put on a thick rubber stem and hung the finished flower on the line she looked up and smiled.

"Want to see a rose-maker's hand?" she remarked, turning her palm up for my inspection. She laughed aloud at my exclamation of horror. Calloused and hard as a piece of tortoise-shell, ridged with innumerable corrugations, and hopelessly discolored, with the thumb and forefinger flattened like miniature spades, her right hand had long ago lost nearly all semblance to the other.

"It is the hot irons do that," she said, drawing her pincers from the fire and twirling them in the air until they grew cool enough to proceed with the work. "We use them every minute. We crease the petals with them, and crinkle and vein and curl the outer edges. And we always have to keep them just hot enough not to scorch the thin muslin."

"How many can you make a day?"

"That depends on the rose. This sort—" picking up a small, cheap June rose—"this sort a fair worker can make a gross of a day. But I have made roses where five single flowers were considered a fine day's job. Each of those roses had one hundred and seventy-five pieces, however; and there was eighteen different shapes and sizes of petals; and besides that, every one of those pieces had to be put in its own place. If one piece had been wrongly applied, the whole rose would have been spoiled. But they don't make many of such complicated roses in this country. They have to import them. They haven't enough skilled workers to fill big orders, and it doesn't pay the manufacturers to bother with small orders."

The girl did all the fine work of the place, and had always more waiting to be done than she could have accomplished with four hands instead of two. She had no rival to whom this surplus work could be turned over. The dull season had no terrors for her, nor would it have had for her comrades had they been equally skilled. She made from $22 to $25 a week, all the year round, and was too busy ever to take a vacation. The other girls averaged $9, and if they got eight months' work a year they considered themselves fortunate. They were clever and industrious, but they had not learned to make the finer grade of roses.

The third week came and went all too quickly, and we were now entering on the fourth. Plainly the season was drawing to its close. The orders that had come pouring in from milliners and modistes all over the land for six months were now dwindling daily. The superintendent and the "boss" walked through the department every day, and we heard them talk about overproduction. Friday the atmosphere was tense with anxiety. The girls' faces were grave. Almost without exception, there were people at home upon whom this annual "layoff" fell with tragic force. I have not talked with one of them who did not have to work, and they have always someone at home to care for. A few were widows with small children at home or in the day nursery. One can tell little, by their appearance, about these secret burdens. Each girl wears a mask.

22.   FROM SALESGIRL TO STENOGRAPHER

I got a position in the notion department of one of the large stores. I received only $4 a week; but, as our rent was small and our living expenses the very minimum, I was able to meet my half of the joint expenditure. I worked four months at selling pins and needles and thread and whalebone and a thousand and one other things to be found in a well-stocked notion department; and then, by a stroke of good luck and Minnie Plympton's assistance, I got a place as demonstrator of a new brand of tea and coffee in the grocery department of the same "emporium." My new work was not only much lighter and pleasanter, but it paid me the munificent salary of $8 a week.

But I did not want to be a demonstrator of tea and coffee all my life. I had often thought I would like to learn shorthand and typewriting. The demonstrator of breakfast foods at the next counter to mine was taking a night course in bookkeeping; which gave me the idea of taking a similar course in stenography. And then the Long Day began in earnest. I went to night-school five nights out of every week for exactly sixty weeks, running consecutively save for a fortnight's interim at the Christmas holidays, when we worked nights at the store. On Saturday night, which was the off night, I did my washing and ironing, and on Sunday night I made, mended, and darned my clothes—that is, when there was any making, mending, or darning to be done. As my wardrobe was necessarily slender, I had much time to spare. This spare time on Sunday nights I spent in study and reading. . . .

When I had thoroughly learned the principles of my trade and had attained a speed of some hundred and odd words a minute, the hardest task was yet before me. This task was not in finding a position, but in filling that position satisfactorily. My first position at $10 a week I held only one day. I failed to read my notes. This was more because of fright and of self-consciousness, however, than of inefficiency. My next paid me only $6 a week, but it was an excellent training-school, and in it I learned self-confidence, perfect accuracy, and rapidity. Although this position paid me $2 less than what I had been earning brewing tea and coffee and handing it over the counter, and notwithstanding the fact that I knew of places where I could go and earn $10 a week, I chose to remain where I was. There was method in my madness, however, let me say. I had a considerate and conscientious employer, and although I had a great deal of work, and although it had to be done most punctiliously, he never allowed me to work a moment overtime. He opened his office at nine in the morning, and I was not expected before quarter after; he closed at four sharp. This gave me an opportunity for further improving myself with a view to eventually taking not a ten-dollar, but a twenty-dollar position. I went back to night-school and took a three-months' "speed course." . . .

One day I answered an advertisement calling for the sort of stenographer I now believed myself to be. It brought a response signed with

the name of a large religious publishing house. I got the position, beginning with a salary of $15 a week, which was to be increased to $20
provided I could fill the position. That I should succeed in doing so,
there was evident doubt in my employers' minds, and no wonder! For
I was the fifth to attempt it.

My work consisted for the most part in taking dictation from the
editor of the periodical published weekly by the house—letters to con-
tributors, editorials, and special articles. Also, when it was found that
I had some intelligent, practical knowledge of grammar and English
—and here was where my studies of the preceding year bore fruit—
I was intrusted with the revision and correction of the least important
of the manuscripts, thus relieving the busy editors of one of their
most irksome tasks.

One day I had occasion to mention to the editor some of the strenuous experiences I had undergone in my struggle to attain a decent
living. He was startled—not to say a little shocked—that a young
woman of apparently decent birth and upbringing should have
formed such an intimate acquaintance with the dark side of life. Inspired by his sympathetic interest, I boldly interviewed the editor of
a well-known monthly magazine, with the result that I immediately
prepared two papers on certain of my experiences; and, to my surprise and delight, they were accepted.

23.   SALESGIRL

My own experience as a salesgirl has been rather pleasant than otherwise, because I have been fortunate in many things. I did not have to
depend absolutely on myself at the beginning, the work was such as I
could do well, and my employers were kind and took a close personal interest in every one of the girls. From them the hundreds of
work people took their tone and the atmosphere was good.

The lowest pay in our store was $3 a week to cash girls, stock girls,
and wrappers. This is pretty generally the lowest pay throughout the
city. . . .

A girl can get good board for $2.50 a week through the Young
Women's Christian Association. There are large boarding houses for
working girls connected with the institution in Brooklyn and Manhattan, and also, I think, in other cities. The charge for board
ranges from $2.50 to $4 a week. The girl who pays $2.50 a week rooms
with a number of other girls, while she who pays $4 has a room to her-
self.

The surroundings are pleasant and homelike, there is a parlor in which to receive one's visitors, and if a girl is sick she is in the hands of friends who will do everything for her. There is supervision, but it is of the kind which one has in a good home and the girls recognize it as proper. They must be in at ten o'clock at night, and when they go away for vacations in the summer time they are expected to let the management know where they are going. . . .

The girl who is all alone and who earns only $3 and pays $2.50 for board must live within walking distance of her store and must have a lunch put up at her boarding house, because she has only 50 cents a week on which to live outside of board. This is $26 a year for clothes and all other things.

If a cash girl is clever with her needle she need not spend more than about $14 a year on clothing. She can make a cloak do two or three years, and her frocks need not cost her more than $2 each, and shoes about the same. Two pairs of shoes a year would be $4, and two frocks $4, leaving $6 for underclothing.

A girl like that is helped by those about her in the store with gifts of clothing or even with money. She buys cheaper than an outsider can, as all employes obtain a reduction on all that they purchase. Then, too, she makes a little extra money running errands outside the store for her head of department or some of the sales people.

A girl who obtains employment at even the lowest work in any department store that I know of must be neat, bright, smart, in good health, and have some education. Girls who are half-starved won't do, as privation makes them stupid.

Their clothes must be at least decent-looking or they won't be taken in. So the new girl has a little start to begin with, and she does not stay at $3 a week. If she suits she is made a wrapper or stock girl, and gets from $3.50 to $4 a week.

The cash girl's duty is to run errands. She must be quick and able to remember a message and the reply, and also able to keep her head when half a dozen people are screaming at her to go to different places at once. The wrapper must be prompt, neat, particular, and accurate. She must keep her wits about her or she will get the parcels mixed, and will send things to the wrong people. The stock girl helps the salesgirl to keep the stock in order, neatly folded, free from dust, unharmed, and looking its best.

From stock girl one progresses to salesgirl at $4.50 or $5 to begin, and then the worst of the economies are over. By the time a girl is earning $6 she's generally helping someone, maybe her mother in the country or a younger sister.

I have been tracing the career of the girl who is successful, the one

who can stand the work, which in the case of the cash girl is running from eight o'clock in the morning till six o'clock in the evening,
with an hour's rest about noon. I have been dealing with the one
who has had steady work and made steady progress. There is also the
unsuccessful to consider, the one who just barely fails for some reason
or another, the one for whom the work is too hard or the one who
falls ill. . . .

As to the sick among our people, there's a good deal of sympathy
and kindness for them. The fact that Miss _____ is lying ill at
her mother's house, that her wages have stopped, and that there is,
quite possibly, want, is soon known throughout the department, and
all her comrades contribute to a fund to be sent to her. Some visit
her; she is not forgotten, and her place is open to her when she is
ready to return to it.

We used to have an employes' association, which ran for about
two years. Each person getting $5 a week or more contributed 25 cents
a week and upward to a general fund, and for this was guaranteed
payment of full wages when ill or out of work and payment of doctor's bills. We had a doctor who undertook all the work of the association. We used to give balls and entertainment to help out the funds,
but the scheme broke down, as we found that we could not keep on
paying out $2 for every $1 we took in without coming to grief.

People may think from what I have said that when one has risen to
be a salesgirl at $5 a week her troubles are over, but they are not. She
can support herself and live in comparative comfort away from the
store, but at the store a new lot of troubles begin—those with the customers.

Our store has a good reputation all over the city for the civility of
the girls, but I must say that it is maintained by a great effort. The
great majority of the women customers who come to us are insolent
and insulting. They seem to put out on the girls any anger that they
have stored up. They treat us like the dirt under their feet, and seem
to think that we never had anything and never will have anything,
and that they can do as they please with us. If a girl allows herself to
be irritated into answering back nine out of ten of the women will report her to the superintendent, and then, if she's a new girl without
a good record to fall back upon, she will probably be dismissed, as
the superintendent generally takes the customer's word.

The rule at every counter is first come first served, but the insolent
woman buying cares nothing for this. If all the girls are busy, and
there are ten people ahead of her, she bustles to the front and insists
on being waited on at once. She can't get that—we dare not leave one
customer to go to another—and then she abuses the girls. It is heart-

breaking sometimes to see the girls trying to please such women, trying their very hardest to suit them and being insulted all the time. . . .

The salesgirl's hours are from eight o'clock in the morning till six o'clock in the evening, with an hour's intermission for lunch about noon. There is a good deal of complaint about standing, but very few of the girls break down. They can sit between whiles when there isn't any rush, and the rush seldom begins before half-past ten o'clock in the morning. Then there's a lull from twelve o'clock till three o'clock, after which business is lively again. The store closes promptly at six, and you see some of those who have complained about standing spend most of the evening in dancing.

A salesgirl can go up in her business till she is earning about $8 a week. Then her next step is to some place of supervision, like head of a small department at $10 a week. About 20 per cent of the women in our store get $10 or more, and a woman gets $15 as head of stock. Here and there you may find a girl who earns more than $15 in a department store, but they are rare.

Pleasures don't cost girls so much as they do young men. If they are agreeable they are invited out a good deal, and they are not allowed to pay anything. The Young Woman's Christian Association only costs $1 a year, and its membership is good wherever there is a branch. That introduces one into a very pleasant society—that is, quite active —and the girls in the store have their own circles, too; those who have comfortable homes inviting others whom they like to evening parties.

Many of the girls are engaged or have young men who are paying attention to them, and, of course, they have all the pleasure they can stand, including theater and dancing.

What I have related is the experience of the salesgirls in the largest and best stores of the city, where there is protection and consideration for the employes, and where the rooms devoted to them are good. One can work in such a place and preserve refinement and self-respect; one who has health can enjoy the work there.

Fully four-fifths of the salesgirls marry, and most of them do well. They prove good wives, for their occupation has made them neat and industrious, they've come in contact with a great many different people, have learned to be tactful and diplomatic, and can make allowances for differences of views in a way impossible to a girl who has been a household pet. Some few may be ignorant about housework, but most of them know all that is necessary for a beginning.

24. *LAUNDRY WORKER*

Once more I scanned the advertising columns.

"Shakers Wanted—Apply to Foreman" was the first that caught my eye. I didn't know what a "shaker" was, but that did not deter me from forming a sudden determination to be one. . . . I found the "Pearl Laundry," a broad brick building, grim as a fortress. . . . Making my way as best I could through the jam of horses and drivers and baskets, I reached the narrow, unpainted pine door marked "Employees' Entrance," and filed up the stairs with a crowd of other girls —all, like myself, seeking work.

At the head of the stairs we filed into a mammoth steam-filled room that occupied an entire floor. The foreman made quick work of us. Thirty-two girls I counted as they stepped up to the pale-faced stoop-shouldered young fellow, who addressed each one as "Sally" in a tone which, despite its good-natured familiarity, was none the less business-like and respectful. At last it came to my turn.

"Hello, Sally! Ever shook?"

"No."

"Ever work in a laundry?"

"No; but I'm very handy."

"What did you work at last?"

"Jewel-cases."

"All right, Sally; we'll start you in at three and a half a week, and maybe we'll give you four dollars after you get broke in to the work. Go over there, where you seen them other ladies go," he called after me as I moved away, and waved his hand toward a pine-board partition. Here, sitting on bundles of soiled linen and on hampers, my thirty-two predecessors were corralled, each awaiting assignment to duty. They were dressed, literally, "some in rags and some in tags and some in velvet gowns."

"Did yez come in the barber's wagon?" asked a stupid Irish girl, looking at me curiously. I looked blank, and she repeated the question.

"What does she mean?" I asked a more intelligent girl who was seated on a bundle in the corner.

"Didn't yez come in Tony's wagon?"

"No; who's Tony?"

"Oh, Tony he's a barber—a Ginny barber—that goes out with a wagon when they run short of help, and he picks up any girls he can find and hauls them in. He brought three loads this morning. We thought Tony picked you up. . . ."

The foreman appeared in the door, and we trooped out at his heels. Down the length of the big room, through a maze of moving hand-trucks and tables and rattling mangles, we followed him to the extreme rear, where he deposited us, in groups of five and six, at the big tables that were ranged from wall to wall and heaped high with wet clothes, still twisted just as they were turned out of the steam-wringer. An old woman with a bent back showed me the very simple process of "shaking."

"Jist take the corners like this,"—suiting the action to the word— "and give a shake like this, and pile them on top o' one another— like this," and with that she turned to her own "shaking" and resumed gossip with her side-partner. . . . For the first half-hour I shook napkins. . . . All the workers were women and girls, with the exception of the fifteen big, black, burly negroes who operated the tubs and the wringers which were ranged along the rear wall on a platform that ran parallel with and a little behind the shakers' tables. The negroes were stripped to the waist of all save a thin gauze undershirt. There was something demoniacal in their gestures and shouts as they ran about the vats of boiling soap-suds, from which they transferred the clothes to the swirling wringers, and then dumped them at last upon the big trucks. The latter were pushed away by relays of girls, who strained at the heavy load. The contents of the trucks were dumped first on the shakers' tables, and when each piece was smoothed out we—the shakers—redumped the stacks into the truck, which was pushed on to the manglers, who ironed it all out in the hot rolls. So, after several other dumpings and redumpings, the various lots were tied and labeled.

The work was now under full blast, and every one of the 125 girls worked with frenzied energy as the avalanche of clothes kept falling in upon us and were sent with lightning speed through the different processes, from the tubs to the packers' counters. Nor was there any abatement of the snowy landslide—not a moment to stop and rest the aching arms. Just as fast as the sweating negroes could unload the trucks into the tubs, more trucks came rolling in from the elevator, and the foaming tubs swirled perpetually, swallowing up, it would seem, all the towels and pillow-cases and napkins in Greater New York.

25. JOBS FOR DOMESTICS

Up several iron steps, along two or three rambling halls, up a few more wooden steps—and here at last was the "intelligence office," in a small three-room apartment. The "office" proper was apparently a bare little kitchen with a table covered with a red and white cloth. The only visible attendant was a sallow slip of a girl with a red pigtail, with long thin arms and clawlike hands, washing dishes at the sink. When applied to for information she obligingly went out on the balcony to call her mother who was visiting in the street below, but who was induced to come in to see her clients.

A second was found in a basement salesroom, where second-hand clothing was piled around in dirty, disorderly heaps, with a living-room curtained off at the back. This so-called office was used as a bedroom at night. A third was a combination baggage- and living-room. The proprietor was an expressman and his wife ran the office. Any left-over baggage was piled in the office at night and utilized for beds or chairs, according to its adaptability. A fourth, literally covered with left-over bundles of waiting employees, had a table in one corner, which contained the remains of a meal, a "day-book," and advertising material. Over in another corner two flashily dressed girls were playing the piano and singing popular songs. In a fifth the proprietor was washing, and we discussed "servants" and "places" to the time of a rhythmic "rub, rub," through clouds of steam and soapy vapor, with an occasional flap of a wet cloth for variation. The sixth was the first floor of a little two-story corner house, in a two-room apartment where the husband worked as a carpenter in one room, while the wife conducted the office in the other. The two rooms were full of children; there was very little furniture, even for living purposes, and no records or system. The seventh was in a two-room apartment, with not a thing more than was required for living purposes. The front room was a bed- and sitting-room where the husband worked on a machine; the other a kitchen and bedroom, where the wife attended to the employment business.

One day, after wandering through a very dirty, disorderly building, an applicant for a job entered a small courtyard. A rough, good-natured Bohemian was washing clothes, and upon the steps sat his admiring wife and three children. When asked where the office was, he tapped himself, and smiling proudly, said, "Me the office; what you want? You want girl? I go out and find her." In another place it was a steaming kitchen, strung with lines of clothes. To meet her patrons a Slavish woman appeared from among the lines, washing in hand, and said: "No girls, me wash day; me open office get girl when wash done."

These are intelligence offices—so-called—in America. These are the forces which America trusts to deal with the unskilled immigrant in domestic service. . . . In the medium and best grade offices especially, the contrast between the treatment of "ladies" and of "servants" is most striking. Merely from the voice of the manager, an observer can tell whether she is in the "ladies'" or the "servants'" room. In the one it is modulated, polite, smooth, pleasing, courteous; in the other, rough, arrogant, and discourteous. This contrast in treatment must impress even the dullest employees. One of the most fashionable offices in New York makes its employees stand all day—"The room holds more," one girl said. . . .

In some agencies these girls are actually herded and treated like cattle. In one Swedish office, run by two young men, one guarded the door of the employees' room and by promises, threats, and actual force made it impossible for girls to get out without paying a fee. Swearing at employees who are restless or who demand their fees back is too common an occurrence to need mention. The means of maintaining order in some of the crowded offices is not only insulting, but brutal, and the best employees seeking housework for the first time will certainly not go there after one or two experiences. In a good office, a woman who insisted upon the refund of her fee was pushed out of the door and downstairs for "creating a disturbance," for she was encouraging others to demand their fees also. She said she had waited two weeks and had not even had an offer of a position. To insist upon "rights" after paying a fee is more often than not the signal for insolence and wrath, and employees are pretty sure to be ignored thereafter in the selection of positions. In one large office the male clerk came into the room and shouted out the positions wanted. When no one replied he then singled out girls. When asked why no one responded, a girl said: "Because he always answers us impudently, and picks out the ones he wants to have anyway." Sodden, uncomplaining, patient, submissive must be the applicant's attitude, unless she responds to the familiarities and "jollying" of attendants. If there is no absolute brutality, there is discourtesy, noticeable lack of respectful address, "bossing," and contradictions. A girl fixes her wages; the office says, "Change it or get out"; another states the kind of work she wants; the office says, "Do something different"; another wants work in a private family; the office cajoles her into going into a hotel; another states she is twenty-five years old, and the office replies, "You are only twenty for our business." In other words, so far as it possibly can, it makes girls over to suit whatever position it has on hand; employees are forced, through such means, into places which they are not fitted to fill and into work in which they have no interest.

26. *WASHERWOMAN*

When I was twenty-four years old my father died, leaving me, to my great surprise, penniless. There had always been enough for comfortable living, but at father's death creditors took everything—even our cozy little home.

I entered my name in every large store in the city. After three weeks notice came that I was to report for service the following Monday. . . .

I will not here take time to relate my eleven weeks' experience in the store. The position was confining and tiresome, but I have no great complaints to make.

The trouble lay in the meager wages—$4.50 per week. Had I been able to have boarded at home this would have carried me through very well. I could have paid $3 a week for my board, had a good home, appetizing food, and $1.50 for clothes and incidentals. But the carfare to and fro—16 cents a day—forbade this. . . . So I sought board near the store. First I paid $3 a week for accommodation in a big dingy house, with a roommate, but I found this unendurable. I was now confined for ten hours a day in a crowded, confused store and spent my other waking hours stretched out resting my back and feet. Of course, appetite was poor, and the cheap boarding house food was quite impossible. I spent the dollar that remained after paying for my board in luncheons, and my stockings!

I was told at the store that, as a rule, it took years of faithful service to get a raise. . . . I began to look for other employment, but oh, the dreary search! No one wanted a poor, inexperienced tenderfoot. At last one Sunday my eyes fell upon the ads for housemaids. How many there were! I thought a few moments, dressed myself plainly, and sallied forth. I avoided all places where more than one maid was kept, for I knew two would mean a roommate, but I answered seven ads for general housework. . . .

I found what seemed ideal—a clean, tidy, little house with a family of two—mother and son. The lady was gentle and refined, but something of an invalid. . . .

Now, as far as the work went I knew my business. I had been housekeeper at home for many years, and had for short periods been without a servant, but the steady continuity of my duties now overwhelmed me. . . . There was no hour from six A.M. to ten P.M. wholly my own for rest.

I had money in plenty; had bought not only stockings, but shoes, gloves, etc., and was saving up a little sum for emergencies. But this was the worst of it. I had many dear friends from whom I was drifting because I could not receive them in my kitchen. One day, in came the washerwoman with her arms full of freshly ironed clothes. . . .

"Beg pardon, but if I might be so bold I was looking for some one to help me, and if the young lady would care to try. . . . Washing by the day is much easier than a housework place," insisted Mrs. Wheelen, "and I would start you in easy. . . . Come to work with me next week. I'll get you $1.50 a day and board. You need not work Saturday or Sunday. I'll start you in easy and you needn't tell your friends what you're doing if you don't want to."

I was bewildered.

"One dollar and a half a day for five days, seven dollars a week and board. Do you mean it?"

"Sure; and Saturday and Sunday for your own."

"And I can have a nice room in a first-class house? Why, of course, I'll come." . . .

Oh, how good it was! And what a delight to use the bath! A pleasant parlor and a piano were at my service, and as I sat playing softly Sunday evening in the dim light of the banquet lamp tears of comfort and content dropped on the keys. . . .

I am working steadily now and do not find it very disagreeable. I do not enjoy washing, but nearly all of my work is ironing, and I take considerable pleasure in that part of it now that I have time to do it well. In my housework days I had to hurry so that ironing was a great trial to me, but now that no cooking, doorbell, or other interruptions occur, and I have time to do each piece perfectly, I find something artistic in the beauty that heat brings to a limp, homely rag. . . .

I am yet boarding in town and receiving my friends in the pretty boarding-house parlor. I have every Sunday an invitation to go somewhere. I have been this summer to week-end parties at the shore and mountains and in the country. I have both time and money for trolley rides and the theater. I have good, appetizing food both at my places and the boarding house—and time to eat it properly. The work is not the pleasantest in the world, but I can recommend it to other unskilled hands. The pay is good—equal to $10 a week without board—the hours are definite, and one is entirely free from working surroundings out of hours. The vigorous labor makes muscle and digests food, and a pleasant Saturday and Sunday are always ahead of one.

27. HOME-WORK

"Home-work" in the tenement is familiar and has been condemned to a considerable degree by public opinion, though not largely prohibited. There is another form of home-work, by which the manufacturer tries by misrepresentation and fraud to get his work done. The home-workers are the handicapped, the unskilled, the "genteel," the misfits, the hard-driven mother, often in small towns, reached by alluring advertisements. The following letter tells its own story, and a careful examination of advertisements in daily and so-called home papers indicates that this kind of imposition is widespread:

Finding it necessary to help somehow to improve the conditions of our home budget, which has sadly diminished on account of my husband's lack of steady work, I decided to find some employment myself. Having three school children, the only thing I could do was home-work, so I set out looking for it.

An ad in a Long Island paper called for women to sew on buttons. With glad heart I went, for what could I do better? Well, I waited in the office for about one hour when a young woman approached me asking had I my reference. No. I was sorry not to have any with me as the ad did not mention any such thing. "You have to have one," she said, "from your butcher, grocer, or landlord just to show that you are an honest woman and we can trust you with our buttons."

Two hours later I was back with the written assurance of all three above-mentioned persons that they had known me long, and the proprietor of the "button works" could sleep at ease although I had the buttons home. After making a satisfactory sample I was told the price was two cents for a gross; no thread supplied. Bewildered, I made some mental multiplication, but I could not think of more than sixty cents for thirty gross of buttons. Of this I subtracted five cents for cotton and thirty cents for car fare, which left a total of 25 cents' earnings.

However, I was elated at being of some help, and set to work as soon as I reached home. It took me one whole week to mount the 4320 buttons, and when I delivered them, using my last five cents for car fare, I was told that ony ten gross were mounted properly; that all I could get was 30 cents, and would I call next Saturday.

My next experience was neckties. I made four samples for a firm in

Broome Street, which took from 9 o'clock in the morning until 3 o'clock in the afternoon. Then when the fourth bow was finished a pimply-faced young woman approached me with outstretched hand. "One dollar deposit, please," she chirped, and I not having any dollar of which I did not know how to dispose, left this "home-work" place, and also my day's work to its benefit.

No. 3: I furnished a sample, received 75 cents' worth of work, and on delivery 15 cents was taken off for a bow for which I did not get any material, being accused of theft, although not directly. . . .

All a woman can earn at home is $1 to $2 weekly at the most, while she has to call for and deliver the work, spend a half-day every time making samples, and cannot get her money before the regular pay-day. Something ought to be done for these poor women whom care of children prevents leaving the house to earn something when the husband is out of work.

Workers in the Slums

28. *SWEATERS OF JEWTOWN*

Take the Second Avenue Elevated Railroad at Chatham Square and ride up half a mile through the sweaters' district. Every open window of the big tenements, that stand like a continuous brick wall on both sides of the way, gives you a glimpse of one of these shops as the train speeds by. Men and women bending over their machines, or ironing clothes at the window, half-naked. Proprieties do not count on the East Side; nothing counts that cannot be converted into hard cash. The road is like a big gangway through an endless work-room where vast multitudes are forever laboring. Morning, noon, or night, it makes no difference; the scene is always the same. At Rivington Street let us get off and continue our trip on foot. It is Sunday evening west of the Bowery. Here, under the rule of Mosaic law, the week of work is under full headway, its first day far spent. The hucksters' wagons are absent or stand idle at the curb; the saloons admit the thirsty crowds through the side-door labelled "Family Entrance"; a tin sign in a store-window announces that a "Sunday School" gathers in stray children of the new dispensation; but beyond these things there is little to suggest the Christian Sabbath. Men stagger along the sidewalk groaning under heavy burdens of unsewn garments, or enormous black bags suffed full of finished coats and trousers. Let us follow one to his home and see how Sunday passes in a Ludlow Street tenement.

Up two flights of dark stairs, three, four, with new smells of cabbage, of onions, of frying fish, on every landing, whirring sewing machines behind closed doors betraying what goes on within, to the door that opens to admit the bundle and the man. A sweater, this, in a small way. Five men and a woman, two young girls, not fifteen, and a boy who says unasked that he is fifteen, and lies in saying it, are at the machines sewing knickerbockers, "knee-pants" in the Ludlow Street dialect. The floor is littered ankle-deep with half-sewn garments. In the alcove, on a couch of many dozens of "pants" ready for the finisher, a bare-legged baby with pinched face is asleep. A fence of piled-up clothing keeps him from rolling off on the floor. The faces, hands, and arms to the elbows of everyone in the room are black with the color of the cloth on which they are working. The boy and the woman alone look up at our entrance. The girls shoot sidelong glances, but at a warning look from the man with the bundle they tread their machines more energetically than ever. The men do not appear to be aware even of the presence of a stranger.

They are "learners," all of them, says the woman, who proves to be the wife of the boss, and have "come over" only a few weeks ago. She is disinclined to talk at first, but a few words in her own tongue from our guide set her fears, whatever they are, at rest, and she grows almost talkative. The learners work for week's wages, she says. How much do they earn? She shrugs her shoulders with an expressive gesture. The workers themselves, asked in their own tongue, say indifferently, as though the question were of no interest: from two to five dollars. The children—there are four of them—are not old enough to work. The oldest is only six. They turn out 120 dozen "knee-pants" a week, for which the manufacturer pays 70 cents a dozen. Five cents a dozen is the clear profit, but her own and her husband's work brings the family earnings up to $25 a week, when they have work all the time. But often half the time is put in looking for it. They work no longer than to nine o'clock at night, from daybreak. There are ten machines in the room; six are hired at $2 a month. For the two shabby, smoke-begrimed rooms, one somewhat larger than ordinary, they pay $20 a month. She does not complain, though "times are not what they were, and it costs a good deal to live." Eight dollars a week for the family of six and two boarders. How do they do it? She laughs, as she goes over the bill of fare, at the silly question: Bread, fifteen cents a day, of milk two quarts a day at four cents a quart, one pound of meat for dinner at twelve cents, butter one pound a week at "eight cents a quarter of a pound." Coffee, potatoes, and pickles complete the list. At the least calculation, probably, this sweater's family hoards up $30 a month, and in a few years will own a tenement somewhere and profit by the example set by their landlord in rent-collecting. It is the way the savings of Jewtown are universally invested, and with the natural talent of its people for commercial speculation the investment is enormously profitable.

On the next floor, in a dimly lighted room with a big red-hot stove to keep the pressing irons ready for use, is a family of man, wife, three children, and a boarder. "Knee-pants" are made there too, of a still lower grade. Three cents and a half is all he clears, says the man, and lies probably out of at least two cents. The wife makes a dollar and a half finishing, the man about $9 at the machine. The boarder pays 65 cents a week. He is really only a lodger, getting his meals outside. The rent is $2.25 a week, cost of living $5. Every floor has at least two, sometimes four, such shops. Here is one with a young family for which life is bright with promise. Husband and wife work together; just now the latter, a comely young woman, is eating her dinner of dry bread and green pickles. Pickles are favorite food in Jewtown. They are filling, and keep the children from crying with hunger. Those who have stomachs like ostriches thrive in spite of them and grow strong—plain proof that they are good to eat. The rest? "Well, they die," says our guide, dryly. No thought of untimely death comes to disturb this family with life all before it. In a few years the man will be a prosperous sweater. Already he employs an old man as ironer at $3 a week, and a sweet-faced little Italian girl as finisher at $1.50. She is twelve, she says, and can neither read nor write; will probably never learn. How should she? The family clears from $10 to $11 a week in brisk times, more than half of which goes into the bank.

A companion picture from across the hall. The man works on the machine for his sweater twelve hours a day, turning out three dozen "knee-pants," for which he receives 42 cents a dozen. The finisher who works with him gets 10, and the ironer 8 cents a dozen; buttonholes are extra, at 8 to 10 cents a hundred. This operator has four children at his home in Stanton Street, none old enough to work, and a sick wife. His rent is $12 a month; his wages for a hard week's work less than $8. Such as he, with their consuming desire for money thus smothered, recruit the ranks of the anarchists, won over by the promise of a general "divide"; and an enlightened public sentiment turns up its nose at the vicious foreigner for whose perverted notions there is no room in this land of plenty.

Turning the corner into Hester Street, we stumble upon a nest of cloak-makers in their busy season. Six months of the year the cloak-maker is idle, or nearly so. Now is his harvest. Seventy-five cents a cloak, all complete, is the price in this shop. The cloak is of cheap plush, and might sell for $8 or $9 over the store-counter. Seven dollars is the weekly wage of this man with wife and two children, and $9.50 rent to pay per month. A boarder pays about a third of it. There was a time when he made $10 a week and thought himself rich. But wages have come down fearfully in the last two years. Think of it: "come down" to this. The other cloak-makers aver that they can make as much as $12 a week, when they are employed, by taking their work home and sewing till midnight. One exhibits his account-book with a Ludlow Street sweater. It shows that he and his partner, working on first-class garments for a Broadway house in the four busiest weeks of the season, made together from $15.15 to $19.20 a week by striving from 6 A.M. to 11 P.M., that is to say, from $7.58 to $9.60 each. The sweater on this work probably made as much as 50 per cent at least on their labor. Not far away is a factory in a rear yard where the factory inspector reports teams of tailors making men's coats at an average of 27 cents a coat, all complete except buttons and button-holes.

Turning back, we pass a towering double tenement in Ludlow Street, owned by a well-known Jewish liquor dealer and politician, a triple combination that bodes ill for his tenants. As a matter of fact, the cheapest "apartment," three rear rooms on the sixth floor, only one of which deserves the name, is rented for $13 a month. Here is a reminder of the Bend, a hallway turned into a shoemaker's shop. Two hallways side by side in adjoining tenements would be sinful waste in Jewtown, when one would do as well by knocking a hole in the wall. But this shoemaker knows a trick the Italian's ingenuity did not suggest. He has his "flat" as well as his shop there. A curtain hung back of his stool in the narrow passage half conceals his bed and fills it entirely from wall to wall. To get into it he has to crawl over the footboard, and he must come out the same way. Expedients more odd than this are born of the East Side crowding. In one of the houses we left, the coal-bin of a family on the fourth floor was on the roof of the adjoining tenement. A quarter of a ton of coal was being dumped there while we talked with the people.

We have reached Broome Street. The hum of industry in this six-story tenement on the corner leaves no doubt of the aspect Sunday wears within it. One flight up, we knock at the nearest door. The grocer, who keeps the store, lives on the "stoop," the first floor in East Side parlance. In this room a suspender-maker sleeps and works with his family of wife and four children. For a wonder there are no boarders. His wife and eighteen-year-old daughter share in the work, but the girl's eyes are giving out from the strain. Three months in the year, when work is very brisk, the family makes by united efforts as high as $14 and $15 a week. The other nine months it averages from $3 to $4. The oldest boy, a young man, earns from $4 to $6 in an Orchard Street factory, when he has work. The rent is $10 a month for the room and a miserable little coop of a bedroom where the old folks sleep. The girl makes her bed on the lounge in the front room; the big boys and the children sleep on the floor. Coal at ten cents a small pail, meat at twelve cents a pound, one and a half pound of butter a week at thirty-six cents, and a quarter of a pound of tea in the same space of time, are items of their housekeeping account as given by the daughter. Milk at four and five cents a quart, "according to quality." The sanitary authorities know what that means, know how miserably inadequate is the fine of $50 or $100 for the murder done in cold blood by the wretches who poison the babes of these tenements with the stuff that is half water, or swill. Their defense is that the demand is for "cheap milk." Scarcely a wonder that this suspender-maker will hardly be able to save up the *dot* for his daughter, without which she stands no chance of marrying in Jewtown, even with her face that would be pretty had it a healthier tinge.

Up under the roof three men are making boys' jackets at twenty cents a piece, of which the sewer takes eight, the ironer three, the finisher five cents, and the buttonhole-maker two and a quarter, leaving a cent and three quarters to pay for the drumming up, the fetching and bringing back of the goods. They bunk together in a room for which they pay $8 a month. All three are single here, that is, their wives are on the other side yet, waiting for them to earn enough to send for them. Their breakfast, eaten at the work-bench, consists of a couple of rolls at a cent a piece, and a draught of water, milk when business has been very good, a square meal at noon in a restaurant, and the morning meal over again at night. This square meal, that is the evidence of a very liberal disposition on the part of the consumer, is an affair of more than ordinary note; it may be justly called an institution. I know of a couple of restaurants at the lower end of Orchard Street that are favorite resorts for the Polish Jews, who remember the injunction that the ox that treadeth out the corn shall not be muzzled. Being neighbors, they are rivals of course, and cutting under. When I was last there one gave a dinner of soup, meat-stew, bread, pie, pickles, and a "schooner" of beer for thirteen cents; the other charged fifteen cents for a similar dinner, but with two schooners of beer and a cigar, or a cigarette, as the extra inducement. The two cents had won the day, however, and the thirteen-cent restaurant did such a thriving business that it was about to spread out into the adjoining store to accommodate the crowds of customers. At this rate the lodger of Jewtown can "live like a lord," as he says himself, for twenty-five cents a day, including the price of his bed, that ranges all the way from thirty to forty and fifty cents a week, and save money, no matter what his earnings. He does it, too, so long as work is to be had at any price, and by the standard he sets up Jewtown must abide.

29. CAPMAKER

My name is Rose Schneiderman, and I was born in some small city of Russian Poland. I don't know the name of the city, and have no memory of that part of my childhood. When I was about five years of age my parents brought me to this country and we settled in New York.

I went to school until I was nine years old, enjoying it thoroughly and making great progress, but then my father died of brain fever and mother was left with three children and another one coming. So I had to stay at home to help her and she went out to look for work.

The children were not more troublesome than others, but this was a hard part of my life with few bright spots in it. I was a serious child, and cared little for children's play, and I knew nothing about the country, so it was not so bad for me as it might have been for another. Yet it was bad, though I did get some pleasure from reading, of which I was very fond; and now and then, as a change from the home, I took a walk on the crowded street.

Mother was absent from half-past seven o'clock in the morning till half-past six o'clock in the evening.

I was finally released by my little sister being taken by an aunt, and the two boys going to the Hebrew Orphan Asylum, which is a splendid institution.

So I got a place in the factory of Hein & Fox. The hours were from 8 A.M. to 6 P.M., and we made all sorts of linings—or rather, we stitched in the linings—golf caps, yachting caps, etc. It was piece-work, and we received from 3½ cents to 10 cents a dozen, according to the different grades. By working hard we could make an average of about $5 a week. We would have made more but had to provide our machines, which cost us $45, we paying for them on the installment plan. We paid $5 down and $1 a month after that.

I learned the business in about two months, and then made as much as the others, and was consequently doing quite well when the factory burned down, destroying all our machines—150 of them.

A little later I became assistant sample maker. This is a position which, though coveted by many, pays better in glory than in cash. It was still piecework, and though the pay per dozen was better the work demanded was of a higher quality, and one could not rush through samples as through the other caps. So I still could average only about $5 per week.

After I had been working as a capmaker for three years it began to dawn on me that we girls needed an organization. The men had organized already, and had gained some advantages, but the bosses had lost nothing, as they took it out of us.

We were helpless; no one girl dare stand up for anything alone. Matters kept getting worse. The bosses kept making reductions in our pay, half a cent a dozen at a time. It did not sound important, but at the end of the week we found a difference.

One girl would say that she didn't think she could make caps for the new price, but another would say that she thought she could make up for the reduction by working a little harder, and then the first would tell herself:

"If she can do it, why can't I?"

They didn't think how they were wasting their strength.

A new girl from another shop talked organization as a remedy for our ills. Finally we went to the National Board of United Cloth Hat and Cap Makers when it was in session, and asked them to organize the girls.

We were told to come to the next meeting of the National Board, which we did, and then received a favorable answer, and were asked to bring all the girls who were willing to be organized to the next meeting, and at the next meeting, accordingly, we were twelve strong and were organized.

Then came a big strike. Price lists for the coming season were given in to the bosses, to which they did not agree. After some wrangling a strike was declared in five of the biggest factories. There are 30 factories in the city. About 100 girls went out.

The result was a victory, which netted us—I mean the girls—$2 increase in our wages on the average.

All the time our union was progressing very nicely. There were lectures to make us understand what trades unionism is and our real position in the labor movement. I read up on the subject and grew more and more interested, and after a time I became a member of the National Board, and had duties and responsibilities that kept me busy after my day's work was done.

But all was not lovely by any means, for the bosses were not at all pleased with their beating and had determined to fight us again.

They agreed among themselves that after the 26th of December, 1904, they would run their shops on the "open" system.

Of course, we knew that this meant an attack on the union. The bosses intended gradually to get rid of us, employing in our place child labor and raw immigrant girls who would work for next to nothing.

On December 22 the . . . notice appeared, and the National Board, which had known about it all along, went into session prepared for action.

Our people were very restive, saying that they could not sit under that notice, and that if the National Board did not call them out soon they would go out of themselves.

At last word was sent out, and at 2:30 o'clock all the workers stopped, and, laying down their scissors and other tools, marched out, some of them singing the "Marseillaise."

We were out for thirteen weeks, and the girls established their reputation. They were on picket duty from seven o'clock in the morning till six o'clock in the evening, and gained over many of the non-union workers by appeals to them to quit working against us.

During this strike period we girls each received $3 a week, single men $3 a week, and married men $5 a week. This was paid us by the National Board.

We were greatly helped by the other unions, because the open shop issue was a tremendous one, and this was the second fight which the bosses had conducted for it.

Their first was with the tailors, whom they beat. If they now could beat us the outlook for unionism would be bad.

Some were aided and we stuck out and won a glorious victory all along the line. That was only last week. The shops are open now for all union hands and for them only.

30. POOR WITHOUT WORK

I liked my work and learned it easily, and father was pleased with me. As soon as I knew how to baste pocket-flaps he began to teach me how to baste the coat edges. This was hard work. The double ply of overcoat cloth stitched in with canvas and tape made a very stiff edge. My fingers often stiffened with pain as I rolled and basted the edges. Sometimes a needle or two would break before I could do one coat.

Then father would offer to finish the edge for me. But if he gave me my choice I never let him. At these moments I wanted so to master the thing myself that I felt my whole body trembling with the desire. And with my habit of personifying things, I used to bend over the coat on my lap, force the obstinate and squeaking needle, wet with perspiration, in and out of the cloth and whisper with determination: "No, you shall not get the best of me!" When I succeeded I was so happy that father, who often watched me with a smile, would say, "Rachel, your face is shining. Now rest a while." He always told me to rest after I did well. I loved these moments. I would push my stool closer to the wall near which I sat, lean my back against it, and look about the shop. . . .

It was "slack" in our shop. Every week Mr. Cohen made me stay home a day or two. It was slack all over the city at all trades. . . .

But when a few weeks passed and father began to stay home three and four days a week, he looked openly alarmed and began to talk of moving back to Cherry Street. And when two brothers and a sister, who were from our part of the country, came one night and asked to be taken in as "lodgers," we finally decided to do it. So, with our lodgers, we moved into a "room and two bedrooms," on Cherry Street again, this time between Jefferson and Clinton Streets. The rooms were on the stoop in the rear. The toilets, for the whole building, were in the yard, facing our windows, the water pump in the street hall. The rent was $10 a month. We gave the two brothers the little hall bedroom with the window, for the sister a cot was put up for the night in the large room with us children. They paid $5 a month. So now we felt easier as our rent was only $5 a month.

But our easy days were not many. One night, soon after we had settled in our new home, Mr. Cohen called me over to his table, just as I was leaving, and told me that he had no work for me for the next day.

A short time after I began to stay home father's shop was closed altogether. Every day now all over the city shops were being closed. Nevertheless father went out every morning, always looking bright, and hopeful of finding at least a few hours' work. He would return at noon looking not quite so bright. He was not discouraged, but as week after week passed, his face grew thinner and the smile that had always lit up his whole face became rare. But still he spoke cheerfully. "This can't last much longer," he would say. "There must be an end to it. It is almost two months now."

All this weighed more heavily on mother. Her face was paler, her features stood out sharply and her eyes seemed to have gone deeper into her head. She was always serious and now she looked as if a dreadful calamity were hanging over us. "Among strangers in a strange country." She began counting the potatoes she put into the pot and would ask the children over and over again when they wanted more bread, "Are you sure you want it?"

Two months passed and a great change seemed to have come over the people. The closed shops turned the workers out into the streets and they walked about idly, looking haggard and shabby. Often as I sauntered along through Cherry or Monroe Street I would meet someone with whom I had worked. We avoided each other. We felt ashamed of being seen idle. We felt ashamed of our shabby clothes. We avoided each other's eyes to save each other pain and humiliation. The greeting of those who could not possibly avoid one another was something like this, "What! A holiday in your shop, too?" Nor would they remain talking long. Both would stand looking away gloomily for a few minutes and finally with a short nod they would walk apart dejectedly.

One day as I was walking on Grand Street toward the Bowery, I saw a tall, slim man, coatless and bareheaded, with a rag bag over his shoulder, bent over a garbage can. There was something familiar to me about him. I was on the opposite side of the street and stood looking at him. And soon I remembered. He was, or he had been, a machine operator. He and his wife had been a merry couple and they had a sweet baby whom they adored. They had lived in our old 338 Cherry Street over the Felesbergs. I had often been in their home and watched them singing and dancing with their baby. Now I hardly recognized him. A ragged gray shirt covered his back. His long thin body was bent. His face looked black and hollow. But what struck me with horror was that he seemed entirely unaware that he was among human beings. . . .

As I recognized him I ran toward him a few steps. Then the full meaning of it all struck me. I threw my arms over my head and ran from him in terror.

One day while mother and we children stood out on the stoop a woman we knew came over to us. . . .

She barely glanced at me and as her eyes returned to her quickly moving needles, "Missus," she said, "I have a place for your girl with a very nice family." Mother's lips drew together tightly. Without looking at mother the woman kept on talking in a slow persuasive tone. "There are only six in the family. They live on Clinton Street near Grand. I think they would pay her $6 a month. Will you let her go?"

My mother's face was white. "No!" she shook her head. She climbed up the stoop steps and went into the house.

I followed her and asked, "Why don't you let me go, mother? Out of the six dollars we could pay our share of the rent for a whole month and have a dollar over."

She turned away from me, leaned against the wall and cried, "Is this what I have come to America for, that my children should become servants?"

It was three months now since father and I had earned anything. We owed the landlord $5 for this third month. We gave him just what the lodgers had paid us. What there was left of our own money we kept just for bread and a little milk for the two smaller children. Father used to bring the big round loaf of bread from the bread stand on Hester Street when he came home at night. We were always in bed then and the light in the lamp was turned low but I was often awake. Mother would sit up to wait for him and open the door and he would come in on tiptoe, lay the bread on the table and sit down heavily beside it. Then mother would cut some of the bread, sweeten some hot water in a glass and give it to him. Then she would sit down on another chair near the table and sit staring on the floor in front of her while he ate his supper. He used to chew every mouthful a long time and drink the hot water slowly. Sometimes in the stillness I could hear a deep half-stifled sigh.

They seldom spoke. Once I heard father ask, "How are the children?"

"How should they be?" she answered. "Hanging onto life." She covered her face and sobbed.

In the morning father was gone on his daily hunt for work before we were up. He no longer came home at noon now, for when he was away he did not have to eat. . . .

The small school which the children attended was, I think, connected with a church or a missionary society. One day when the children came home they told us that any child in the class who would say a prayer received a slice of bread and honey. Mother looked at them and asked them to tell her about it. Sister said, "There is nothing to tell. If you just bow your head as you sit at the desk, and repeat the prayer after the teacher you receive a slice of white bread and honey."

We heard a great deal about the missionaries that winter. On Grand Street, at the corner of Attorney Street, there was a big store with green shades which were always drawn. In this store we knew the missionaries held a meeting every Saturday. We heard that the head of the missionaries was a baptised Jew. I heard my parents express their anger because they came and settled right in the heart of the Jewish neighborhood. We children used to run past the store with a feeling of fear and then stand at a little distance and look at it. I often went back to look inside through a worn part of the shade, and saw a man standing up and talking and a few people in the back of the room listening. Week after week the man preached almost to an empty room. Still we hated to have them in the neighborhood to tempt our people.

One Saturday afternoon father came home and said that he had just passed the missionaries' store on Grand Street. "They are doing good business these days," he said. "As I passed, the door opened and I saw the place crowded with people." We heard that anyone who went there and listened to the lectures received food and clothing.

A young man, who was a friend of our lodgers, used to come to visit them. When he became well acquainted with us he would come in at any time during the day, even when his friends were out. Of course he was out of work. It was six months now since he had earned anything. He looked like the rest of us, shabby, despondent, half-starved. If he happened to come in when we were having a meal mother always invited him to eat with us. He would take the bread which, like father, he chewed slowly, and often said, "This is very good bread."

He would sit and argue with mother, trying to convince her that it was no sin to accept food from missionaries when one was almost starving.

"But do they give it to you? You have to show that you believe with them, that you accept their religion." . . .

Another month passed and all our money was gone. For a week or so we borrowed from our lodgers 10 and 15 cents at a time until we had a dollar. Then we did not know what to do. We would not ask the coal man and the grocer to "trust" us. We had never owed anyone, and father and mother shrank from the very thought of owing. Besides, the coal man and the grocer hardly knew us. We had not bought much coal and bread was a cent cheaper at the big stand on Hester Street. On the morning when father took the last few cents he went away earlier than usual. And mother walked about with slow shuffling steps from room to room. As the children were leaving for school she asked them without looking at them, whether bread and honey was still given to the children at school.

"Yes," sister said, "to those who bow their heads and pray."

The boy was already out of the room when mother called after them. "You can bow your heads and pray."

Then she went into her dark bedroom.

31. SWEATSHOP GIRL

When mother died I thought I would try to learn a trade and then I could go to school at night and learn to speak the English language well.

So I went to work in Allen Street (Manhattan) in what they call a sweatshop, making skirts by machine. I was new at the work and the foreman scolded me a great deal.

"Now, then," he would say, "this place is not for you to be looking around in. Attend to your work. That is what you have to do."

I did not know at first that you must not look around and talk, and I made many mistakes with the sewing, so that I was often called a "stupid animal." But I made $4 a week by working six days in the week. For there are two Sabbaths here—our own Sabbath, that comes on a Saturday, and the Christian Sabbath that comes on Sunday. It is against our law to work on our own Sabbath, so we work on their Sabbath.

In Poland I and my father and mother used to go to the synagogue on the Sabbath but here the women don't go to the synagogue much, though the men do. They are shut up working hard all the week long and when the Sabbath comes they like to sleep long in bed and afterward they must go out where they can breathe the air. The rabbis are strict here, but not so strict as in the old country.

I lived at this time with a girl named Ella, who worked in the same factory and made $5 a week. We had the room all to ourselves, paying $1.50 a week for it, and doing light housekeeping. It was in Allen Street, and the window looked out of the back, which was good, because there was an elevated railroad in front, and in summer time a great deal of dust and dirt came in at the front windows. We were on the fourth story and could see all that was going on in the back rooms of the houses behind us, and early in the morning the sun used to come in our window.

We did our cooking on an oil stove, and lived well, as this list of our expenses for one week will show:

ELLA AND RADIE FOR FOOD (ONE WEEK)

Tea	$0.06
Cocoa	.10
Bread and rolls	.40
Canned vegetables	.20

Potatoes	.10
Milk	.21
Fruit	.20
Butter	.15
Meat	.60
Fish	.15
Laundry	.25
Total	$2.42
Add rent	1.50
Grand Total	$3.92

Of course, we could have lived cheaper, but we are both fond of good things and felt that we could afford them.

We paid 18 cents for a half pound of tea so as to get it good, and it lasted us three weeks, because we had cocoa for breakfast. We paid 5 cents for six rolls and 5 cents a loaf for bread, which was the best quality. Oatmeal cost us 10 cents for three and one-half pounds, and we often had it in the morning, or Indian meal porridge in the place of it, costing about the same. Half a dozen eggs cost about 13 cents on an average, and we could get all the meat we wanted for a good hearty meal for 20 cents—two pounds of chops, or a steak, or a bit of veal, or a neck of lamb—something like that. Fish included butterfish, porgies, codfish, and smelts, averaging about 8 cents a pound.

Some people who buy at the last of the market, when the men with the carts want to go home, can get things very cheap, but they are likely to be stale, and we did not often do that with fish, fresh vegetables, fruit, milk, or meat. Things that kept well we did buy that way and got good bargains. I got thirty potatoes for 10 cents one time, though generally I could not get more than fifteen of them for that amount. Tomatoes, onions, and cabbages, too, we bought that way and did well, and we found a factory where we could buy the finest broken crackers for 3 cents a pound and another place where we got broken candy for 10 cents a pound. Our cooking was done on an oil stove, and the oil for the stove and the lamp cost us 10 cents a week.

It cost me $2 a week to live, and I had a $1 a week to spend on clothing and pleasure, and saved the other dollar. I went to night school, but it was hard work learning at first as I did not know much English.

Two years ago I came to this place, Brownsville, where so many of my people are, and where I have friends. I got work in a factory making underskirts—all sorts of cheap underskirts, like cotton and calico for the summer and woolen for the winter, but never the silk, satin, or velvet underskirts. I earned $4.50 a week and lived on $2 a week, the same as before.

I got a room in the house of some friends who lived near the factory. I pay $1 a week for the room and am allowed to do light housekeeping—that is, cook my meals in it. I get my own breakfast in the morning, just a cup of coffee and a roll, and at noon time I come home to dinner and take a plate of soup and a slice of bread with the lady of the house. My food for a week costs $1, just as it did in Allen Street, and I have the rest of my money to do as I like with. I am earning $5.50 a week now, and will probably get another increase soon.

It isn't piecework in our factory, but one is paid by the amount of work done just the same. So it is like piecework. All the hands get different amounts, some as low as $3.50 and some of the men as high $16 a week. The factory is in the third story of a brick building. It is in a room twenty feet long and fourteen broad. There are fourteen machines in it. I and the daughter of the people with whom I live work two of these machines. The other operators are all men, some young and some old.

I get up at half-past five o'clock every morning and make myself a cup of coffee on the oil stove. I eat a bit of bread and perhaps some fruit and then go to work. Often I get there soon after six o'clock so as to be in good time, though the factory does not open till seven. I have heard that there is a sort of clock that calls you at the very time you want to get up, but I can't believe that because I don't see how the clock would know.

At seven o'clock we all sit down to our machines and the boss brings to each one the pile of work that he or she is to finish during the day, what they call in English their "stint." This pile is put down beside the machine and as soon as a skirt is done it is laid on the other side of the machine. Sometimes the work is not all finished by six o'clock and then the one who is behind must work overtime. Sometimes one is finished ahead of time and gets away at four or five o'clock, but generally we are not done till six o'clock

The machines go like mad all day, because the faster you work the more money you get. Sometimes in my haste I get my finger caught and the needle goes right through it. It goes so quick, though, that it does not hurt much. I bind the finger up with a piece of cotton and go on working. We all have accidents like that. Where the needle goes through the nail it makes a sore finger, or where it splinters a bone it does much harm. Sometimes a finger has to come off. Generally, though, one can be cured by a salve.

All the time we are working the boss walks about examining the finished garments and making us do them over again if they are not just right. So we have to be careful as well as swift. But I am getting so good at the work that within a year I will be making $7 a week, and then I can save at least $3.50 a week. I have over $200 saved now. . . .

I am going back to night school again this winter. Plenty of my friends go there. Some of the women in my class are more than forty years of age. Like me, they did not have a chance to learn anything in the old country. It is good to have an education; it makes you feel higher. Ignorant people are all low. People say now that I am clever and fine in conversation.

We have just finished a strike in our business. It spread all over and the United Brotherhood of Garment Workers was in it. That takes in the cloakmakers, coatmakers, and all the others. We struck for shorter hours, and after being out four weeks won the fight. We only have to work nine and a half hours a day and we get the same pay as before. So the union does good after all in spite of what some people say against it—that it just takes our money and does nothing.

I pay 25 cents a month to the union, but I do not begrudge that because it is for our benefit. The next strike is going to be for a raise of wages, which we all ought to have. . . .

Some of the women blame me very much because I spend so much money on clothes. They say that instead of $1 a week I ought not to spend more than 25 cents a week on clothes, and that I should save the rest. . . . Those who blame me are the old-country people who have old-fashioned notions, but the people who have been here a long time know better. . . .

I have many friends and we often have jolly parties. . . .

32.   CHILDREN IN A SOUTHERN COTTON MILL

The mill-hands are not from Columbia. They are strangers brought in from "the hills" by the agents of the company, who go hither and thither through the different parts of the country describing to the poor whites and the hill dwellers work in the mills as a way to riches and success. Filled with dreams of gain and possessions, with hopes of decent housing and schooling for their children, they leave their distant communities and troop to the mills. These immigrants are picturesque, touching to see. They come with all they own in the world on their backs or in their hands; penniless; burrs and twigs often in the hair of the young girls. They are hatless, barefooted, ignorant; innocent for the most part—and hopeful! What the condition of these laborers is after they have tested the promises of the manufacturer and found them empty bubbles is the tragedy of this population. . . .

The mill houses are all built exactly alike. Painted in sickly greens and yellows, they rise on stilt-like elevations above the malarial soil. Here the architect has catered to the different families, different individual tastes in one point of view alone, regarding the number of rooms: They are known as "four- or six-room cottages." In one of the first cottages to the right a wholesome sight—the single wholesome sight I see during my experience—meets my eye. Human kindness has transformed one of the houses into a kindergarten—KINDERGARTEN is over the door. A pretty Southern girl, a lady, stands surrounded by her little flock. The handful of half a dozen emancipated children who are not in the mills is refreshing to see. There are very few; the kindergarten flags for lack of little scholars. . . .

I see for the first time my dwelling part of this shanty.

A ladderlike stair leading directly from the kitchen takes me into the loft. Heavens! The sight of that sleeping apartment! There are three beds in it, sagging beds, covered by calico comforters. The floor is bare; the walls are bare. I have grown to know that "Jones' " is the cleanliest place in the Excelsior village. . . . Around the bare walls hang the garments of the other women who share the room with me. What humble and pathetic decorations! poor, miserable clothes—a shawl or two, a coat or two, a cotton wrapper, a hat. . . .

The nourishment provided for these thirteen-hour-a-day laborers is as follows: on a tin saucepan there was a little salt pork and on another dish a pile of grease-swimming spinach.

In my simple work garb I leave Columbia and take a trolley to the mill district.

Before the trolley has arrived at the corporation stores Excelsior has spoken—roared, clicked forth so vibrantly, so loudly, I am prepared to feel the earth shake. This is the largest mill in the world and looks it! A model, too, in point of view of architecture. I have read in the prospectus that it represents $1,750,000 capital, possesses 104,000 spindles, employs 1200 hands, and can, with crowding, employ 3000. I am consigned to a standing job. A set of revolving spools is designated, and a pretty young girl of about sixteen comes cheerfully forward and consents to "learn" me.

Spooling is not disagreeable, and the room is the quietest part of the mill—noisy enough, but calm compared to the others. In Excelsior this room is, of course, enormous, light and well ventilated, although the temperature, on account of some quality of the yarn, is kept at a point of humidity far from wholesome. . . . "Spooling" demands alertness, quickness, and a certain amount of strength from the left arm, and that is all! To conceive of a woman of intelligence pursuing this task from the age of eight years to twenty-two is not salutary. . . .

At 5:45 we have breakfasted—the twelve of us who live in one small shanty, where we have slept, all five of us in one room, men to the right of the kitchen, women and children on the left. To leave the pestilence of foul air, the stench of that dwelling, is blessed, even if the stroke that summons is the mill whistle. . . .

It is early—"all the yarn ain't come yet." Two children whose work has not been apportioned lie asleep against a cotton bale. The terrible noise, the grinding, whirling, pounding, the gigantic burr renders other senses keen. By my side works a little girl of eight. Her brutal face, already bespeaking knowledge of things childhood should ignore, is surrounded by a forest of yellow hair. She goes doggedly at her spools, grasping them sullenly. . . .

"She's a mean girl," my little companion says; "we-all don't hev nothin' to say to her."

"Why?"

"Her maw hunts her to the mill; she don't want to go—no, sir—so she's mad most the time." . . .

Through the looms I catch sight of Upton's, my landlord's, little child. She is seven; so small that they have a box for her to stand upon. She is a pretty, frail, little thing, a spooler—"a good spooler, tew!" Through the frames on the other side I can only see her fingers as they clutch at the flying spools; her head is not high enough, even with the box, to be visible. Her hands are fairy hands, fine-boned, well-made, only they are so thin and dirty, and her nails—claws: she would do well to have them cut. A nail can be torn from the finger, *is* torn from the finger frequently, by this flying spool. I go over to Upton's little girl. Her spindles are not thinner nor her spools whiter.

"How old are you?"

"Ten."

She looks six. It is impossible to know if what she says is true. The children are commanded both by parents and bosses to advance their ages when asked.

"Tired?"

She nods, without stopping. She is a "remarkable fine hand." She makes 40 cents a day. See the value of this labor to the manufacturer —cheap, yet skilled; to the parent it represents $2.40 per week.

I must not think that as I work beside them I will gain their confidence! They have no time to talk. Indeed, conversation is not well looked upon by the bosses, and I soon see that unless I want to entail a sharp reproof for myself and them I must stick to my "side." And at noon I have no heart to take their leisure. At twelve o'clock, Minnie, a little spooler, scarcely higher than her spools, lifts her hands above her head and exclaims: *"Thank God, there's the whistle!"* I watched them disperse: some run like mad, always bareheaded, to fetch the dinner-pail for mother or father who work in the mill and who choose to spend these little legs and spare their own. It takes ten minutes to go, ten to return, and the little laborer has ten to devote to its own food, which, half the time, he is too exhausted to eat.

I watch the children crouch on the floor by the frames; some fall asleep between the mouthfuls of food, and so lie asleep with food in their mouths until the overseer rouses them to their tasks again. Here and there totters a little child just learning to walk; it runs and crawls the length of the mill. Mothers who have no one with whom to leave their babies bring them to the workshop, and their lives begin, continue and end in the horrible pandemonium.

One little boy passes by with his broom; he is whistling. I look up at the cheery sound that pierces fresh but faint and natural above the machines' noise. His eyes are bright; his good spirits surprise me: here is an argument for my comfortable friends who wish to prove that the children "are happy!" I stop him.

"You seem very jolly!"

He grins.

"How long have you been working?"

"Two or three days."

The gay creature has just *begun* his servitude and brings into the dreary monotony a flash of the spirit which should fill childhood. . . .

I asked the little girl who teaches me to spool who the man is whom I have seen riding around on horseback through the town.

"Why, he goes roun' rousin' up the hands who ain't in their places. Sometimes he takes the children outen thayre bades an' brings 'em back to the mill."

And if the child can stand, it spins and spools until it drops, till constitution rebels, and death, the only friend it has ever known, sets it free.

Besides being spinners and spoolers, and occasionally weavers even, the children sweep the cotton-strewed floors. Scarcely has the miserable little object, ragged and odorous, passed me with his long broom, which he drags half-heartedly along, than the space he has swept up is cotton-strewn again. It settles with discouraging rapidity; it has also settled on the child's hair and clothes, and his eyelashes, and this atmosphere he breathes and fairly eats, until his lungs become diseased. Pneumonia—fatal in nearly all cases here—and lung fever had been a pestilence, "a regular plague," before I came. There were four cases in the village where I lived, and fever and ague, malaria and grippe did their parts.

"Why, thar ain't never a haouse but's got somebody sick," my little teacher informed me in her soft Southern dialect. "I suttinly never did see a place like this for dyin' in winter time. I reckon et's funerals every day."

Here is a little child, not more than five years old. The land is a hot enough country, we will concede, but not a savage South Sea Island! She has on one garment, if a tattered sacking dress can so be termed. Her bones are nearly through her skin, but her stomach is an unhealthy pouch, abnormal. *She has dropsy.* She works in *a new mill* —in one of the largest mills in South Carolina. Here is a slender little boy—a birch rod (good old simile) is not more slender, but the birch has the advantage: it is elastic—it bends, has youth in it. This boy looks ninety. He is a dwarf; twelve years old, he appears seven, no more. He sweeps the cotton off the floor of "the baby mill." (How tenderly and proudly the owners speak of their brick and mortar.) He sweeps the cotton and lint from the mill aisles from 6 P.M. to 6 A.M. without a break in the night's routine. He stops of his own accord, however, to cough and expectorate—he has advanced tuberculosis.

At night the shanties receive us. On a pine board is spread our food —can you call it nourishment? The hominy and molasses is the best part; salt pork and ham are the strong victuals.

It is eight o'clock when the children reach their homes—later if the mill work is behindhand and they are kept over hours. They are usually beyond speech. They fall asleep at the table, on the stairs; they are carried to bed and there laid down as they are, unwashed, undressed; and the inanimate bundles of rags so lie until the mill summons them with its imperious cry before sunrise, while they are still in stupid sleep.

"What do you do on Sundays?" I asked one little girl.

"Why, thare ain't nothing much to dew. I go to the park sometimes."

This park is at the end of a trolley line; it is their Arcadia. Picture it! A few yellow sand hills with clusters of pine trees and some scrubby undergrowth; a more desolate, arid, gloomy pleasure ground cannot be conceived. On Sundays the trolleys bring those who are not too tired to so spend the day. On Sundays the mill shanties are full of sleepers. . . .

Several little children, who have no clothes but those they wear, cling close to the side of a gaunt, pale-faced man, who carries in his arms the youngest. The little girl has become a weight to be carried on Sundays; she has worked six days of the week—shall she not rest on the seventh? She shall; she claims this, and lies inert on the man's arm, her face already seared with the scars of toil. . . .

The file of humanity that passes me I shall never forget! The Blank Mill claims 1500 of these . . .

33. BOYS AND GIRLS SHOULD WORK

Q. . . . In visiting the homes, how did you find the condition of the children who had been employed in the mills?—*A.* It is the rule in these mills to employ all the children, too. They won't have a family unless they employ the children.

Q. From what ages?—*A.* Six years up.

Q. You found some employed at six?—*A.* The parents told me that was their age.

Q. . . . What can a child of six do in a cotton mill?—*A.* They use them as doffers in the spinning room.

Q. They must be very precocious children?—*A.* They develop rapidly in the South, but they are very small. You discover little ones coming out of the mill at half past six in the evening.

Q. . . . That is the exception, is it not—children of that age?—*A.* From six to eight or ten years old you will find plenty of them. I made an investigation last December at the Exposition Mills, and while I did not make any attempt to count and could not, an inquiry among the operatives working there showed that there was something like 150 children under twelve years of age—from six to twelve. At this time we had before the legislature here a law that would prohibit the employment of children under twelve years of age, and in my efforts to assist in the enactment of that law I made this investigation in that mill to discover how many children were there under twelve years of age.

Q. Do not the mills have a rule that twelve shall be the minimum age?—*A.* Some claim to have such a rule.

Q. And that children are employed younger than that only on the solicitation of their parents?—*A.* That is what the mill presidents say, but I find they will take a family—the larger the family the more acceptable to the mill people.

Q. Do you regard this as very laborious work?—*A.* No, sir. It is the confinement more than anything else that is detrimental to the children, and, of course, in a room where there is more or less dust—.

Q. . . . You are familiar with the operation of our large department stores in the cities?—*A.* Fairly well.

Q. You are acquainted with the fact that there are a large number of cash girls employed there under twelve years of age?—*A.* Yes, sir.

Q. And hours of labor about ten?—*A.* Yes: ten to eleven.

Q. You think the work is about similar as regards the physical requirements?—

A. I think the physical requirements are greater in the cotton mills: that it has a greater tendency to retard the development in the cotton mill than in the store, and a glance at the children working in the mill compared with those in the stores will prove that the physical conditions and the exactments are harsher than in the stores.

Q. Suppose a compulsory education law required these children to go to school at least six months in the year, would there be a great objection to keeping them in the mills the balance of the time?—*A.* Not if necessary to support the families.

Q. Is it not true that it is better for all children to be employed than loafing around the streets so long as the work is fitted for their shoulders?—*A.* I do not think a child should be permitted to enter into manual labor under twelve years of age.

Q. How about the farms?—*A.* You can make no comparison between life in the city and on the farm.

Q. I think there is quite a comparison, because the work is harder.—*A.* You are out in the open air. You are breathing pure oxygen, while in the mill you are breathing deadly vapors and dust.

Q. Your windows are open eight or nine months in the year?—*A.* Sometimes you find the mills require them to keep the windows closed and they have them frosted.

Q. It seems to me that the main difficulty is the educational one, and if the children were put to school for six months it would not be detrimental to have them employed the rest of the time.—*A.* There is another thing that should be considered. These children employed in the factories displace adults, and by putting the children in there it—does not make any difference whether it is three or six months—it leaves an avenue by which the adult labor can be displaced.

Q. That is true generally over the country, and yet it is hard to say that my child shall not work. My father brought up a large family on the farm and they were put at the plow at ten years of age. It would be hard for people to say to him, you cannot employ your children but must employ a man at so many dollars a month.—*A.* After you come to a certain age it is expected that the boy or girl should work, but I do not think under the conditions that exist the law ought to permit such children to work.

Q. . . . . Organized labor has never offered any protest against the farmer putting his children to work on the farm?—*A.* Never.

Q. Would it not be better to provide about nine months' school in the year and compel them to attend?—*A.* The Georgia Federation of Labor has advocated compulsory education, and in fact, the law that we presented to the legislature last winter, as originally presented, had a clause to that effect—that children under twelve years of age should be required to attend school a certain number of months during the year, and could not be taken into the factory unless they showed a certificate from the teacher or county board of education that they had attended school. Then, under the law, they would be permitted to go into the factory if necessary.

Q. What age did that bill provide for?—*A.* Twelve years.

Q. Is that satisfactory to the organized trades of the State?—*A.* Yes, sir; we believe that, while it would not eradicate the evil existing, it would be a great step in advance of anything we have.

Q. You are willing to accept that as a beginning?—*A.* Yes.

V

Workers in a
Free Economy

THE purpose in presenting such a wide array of life histories of workers at the turn of the century is to afford the reader an opportunity to respond directly to these first-hand materials. It is hoped that they have provided much new knowledge and detail about the ways in which Americans worked, lived, and thought. It would be possible to let the record speak for itself. But it may add yet another dimension to a consideration of the lives of these workers if an evaluation is made of some of the salient points which these case materials reveal. Attention will be directed to those aspects which shed new light on issues of fact or interpretation. For convenience, this evaluation will be subdivided into three sections: the conditions under which workers worked; the conditions under which they lived; and their aspirations.

Working Conditions

One cannot fail to be impressed with the fact that a great many workers in the years prior to World War I were employed from sun-up to sun-down. This was true for women as well as men, and it was true for children. In some extreme situations such as in the sweatshops of New York City the hours were even longer, especially in the busy season when they stretched from 6 A.M to 9 P.M. And in some service sectors such as hotels and bars we have records of work-days that stretched over eighteen hours.

For the most part these hours held for a six-day week but many found it necessary to work seven days either because these were the terms of employment or because they could not afford to work fewer hours. One of the reasons that many workers did not balk at such long hours was that they knew that at some later time during the year they were likely to be on short time or even unemployed because of the seasonal nature of their work. Early in this century, seasonality was a much more pervasive fact of our economic life.

Economic pressure was also an important factor which influenced workers to accept these elongated hours—and they were very elongated since to the hours actually worked must be added additional time to get from home to plant or shop. Many of those who had arrived in this country with no capital wanted to become self-supporting as quickly as possible. They were in no position to be selective about their jobs. They had to take what was offered. And the employer did not have to offer very much for unskilled labor—because so many in need of employment were arriving daily from the farms and from abroad.

Nevertheless, although many worked a very long day, some workers had already succeeded by the first decade of this century in forcing down the standard work week. In the Colorado mines the eight-hour day prevailed, and in fact it was closer to a seven-hour day for the management paid on a portal to portal basis. As labor gained strength the hours of work declined, but much of the momentum for the decline came from social reformers who believed that working men and women should have more time for constructive activities off the job; from health officials who warned against the dangers to the health of women and children from excessive hours of labor; and from the belief on the part of workers themselves that if they worked less their jobs might be more secure, and that if they had more time to increase their education and training they stood a better chance of pulling themselves up the economic and social ladder.

Many of the new entrants into the labor force who had been used to long hours of work on the farms on which they had lived in this country or in Europe did not see the long industrial work day as particularly burdensome.

There were other aspects of their working environment which concerned them much more. They were greatly concerned about what would happen to themselves and their families if they were injured or contracted a serious occupational disease. Many faced this problem. Frequently, they were seriously ill before they realized it, as happened to many miners who contracted silicosis and painters who developed lead poisoning.

Among the primary objectives of trade unions was the establishment of mechanisms that would provide assistance to those who could not continue to work because of injury or illness. The miners' unions were among those that took the leadership in developing such plans but the scale of contributions to the union fund was usually so modest and the number of claimants so large that only a limited amount of help was available for the worker in need. Moreover the employer frequently refused to make a disability payment from the fund unless the injured worker waived all of his rights to bring further action. In most instances close relatives assumed the burden of caring for those who were unable to work. The need that workers felt for some type of protection in the event that they could not support themselves because of sickness or injury led to the establishment of a great many self-help plans under other auspices when there was no union to take the lead.

Because so much of the work that had to be done in those days required a high order of physical strength, men in poor health as well as older men were frequently in a very vulnerable position. It should be observed, however, that long before the advent of widespread unionization, employers frequently found lighter work for older men who had served them faithfully. Strength also played a part in the work assignment of younger persons, many of whom started work at ten or twelve years. For instance young boys first picked slate at the mine head; then they became drivers; and only when they were full grown did they become miners.

Constant technological innovations contributed greatly to expanding employment opportunities for women by reducing the importance of physical strength in the performance of work.

While there was only a minimum of state or federal legislation that bore directly on the conditions of work at the turn of the century, even that minimum was more frequently ignored than obeyed. With a constant flow of new workers available, many of them unable to read or speak English, it was a relatively easy matter for employers to ignore laws that they found cumbersome or costly. The worker knew, or he soon learned, that insistence upon his rights could lead to dismissal.

There was considerable victimization of the most vulnerable groups of workers, such as the wives of immigrant workers in the larger urban centers who sought to supplement their meager family income by doing some work at home. Frequently these women paid more for the materials on which they worked or for the machine which they used than they were able to earn. Frequently the employer refused to pay them in full on the ground that their work was imperfect. Large-scale cheating of workers was also common practice in mining where docking bosses were empowered to reduce the tonnage record of a miner if his car had too much slate. The opportunity for this type of exploitation of his work force was a temptation that many an employer could not withstand.

Some workers, especially immigrants and women, were even more abused. While there were laws to prevent employers from physically chastising their workers, many actually were beaten. Since workers could usually quit and find another job without too much difficulty there was a limit to what employers attempted. However, the work force always included a considerable number of mentally retarded and emotionally unbalanced individuals, and these were frequently subjected to severe abuse.

Since many women who worked were completely supporting themselves and frequently also an aged parent or a young child, they were particularly vulnerable. Often the wages which they were able to earn were so low that they were forced to supplement them by establishing relationships with men. This explains why so many parents were concerned when their daughters had to enter paid employment. There was a widespread presumption that women who worked were likely to be immoral, and this presumption was based on fact.

Many immigrants were struck with the fact that the pace of work in the United States was much faster than what they had known at home. Often, an energetic and able worker earned a respectable wage through keeping a fast pace; since every plant had pace-setters there developed an atmosphere of speed and attention to the job at hand. But when they wanted to, workers found ways to control, if not to beat the speed-up.

In the Southern textile mill towns, employers tried to attract not the individual worker, but a family with many potential workers—husband, wife, children. Such a pattern made it easier for him to establish a low wage scale and at the same time the family could earn enough to exist. While a rough counterpart of this pattern can be found in the tenement families in the larger Northern cities, the fact that compulsory school attendance was fairly well established in the North gave the employment pattern a different cast.

A word should be said about the strategic role of the foreman. He was in most instances the key to whether a new worker got a job and whether an older worker held on to one. He had considerable latitude and often used it to abuse and exploit the workers, especially those recently arrived from overseas. The difference between a man who got ahead and one who did not frequently was a reflection of the former's quickly learning the way in which the game was played. Among the earliest and most persistent aims of trade unions has been to restrict and restrain the arbitrary power of the foreman.

An interesting system of exploitation which developed among immigrant labor, especially among the Italians, was the padrone system. A padrone was an entrepreneur whose business consisted of collecting and selling labor. Since his compatriots were frequently incapable of making their own way in a land whose language and customs they did not understand, the padrone acted as boss, instructor, negotiator, counselor, and even banker. Sometimes his charge was reasonable for the services rendered; more frequently it was as much as the traffic would bear. But here too the market acted as a corrective. It did not take many immigrants very long to learn the ropes.

A few highlights can be ventured of the conditions under which American labor worked in the two decades prior to the outbreak of World War I. The American economy fulfilled the major needs of the large stream of new entrants into the labor force. It provided jobs for all who were able to work. The hours of work, while long and arduous, were not a source of major dissatisfaction. But the fear of loss of work from injury or illness was oppressive. Many workers built up deep antagonisms toward employers who cheated them, who sweated them, and who otherwise dealt with them arbitrarily and unjustly. These were the major foci of discontent but even these were in many instances mitigated by what workers were able to earn and what they could look forward to in the future.

Living Conditions

With good results and bad, students frequently oversimplify points of history. An advantage is that it enables them to establish a clearer base from which to measure change. A disadvantage is that they are likely to focus on special rather than general conditions and thereby convey a false picture of the circumstances of an earlier day by taking the unrepresentative and establishing it as the norm.

The life histories of immigrants and migrants should help to correct the widespread impression that most members of the non-agricultural laboring force at the turn of the century lived under severely straitened conditions—at, or very close to, the poverty line. While it was true for some, it surely was not true for most.

First of all, except in years when jobs were hard to find, and there were not many such years except in regions such as the South where industrial jobs were scarce and except for those workers who because of age or lack of skill had little to offer an employer, most members of the working population earned enough to support their families. They were even able to put some savings aside which would enable them to raise their living standards, buy a house, start a business, or meet an emergency.

The factors which determined how the working man's family lived were: the amount of money that the head of the household was able to earn during the course of a year; the number of other workers, usually adolescent children, who contributed to family income; and the extent to which the woman of the household contributed indirectly by raising vegetables, keeping a cow and chickens, taking care of boarders or lodgers, and by using skills in the management of the household.

When a worker earned $15 to $20 during a two-week period—or between $400 and $500 per annum—he was frequently able to put some savings aside, especially if he did not have a large family to support and if his income was supplemented by $3 or so per week for a boarder. He frequently was able to walk to work, and with a 5 cent beer he could eat a free lunch. Since he worked such a long day his expenditures beyond food, work clothes, and a good suit for Sunday, most frequently went for drink, tobacco, newspapers, and lodge fees. Often differences between the standards of living of two working class families reflected an addiction to drink on the part of one worker and a general abstemiousness on the part of the other.

In coal mining there was a spread in earnings of approximately 70 cents a day between the man who performed unskilled labor and the skilled miner—one earned about $1 a day, the other about $1.70. In point of fact the full range was considerably greater, for within the skilled group were men who as a result of strength, aptitude, favoritism, or just good luck in mine sites could earn very much more than most of their co-workers.

In fact there was an elite among highly skilled workers in many sectors of the economy whose annual earnings were strikingly high—three and four times, sometimes even more, what their fellow workers made. Their high earnings usually reflected the fact that they operated more as entrepreneurs than as paid workers. They were paid on a piece basis but they hired and paid others who helped them; employers often were afraid to readjust the terms of their contract since these were key men who, if they left, could put a major snag in the entire operation.

It is difficult to reconstruct how much good food workers were able to buy at the turn of the century. Time and again workers reported how well they were fed in homes or boarding houses for $3 to $4 a week. They had to work hard and for long hours and these men ate heartily: meat three times a day was not exceptional for the steel worker, the lumberjack, and others who were engaged in strenuous physical labor. And in most instances the laborer on the farm was able to eat his fill —perhaps not in the impoverished South but certainly in the rich farm lands of the Midwest.

We know that single men were able to find room and board for about $11 to $12 a month. And in steel and other heavy industry they were frequently able to earn $10 per week or over $40 a month. A great many single men had come to this country to get a start with the intention of bringing their wives or fiancées over just as soon as they had put some money aside. Most of them were able to send for their families or future brides within two or three years, many within a year. As always happens with large-scale relocations some men used their separation from home as an excuse to break ties. They left their wives and children behind and frequently started second families in this country.

Other single men had a pattern of life which was quite different. They were restless individuals who moved around the country, staying with no job long, working in spurts, and playing hard when they had money. Whiskey, women, and gambling were their recreation. Much of the hard work that had to be done in isolated places—laying railroad tracks, cutting virgin forests, opening up new mines—was performed by these rough fellows, usually as members of a work gang. It is not surprising that some of the most aggressive trade union and political activity was centered in the West which drew so many of these men.

There are many reasons why students of society should exercise caution in generalizing about the motivations and behavior of any large group of men and there is particular reason to avoid generalizing about American labor at the turn of this century when those who composed the laboring force were drawn from such diverse backgrounds, had such different aims and ambitions, and were confronted with such different conditions. There was indeed little in common between the Italian shoemaker in New York and the Slovakian lumberjack in Oregon; or between the steel worker in Chicago and the anthracite coal miner.

Among the special problems faced by many workers during this period of the country's history was the method of wage payment. In many mine areas, for example, workers were paid monthly despite the fact that the law said that they had to be paid at least semi-monthly. By paying the miners only at the end of the month, the owners assured that most of the workers would have to trade at the company store, where they were extended credit. But most company stores charged considerably above competitive prices. It was not unusual for the company store to ask $2.50 or more for a keg of powder while it could be bought on the open market for half that.

Some employers in the cities also victimized their workers when it came to paying them. They might insist on paying them by check, having worked out a mutually advantageous arrangement with a neighboring saloon which would cash them and in turn get back a considerable part as payment for drinks.

Special reference should be made to women workers, who were generally at the bottom of the wage scale. The question arises whether and to what extent they were able to make ends meet. Several qualifications are in order. If a girl were able to live at home, and particularly if she were able to walk to and from work, she was likely to have some spending money even if her weekly wages were as low as $3, which was typical. But if she had to pay for room and board, and particularly if she also had to pay carfare, she could barely make ends meet. Most girls in this situation worked out arrangements with other girls to share the expenses of room and food.

Most young women who worked at this time did live at home, and even if they contributed to the family's income they frequently had some money left over to spend on themselves. In fact one of the most potent factors that helped to draw young women from working class homes into paid employment was their desire to earn some money so that they could dress better. Some historians have assumed that the only reason that women worked during this period was economic necessity. Many of them, however, thirsted after independence. They did not want to be completely dependent on their fathers or brothers for their clothes and the extras which could add zest to their growing up. A job also gave them an opportunity to escape from the strict supervision of their mothers and brought them into close contact with other girls and, equally important, with boys of their own age. In many mills, despite the relatively hard work and the steady pace, the girls found great satisfaction in being able to talk with their fellow workers. Contemporary reports stress the importance of the plant in facilitating socializing, especially among young girls. Here is a harbinger of later sociological investigations which relearned this basic fact.

Although many workers were unable to earn enough to support

their large families adequately, most working class families, in which
the head of the household was able to hold a full-time job, were able
to eat adequately and to cover other basic needs. If a family had multiple earners, and particularly if the head was a skilled worker, it was
likely to live quite comfortably. There would be ample food, good
clothing, and money for extras. Moreover the family would be able
to save.

Aspirations

Many lived only for the day but many more lived for the morrow.
The principles which underlie the selection of these life histories
tended to exclude the large numbers of workers who succeeded in rising on the occupational and income scale until they cut away from
the class to which they had belonged. The people who are included
in this collection were, with few exceptions, workers throughout their
entire lives.

The workers who found that they could save part of their earnings
frequently converted much of their savings at some point into a home
and furnishings. Visitors to these shores frequently remarked on the
comfortable homes of workers and the substantial manner in which
they were furnished. Part of the explanation lies in the fact that many
who had moved from farms had come from families which had owned
their homes. And it was only a short step for the land-hungry peasant
from Europe who settled in an American city to seek stability and
status through the ownership of his home.

The carpeting, bathrooms, pianos, and other hallmarks of economic
well-being helped the worker, even the immigrant, to consider himself as good as any other man. The fluid class lines made it possible
for any worker to move into the class above as soon as he had acquired the emoluments characteristic of it. While vast differences in
income established vast differences in the way in which different groups
lived, once the income differentials had narrowed or disappeared, there
were few psychological or social barriers to spending money as others
in the community spent theirs.

The burgeoning of consumer credit in the 1920's and later was in
direct line with the substantial indebtedness assumed by many who
had in an earlier day mortgaged their futures so that they could own
their homes. While the fulcrum of this development was to improve
the family's living standard, it also frequently contained an element of
speculative investment. With ever larger numbers pouring into the

cities, workers who bought a sound house for their use were likely to make a profit on it when they decided to sell. Others purchased land or houses or both more directly for speculative purposes, in what Veblen called "the great American game."

While many were able, after years at work, to "have more time, more money, and to live better," a substantial minority fared poorly. This was especially true for those who depended on a single industry when that industry came on evil days, as happened from time to time in mining and in other sectors of the economy. We read of a marked redundancy of labor in the anthracite coal mining regions of Pennsylvania during depressed years, when children had to be kept home from school because they had no shoes. During these years, immigrants of an earlier day began to press for restrictive legislation so that their difficulties would not be compounded through further flooding of the labor market.

Relatively few escaped from the mine villages to return to Europe. But we know that every year many who had been successful, and many more who had not, decided to go home. The unsuccessful had an opportunity, if they were strong enough, to work for their passage on cattle boats, but many of these jobs were little short of slave labor. It is worth noting that the return to the old country frequently turned out to be temporary and before long the one-time immigrant was on his way back, usually with the intent to make his home permanently in the United States.

Different groups of workers fared completely differently in the early years of this century. When business was active, young men and women could get jobs readily, and while their earnings were not very high they usually made enough to enable them to marry and start a family while they were still young. There were few bachelors in the coal mines older than twenty-three. But on the other side is the testimony that a miner of thirty-five was already old—worn out by two decades below ground.

When death or illness struck the impact could be very serious indeed, especially for the women and young children who had not expected to have to work for their bread. But on the other hand there were many young girls living at home who were able to get jobs which enabled them to dress much better and to have more fun out of life.

Although the basic wage level was low, the steady expansion of the economy plus the large-scale inflow of new workers at the bottom of the ladder implied that those who were already established in their jobs were likely to be pushed up, at least one or two rungs.

Even an immigrant shoeshine boy could accumulate many hundreds of dollars of savings during a relatively few years. Young women who were paid only $3 to $4 a week as stock clerks might work their way up over a period of time to become supervisors earning $10 to $12 weekly. The more ambitious, especially those who lived in large cities, could avail themselves of the opportunity to attend school at night to add to their knowledge and skills. It was surely not easy for a young man or woman after a strenuous ten hours or more at work to apply himself to study, but many did. The clear and unequivocal evidence in their environment that others had been able to pull themselves up through education served as a great stimulus to educate themselves.

Even many tenement workers dreamed of the day when they could accumulate enough capital so that they themselves could "sweat" others and earn their 50 per cent, just as they were now being forced to divide their earnings with their "sweaters." The transition from worker to businessman was but one short step, a step that many workers were able to take. For teamsters the jump was more difficult and fewer dreamed such dreams. In the coal mines, cotton mills, and other large undertakings even the prospect of making the jump was beyond the imagination of most workers. The more ambitious might see a possibility of moving sideways and then up—by opening a store or getting a job with local government, but the direct leap into ownership was beyond their expectations.

But there was no need for the ambitious person to try the impossible. While the rapid expansion and transformation of the economy frequently brought hardship to some workers, it created a great many new opportunities for others. Those who had drive and intelligence —and some luck—had no reason to fear. The odds were good that they could move ahead rapidly. And even the large majority could afford to be content, for they were able to advance even while standing still. They were on a moving escalator. And the prospects for their children were dramatic; with the advantages of free schools, they could aspire to much more.

Part
THREE

Part

THREE

VI

The New Era
and the Great Depression

THERE is no simple and surely no certain way to divide the past into significant periods so that the events in one can be clearly and sharply differentiated from those in another. And yet without some temporal distinctions it is almost impossible to order the multitude of events that give shape and direction to the lives of men and nations.

It was cumbersome to include in Chapter IV the rich diversity of experience that characterized the American economy and society between the depression of the early 1890's and the outbreak of World War I. It will be even more cumbersome to include within Chapter VII the even more diversified experience of the period which included the war boom and the sharp postwar reaction of 1920–21, the prosperous twenties that are known as the New Era, and the years of deep depression that swept over the land in the 1930's.

Why, if it is so difficult to compress so much diversity into a single period, would it not be sensible to increase the number of periods into which reality is forceably subdivided in order to be able to distinguish them more clearly? The answer is that the diversity existing at any point in time within an economy of continental proportions with markedly different regional substrata would prevent the establishment of neat homogeneous time periods. In every period of American his-

147

tory, the diversity of economic and social conditions existing includes differences in levels of employment, income, standards of living, prospects for the future. Even at the height of a war boom or in the depth of a depression the range of variations remains substantial. Since, then, there is no escape from the inherent limitations of historical periodicity, this part of the book covers once again a quarter-century, from the outbreak of World War I to the outbreak of World War II. To help the reader keep in perspective the major alterations in the framework within which people worked and lived, the following pages will describe some of the major transformations brought about by the United States' involvement in World War I, the prosperity of the twenties, and the acute depression of the thirties.

World War I

In the year when war broke out among the world powers, over 1.2 million immigrants arrived in the United States. This number exceeded the total that arrived in this country during the next five years. While the restrictive legislation with regard to immigration did not take full effect until 1925, following passage of the acts of 1921 and 1924, the very large-scale inflow of immigrants that had been characteristic of the last decade of the nineteenth century and the first decade of the twentieth was radically reduced with the outbreak of World War I and never regained its prior level.

While the first consequence in the United States of the outbreak of hostilities was to unsettle the American economy and to increase the unemployment rate in 1915 to about 10 per cent,[1] more than double what it had been two years earlier, economic conditions began to right themselves by 1916. The next few years saw a substantial expansion in employment and substantial increases in wages which, together with other war developments, made substantial changes in the position of the American worker.

Some measure of the effect of the war on expanding employment is suggested by the fact that in the five years prior to 1914 the total number of persons engaged in manufacturing had increased from approximately 7.9 million to 8.4, or less than 7 per cent. In contrast, there was a gain of about 2.6 million, or more than 30 per cent, between 1915 and 1918.[2] But even this increase understates the rate at which opportunities were opening up. For during World War I the United States mobilized in excess of 4 million men; many of them had formerly been employed in manufacturing, and replacements had to be found for them.

Among those who gained from the tight labor market conditions of the war years were Negroes. Before 1920 there were relatively few Negroes in the North and they had had little opportunity to obtain jobs above the unskilled level. But in the rapid expansion of the war years they made some progress up the skill and income ladders in industries such as meat packing, automobiles, and metal-working plants.[3]

The shortage of labor precipitated by the involvement of the United States in World War I accelerated trends that were already under way more frequently than it instituted entirely new developments. This surely was the case with women who worked outside of the home. The big change in the employment of women that occurred between 1910 and 1920 was not in the total numbers or the percentage of women who worked but rather the opportunities that were opened for women to rise in the occupational hierarchy. In 1910, two-thirds of all women employed were working at semi-skilled or unskilled jobs. Only one in eight was a teacher, a nurse, or in another professional field; and about one in six was employed as a clerical or sales worker. A decade later only slightly more than half of all women who worked were still classified as semi- or unskilled workers; the percentage in sales or clerical work had increased to about one in three. The other categories showed little change.[4] The war opened opportunities for women in local transportation, high school teaching, munition plants, and many other sectors. In many instances the breakthroughs were temporary, but in other areas they were permanent.[5] Their most significant gains resulted from the great expansion in office and clerical work required by the wartime economy.

The tightness of the labor market brought with it marked upward pressure on the wage structure, especially since the government's method of financing led to such a marked increase in the money supply that strong inflationary pressures were unleashed. Workers sought to take advantage of the rising demand for labor by seeking and obtaining large wage increases. In 1914 average earnings per hour of work in manufacturing stood at 22 cents; by 1916 they had risen only to 26 cents, but thereafter the rise was spectacular. By 1920 the average wage per hour of work was 55 cents—more than double what it had been five years earlier.[6]

This rapid increase in average earnings for all non-agricultural employees resulted in an increase in annual earnings from under $700 in 1914 to just under $1500 in 1920.[7] Its true impact, however, can be gauged only if consideration is also taken of changes in the cost of living and in the hours that people customarily worked. As for the former, the rise was sufficiently rapid to eat up most of the gain: total real compensation of workers improved only about 20 per cent during this period.[8] But the average work week decreased from 51.5 to 48.2, or by over 6 per cent—so that the gains of the laboring man in real wages and leisure combined were approximately 25 per cent within this five-year period.[9]

The wartime gains of labor were not limited to increases in wages and reductions in hours. This period witnessed a very substantial strengthening of organized labor. Union membership stood at approximately 2.5 million in 1915 and it was still under 3 million in 1917. By 1920, however, it had broken through the 5 million mark, which represented a gain of 100 per cent in the five-year period.

The increases in union membership were not evenly spread throughout the economy. The most substantial gains were realized in "metals, machinery, and shipbuilding" where membership increased from approximately 250,000 in the middle of the decade to over 850,000 in 1920, and in "transportation and communication," which saw a rise from about 570,000 to 1,250,000.[10]

Labor's gains were not made without struggle and strife. In 1915 there were less than 1600 work stoppages; in the succeeding years there were between 3500 and 4500 strikes each year, which indicates the mounting tension between labor and management.[11]

In preparing for the election of 1916, President Wilson had taken the leadership in pushing forward labor and social welfare legislation. Once the United States entered the war, the federal government had to act on many fronts involving economic and labor control measures. In establishing various boards and commissions, Wilson gave public recognition to the role of labor and placed representatives of organized labor on many of these public bodies. By such action he went far to legitimize the new place of labor in American society.

Many industrialists and businessmen were concerned about these wartime gains made by labor and struggled to keep them to a minimum. Their chance came at the end of the war, and particularly with the election of a new president. Harding's slogan is indicative of the mood; he pledged a return to normalcy. And soon conservatives had a new ally: the acute depression of 1920–21 acted to erode many of labor's gains.

At the height of the war (1918), the total number of unemployed was only about half a million, or 2 per cent of the non-farm employees. In 1921, at the bottom of the postwar depression, 5 million, or 17 per cent of all non-farm employees, were out of work. In 1922 the percentage had dropped, but almost 3.2 million, or approximately 10 per cent, were still unemployed.[12]

While wage rates were reduced by about 20 per cent during the depression, the consumer price index likewise declined by about the same amount, with the result that those who were lucky enough to retain their jobs did not suffer any real worsening in their positions. And even some of the unemployed were not too badly pressed during the first year of the crisis because many of them had accumulated considerable savings during the preceding boom years. But when President Harding called a conference on unemployment in September of 1921 at the suggestion of Secretary Hoover the situation could no longer be ignored. Hoover warned that unless the unemployed were speedily reabsorbed, the entire moral and economic system might disintegrate. Fifteen thousand enterprises had already gone bankrupt; many more were operating at a loss; and the physical value of production had declined by about 17 per cent. But just as the outlook was darkest, powerful forces started to turn the economy around. The price liquidation was nearing its end; pent-up construction demand was making itself felt; and most important, the automobile industry was set to start on a major expansion which would transform the face of America during the 1920's and would provide the basis for a sustained industrial prosperity.[13]

The New Era

The 1920's were unique in many regards. First of all was the widespread belief, especially toward the end of the decade, that the American economy had a new complexion: it had become one where high-level employment and high-level profits would be permanent. While it is relatively easy in retrospect to identify the signposts which misled both amateur and professional economists, the seven good years that followed the recovery from the 1921–22 depression did contain many new and surprising aspects which contributed to error. Perhaps the most important was the relatively stable prices and wages which were assumed to reflect the soundness of the underlying economy.

As we suggested earlier, a cross-sectional view of the American economy is unlikely to reveal a picture in which light or darkness is evenly distributed. It is much more likely to disclose an economy in which some sections are more prosperous than the average while others are moderately or even severely depressed. What in fact do the figures tell us about the New Era?

National income increased from a low of $63 billion in 1922 to a high of $88 billion in 1929, an increase of no less than 40 per cent in seven years—indeed an impressive record. Even after allowance is made for the increase in population the record is still impressive. Per capita income, in stable prices, advanced from about $660 to $855 between 1921 and 1929, or approximately 30 per cent in eight years.[14] There was surely a basis for the widespread satisfaction with the performance of the American economy during these years.

Yet there were developments that should have precipitated some disquietude about the position of the American wage earner. First, the number of employees in non-agricultural establishments increased very slowly after 1923; it was only 6 per cent higher in 1928, and at the peak of the boom in 1929 it was only 10 per cent higher, than in 1923.[15] In several major areas of employment, such as mining, transportation, and public utilities, there were actual declines. Even more striking is the fact that in manufacturing—the backbone of the American economy—the number of employees was smaller in every year after 1923 except for 1929, when the total was only slightly in excess of what it had been six years earlier.[16] The strong sectors were construction and the service industries, which expanded rapidly. Even so, in four out of the seven years after 1922, there was an unemployment rate for nonfarm workers of just under 6 per cent or more.[17]

The industrial work force had always recruited large numbers from the farm, and the 1920's saw an intensification of this long-time trend. During the war the remaining farm labor had been inadequate to meet the rapidly expanding demand for agricultural products and advances were therefore made in the use of power machinery on farms. The use of advanced technology was continued on farms during the postwar years, but now demand had slackened; the war-devastated regions in Europe were on the road to recovery, and new competitors were entering the international market. This resulted in severe pressure on prices and profits—the more so because American farmers had expanded at an inflated price level and were now receiving for their crops prices which were much below the wartime and immediate postwar levels.[18]

Experts talked about the "large gross movement from farms to cities" during the 1920's. In point of fact the numbers of gainful workers in agriculture, which had totalled 10.7 million at the beginning of the century, was slightly less in 1930—10.5 million—despite the fact that in the intervening three decades the total of all workers had risen from approximately 20 to 49 million.[19]

Agriculture was by no means the only "distressed industry" during the prosperous twenties. The decade saw a drop of about 10 per cent in the number of coal mine operatives and laborers; and if allowance were made for the short time that many miners worked during the period, the figures would be much more depressing. Many workers attached to lumbering, tobacco, textiles, footwear, and still other industries fared poorly, especially if they lived and worked for firms in areas of the country which had been left behind in the competitive struggle, such as many localities in New England.

It is worth noting, especially because of the renewed concern in the 1960's with accelerated technological change, that the term "technological unemployment" came into prominence toward the end of the prosperous twenties. The rate at which industry was investing in new and more productive machines appeared to be in excess of the economy's ability to absorb all who were looking for work. While there was no agreement among economists or politicians, then as now, as to the short- and long-run implications of these trends affecting investment and employment, there were a growing number of observers, toward the end of the decade, who were concerned about the widening gap between the number seeking work and the number of jobs available.

There were other untoward developments during the New Era which affected the American working man that should be at least briefly noted. Harding had won an overwhelming victory in 1920 based on a return to normalcy; "big business," which had succeeded in breaking the steel strike in 1919, continued to ride high in the centers of power, both private and public—witness Andrew Mellon's incumbency as Secretary of the Treasury—throughout the whole of the era.

Organized labor was unable to maintain its wartime gains. Each year saw the rolls of the unions decline from a membership in excess of 5 million in 1920 to a total of about 3.4 million at the end of the decade, or a loss of about one-third. When allowance is made for the substantial increase in the numbers of non-agricultural employees, the proportion of the total represented by union members in 1930 was lower than it had been two decades earlier.[20] Union membership was very heavily concentrated in five industries: transportation, building, printing, public service, and theatre accounted for about 70 per cent of the total membership.[21]

The difficulties that organized labor experienced during the twenties reflected more than an unequal power struggle between them and the employer group. There were important transformations under way in the structure of American industry, in the functioning of management, in the characteristics the labor force, and above all in the prevailing ideology. All of this helped to block organized labor's ability to organize or even to keep its members.

In the manufacturing sector of the economy substantial capital investments not only led to enhanced mechanization but also facilitated a vast array of improvements that contributed to a marked increase in productivity. When employers closed down old plants in the North and opened new ones in the South or West they were able to take advantage of all that the industry had learned about plant layout and plant management. Among the most important of these lessons was the recognition that if costly capital was to be efficiently operated and maintained, it was desirable to establish and maintain a high level of worker morale and satisfaction. At a minimum, management had learned, it was desirable to eliminate all dangerous and disagreeable aspects of the working environment just as expeditiously as possible. Small firms that operated on very close margins were frequently unable to take constructive steps to improve their working environment, but large profitable companies had considerable leeway. The twenties saw the rapid growth through the success in the market place, aided and abetted by mergers, of the large profitable corporate unit. In 1920 the manufacturing companies in the top 5 per cent according to size accounted for about 75 per cent of all net income reported by companies that ended the year with a net profit. In 1930, the corresponding companies accounted for approximately 85 per cent of the total.[22]

Many of these very large companies, as well as others of more moderate size, responded to the promptings of spokesmen in business, academic life, and government who advocated that scientific personnel policies and humane labor relations would contribute to company profitability. The twenties saw a rapid growth in what has been called "welfare capitalism." The thrust of the effort was to create good employment conditions; to give workers new types of benefits, such as free lunches, recreational opportunities, various types of insurance, pensions after long years of service, and similar emoluments. These efforts were in considerable measure motivated by management's desire to prevent the growth of unionism. But by providing these benefits, by acting to reduce the arbitrary power of the foreman in hiring and firing, by establishing some mechanism for consultation between workers and management, the more progressive sectors of industry acted in recognition of the fact that American working men and women had many legitimate aspirations which industry had in the past failed to meet.

Irrespective of the reasons why management acted to improve the conditions of employment, the fact is that a significant minority of American workers who were employed in the more advanced technological sectors made substantial gains during the 1920's as a result of these welfare plans.

Another source of gain that affected many more fell completely outside the framework of labor-management relations. A significant determinant of employee welfare has long been the extent to which he has been able to obtain various services from government. What a worker is able to earn after he starts to work and how high he is able to rise on the occupational and income ladder is greatly affected by the type of educational and other developmental opportunities available to him. Government has long been the agency in American society charged with the responsibility of providing educational opportunities. Government has also long contributed, along with private philanthropy, to the support of a wide range of services that play an important role in mitigating the impact of adversity or in broadening the scope for opportunity. Between World War I and the end of the New Era the scale of expenditures by government and philanthropy on social services, including education, increased more than four-fold annually—from under $900 million to over $3.7 billion.[23]

Indicative of the rising standards is the increase in the percentage of various age groups enrolled in school in 1930 compared to the same figures in 1920. By the end of World War I, most young people (92.5 per cent) remained in school until their fourteenth year, but in the older groups the percentage declined rapidly. In 1930 a much higher percentage of adolescents and young adults were in school than ten years earlier. The gain among sixteen-year-olds was from half to two-thirds; among eighteen-year-olds from about 21 to 31 per cent; among twenty-year-olds from 8 to 13 per cent.[24]

Among the more subtle changes wrought by World War I was the acceleration in the Americanization of the labor force and of the total society. The foreign-born sectors declined both absolutely and relatively. Many men with foreign-born parents who served in the Army during the war now stepped forward to claim their full rights as American citizens. Many Negroes likewise had a first chance to improve their disadvantaged position as a result of the war by joining one of the services or moving North and getting a job in industry or trade. The position of women was greatly improved by the passage of the Nineteenth Amendment which gave them the right to vote. While there were no spectacular changes in the employment pattern for women during the New Era either in terms of the percentage who worked or the types of jobs that were opened to them, the earlier trend was maintained and reinforced. More women worked, including a small but growing number of married women from middle and upper class homes.

The New Era, like every distinctive period in American history, is characterized by contradictions. While most workers shared in the prevailing industrial prosperity, a sizable minority did not, either because they were attached to weak industries or because they were the victims of technological change. With wages advancing only moderately and hours declining hardly at all, the wage-earning population was surely not the major beneficiary of the expansion and prosperity. Some speculated successfully in real estate or the stock market, and some improved their position by virtue of their wives' also holding paid jobs.

Some had employers who introduced attractive benefit plans and some lived in communities where the quality and quantity of public services were significantly expanded. But even after account is taken of these favorable trends, it is clear that the New Era as such, no matter how attractive it might have appeared to the business community and even to many academic economists, did not result in substantially improving the lot of the American working man. The improvement that he did experience had more to do with changes in the national scene—the control of immigration, the expansion and improvement of governmental services, and the breakthroughs in technology and medicine—rather than with his strengthened position in the labor market.

The Great Depression

Just as it was difficult for contemporaries to recognize the end of the New Era it is difficult even now to reach agreement as to when in the 1930's the forces unleashed by the Great Depression had spent themselves. Some contend that in the all-important matter of employment the depression failed to lift throughout the whole of the decade —although it was mitigated after Mr. Roosevelt took office. They say that the major upward movement in the economy, at least as measured by the full recovery in employment, did not begin until the war mobilization boom of the early 1940's. The student of business fluctuations dates the Great Depression from 1929 to 1933; he notes that the recovery in the following years left large numbers of the labor force still on the unemployment rolls; he calls attention to the sharp depression of 1937–38 but he insists that a strikingly rapid recovery followed 1938.

The economic historian has an alternative interpretation: his reading that the whole of the 1930's was a period of poor economic performance is underscored by the fact that the basic indices for 1939 showed no significant gains over 1929. The most telling support for this appraisal is the fact that a high level of unemployment persisted, the key measure of the performance of a modern industrial economy.

The index of common stocks—the important harbinger of the prosperous twenties—had risen from about 8.5 per cent in 1923 to over 26.0 in 1929, or a gain of more than 300 per cent. By 1932 it had fallen to under 7, a decline of over 70 per cent within a period of three years.[25] An interesting point to recall is the failure of so many to acknowledge that the economy had run into stormy weather.

There was a decline of almost 26 billion dollars in the value of securities listed on the Stock Exchange in the fall of 1929. Irving Fisher, an economist of international repute, commented on this tremendous drop as being "so full of sound and fury, signifies little." He argued that since only about 1 per cent of the population earned over $9000 per annum, the vast majority of the population would not be affected by the vagaries of the stock market.[26] Henry Ford, an early apostle of the doctrine of high wages as a lever to economic prosperity, publicly reaffirmed his faith in his theory shortly after the stock market broke by recommending that: "Wages must not come down, they must not even stay at their present level; they must go up." [27]

Since the seven good years of the 1920's had been preceded by the expansion of World War I and the immediate postwar years—marred only by the sharp liquidation of 1921–22; and since, in the much larger sweep of time from the recovery of the economy after the depression of the mid-1890's until the outbreak of World War I, business had escaped any serious period of liquidation (for the panic of 1907 was quickly contained)—it is not surprising that the country's leadership remained optimistic after the stock market collapse of 1929. They had good reason to hope and expect that at the worst there would be some radical readjustments in financial markets and possibly even in commodity prices. But in light of their experience, and more particularly because of the absence of overt inflationary trends during the 1920's, they did not anticipate a major falling off in production, employment, or income.

But as it turned out they were completely wrong. President Roosevelt stated that "the almost complete collapse of the American economic system marked the beginning of my administration." [28]

A few figures can go far to substantiate the correctness of the President's judgment. The number unemployed in 1929 was about 1.5 million, just over 3 per cent of the labor force; in 1933 the total number out of work was just under 13 million, approximately 25 per cent of the entire labor force. At no time during the rest of the decade did the total drop below 7 million or 14 per cent; in three years—1934, 1935, and 1938—the total fluctuated around 10 to 11 million, or in the neighborhood of 20 per cent.[29]

But even these figures understate the plight of the working man during these years. If the work force is defined in terms of non-farm employees, then at the height of the depression more than one out of every three workers was out of a job and at no time throughout the rest of the decade did the percentage drop below one in five.[30]

While, of course, those who lost their jobs suffered the most, many who held them also endured privation. There was for instance a decline in the average weekly hours of work for production workers from over 44 in 1929 to under 35 in 1934, a reduction of about 20 per cent. Average hourly earnings declined during this same period by about the same percentage, with a resulting drop in average weekly earnings of almost 33 per cent. While the price index of consumer goods also declined during those years, many workers were attempting to pay off debts that they accumulated earlier with dollars that had become more valuable.[31]

These averages hide about as much as they disclose. In a decade in which many more were seeking work than there was work available, a great many in the laboring population were hardly able to support their families. Some employers paid as little as 5 cents an hour; others were unable to meet their payrolls at all; many could offer only a few days of employment a month to the few members of their work force for whom they felt a special obligation.

In recognition of the enormity of the problem, particularly the inadequacy of the job market, the New Deal was established to provide income and to put people to work on projects financed and operated by the federal government. Between 1934 and 1940 there were approximately 300,000 young men at all times in the Civilian Conservation Corps. The National Youth Administration provided part-time employment for between 500,000 and 750,000 students during those five years. Thus, more than a million young people directly benefited from these two programs. Between 2 and 3 million men and women were on the rolls of the Work Projects Administration, which spent in the neighborhood of 1.5 billion dollars annually. Other federal programs provided employment for an additional half million persons or so.[32]

In the depression years the various programs of the federal government gave direct employment to almost 4.5 million persons. This represented almost half of the total employment provided by manufacturing.

In addition to the New Deal's direct efforts to provide employment, it acted on two other fronts which had tremendous impact in the long run: it altered the power of labor in the market and provided a large number of new benefits to the working man through the development of a social security system.

As might have been expected, the trade union movement, which had been losing ground steadily since the end of the World War I boom, was all but extinguished in the collapse of the economy during the years of the Great Depression. Reported membership declined from about 3.6 to 2.9 million in the four years 1929 to 1933, but many who were carried on the rolls had long before stopped paying their dues. The American Federation of Labor, with a membership of only slightly above 2 million in 1933, was back to the level where it had been on the eve of World War I, two decades previously. In the interim, of course, there had been a marked expansion of the industrial sector, which means that organized labor's relative position had worsened appreciably.[33]

When President Roosevelt established the National Industrial Recovery Act in 1933, a section was inserted which provided "that employees shall have the right to organize and bargain collectively . . . free from interference, restraint and coercion of employers of labor. . . ." In large part, this provision was made in order to balance the opportunities offered industry under the NIRA codes to establish prices through joint action. Two years later Congress was ready to incorporate into permanent legislation the right of workers to join unions of their own choosing. The National Labor Relations Act went far to alter the relative power of employer and employees in the struggle of the marketplace. Among the potent factors operating in this direction was the National Labor Relations Board, established under the provisions of the Act, which through interpretation and administration reinforced the expanding strength of organized labor.

A friendly President, supportive legislation, and administrative agencies that were inclined to be sympathetic to its claims all contributed to the truly spectacular gains made by organized labor in the latter part of the decade. The ranks of organized labor swelled from under 3 million members in 1933 to over 8 million in 1938—a gain of 170 per cent in five years.[34] It is probable that an important precipitant of the sharp business depression of 1938–39, which reinforced the effect of the drop in governmental spending, was the immobilization and frustration which beset the business community as it watched the ever-greater accretion of power by the trade union movement. Except for two unusual years—1919, which marked the postwar inflation, and 1934, which marked the beginning of the recovery from the depth of the Great Depression—wages rose more in 1936–37 than in any previous year in American history: average earnings per hour of work in manufacturing rose almost 7 cents on a base of 54 cents or by approximately 13 per cent in a single year.[35] Much of the momentum which helped to increase membership and improve conditions came from the industrial unions, old and new, which had formed themselves into the Congress of Industrial Organizations under the leadership of John L. Lewis.

The year 1935 was significant beyond all other years in American labor history because it saw the passage not only of the Wagner Act but also of the Social Security Act. It is ironic but nevertheless revealing of the ideological orientation of American labor that as late as 1932 the Convention of the American Federation of Labor looked askance at governmental programs of unemployment insurance. Labor was almost as wary of governmental action as was management. Nevertheless the lesson of the Great Depression and its aftermath of continuing high-level unemployment was finally learned. One important segment of the legislation passed in 1935 was the establishment of a federal-state unemployment insurance system.

The Act also set up the first system of general benefits for workers who were no longer able or willing to work. Benefits were paid to workers after they reached 65, on a sliding scale depending on their previous earnings and contributions. Later amendments, in 1939, made benefits available to certain dependents of the wage earner after his retirement or death.

Unemployment and old age benefits were based on the contribution principle, but the Social Security Act also provided for public assistance programs financed by federal, state, and local governments to provide essential assistance to persons on the basis of need without reference to their past earnings or contributions. While several states had been providing various types of assistance to needy persons for some years, their programs had been very uneven and a great many persons in want had been receiving nothing or very little.[36]

The impact of the new federal legislation in the area of labor relations was immediate; more time was required before the economic and social implications of the new social security system became manifest.

The position of the American worker had been reduced in the 1930's to a theretofore unknown low. Millions lost their jobs and homes, and the prospects were dim for many ever again to improve their positions. Their hopes were shattered. But at the very same time, organized labor gained a new lease on life, and government acted to insure that in the future the working man would never again have to bear so much of the costs of the instability that are characteristic of a dynamic industrial economy.

VII

Prosperity and
Depression: Life Histories

Up the Skill Ladder

34. HOT BLAST MAN

THE twelve-hour day makes the life of the steel worker different in a
far-reaching manner from the life of the majority of his fellow workers.

It makes the industry different in its fundamental organization and
temper from an eight-hour or a ten-hour industry.

It transforms the community where men live whose day is twelve
hours long. . . .

To tell it exactly, if I can: You go into the mill, a little before six,
and get into your mill clothes. There may be the call for a front-wall
while you're buttoning your shirt. You pick up a shovel and run into a
spell of fairly hot work for three quarters of an hour. On another day
you may loaf for fifteen minutes before anything starts. After front-
wall, you take a drink from the water fountain behind your furnace,
and wash your arms, which have got burned a little, and your face, in
a trough of water. A "clean-up" job follows in front of the furnace,
which means shoveling slag—still hot—down the slag-hole for ten

161

minutes, and loading cold pieces of scrap, which have fallen on the floor, into a box. Pieces weigh twenty, forty, one hundred pounds; anything over, you hook up with a chain and let the overhead crane move it. This for a half-hour.

Suddenly someone says, "Back-wall!" Lasts say thirty or forty minutes. It's hot—temperature, 150 or 160 degrees when you throw your shovelful in—and lively work for back and legs. Everybody douses his face and hands with water to cool off, and sits down for twenty minutes. Making back-wall has affinities with stoking, only it's hotter while it lasts. The day is made up of jobs like these—shoveling manganese at tap-time, "making bottom," bringing up mud and dolomite in wheelbarrows for fixing the spout, hauling fallen bricks out of the furnace.

I have had two or three hours' sleep on a "good" night-shift; two or three "easy" days will follow one another. Then there will come steady labor for nearly the whole fourteen hours, for a week.

So, briefly, you don't work every minute of those twelve hours. Besides the delays that arise out of the necessities of furnace work, men automatically scale down their pace when they know there are twelve or fourteen hours ahead of them: seven or eight hours of actual swinging of sledge or shovel. But some of the extra time is utterly necessary for immediate recuperation after a heavy job or a hot one. And none of the spells, it should be noticed, are "your own time." You're under strain for twelve hours. . . .

Inseparable from the twelve-hour day in the open hearth where I worked were the twenty-four-hour shift, and the seven-day week. . . .

I've worked "long turns" that I didn't mind over much, and others that ground my soul. If you are young and fit, you can work a steady twenty-four hours at a hot and heavy job and "get away." But in my judgment even the strongest of the Czechoslovaks, Serbs, and Croats who work the American steel furnaces cannot keep it up, twice a month, year after year, without substantial physical injury. "A man got to watch himself, this job, tear himself down," the second-helper on Seven told me. He had worked at it six years, and was feeling the effects in nerves and weight. . . .

The "long turn" leaves a man thoroughly tired, "shot," for several shifts following. . . . The nervous excitement that helps any man through the twenty-four turn has gone—quite. The seven or eight hours of day-sleep seem to have taken that away without substituting rest; and what you have on your hands is an overfatigued body, refusing to be goaded further. My observation was that, on this Monday after, men made mistakes; there were arguments, bad temper, and fights, and a much higher frequency of collision with the foreman. Efficiency, quality, discipline dropped. . . .

"The twenty-four hours off" . . . comes at the conclusion of fourteen hours' work on the night-shift, and is immediately followed by ten hours' work on the day-shift. As far as I could observe, men went on a long debauch for twenty-four hours, or, if the week had been particularly heavy, slept the entire twenty-four. In the first instance they deprived themselves of any sleep, and went to work Monday in an extraordinarily jaded condition. In the second, they forfeited their only holiday for two weeks. . . .

Another feature . . . is that the sleep you get is troubled, at best. You are compelled to go to bed one week by day, and the next by night. . . .

The body will adjust itself to continued day-sleeping, I know; but apparently not to the weekly shifts, from day-sleep to night-sleep, customary in steel. . . .

The twelve-hour day gives a special character to the industry itself as well as to the men. I remember noticing the difference in pace, in tempo, from that of a machine shop or a cotton mill. Men learn to cultivate deliberate movement, with a view to the fourteen-hour stretch they have before them. When I began work with a pickaxe on some hot slag, on my first night, I was reproached at once: "Tak' it eas', lotza time before seven o'clock." And the foremen fell in with the men. They winked at sleeping, for they did it themselves.

Another kind of inefficiency that flowed quite naturally from excessive hours was "absenteeism," and a high "turnover" of labor. Men kept at the job as long as they could stick it, and then relaxed into a two or three weeks' drunk. Or they quit the Company and moved to another mill, for the sake of change and a break in the drudgery. . . .

Now it should be mentioned that some of the social life that most workers find outside the mill gets squeezed somehow into it. In the spells between front-walls we used to talk everything; from scandal about the foreman to the presidential election. The daily news, labor troubles, the late war, the second-helper's queer ways passed back and forth when you washed up, or ate out of your bucket, or paused between stunts. Then there was kidding, comradely boxing, and such playfulness as hitching the crane-hooks to a man's belt. One first-helper remarked: "I like the game because there's so much hell-raisin' in it."

But this is hardly a substitute for a man's time to himself, for seeing his wife, knowing his own children, and participating in the life of larger groups.

The twelve-hour day, I believe, tends to discourage a man from marrying and settling into a regular home life.

35. FIFTY-FOUR YEARS IN THE MILL

I have been retired since 1946—five years ago. I was pretty happy to leave, too, after fifty-four years in the mill. I had a pretty easy job there at the last and I might have worked a little longer if I could have, but I wasn't sorry to go. . . . I was a test carrier and worked around in the lab a little helping the chemists. I could do it all right even when I was getting old. It only paid labor wages, though, not like the money I made in the sheet mill. They had to keep us old-timers on those jobs—young people wouldn't stay but a day or two and then quit. . . .

I started at D. in 1902, when they first started the I.H. plant. Yes sir, D. is a good Company to work for. They treat you right. If a man is willing to work, he can really get ahead. . . .

My mother and dad wanted me to finish high school and even go to college. But I was just stubborn. I thought I wanted to go mine coal. That's all I thought people did in those days. I was just a young tad and my uncle took me through the mill. They dug their own coal for the mill, and I guess that's all I remembered. I should have gone on to school. I never even finished high school, but it's my own fault. I used to work summers sorting nails in a nail factory. I got 30 cents a day for that. I started at the mill at a dollar a day, and worked up to $2.50 a day as a puddler. And that was hard work—people don't have to do jobs like that any more, machines do it all. One of the superintendents from the Sharon Mills came to E_____ and built a steel plant there. Then he came up to the Harbor when they started. I figured he'd push me along, so I came to work for him. A lot of men from Sharon came to D.

If I had it to do over again, I'd never go into the sheet mills. That work is too hard and too hot. I was lucky because I never got cramps in my stomach, but sometimes I'd come home and couldn't raise my arms to reach my neck. . . . That was hard work in those days—you'd move the steel by hand onto the rolls and pull it back and forth, hot steel, too. Many's the time I've come home feeling so bad, I didn't think I could make it back. But my wife would work over me and somehow I'd go back the next day. It didn't need to be so hard when I started there. The only thing I liked about it was the money. I couldn't think of anything else. Once I got started, I couldn't quit or I'd have had to start all over someplace else at the bottom. If I could be young once more I'd go to school. I'd get all the school I could get, go to college. That's the way to get good jobs. All the superintendents are college men, even though they don't know anything about steel. If I couldn't go to college and had to work for a living, I'd want to go into carpenter work or farming. I like to work with my hands, and I like to be outdoors. . . . You live longer that way. Besides, you're running your own place. And carpenter work is good, too. But when I started in the mill, carpenters weren't making good money, not as much as I was in the sheet mill.

36. THE AIR HAMMERER

Mr. B., a fifty-nine-year-old steel worker, . . . speaks about his job at the D. Steel Company:

I am an operator. I operate a billet machine. I am a billetier. . . . It's not hard work like I used to do. I used to be a chipper. I used to scrape the bad spots off steel with an air hammer. It was very hard work. I operated an air hammer for thirty-one years. I held it under my arm . . . and stood over it. For thirty-one years, it went up and down. It ruined my leg; I can hardly stand on it any more. To operate a machine you have to have good legs, good eyes, and good brains.

I always worked in a steel mill. If I had my life to live over again I'd be a chipper again. I was a good chipper, the best they had in Granite City. I made good money, and all the bosses knew I was the best man they had. When I went up to D., the boss asked me to come back. But I stayed at D. You know, I came to this country from Europe when I was a boy of twenty. I came to find a good job. I went down to Granite City, Illinois, and I got it. The only thing I did not like there was what they called "the blue laws." You know, no drinking, or dancing, or gambling allowed on Sundays. I did not like that, but I never drank too much anyhow. I wrote my mother in the old country that I liked it there in Granite City and that I was not coming back. . . .

Young men today do all right. They go to school and get good jobs in the mill. There are lots of machines in the mill now, and everything is made easy for them. But they could not do the work I did when I was a chipper. They could not hold an air hammer, and even if they did, they would not know how to use it. Now they have inspectors who make chalk marks on the places they want scraped off. In Granite City, I looked at the slab of steel and decided for myself the spots that needed chipping. . . . My helper here at *D*. thought he was pretty good—it took him only a few weeks to learn how to be a billet operator, and now he is a good man on it. I told him you are a good man, but you can never handle the job I used to. He said he could. I told him to go ahead down there then, tell them that I sent him, and they would give him a job. I told him he could make a lot more money down there than he is making here. They pay a lot more money for chippers than they do for billet operators. So he went down there and told them I sent him. They gave him a job right away. But it only lasted two weeks. He came back and said it was too hard.

37.   THE OLD-TIME ROLLER

Mr. K., an employed, seventy-one-year-old steel worker, lives in East Chicago. . . .

I'm seventy-one now. When I was hired, the son of one of my friends took my application. I was fifty-five then, but he just put down forty-seven. I keep telling them how old I am, but they don't want to change their records. As long as someone does his work, no one cares. That mill has no heart. If you're gone one day, no one misses you. They just get a new man and go right ahead. . . .

I'm a roll grinder at *D*. That's in the machine shop. We don't handle the big rolls that they use on the rolling machine but any of the smaller rolls they need, they bring over to us. I operate a machine like a lathe. It's pretty easy, except you have to be awful careful about measuring. I started that job in 1935. I'd never done any machine work before. It was an entirely new trade. . . . I've been a mill man all my life. I started to work when I was seven years old. I only had one year of school in my life. . . .

My first job was in a glass factory. I was just a little shaver but I was careful and pretty quick with my hands. After a couple of years I did all kinds of jobs. . . . I was a rougher when I was seventeen. They don't have any jobs like that any more. That was man's work. The oldest man they had on that job was nineteen. You couldn't stay on it long or you'd kill yourself. I liked that job though. There's never been anything else like it. I worked up to roller in the mill. . . .

In those days we made good money at the mill and we spent good money too. During the first war I made up to $100 a day. They don't pay you like that for any job out there now. That was a lot of fun. . . .

I think my best job was when I was roughing. The men on that job were young and tough. It was interesting work. It looked dangerous, but people never got hurt if they knew what they were doing. It was really a spectacle to see the mill going at night. There were no lights in the plant and you worked by the light of hot steel. The whole plant was open and people used to walk through in the evenings for entertainment. They didn't have any shows or nightclubs then. You'd see those ingots coming so close to a man that you'd think he'd be burned for sure. The roughers just had a pair of tongs like ice tongs. There were two of us, one on each side of the rolling strip. We had to work together pulling the ingot back to the rolls, flipping it over, then throwing it down the line. It was fast work. After you worked with another man for a while, you'd go so fast you couldn't even see what you were doing. You just moved by instinct. At the end of the line a man stood and pushed ingots off the rolls. It would look as though he would be run down every time. The steel would practically go between his feet. He was the one the people liked to watch the most. It always looked like he'd be killed but you get pretty nimble when you have to do a job like that every day.

38.   PAINTER BY TRADE

Mr. N., a fifty-nine-year-old steel worker, is a scarfer at *D.:* a scarfer burns scales off strips of steel with a torch. Sometimes he works with hot steel, and sometimes with cold strips.

I've been at *D.* for almost thirty-five years now.

I worked as a painter for a long while, and in the carpenter shop before that. . . .

Which job did I like best? What difference does it make? If you have a family—I have a wife and four children—you have responsibility. You have to work steady. If a man has a family, he can't get drunk and leave his job; he has to keep working.

But the honest truth is I like my job as scarfer because it is easy work. We have two men on a torch. One works for an hour while the other sits around and takes it easy. We have a good foreman over here, too. He does not squeeze us. It's not like the old days when the foreman carried the time sheet around in his shirt pocket. If he saw you taking it easy, he would push you along. He could fire you just like that, if he wanted to. The worst part about this is when you are working the hot strips, the heat is pretty bad. Then, of course, there is always the gas, the smoke, the fumes out there in the steel mill. . . . I could not be a painter now. I am too old. But when I was young, I could do it. I liked it best of all. . . . It's good work for a young man. You can climb around and keep busy all the time. They'd call us from one place to another. "Paint this, paint that," they'd say. You did not kill yourself working, but you always had something to do. I like to work, but I don't like to work too hard. . . .

. . . I started to work on the railroads out West, out around Montana and Idaho. That was in 1912, 1913, and 1914. Things were pretty bad then, not like now. We worked like animals. If the foreman saw somebody resting for a minute, he was out on them, pushing them along. I moved around a lot then, looking for steady work. I heard there is work in Chicago. At the stockyards I heard they put men on around Christmas time. I did not know anything about that work, about animals or butchering. But it was close to Christmas and I wanted some work. I went out there. They let me work a couple of hours the first day, a couple of hours the second day, and a couple of hours a third day. Then they told us there was no more work; we could go home. Do you know what my check was for that work? I never forgot it. For three days' work, a few hours each day, I got a check of $1.65. In those days you did not ask how much a job paid, you just asked for work. . . .

. . . I came from Greece. I came to this country just like all other immigrants, because we heard there were jobs here and that we could make some money here. Over there, there were lots of people without work, starving. Our family had a small farm, we were poor people. I wanted to earn some money so I could go back, buy a farm, and start a family. That's what everybody wanted, just earn some money and then go back home.

. . . But when I was over in America the war started, and I got married over here and started to raise a family. When that happens you never go back.

39. STEEL AND ALL THAT

Did I work in steel? Why, I found more work than I had supposed was still in the civilized world! Twelve hours of the hardest kind of back-testing labor under what I would call difficult conditions.

We began at five-thirty—three of us Americans, one Italian boy, one Mexican, one Greek, and several Slavic and Russian fellows—all of them hardly able to say more than a very few English words, though they had all been in this country a number of years. It was bricks and brickbats, and then more bricks and more "bats." We shovelled or pitched broken bricks into big ladles or boxes in the "cinder-pit" beneath us at the back of the furnace; we piled good ones; we took turns getting into the hot ruins of the furnace substructure and lifted and tossed and shovelled them up to the platform for the others to carry and shovel. Occasionally we rested a few moments. At all times we sweat—especially when down in the ruins. Indeed we had trouble to keep from fainting with the heat as we got farther down into the hot "down-take" or vertical passageway at the end of the furnace. After an hour or two the Greek grew so dizzy that he was let off from his turn of going down—which meant more frequent turns for the rest of us. . . .

The twelve-hour shift is mainly responsible for the attitude of all of us toward brickbats. When I started in I figured I'd keep going as long as I could and loaf after I was played out. I couldn't get on with the program. First the little Italian boy tapped me on the shoulder and advised, "Lotsa time! Take easy!" I slowed down a notch or two. A little later the Russian, wiping off the sweat as he sat for a moment advised: "You keel yourself. Twelve hours long time." Finally, after everyone had remonstrated, I got down to a proper gait. . . . But at that I guess they knew better than I—I'm certainly tired enough as it is.

But we were not the only ones who tried to adapt the job to our capacities. A large part of the after-midnight portion our boss sat with his head on his hands and slept while we kept on working at, say, 55 per cent regular "load." At about four he varied the monotony by taking us out in the rain to carry in some back-breaking iron roof beams for the rebuilt furnace. After that it was a contest to see who could keep out of his sight and move the fewest bricks. At five everybody sat down and smoked and dozed, waiting for five-fifty to start back with our shovels to the shanty. As a matter of fact, we had given all the energy we had. . . .

The men, of course, get to feeling that their work is never done. They have then not the slightest interest in what it means or how it affects the operations of the mill around them because, I *will* say, nobody tries very hard to give it to them. It is all just a matter of doing as little work as the boss will allow. . . .

In all of these jobs there comes finally a skill which enables the experienced worker to do with sleight what the greenhorn has to do by main strength. The trouble is that no arrangements seem to be made for giving the greenhorn the proper instruction. So he learns only after the discomfort and more or less disgrace of initial failure. . . .

Steady work is just about as important, it seems, as good day wages. It seems to be felt, also, that this steadiness of the job is often more subject to the management's good will than good wages.

Listen to my neighbor at a long and crowded bar in a neighboring town. He happened to be an old machinist I'd seen in the mill.

"Yes, sir," said he, "I'm near seventy years old, and I've been in the steel line, one way or 'nother, forty-two of them—sheet floors mostly, I guess. I've made big money too, but I never saved nothin' till just lately—now that my children are all well married and I hain't no bad habits to spend nothin' on 'cept my board and room —and that's less'n ten dollars a week. . . .

"Just two year I been here in the mill, and for a seventy-year-older, I'm making pretty good money. The foreman—why, I wish't you could see the long hours he gives me—and pay-and-a-half for everything over eight hours! I tell you he's fine. Sometimes I work eighteen hours and take home money for, let's see, yes, that's right, twenty-three hours. Yes sir, you're right, that's $9.86. And it's steady work too. And when one job gets too heavy for me he puts me on somethin' easier. . . ."

The foreman is everything to the worker, all right, but it doesn't fix matters any for the worker if the manager says, "Speak to your foreman about that," and then turns around and rides him down too hard.

"Alla time 'hurry-up, hurry-up, hurry-up'—*no good!*" said my Greek "catcher" the other day, with a grimace as we walked out together, both very tired. He has to "hurry-up, hurry-up" me because the roller hurry-ups him, because Jo hurry-ups him, because Shorty hurry-ups him, because Jack shakes his head and makes a wry face as he looks at the sheets and hurry-up, hurry-ups him. Who or what does it to Shorty and Jack I don't know, but it's something or somebody, and it looks to me as though all of us from Jack down are doing the best we can, though I'm mighty sure that nobody is very happy about it.

Maybe, by the way, that's the reason so many on all sides speak enthusiastically of coal-mining—"You go down and get your coal and when you've got it you're through and nobody to say nothin' to you."

On my advance trip down here last week my eyes and nose noticed too many things to make my prospective coal-mining altogether a delight to think about. The little old Irish landlady, too, had a good deal to say about my having three or five roommates. . . . But I confess I was stumped when I arrived and found that the three beds were all double.

The children were out on the road dragging home over the rough cinder ruts their little wagons full of coal, picked up at the company dumps, while others carry water from the wells. And as they work they follow the example of their elders; little tots of eight and ten curse at each other shockingly. . . . Under the bridge other dirty little tikes play in the stream in the midst of the sea of little rusty tins and irons and rags and papers. . . . From downstairs for the tenth or fifteenth time . . . comes the scream of exasperation from shrill-voiced and overworked mothers. . . . Up the road loll with obvious unconcern two young miners who turn in toward the kitchen of a neighbor woman. Her nine-year-old daughter will help her hand out the beer or whiskey. . . .

I was delighted, after I adjusted my lamp and reported for duty, to be assigned to an experienced miner who was able to speak my own language—almost; his Scotch was very burry. . . .

"Mac" was sure enough born for a mine; in fact his shortness makes him a perfect fit for our five-foot seam of coal. In spite of his fifty-three years he's a hard worker and a real shovel-wrestler. . . .

And always his words were followed with the chance to do the thing —which is good teaching. . . .

The amount of pride he took in his possession of all the mysteries of mining was splendid. . . .

His skill represented, to be sure, forty-three years in the dark hallways of the school of pick and shovel. . . .

Of schooling he had practically none at any time. . . . But, I brought away with me huge respect for the contribution he has made to the doing of the world's work and the meeting of the world's needs with the untiring energy of his hands and shoulders and the interest and enthusiasm of his heart and head.

There is no boss nearby to take away the pleasure of working as much or as little as you like, or to steal the job of using your own skill and "know-how" for getting your results. Furthermore, these results, with the help of the watchful "check-weightman" paid by the union to sit alongside the company's man and note all weights, can be depended on to represent a certain definite amount in dollars and cents.

We used to agree in the sheet-mill that the foreman did not want to answer our questions for fear he'd lose his monopoly of the "know-how" and how on the open hearth we usually learned things only by being cursed in everybody's presence when we made mistakes. No wonder these men here feel independent and self-respecting. Especially when the tonnage men can take their dinner-bucket and go "outside" and home at any hour they feel like it. Still more important, once a year anybody can go to the county-seat and take an examination to become a fire-boss, and then a pit-boss, and so rise almost indefinitely.

In other words, the State, as it were, furnished in coal that pull-less promotion which is felt by many workers to be so missing in many plants.

Altogether, it looks as though the independence of the workers, a proper day of eight hours with good pay, either according to your own efforts or to an agreed, liberal day-rate, with "alla time good air and no cold—no hot," justifies the country's miners in thinking highly of their work, their service, and therefore themselves as useful and self-respecting persons.

It also appears to me unquestionable that the miner's work carries him much closer to a genuine self-respect than does the steel-mill laborer's job.

But in a community where no house can be bought—because the town may not be there a few years later—and where the roads may be too bad for a flivver, then the only other way of indicating the status of a self-respecting man who is "as good as the next one" would seem to be by that "conspicuous leisure" which is obtained, not in the ordinary way of working, earning, and then buying, but by not working—by walking out of the mine at two o'clock while some other chap is so much a dub of a worker that, in order to make a living, he has to stay in till the day is ended at four!

At the mine the most serious moment of the day was at five o'clock. Then everybody began to listen and I wouldn't be surprised if many prayed. Finally the whistle would boom and re-echo from the sides of the valley: One-two-three! With that, the tension was over and everybody smiled. "Work tomorrow! Thank God!" But when it went only one-two! you saw men taking it pretty hard—running their hands through their hair and saying: "My God!—How can live! What can do? No work tomorrow!"

There's plenty of loafing now that we're all on day rates. But there was twice as much when we were on piece rates—only that loafing didn't cost the company anything; we just waited around to get a chance at some job; only on special rush times were all of us busy. But the company didn't save very much at that, either. Because when we did get a job, 'course we tried pretty hard to make it a big one. We'd see maybe that several other things ought to be done to the engine besides the things called for on the card—and the foreman or the "super," he didn't take the time to check up too carefully; and besides it was a matter of opinion. So a thirty-cent job might be made into a two-dollar proposition—and besides helping the machinists that would make a better showing of work done for everybody all up the line, from the foreman to the "super" himself.

The Job Is Satisfactory

40. G.M. DRAFTSMAN

I am a draftsman in the Tool Design Department of the General Motors Corporation.

In such department we design the special tools, jigs, dies, fixtures, and gauges required by the Production and Inspection Departments.

That, briefly, is the classification and nature of my job.

However—there is nothing brief about the reasons as to why I like my job; there is a multiplicity of them. . . .

In order to clarify a few of these many reasons I shall outline a bit of personal background.

When the Japs launched their sneak attack on Pearl Harbor I had been retired from active business participation some six or seven years —doing all the things for which one strives and to which one looks forward—golf, hunting, fishing, Florida in the winter and my northern Michigan home in the summer; in short, a life of ease, relaxation, and enjoyment.

I was then nearly 62 years of age, much too old for any military participation, but being healthy and active, with unimpaired faculties, I felt that I must contribute to the best of my ability in the national emergency.

As a young man, in the early 1900's, I had been employed as a draftsman by some of the leading automobile manufacturers. . . .

I, therefore, communicated with the employment division of General Motors Corporation.

This return to factory and production activities has been to me a revelation indeed and has impressed me profoundly.

Back near the turn of the century, a time to which we glibly refer as "The Good Old Days" . . . I worked at a "Model Factory." This "Model Factory" was inadequately lighted in many areas with windows unwashed from one season to the next. It was not comfortably heated in the winter; the floors were dirty and the machine tools were unkept. Even the workmen were frowsy, unshaven, and with overalls so shiny and stiff with grease, oil, and dirt that the "proud" owner thereof could lean them against the bench when the quitting whistle sounded, secure in the knowledge that they would be leaning right there the next morning for him to step into.

Also—the hours were long and the remuneration was "short." . . .

Now I find in this Division of the General Motors Corporation a plant that is light; that is airy; that is clean.

Nearly 50 per cent of the wall area is glass; not dirty, grimy, dingy glass, but glass that is kept clean by a crew of workmen whose exclusive duty is to keep it that way. When they have washed all the windows from one end of the factory to the other end, they start all over and—wash them again. These windows are hinged and can be opened as occasion requires.

As a result such windows, although placed high in the walls to eliminate distracting views of external goings-on, do let in a flood of God's sunlight and a sight of the Heavens from which it emanates.

For those days when overcast renders the sunlight inadequate, and for the carrying on of nighttime activities, there is a flood of restful, all-pervading fluorescent light—dark areas and blackout corners just don't exist.

Lusterless white painting of walls, ceilings, and columns further enhances illumination and reduces eye strain and fatigue to a minimum.

The ceilings are high and there are no obstructing interior walls—in short, the factory is (to use a paradox) an open, enclosed shell from end to end and side to side.

This, together with the open windows, provides a natural air conditioning during the warm seasons and permits of an even all-pervading distribution of heat in the winter.

During those seasons of the year when it is necessary that windows be kept closed, rotary roof ventilators dispel into the outer air any smoke and noxious odors which may emanate from production operations; and at grinders and other sources of hygiene hazard, masks connected to powerful suction conduits whip away and deposit in receptacles outside of the factory every trace of abrasive particles, thus eliminating this vicious source of respiratory irritation and silicosis so prevalent in the "Good Old Days."

And particularly outstanding among these many vast differences over the old days is the matter of cleanliness.

A crew of sweepers is constantly at work throughout the factory: The regular use of electrically operated, mobile scrubbing machines keep the floors free of any accumulation of grease or oil and the machine tools are not encrusted with filthy and unsightly coatings of sludge and dirt. . . .

And all of these wonderful developments and improvements in

working conditions and manufacturing procedure have had their inevitable effect on the workman himself. . . .

He arrives on the job every morning clean shaven, neatly attired, and usually in his own car which he parks for the day in the space provided for that purpose by the Corporation.

If his duties are such as to make probable the soiling of his garments he changes into suitable work clothes in the spacious room also provided for that purpose.

If he is employed on the normal day shift his day's work is finished at 3:30 P.M., and the balance of the day is his own to do with as fancy dictates. . . .

There is the inestimable physical safeguard and mental equanimity of having a competent medical man and an efficient corps of nurses ready at all times to render instant aid and relief to any injury or illness which may arise during the work day. . . .

Back in those days the wage earner did not have the very great advantage of material reductions in premium for insurance against medical, surgical, and death hazards and which reductions we now enjoy. . . .

Now . . . we can, at a minimum monthly cost, insure ourselves and our immediate families against the exigencies arising from illness or accident and can assure our dependents of a substantial and immediate cash payment in the event of the demise of the wage earner.

41. NEGRO WORKERS

At that time, father had become the outstanding stone mason and bricklayer of the town, surpassing even Bill S. (white) from whom he "stole" his trade. On excursions father would take us to the houses he was building and to the bridges that were in process of construction and my youngest sister and I would be awestruck with the wonder of it all. Dad would allow us to climb in and about the houses and he would show us how to mix mortar, handle the trowel, etc. I remember how he used to love his tools and when folks would come to the house to borrow them, we wouldn't let anyone have them.

So it was very early that we acquired a deep and abiding respect for the people of the working class because we were and are part and parcel of them. We were taught early by both our parents to respect personality as it showed itself through constructive labor. The men who worked for Dad, the mechanics as well as the laborers, we thought of as constructive forces in the community.

The standard set by the Negro leaders in the community was, we thought, false. The inclination was to set on a pinnacle the Negroes who were of the professional class. There weren't many, very few in fact, and probably because of this rarity there was much abject worship. Everything my father and mother did helped to confirm our judgment that the people of the professional class were only a different kind of skilled worker and respect for them and their opinion came to being only in so far as they were masters of their trade.

Because our family on mother's side of the household was very well known and respected, our relationship with the elite of the white group was casual and usual. But, although we were often in the homes of the most wealthy, mother took care that our house while comfortably furnished, was in keeping with our economic status. It was simply but tastefully furnished.

We did have a piano—and a very good one because mother thought that there should be entertainment in the house and she believed in the cultural influences of music. While many colored people had big houses, expensively furnished, we were the only colored children who belonged to the private library. There was no public one and mother had to pay for cards. We always had three cards, one for each two of us. As to politics, I can remember only that father thought a man was a good candidate if he sympathized with the aims and aspirations of the working class group. . . .

At the time of my parents' marriage my father was only a laborer in the town and he never advanced beyond this stage. My mother was a cook and washwoman. . . .

From 1899 to 1914, my parents lived in the same three-room house in a town of about 1500 people. In 1912 my mother, who was the more thrifty, and the business manager of the family, bought four lots in a new section of the town (and soon we built a house on it).

In 1914, we moved into the new house, where my parents lived until their deaths in 1927. For 22 years, 1899 to 1921, my father worked regularly as a laborer for two families, a physician's and a merchant's. His weekly wages from the two families ranged from $6 to $10. For about the same time my mother cooked out and took in washing, receiving for her labor from $3 to $10 per week. As soon as we children became old enough, we (boys as well as girls) did as much of the washing and ironing as we could. The training I gained enabled me to spend 7½ years in boarding school and spend only $3.65 for laundry during that time. At the age of ten I was hired out to a family to be the companion and guardian at play of their three little sons. For four years, before and after school hours and in the summer, I worked for this family, receiving $1.75 plus meals per week.

Mother hated a quarrel and never, to my knowledge, engaged in vulgar gossip in the presence of her children. She was an advocate of patience and tolerance, and often said, "It is better for you to suffer unjustly than to cause another to suffer: rather than wrong another, run the risk of being wronged."

* * *

My mother and my father began their married life in Savannah, Georgia, in 1910. . . .

Mother found many things which tended to put their marriage on the rocks at the start. Her personality and traditions were so different from Father's. She was a quiet, home-loving person with no desires for dances, parties, and good times. But Father was just the opposite in those days; he loved to dance, go to all-night parties, and run with the fast crowd. He was bored staying home after working hours. Mother used to tear his shirts off of him to keep him home, but he still went.

Then the war came and Father did not want to be sent over to fight so he decided to move away. Then too the blacksmith business was slowly dying. There was a chance to make money up North, so Father moved to a northern city and found work there. He sent for Mother and me. We lived there for five years. Father worked hard and saved his money. Mother made all of my clothes for school. It used to be very cold there then, and Mother being fresh from the South thought I would freeze to death, so she used to pile me up with clothes. However, I was never sick a day during those days.

Our family lived down in the Negro section of S_____ until Father had the house in Savannah paid for, then we moved up on "the hill," where the better-class Negroes lived. By moving up into this new district, I had a better chance in school because there were not half as many Italians and Jews in the new school. There were also fewer colored children and the teachers were far nicer. Father worked hard to keep the family up economically, and Mother did her share in the home to keep things balanced. My family did very little socializing. They went to church socials and parties where the church minister was always present.

A great crisis came to our family in 1926 when Father lost his job as a mechanic which he had with a packing company. He had been with that firm since he first moved to S_____. He looked everywhere for work and found none so he decided to go to New York City, and look about. He found work there and sent us money to keep up our expenses in S_____.

Then Father became ill. We lived one year off of our savings account until Father was good and well. Mother went out to work two days a week to help keep up the expenses of the home. During all that time we never missed the payment of the rent and there was always plenty of food. We did not buy many clothes and I made over things for Mother and myself. We could always buy things for my little brother at a small price. . . .

After Father had been on the new job a year we started buying our home. We bought a two-family house with plenty of front lawn, and room for a garden in back. Father instantly began to remodel the house, and Mother and I did all we could to help him. He papered, put in new plumbing, and put in the electricity himself.

I got a job after school so as to buy my own clothes, and then to save money for college too. I worked on Saturday mornings. For four summers I had a job as a cook and made quite a large sum of money during the vacation. During all this hard struggle we never failed to attend church on Sunday, and Father even went to prayer meeting as he was a deacon. We always had Sunday clothes even if our neighbors did wonder how we managed.

I graduated from high school the second year we had the house. Father didn't see how he could send me to college with the house to be paid for, but since I had saved $500 for college he would send me. He paid my train expenses and bought my clothes and I worked for my tuition. . . .

It makes me happy to know that my family has paid for our home, and that they are now able to enjoy life after the hard struggle which they have put forth to have a few of the necessary things.

42.   EX-ELECTRICIAN

In 1909 I was an electrician but there wasn't much work available. My uncle was a machinist who worked for a fellow who owned a phonograph repair store. This fellow opened a motion picture place in a converted store and my uncle learned how to operate the machine. Since I wasn't making any money as an electrician and I was too old for a youngster's job, and looked too young for an old man's job, I went in with my uncle. He taught me how to operate the machine, and between the two of us we earned $11 a week working a seven-day week twelve hours a day.

Before I started I knew what the conditions were, but it was either that or not making a living at all. At first, I thought the job would be only temporary, since then there was a great deal of doubt as to whether the motion picture industry would last. . . .

I sent my daughter through college. She graduated from Brooklyn College two years ago and now has an executive position with the Telephone Company as a business representative in a local office.

When my son got out of high school he didn't want to go to college, . . . I taught him two jobs. He learned how to be a printer and a motion picture operator. He now works for The Morning Telegraph as a printer. The job calls for 35 hours a week and he makes slightly more than I do as a projectionist. Four years ago, while he was in the army, I got him admitted to the union; when an opportunity arises he wants to quit printing and go into projecting even though he would make a few dollars less. He would rather have the extra leisure time. For instance, I figure my work week averages 24 hours. Now that he has a child, he'd like to spend more time at home with his family. I'd recommend projecting to anyone. The pay is good. The hours are short. And if you take care of your health you're all right. The only thing that's difficult about the whole thing is getting into the union. For a long time they have been letting in only sons or brothers of existing members. And even then it isn't so easy because you have to wait years before you can get a full-time job at a regular theater. The trouble was that years ago too many projectionists boasted to their friends and relatives about what good jobs they had. They made from $65 to $85 a week, and worked much fewer hours than other workers. The result was that a lot of people decided to get in on the deal. They went to school for six weeks, with a little political pull they got a license from the city, and with a few connections in the union they were admitted to the union. In one year they admitted over 600 members. (The total membership is now only 2400.) Now the industry is overcrowded since the market is saturated with projectionists. . . .

I don't have any other job, and, in fact, very few of the other men have other jobs. There's always a lot of talk about many of the men taking other jobs, but that really isn't true. There are a lot of men in this neighborhood who are projectionists—they came into the union after we pioneered the way for them—and you see them all the time outside wheeling their children. . . .

I like practically the whole set-up about my job. I like the short hours; I like my schedule—seven days on, two days off, seven days on then five days off. I find the work pretty interesting; I like to tinker with things and as an old timer in this business I keep my machine in very good order—much better than the newcomers. I look at the pictures all the time, but I look at them objectively; I usually don't know what's happening on the screen. To me every picture has one face; just like a doctor, to whom all women have the same face. I look at the screen professionally just to see if the image is clear and if the sound is all right. . . .

I don't feel that my job is monotonous. I manage to keep interested. The other day my partner walked in and said, "What a long day this is going to be." I hate those kind of guys. . . . I sort of divide up the day. I come in and say to myself, "I only have two more hours till lunch." I eat lunch, then a little while later I do a little something around the machine—I oil it up or something like that; then I figure there are only two or three hours before I go home for the day. So it doesn't bother me. . . .

The mental trouble results from two sources—the one-man operation and the two-man operation. In the smaller theaters they can't get paid the full union scale so in order to get a decent wage one man operates the machine without a partner. He's in a very small booth all by himself. Many times they report cases of claustrophobia or go "stir nuts." Once, about thirty years ago, I got a case of claustrophobia; I was terror-struck in the booth by myself for a period of a few minutes. I was seized by such fear that I was ready to run out of the booth and quit this line of work. Then I began to think about my family. Then I realized that in a few seconds I'd have to put myself into action and change reels. That made me snap out of it.

The two-man operation has another sort of mental hazard. You have to be compatible with your partner—it's just like being married to him. You live with him alone in a small booth for a good part of your time. Only once in my career did I find it intolerable to be with a partner. I was with him for six years and almost quit in disgust several times. . . . There are many cases where partners in the same booth have fought each other. You must have read in the papers about the operator who killed his partner with the fire extinguisher in the booth, or the other case where the operator knifed his partner with a screwdriver.

It is also a nervous business. You are always on edge waiting for something to go wrong with the machine or with the sound. It's just like the story about the fellow in the downstairs apartment waiting for the other shoe to drop.

I always planned that when I was sixty I would stop work and go to someplace like Arizona, maybe, and take it easy. But I'm almost sixty now and I find myself financially unable to do so. In a few years, I guess what I'll do is work just three months in the summer and three months in the winter . . . by quitting my regular job and joining the ranks of the union's "unemployed."

43. GROCERY CLERK

My first job in the grocery business was with Piggly-Wiggly Stores. . . . I was employed at $20 a week, to work from the hours of eight to six, six days a week, with the exception of Sunday. Saturday we stayed until the store was cleaned up for the weekend, which generally took us to twelve o'clock. . . .

I stayed with the Piggly-Wiggly firm up until 1928, advanced from clerk to store manager. The time I terminated from Piggly-Wiggly employment, I was making $47.50 a week as a store manager. I returned to Piggly-Wiggly in the middle of 1929, at a salary of $25 a week.

. . . The Piggly-Wiggly store where I first worked was a small store in volume of business; as far as floor area, it would be considered a medium-sized store in a present day concept. Number of employees were: two butchers, and three food store personnel . . . including a manager.

As a clerk in 1926, I did very much the same work that is being done in grocery stores today. Setting up a produce stand is a first job to be performed in a day's work. The receiving of the merchandise for the food store operation thereafter; that is, the sales and delivery of merchandise from bakery wagon drivers, milk wagon drivers, and others, and deliveries from the Piggly-Wiggly warehouse. Besides checking those orders in and putting the orders into stock, I stocked the shelves, waited on customers, and did any clean-up work around the store that had to be done.

The turnover in the grocery business has always taken its toll. Of the original people that I knew when I first started in the grocery business, few remain today. . . . From my start in the grocery business up to the depression years . . . a grocery clerk from the time he started up to the time he was a store manager could achieve a rate pretty close in line with the differential now existing between grocery clerks and butchers. But after the depression had started, grocery clerks' wages were severely reduced, and the new hires especially were hired at then existing minimums or whatever price they could be employed at. However, we found the butchers, who had their scale in 1927 around $47.50, through the depression years were finally reduced down to $37. We find the grocery clerks, who were checkers in 1926 and made between $30 and $35, reduced to $16 and $18. . . .

I feel that the chains made a complete switch-over by 1932. They started as early as 1929. So that by 1932 they had most of their clerks at or near the minimum wage.

44.   THE CUSTOMER IS ALWAYS RIGHT

I'm an assistant to the buyer. I handle complaints, refunds, exchanges, in the bedding department. I don't sell much any more. I do a little, but you can't take sales very much or you're not available when you're needed to settle something. I help the buyer. And I take care of customers' difficulties. I make a living, and I don't ask for the moon.

Selling is practically in my blood. I've got it from both sides of the family. It's the only thing I've known. I started when I was a kid while I was still going to school.

I lived in a little town in Iowa, and we used to have this little store, and I'd see the salesmen come into town. And I'd read Horatio Alger stories—found them somewhere. I thought the salesmen that traveled around were just the top of everything. That's what I wanted to be more than anything.

So I came to Chicago, and I was walking in the streets. I'd been three days without anything to eat. I came to *L*.'s then and asked for a job. Any job. They told me they didn't need anyone. I said, "You can't mean that. I've just walked through this store and you can't tell me with all this merchandise you can't use a man who can sell." And I convinced him. I had to do it with three of them, as a matter of fact. But I got the job.

L.'s is the model for every store. Lots of them try to be like *L*.'s, but none are what *L*.'s is. *L*.'s made the "customer always right." Lots of times it's something that just doesn't seem right, but if the customer wants it, it's okay. He's taken care of, no matter what his complaint. You can't beat it anywhere.

If I knew what I know now about business, I'd be able to make a go of my own place. I had my own place once, but I lost it. I was young and didn't know anything about business. I didn't even know what "ten days net" meant. I paid the bills and didn't deduct for it, and I didn't know what it meant. I didn't know anything. I was too young and inexperienced.

Even if I didn't have to work, I wouldn't quit. I've seen men that quit work. They don't last too long. I had an uncle once—more active than many men younger than he was. And after he quit work, he just went downhill so fast; he only lived two years after that, and he just wasn't the same person. I've seen others too, now that they've put in this retirement plan. They change as soon as they hear that they have two years to go.

I don't want the store to get me like that. I don't want to feel that way. I've seen the old-timers come in. The store's their pet. They look at it, and you can see that everything in it is part of them.

We travel on our vacation. I'm always glad to get off to places, but I'm almost nuts to get back to work when it's over—not right when it's time to start back. But as soon as I *start* back, I can't wait to get back at it.

Selling's practically born in me. It's what I know best. There isn't anything that isn't selling—your doctor or dentist—if you have an invention and you can't sell it, no matter how good it is it doesn't go anywhere.

I like good merchandise. And honest-to-God customers. You can tell them. They really want to buy. I like to sell good merchandise to good people. If I had a store of my own, I'd sell nothing but the best, nothing but the very best possible product.

45. SELLING BOOKS

I was a school teacher at one time but I went into selling books at about 1923.

The Book House for children was what I sold. It was a set of books sent to me by my sister to use in school. Well, then the parents said the children wouldn't listen to their stories because they liked my stories better, and they wanted to know where they could buy the books; so I wrote the company in Chicago and they said they didn't have any sales people out there—and would I mind taking their order? So, I just started by sending in orders for my friends. I was well acquainted there, naturally, and they respected my opinion on things —really, it wasn't much selling. I just ordered, just as long as I had friends to go on. And then I decided to give up the school and do that altogether. At first I just did it after school, a couple of hours in the afternoon and on Saturdays. But it really wasn't much to it because one person told another and they bought because they liked the book.

Then, in two years, I had sold so many in Oregon that there wasn't any place left for me to sell. Then I moved to San Francisco and traveled places in northern California. I worked there for three years and then the manager said if I wanted to go farther, I'd have to go to the Chicago office. And so I picked up and went to the Chicago office. And they started me out supervising—I supervised several states— and trained their salespeople. Then from that I taught classes in the various offices and wrote a sales book for them and started their history book and did things like that until 1935. . . .

In just three years I was making $75 a week—and then with the Book House for children, I got up to $90 a week and expenses. So, you see, you never make that in the book department. But there are expenses connected with that too—you have to have a car, have two homes almost, and there were expenses too, so sometimes what it costs you to keep a job is as much as having it, but I liked it.

Then my daughter was graduated and married and I didn't have to travel or make much money. I'd always wanted to work in a bookshop. That was my idea, working in a bookshop, and so I started to work at *V*.'s in their bookshop in St. Louis. I worked there for three years and then I came here—and I've been here for about ten years. I have worked on books a long time. I prefer the bookstore because it's much more expanding to have all of the books at your fingertips than it is to just be selling one set of books. You're so apt to confine your interests to one set of books—because it takes up so much of your time. So I think that what I have learned in book-selling—would be more valuable than any experience I've ever had in my life—even travel or meeting people or anything. You're always meeting and coming in contact with specialists in various fields, so you're apt to weed out the ones that aren't much good in fields and know which ones are considered better; even though you might want to read the good and the bad, you at least know what specialists in every field think about different types of books.

When I first came here I used to keep changing the stock, trying to change it around so it would sell better. The only way to do creative work is if a customer comes in and asks for one book, you can think of half a dozen others he'd be interested in. If you just gave him the one book and he walked out it wouldn't be creative. Outside selling is more creative than inside selling because you really have to understand a person and know their needs and decide quickly, whereas inside they know what they want before they come in.

46.   I HAD TO BE BUSY

In my first years of married life, we had three ready-to-wear stores and were doing very well. Then the depression came . . . and we lost everything. It did something to my husband I think more than it did to me. Of course, I was younger and I forged on and I became a buyer of ready-to-wear, and it took many years before my husband could really get back on his feet. And so the years went by with me as a buyer, and then we went back into business. But when my husband passed away, I didn't like the little shop at all. I was unhappy in it because he was everywhere in the store, and I sold it. And I came right back here, to the department I had left. I like it.

When you don't work . . . there's so much you'd miss, of course. I think there's nothing better for an individual like me than to meet people and even serve people. Sometimes it's very difficult and sometimes it's very beautiful and pleasant. I like people, and I'm very unhappy when I haven't them around, and therefore, working gives me that opportunity.

Working for yourself is much better than working for a store. It's a much better feeling when it's your own. Working for a store like N.'s is quite a different thing! When you work for yourself, no matter what you do for yourself, you know you have done your best. . . . But working for other people, you must always do more than your very best, and even then you don't know whether they appreciate it. When you have your own business you can do as you wish and you alone are responsible.

Selling is sort of a challenge. I like it when I've had a good day. I feel fine. I think it's a wonderful job. I feel as though I can do anything. When it's a bad day I think, "Isn't there anything else I can do? What a horrible way to earn a living!" But it isn't the money—I don't think of it so much in terms of money. It's the accomplishment; it's knowing that you have done the job, that you have made sales, that you have accomplished something that you set out to do.

I find selling here physically hard. Not so much mentally—I'm not mentally tired at the end of the day. I'm just physically tired out. You have to drag heavy coats and lift dresses by the thousands. You have to make every customer feel that you're doing something for her. She wants to see things. If she's going to buy, she doesn't want just anything, she wants something that does something for her. And she expects a lot from you. It's natural. You feel the same way and so do I. But it's just a lot of hard physical labor. And sometimes you spend an hour just showing things. Sometimes you think what the customer has on does something for her, but *she* doesn't. And then you have got to change her mind—if that's possible.

So sometimes I think, "Well, I guess I'm too old. I guess I get tired too quick." And then I see the young kids in the section—they get more tired than I am. I've seen them. Yesterday we had a couple of flyers—they just come in and work wherever it's busy—and they were just young kids, two very young girls, at the end of the day they were fit to be tied. So I guess it isn't me after all.

If I could do anything I wanted to do, without caring about money . . . I think I would still handle people. I'm a natural executive—you might say a born executive . . . unless my years as I grow older have changed me so much. They tell me no, that I am still capable of it. Sometimes I wonder, but still I feel sure that I could take a group of girls and train them; I could handle people always in my younger days. . . .

I never earned less than $75—even in the worst days, I never earned less than $75 plus a bonus. Now I don't earn that much, but I don't think that it's that I'm any less efficient. I think the whole department feels it.

47. THE MILK DRIVER

I was in San Francisco in 1920. . . . I went around to the different dairies. A fellow told me, "If you want to get a job driving a milk wagon, you should continually go back, call on them about once every week or every ten days." So I did. I'd go around to the different dairies and say, "Well, I was just dropping by to see if anything was doing." I had my application in about approximately ten months, waiting for a milk driving job. I just thought I could do it.

Finally I returned home one day and the hotel clerk told me there was two calls in for me. I had heard the Dairy Delivery was the best one to work for (and they were, very considerate) so I went down there and I got the job. . . .

I drove a horse and wagon retail for Dairy Delivery for . . . approximately eight months. . . . Incidentally, . . . my relief man . . . relieved me four days a month. At that time, if I recall right, I was serving approximately 450 customers retail. At that time, also, there was more retail business than what there is at the present day. . . . I don't recall of any credit problems at all on the routes that I was serving. . . . You had a different type of person to deal with in the twenties than you have now. Very few of the people who were served tempted to beat you out of any money, where now there's quite a bit of that going on. I really couldn't say why, but I know that that is quite a problem now—credits. . . .

In the first ten years that I worked for the company they never said anything about new customers. We naturally went out and got all the new business we could. We took an interest in our routes and tried to keep them up. Then as time went on and business wasn't quite as good, there was a little more pressure put on to get new customers and sell byproducts. . . .

The horses done a good job. If you tried to overlook a customer or just forgot him, the horse would stop and remind you that you had to serve Mrs. So-and-So, whereas right now with the automobile you can pass by Mrs. Brown and forget her and then you get an overlook when you get in.

. . . I would say the men loved their horses because they had those particular horses and they just babied them right along. I know I did because I had three horses that were really nice horses. I babied them and I know the other boys did also. They enjoyed having the horses, and they wanted to keep them good so they could do a good job for them. And the horses really helped the men out lots.

. . . When we were delivering we had a coverall. That was the uniform of the Dairy Delivery at that time, white coveralls and we also wore a white-topped hat. We bought the uniform but they would wash them. That was in the union agreement.

. . . I think all the men more or less were proud of their particular rig, and I think every one of them had a ribbon, especially on the whip. The longer the ribbon, the better it looked.

After approximately eight months the Dairy Delivery switched me over to wholesale.

. . . This was better than being a retail driver. . . . In this respect, that you didn't have the stairs to be climbing all the time and you could jolly with the customers during the day, while on retail you'd just be running up and down steps. The wholesale is, I think much more pleasant.

The Dairy Delivery had about 150 employees. . . . Maybe ninety were drivers and the rest were inside men. . . .

When I started in 1921, I figure the average man possibly would have a grammar school education. Most of them seemed to me were fellows from large families, and at that particular time had to get out and hustle and make a living. . . . A majority of our members were married and it's still so today. . . . The turnover at that particular time was very, very low. If we had fifty a year initiated into the union at that particular time in the twenties, that would be a big majority. So it just shows that the men would get on the job and they would stay there. Very little turnover.

. . . In the twenties we were getting $182.50, working an eight-hour day with four days off a month. The extra man was getting $197. . . . And then we got a cut, $12.50, and to my knowledge, that was the only cut in wages that we ever got in our organization. This cut was around the latter part of the twenties or just about the thirties, after the stock market crashed. . . . We got cut to $170, and from then on we have never taken a cut in wages. And in our organization, we had no voice in the matter either. To my knowledge, it was the first time it had ever happened. They just agreed between union and employer and said to us, "Commencing, say, the first of the month, wages are now going to be $170."

Prosperity Passed Them By

48. A TOPPER

I left school on December 11, 1914, my fourteenth birthday, hoping that I could help with the bread-winning, but after a few trials found that the proposed bill forcing the manufacturers to allow children under sixteen to go to school one day a week made it impossible for me to get work. I had started work in a spinning mill, but was laid off because I was under sixteen. After several other jobs I was afraid I would have to go back to school. How glad I was when a neighbor told my mother that I was to learn hosiery topping with her.

It was in May that I started to learn topping in Brown and Aberle's mill. The season was dull and we worked only two or three days a week. This meant that I earned very little as my weekly pay was just $3.50 for a full week, but I was glad to have work. In those days a learner had to do all the loose-coarsing and if she finished before time to go home she was allowed to try to top a stocking once in a while. After I knew how to top I was allowed to work in a girl's place when one stayed out. . . . We got 5 cents per dozen and could do twenty dozen a day. My first day was very trying and by noon I was almost in tears, but the boss, a fatherly soul, told me to try it a while and after that I didn't even mind the Polish men who were knitters; although they never spoke to us, the way they looked at us made me uncomfortable. After a while I really got used to the work and the men.

In January all the children under sixteen were sent to continuation school. This meant that we would lose our jobs because, if we had off, the knitter would lose time while we were in school. We were then made "extra girls" who had to work in other girls' places when they were out.

On my sixteenth birthday another girl who was to be sixteen in January and I were given steady jobs on the first Reading machine installed. . . . We made mercerized stockings and did about forty-five dozen a day at 8 cents a dozen. We worked fairly steadily, but during the summer and fall we frequently went on strikes. Sometimes they lasted a day or two or even a week. We were not organized and as a rule we had few victories because we had no leaders. We would walk out, then have a meeting. When it was cold, we went in a store across from the factory—if it was warm, we stayed in the street. Sometimes representatives came from the union, but we never joined.

After we had worked on this machine for almost a year we had our biggest strike. We paraded around other hosiery mills in an effort to have them join our formation, but they shouted for us to get back to work. We stayed in formation out of sight of the mills, then went our separate ways. After about a week of it we just went back. The men realized by this time that it was necessary to belong to a union. They got busy and started to organize. My knitter, who had come from another shop, asked me to carry the cards in the pocket of my coverall apron to the knitters in other rooms. This was easy for me to do because, as spare hand, I worked all over the plant, and so no one noticed the cards as I silently laid them on the machine and moved off. I knew nothing of trade unions, but realized that if I was caught it would mean my job.

In September of 1917 . . . I quit and got another job. . . . The firm guaranteed us $24 a week, but when we made over that we got it. Conditions were greatly improved, but by this time we wanted shorter hours. Government workers had them and our increased efficiency made it seem necessary for us to have them too. Our men were organized too by this time; they also had a shop association. We usually knew when they met and decided to ask the firm for some improved conditions. We girls got so mad because we were ignored when the men stopped the machines to hold a meeting to take a vote on some motion made in the shop meeting. These meetings were held in the shop; a committee was selected to go up to the office. If the request was granted the men started up the machines. It was wartime so we usually got what we asked for, but we had to strike for an eight-hour day. The girls had been organizing by this time and we were all set for the strike when it was called on January 1, 1918.

In March we went back to work; we had won the 48-hour week with no increase in wages. We did prove that we could produce as much in a 48-hour week as we could in the 54-hour week. We limited our production to forty dozen a day. The knitters also limited the number of knitters turned out by increasing the years of apprenticeship from two or three years to four years. Things ran smoothly for a while. We were getting good wages, buying bonds, giving a day's wages for the war chest, observing heatless, meatless, wheatless, and other days.

January 1919 work became slack, some of our boys came back from

France, and the men had organized the loopers, seamers, and menders preparatory to going on strike.

At last the strike was over—October 1920—no reduction of wages, recognition of the union, all single jobs; all our hardships were forgotten. Nothing mattered now except that we won and were at work.

. . . We finished over 120 dozen by Friday and did not work Saturday. The toppers made about $39 per week.

The trade on the whole progressed rapidly; on account of the style for shorter skirts, lighter weight and finer weave stockings were introduced. The machines were improved, made faster and longer sectioned. There seemed to be no limit to our prosperity until the bottom dropped out in 1929–1930.

49. RHODE ISLAND SILK WEAVER

I got my first job when I was fourteen, in a Rhode Island silk mill once reputed to be the largest under one roof in the world. I was very proud to be working and contributing $7.50 to the family income, for that was hastening the time when my mother, who was weaving in a cotton mill, could stay at home. I enjoyed my work as a quiller (making filling for the weavers) and remember how I used to hurry to fill as many boxes as the other girls. I also remember that I early learned to be frightened by anyone in a supervisory capacity and was appalled at having to use a toilet which exposed one's feet and legs to every passer-by.

A new department was being installed and I was sent to work there. Here I learned to reel silk into skeins and found it difficult but enjoyed the easier discipline. For about nine months I worked here, then left when my mother decided to teach me to weave.

Young boys and girls under fifteen were not allowed to weave, so I, not yet being fifteen, was put to filling batteries; that is, putting bobbins in an automatic device at one side of the loom which feeds them into the shuttle as it empties. The weave shop was very large, which gave me a feeling of being lost, at first; the noise was tremendous, but I soon became accustomed to that. I enjoyed the jolly "comraderie" of the older weavers and made many friends among the younger ones. Then after five weeks "standing in" with my mother, I became eligible for looms of my own.

It was during those first few weeks of weaving that I learned, unconsciously, what skill meant. To do this job well, I must work hard, conscientiously, and be very painstaking. I envied the apparent ease with which the older women weavers did their work and wondered if I would ever attain that stage.

Many things I accepted unquestioningly as part of the job: the long work week (54 hours); the faulty humidifiers, which often threw off sprays of water instead of steam; the "blower" used to remove the lint which collected like snow on and under the looms. The English and Belgian weavers seemed to be immune from the evil effects of these things, perhaps through generations of factory workers before them, but the Italians often seemed languid and wan-faced, and the German woman who worked next to me complained that the humidifier made her shoulder ache, and often with an angry gesture she shut it off.

My mother had learned of the better working conditions in the silk industry; wages were higher, hours shorter, and the jobs were cleaner. After two years of work in the woolen mill, I left with no regrets when the opportunity came to learn silk weaving. Because the industry is newer, sanitary conditions are usually better, and by far the largest majority of silk mills run only 48-hour shifts. After learning that I must acquire a delicate and lighter touch necessary in handling silk than in cotton and something of the complicated mechanism of the silk loom, I was put to run two looms, then three. Here I worked for six years, always conscious that I must acquire, and always striving for, greater skill, not so much because I wanted to become skilled, but because there was a constant demand on the part of the management for the elimination of imperfections.

It was here I was working when I took my first summer off to attend Bryn Mawr Summer School. Since my health was not good, upon returning I decided that I would look for an easier job. I applied at the employment office of a great cotton mill and after having my eyes examined and found good was given a job in the spinning room at $12.50 a week. Knowing the wages were much less than I had received for weaving, I thought the work would be less fatiguing and less exacting. I had great difficulty in learning to keep a small leather pad in place over my right knee, this being used to protect the knee when it was brought into position to stop the spindles spinning at a rate of 8000 revolutions a minute, in order to piece the broken ends. Within a few days I was able to run three sides; these being near the door, I was instructed to keep them well cleaned in order to make a good impression upon visitors entering the room for the first time. After four weeks of this work I decided that it was just as strenuous, if not more so, than silk weaving and the compensation far too small, so I gave up the job.

Through my studies in economics at Bryn Mawr I had become interested in discovering for myself just what conditions in Rhode

Island industries were, so while I was unsettled I thought I would try night work. I applied at the office of a silk plant, one of the large factories on the river bank, which ran three and four shifts, for a job on the night shift. I was informed that they employed no women at night, but was offered a job on the afternoon shift. This meant working from three in the afternoon to eleven at night, on Saturday nights till twelve. This I did for one year.

It was a joyous thing to have my mornings free. I learned to swim, I worked in the garden, and did many other things I had always wanted to do. Then thinking this time too precious to spend on such trivialities I spent my morning hours in school for a few months. I found, however, that in order to keep fit and well I must live a very regular life, also that one loses contact with one's friends and that there is little or no social life. Absences were allowed occasionally but these gotten with difficulty, for too frequent absences from this shift would break down the discipline, resulting in too large a labor turn-over. Sanitary conditions were good: white-tiled lavatories with hot water, weave-shop floors washed at least once a week, machinery kept clean, and a cafeteria where hot food could be bought; no interval provided while eating it, however.

What of the workers? The majority were Polish and French Canadians, with a goodly number of Syrians—a typical silk-mill crowd. The men, mostly married, seemed indifferent as to what hours they worked as long as they made a fairly decent wage. And the women—Mary, who worked next to me, said: "Workin' dis way, I can do my wash and sew for my kids." Her husband had only one eye, was unskilled, and was unable to find a job. He cared for the children while she worked "afternoons." Several widowed mothers found this shift convenient. Usually the children "stayed with the lady downstairs" or were "old enough to take care of themselves." A little widowed Polish mother very proudly one night showed me a photograph of her daughter who was attending high school. I never saw a more woebegone face than hers when one day she passed my looms on her way to the first-aid room. She had been hit in the chest with a flying shuttle. What was she thinking? Perhaps what so many workers often think with terror. "Suppose some day something happens to disable me permanently, so that I can not work any more, what shall I do?" The courage and patience of these women is great to stand these hours day after day and year after year. When a year later I was offered a job on the day shift, I took it gladly.

After working some months on the day shift, running four looms, the mill closed for a two-week period. When the workers went for their wages, a notice was posted on the door to the effect that workers desiring a job after that period must reapply to the employment manager. This meant the "stretch-out" system; only the most efficient workers would be given employment on six looms, whereas formerly they had run only four. There was much talk against this and much harsh criticism, but the system was being introduced into other shops and the workers thought it useless to make a formal protest. Gradually the shop resumed the three-shift schedule, with the 1000 looms running with a dimished labor force.

The first few days under this system I remember very clearly. One day I had mastered those six looms and I stood for a moment watching them run. All in good order, all running smoothly. At a moment such as this there is a rhythm to the clattering thunder of a thousand looms that is music to a weaver's ears. As I stood listening, watching, I became conscious that my body was wet with perspiration, every muscle taut, every pulse beating hard, and my heart pounding within my breast. I felt for a moment that I wanted to shriek and make my voice heard above the clattering thunder. A suggestion of a thought— "I can't stand this long"—but my mind does not dwell on it for my trained eye went instinctively back to the loom where I saw work to be done. And so it was day after day, a constant effort to master the machine.

Perfect cloth was not demanded at first under this new system, but as the weavers became more accustomed to operating more looms the managers became more exacting until perfect cloth was demanded constantly. Weavers were fined for imperfections, often they were told not to report for work for one day, two days, and sometimes more, this being the manager's method of teaching the weavers to be more careful. Oftentimes the imperfections were not the fault of the weavers but of the loom—but this was not always taken into consideration. Fines and lay-offs were imposed just the same and weavers were often fired.

For two years I worked under this strain (as did every other worker) of fear of being laid off, fear of losing my job, and the constant physical effort necessary to keep the looms running. . . .

The story is the same in every silk shop today. The workers are constantly beset with fears of the "stretch-out" system, wage cuts, and the ever-present demand for perfection and production. Each realizes that eventually some of their number will have to go—all will have to concede to the demands of the industry.

50.   FROM NORTH TO SOUTH

When I moved from the North to the South in my search for work, I entered a mill village to work in a cotton mill as a spinner. There

I worked eleven hours a day, five and a half days a week, for $7 a week. In a northern mill I had done the same kind of work for $22 a week, and less hours. I worked terribly hard. My boss was a farmer who knew nothing about regulating the machines. I had not been there long when he was fired and an overseer from the North with his speed-up and efficiency system was hired in his place. I do not know which was worse: to work under a man who did not know how to make the work run well but who was pleasant to work with, or to have well-regulated machines which ran better but a driving boss.

The sanitary conditions were ghastly. When I desired a drink of water, I had to dip my cup into a pail of water that had been brought into the mill from a spring in the fields. It tasted horrible to me. Often I saw lint from the cotton in the room floating on top of the lukewarm water. All of the men chewed tobacco, and most of the women used snuff. Little imagination is needed to judge the condition of the water which I had to drink, for working in that close, hot spinning room made me thirsty. Toilet facilities were provided three stories down in the basement of the mill in a room without any ventilation. Nowhere was there any running water; even in the houses provided by the company there was no running water.

The married women of the South work extremely hard. The majority of them work in the mill besides having large families to care for. They arise about five to take the cow out to the pasture, to do some weeding in the garden, and to have hot cakes ready for their husbands' breakfasts when they arise. Then they prepare their children for school and finally start their work in the mills at six-thirty, where they work for eleven hours. Upon their return to their homes, they have housework to do. They have no conveniences. Instead of a sink they have a board stretched across one corner of a room. When the washing on the dishes is done, the refuse is thrown out of the back door. When a woman desires meat for her family, she orders it at the company store. When the manager has enough orders of meat, he kills a cow.

Everything in the village is company owned. The houses look like barns on stilts, and appear to have been thrown together. When I would go inside one of them, I could see outside through the cracks in the walls. The workers do all of their trading at the company store and bank, and use the company school and library for they have no means of leaving the village. The money is kept circulating from the employer to the employees, employees to company store, store to company bank, and from the bank to the company again. The result is old torn bills in the pay envelope each week.

I worked in the South for nine months, and during that time I could not reconcile myself to the conditions of the mills and village. Therefore, I left the South and returned to the North—back to the clock punching, speed-up and efficiency system of the northern mills.

Five years have passed since then, and I have learned through experience that I may go North, South, East, or West in my search for work, and find miserable working conditions for miserable wages. I know that the workers in any industry are in a most deplorable condition, but the workers of the South are in virtual slavery.

51.   LACE CURTAINS

. . . I do wish we could afford some real lace curtains but I've done give up hope of that. I used to hope that some day we could have things but times gits worser and worser. We ain't never had nothing and we won't never have nothing.

All of our folks before us was tenant farmers and that's all we've ever done. If you know anything about tenant farming you know they do without everything all the year hoping to have something in the fall. Well, it's very little they ever have, but it's a hope to live and work for all the year just the same. I was raised hard and so was John. We had plenty to eat and that was all. No nice clothes and never a cent to throw away. The first years after John and me got married was hard aplenty but they ain't nothing to what we've had lately.

We started off on a ten-acre farm, four acres of tobacco, two of cotton, and four acres of corn. That didn't include the garden and the 'tater patch. We raised enough vegetables, hogs, and chickens for us, and our money crop bought the rest—you know, sugar, coffee, and a piece of clothes now and then.

We worked early and late that first year and we made a good crop. In a little over a year after we married Lucy come, and as she come in August I won't worth much to John the whole year. He was good to me, too, and tried to keep me out of the field when I was so heavy.

The next year I worked like a nigger and that fall John bought me a coat suit, come the time he sold the first load of tobacco. If he'd waited till the last load I wouldn't of got one because the last load got wet and we got just $35 for it when it was worth pretty near $200. The coat suit didn't do me much good that winter because I was in the family way again and it was the next winter before I could wear it. John bought hisself a suit of clothes, too, and he shore was proud of it because it was the first whole suit he ever had.

Macy was born in March and I was pretty sick. John was mighty disappointed because he had his heart set on a boy. He said that the younguns was coming too fast and that with more mouths to feed and me not able to work half the time we'd soon find ourselves starving to death.

When Jack was two years old the twins come. It had got harder to feed the new mouths and even if John had been mighty worried all the time I never did worry till Amy and Joyce got here; then I was in despair. We hadn't paid the doctor for bringing Jack yet and we still owed a little on Macy. He charged us double the usual price when he brought the twins and from that minute on ever' bill has doubled it seems like.

We just played the devil by not farming this year. We thought that we'd make a whole heap more working out by the day but we found out different pretty quick. A heap of folks wanted work done but they ain't had no money on hand. A heap of them give us vegetables and stuff for our work. Some of them hired us on credit to chop cotton and barn and grade tobacco. When the boll weevil eat the cotton up they thought that we was no better to lose than them. When tobacco brought little prices they thought that we hadn't orter charge for our work.

We are going to farm this land around here next year and so we don't have to pay no rent nor for wood we burn. It shore is a big help, too, not to have to pay for them things when gitting a little to eat's such a problem.

Diet? Well now, I don't know. I always thought that just so a person eat aplenty it didn't matter much what he eat. Of course I think vegetables, eggs, milk, and butter is good for folks and I believe in plenty of hot coffee in cold weather. Then I believe that corn bread is better for a body than biscuits. We always did have enough of something till the last year or so. My worry's not diet but where to git any kind of rations from.

When we have cereal for breakfast or meat and bread we don't have no dinner at all and we have supper at four o'clock. As we set down to the table we play like all of us had been to dinner with friends. We ask each other what he had and we all make out we had turkey, chicken, cake, pie, and a heap of other fancy stuff. Sometimes when one's telling what he had somebody will say, "That's funny, I had the same thing." You'd be surprised how much that helps out. . . .

I'm sorry my younguns can't git a education because that is the one thing a feller has got to have to git a job. Shucks, you can't dig ditches now unless you got a high school education and you can't put up a hawg pasture unless you got a college education. I wish things was back where they useter be when a feller just had to be strong and honest and have a little horse sense to git any kind of job. . . . The biggest problem I see here is the landlord that has a bunch of tenant farmers on his place. They work like niggers all the year and he gits rich. They can't even make enough to eat on through the winter. I've had some pretty good landlords and some pretty bad ones but I reckon that I'll have to put up with them all my life. I hate the thieving rogues anyhow, good or bad. I'm proud of our United States though, and every time I hear the "Star-Spangled Banner" I feel a lump in my throat. There ain't no other nation in the world that would have sense enough to think of WPA and all the other A's. . . .

Speaking about money; well, I reckon we live on about $4 or $5 a week now but it ain't exactly what you call living. I git a day's work here and yonder digging ditches or wells, chopping wood, or killing hogs. Some of them pay me off in meat or potatoes. Some weeks we don't have but a dollar or two and so we go in debt for groceries and have to pay it out of the next week's money. We've never had more than about $12 a week to live on except in wartime and you know the high prices of everything then. I think we could do good on $15 a week and pay our bills good. . . . Why we might even be able after a while to buy some lace curtains.

52. FARM AND FACTORY

Hub's hired solid time and has been for two years. He works every day from six in the morning till six at night in Mr. Hunter's brick plant across the tracks. Some day's more'n that—twenty-four hours on a stretch. That's overtime, but don't mean no extra pay. It's $40 a month straight, no matter what.

Hub fires the boiler most of the time. Then when they're drying bricks, he has to run the fan for twenty-four hours. They couldn't make out in that kiln unless Hub was there.

He ought to git more for the work he puts out. Forty dollars just ain't enough for us to live on. Me and Hub and the three children. We have to pay $4 out every month for this shack. Mr. Hunter makes the hands live close by the plant. And he gits ahold of that $4 for the rent before we ever see a cent of Hub's wages.

We ain't been to church for years. I was taught working on Sunday was wrong. Folks that holds out against working on Sunday don't have to hire others to work for 'em if they don't show up. Hub had to pay a dollar and a quarter yesterday to git a man to turn the fan so's he could see after his sister. She's about to die. Dirty shame for a man to have to pay to go see his own die. I sure wish he could find hisself a better job.

They's been talking something about a new law on hours and wages. I've heard folks in town that knows say Mr. Hunter ought to be forced to pay us more. Twelve cents ain't no decent price to pay for a hour's hard work. But what you going to do? Mr. Hunter's got the jump on us. Hub ain't got nothing good in sight right now. Last year Mr. Hunter had every hand to sign a paper or quit. Hub he let 'em put his name down. He couldn't quit not knowing of a job nowhere else.

Mr. Hunter made a big blow about a bonus he give the hands every January. But they fired a man last year in December. He'd worked steady all the year, solid time. They fired him so's to make sure he didn't draw no bonus.

Hub's going to hang on this year till after he gits his bonus. What he aims to do is to turn over every stone he can to git back on the WPA. We got along a lot better on the WPA. We had our check regular and had good warm clothes for the girls. And they give Hub clothes, too, because his work kept him in the open. I didn't git none but I could manage all right when the others was gitting all they did. Whenever one of us would git down, the WPA would send a doctor and medicine. They give us food too. Things that are supposed to be healthy for eating such as prunes and raisins. We can't buy 'em now.

53.   A DAY AT KATE B'S HOUSE

"Before we moved to the mill Ma had already got jobs fer me and her and Alice. She drawed 25 cents a day and we drawed 10 cents apiece. Pa stayed at home with the children. It was winter time when we first went there and we started to work by lantern light and quit by lantern light, the kerosene lantern swinging down from the ceiling.

"Pa's death was jest the beginnin' of a long, hard time. Clarence had growed big enough to go in the mill, makin' four of us to draw money. Come summer, Alice tuk the typhoid. Then Clarence. Ma had to stay outa the mill to wait on 'em. That left lone me makin' 10 cents a day fer the family to live on. But the neighbors was awful good to us and they brought in rashins. If they hadner we woulder starved, I rekin. Alice was still awful puny when she went back to the mill. And the very day she went to work I tuk down with the fever. It was hard times fer us and hard on poor Ma.

"But . . . I'd learnt that a little grit'll help a body along. I hadn't been back to work long after the typhoid when I went to my boss and done straight talkin'. 'I think I'm wuth more than 10 cents a day,' I said to him. And he raised me to 20 cents. Ma had got up to 50 cents and he raised Alice same as he did me.

"I learned mill work from *a* to *izm*. I could do anything they was to do but run the cards and the lappers. In them days machinery weren't speeded up and a body could catch up with his work and go over to see what his neighbor was doing. When I went avisitin' I went alearnin'. That's why they could put me in pretty near any part of the mill and I could hold down the work. . . .

"Nearly every day I cook Irish potatoes and pintos, and I'm glad when I have a change. We don't care much fer meat and I reckin it's a good thing we don't. On the little bit Iry makes we couldn't buy steak and roast, and sech like. Iry gits him a little mess of liver puddin' near bout every pay day and that's all the meat we buy. I don't like it myself and it gen'ly lasts him for two meals. The doctor tells me to eat chicken and fish. I get my chicken when I go to a supper at the church—and fish too if you count oysters. The members of my class know I ain't makin' nothin' now and they don't expect me to pay. I go over and stay all day to help with the work and that pays fer my meal.

"What we have we uses and what we don't have we do without. I don't believe in makin' no big debts. Hit's jest been fer the past three months that Iry has had regular work. Fer five or six month he'd been gettin' one, two, or three days a week. We done what we could during work times to prepare fer short times. We'd buy up flour, lard, and coffee knowin' we could make out if we had bread and coffee. But one time when things was so bad and the mill w'an't runnin' atall we never even had bread in the house. I went up to Robert's office and I said, 'Robert, I'm hungry.' He looked at me jest like he never knowed what to say fer a minute, and then he spoke, 'Miss Kate, haven't you got anything to eat at your house?' I said, 'Not a bit.' He run his hand down in his pocket and pulled out a $10 bill. He said, 'Miss Kate, go buy yourself somethin' to eat.' Robert Hall's a good-hearted man. I've knowed him ever since he was a child.

"Last year I was sick with the bloody flux, been in bed from Tuesday to Saturday. I hadn't no doctor, and I kept hopin' I could pull through without one. Then Saturday morning in come Dr. Brown and asked me how I were gettin' along. Said he'd heard I were a little sick and he thought he'd come to see about me. It turned out Robert had heard about me bein' sick and he sent the doctor. That evenin'

Robert hisself come by. When he left here he went by the store and ordered chicken soup and fruit juices and told 'em to bring it up here to me."

"A man workin' as hard as I do oughter make $15 a week," Ira said after conversation had been dead for three or four minutes.

"We could make out pretty well with that much," Kate said. "Buy meat now and then, though neither one of us is much a hand fer it."

"They could pay me that much too," Ira continued as he scooped up a spoonful of beans. "The mill's makin' money and I know it. They sell enough cloth."

I sat and rocked slowly in my chair while Kate took a tin box from her dress pocket and poured snuff into her mouth. Once the snuff had settled into position so that speech was easy, Kate said, "It costs when a body gits wrong. Back in 1912 I was in the hospital fer a operation and it cost me $75. I were there agin in 1922 and it cost me $230. Three year ago Iry had a operation for rupture and it cost him $150. Hit looked like he'd never git that one paid fer. Robert Hall had made the arrangemints at the hospital and when Iry went back to work he took out so much a week. 'Tain't been long neither since he stopping takin' out for it."

I agreed with Kate that doctor's bills were always hard for most of us to pay, and from that we went to other things.

Finally Kate got around to talking about education again. It was such a handy thing to have, she said, and a body didn't know how inconvenient it was not to know how to read. She'd told her children, "I want you all to get a education. I never got nary one, and I know how bad a person needs one. Hit'll be nice fer me too, havin' my children with learnin' enough to read to me."

"Jessie, she went to the seventh grade," Kate had continued, "and Iry he quit in the sixth. Charlie—he's the one that's dead—went as fer as the sixth too.

"They's one thing I'd like to ask you before you go. Do you think I'll git the old age pension if I live to be sixty-five? Even if Iry ain't married by then? They say you don't git it if you've got somebody able to take care of you. Married or not, Iry ain't able to take care of me on what he makes. A little money of my own would help out a sight. Do you think I'll git it?"

"I don't know all the provisions of the law," I answered, "but I believe you'll be eligible for a pension when you reach sixty-five."

"I worked as long as I could and I'd work agin if they'd give me a job. That is if I could hold out. Hit may be, like they've got things speeded up in the mill now, I wouldn't fit in atall. But I shore did once; I run everything but the cards and the lappers."

Kate followed me out on the porch, and called my attention to a plant of green moss which hung in long streamers over the sides of the bucket in which it grew. "Stays green all winter," she said. "I'd better bring it in tonight too, because the air is blowing up chilly. I do love to tend my flowers."

54. GREASE MONKEY TO KNITTER

I am a knitter, a full-fashioned knitter. I was born on a little cotton farm near Fort Worth, Texas, August 18, 1912, I am twenty-six years old, been married three years, and have one baby, a little girl, two years old.

In January, 1930, the cafe where I worked went busted. I was out of a job and I couldn't find a single thing to work at. I was young and had no training, and lots of people were out of work. I had nothing to do all the balance of that winter, and when spring came I was down to $30.

We traveled around over Texas—but we didn't find any jobs. I bummed around in Georgia and South Carolina. Everywhere I went it was the same old story—"No help wanted."

But there were lots of people on the road worse off than me. I was young, in good health, and had only myself to look out for. That summer I met whole families wandering around homeless and broke, even women with babies in their arms.

Between Augusta and Charlotte I met a man, his wife, and seven children. The oldest child was only eleven and the youngest was a nursing baby. I guess that baby was the luckiest in the lot because he had something to eat. The other children were all hungry. Some of the little ones were crying for food.

The family was stranded on the highway. It was late in the evening, and neither the mother or the father seemed to know what to do. They just stood there on the outskirts of a little town, hoping.

. . . Finally in September I got a job learning to knit. . . . They told me that if they didn't have a machine for me when I learned they'd give me something at which I could earn expenses. It was understood that I was to learn three months without pay.

I worked the rest of that year for nothing. I got a machine on the night shift the first of January, 1931. I'm still on that same machine, but I'm now on the first shift, from seven in the morning to three in the afternoon. I saved enough money the first year to buy a car. In 1935 I married. My wife is a looper. She worked on for awhile after we married and we bought a lot and had a house built on it. But we've never lived in the house. When it was finished a fellow wanted to rent it. He offered a good price, so we rented the house to him and we lived on at the boarding house. . . .

Before the baby was born we bought some furniture and rented a little place in the country. Maybe I am just a farmer at heart. Anyhow, I love to putter around in the garden, and my wife does, too. We keep some chickens scratching around. It's only three miles from town and I can be home in five minutes after I get out of the mill.

Knitting may look like an easy job, but it's not so easy as it looks. For one thing, it is hard on the eyes; for another it's exacting. The full-fashioned knitting machine is a delicate and highly complicated machine. A knitter must keep his wits about him constantly. It's very easy to smash a machine, doing hundreds of dollars' worth of damage and maybe putting that machine out of commission for a couple of months.

If you want to understand why knitting is such a particular job, and puts such strain on the eyes, spread out a silk stocking and examine the weave or mesh. Then try to stick a fine needle through one of the spaces in the weave. The silk threads are fine and the needles are small and slender. Unless a man has very good eyes he will have to wear magnifying glasses soon after beginning to knit. Knitting is a young man's job. You'll see ten times as many knitters under thirty as you will over thirty. A man's eyes were not made for such fine work. The eyes of some knitters go bad after five or six years, sometimes sooner than that. In fact, unless a man has good eyes he can't learn to knit. Some learners fall down the first week on account of their eyes.

The mills around here teach their own knitters. Some of them have an age limit of twenty years for learners. They prefer young fellows under twenty just out of high school. I imagine a knitter would have to have very good eyes to last ten years. But knitting pays well, comparatively speaking, and there's no lack of applicants. A full-fashioned knitter is considered to have a good trade hereabouts. The wage is much higher than common. A good knitter can average $40 a week the year round. The work is not hard except on the eyes. The light isn't always good. If a man had daylight to work under it wouldn't be so bad, but that can't always be. Most of the mills around here run three shifts, and some are naturally dark and require artificial light even at midday.

There's a boom on in the silk hosiery trade. All the mills around here are running full blast, and those that don't have third shifts are starting them. Many new mills are being built close to Burlington. I've heard that the mills up around Philadelphia are not doing any good. Silk hosiery is a new industry in the South, but it's growing fast.

55.   I'D RATHER DIE

I went to work for Travis and Son a few weeks after Dad died. It's an overall factory—run by Old Dave MacGonnigal and his four boys.

Dad was a pattern-maker there and worked for Old Dave over forty-five years. If things hadn't gone the way they did, I'd never known what he went through to keep us alive all those years. After Dad's death when the bottom dropped out from under the family I couldn't find a job anywhere. Finally I applied to Old Dave MacGonnigal.

". . . Well," he said to me, "you needn't think that because you've got that high school diploma you can sit around on your tail here and talk Latin. We work here, boy. I put on overalls and work like the rest. You soldier on me and I'll fire you like a shot—understand?"

Seemed to me at the time that the job was something handed down out of heaven. I was so happy and relieved I didn't even ask the old man how much he was going to pay me. Rushed on home as fast as I could go to tell Mom.

I can tell you I didn't feel that way when the end of the first week came around. I drew six dollars and fifty cents.

I don't ever remember want or any feeling of insecurity when I was little. Dad made good money in those days—say, about $50 or $60 a week. You know, a pattern-maker has a pretty important job in an overall factory. If the patterns he lays out aren't right to the fraction of an inch the cutters will ruin a lot of goods. There's a good deal of figuring to it, complicated figuring, and he can't make mistakes. Dad never learned mathematics because he hadn't a chance to go to high school. But he'd worked out a system of his own with all sorts of funny little signs and symbols. Nobody else undertood it. He could take a problem of figuring up goods and have it done in a minute where some of the efficiency experts Old Dave had in from time to time would take an hour to work it. And Dad's would be nearer the right answer than the experts'. The boys in the cutting room told me all about it when I came there to work. So they paid Dad a pretty good salary, though not what he was worth.

We had our own home . . . and we had a car. My two older brothers and my sister finished high school. My oldest brother, after being a salesman for a few years . . . worked his way through Columbia University. I don't guess he could have done it by work alone. But he won one scholarship after another and finally a travelling fellowship that gave him a year in Europe. . . .

The first hard times I remember came in 1933, when I was in the eighth grade. Travis and Son shut down and for six months Dad didn't draw a penny. Things must have been pinching for two or three years before that because by that time the house was mortgaged and the money spent. I don't know much about the details. Anyhow, my brother . . . couldn't help much.

Then we were really up against it. For a whole week one time we didn't have anything to eat but potatoes. Another time my brother went around to the grocery stores and got them to give him meat for his dog—only he didn't have any dog. We ate that dog meat with the potatoes. I went to school hungry and came home to a house where there wasn't any fire. The lights were cut off. They came out and cut off the water. But each time, as soon as they left, my brother went out and cut it on again with a wrench.

I remember lying in bed one night and thinking. All at once I realized something. We were poor. Lord! It was weeks before I could get over that. . .

. . . We lost our car and house and kept moving from one house to another. Bill collectors hunted us down and came in droves. Every now and then my brother or Dad would find some sort of odd job to do, or the other brother in Chicago would send us a little something. Then we'd go wild. I mean we'd go wild over food. We'd eat until we were sick. We'd eat four times a day and between meals. We just couldn't help ourselves. The sight and smell of food sort of made us crazy, I guess.

The winter of 1934 was the hardest time of all. . . . We were completely out of coal one time when we were living away out at the edge of town. The weather was freezing bitter then, so at night my brother and I would bundle up and go about a quarter of a mile away to a big estate on the Tennessee River. We made a hole in the fence and stole some of the wood that was piled a good distance from the house. We just walked in and got it. I don't remember that we tried to be quiet about it in particular.

After awhile things got some better. My brother in Chicago got so he could send money home and my other brother got another newspaper job. Dad went back to regular work at Travis and Son, though he only got about $20 a week. . . .

I went on through high school and made good marks. In my senior year I had an average of 98 and was elected class president and was valedictorian at graduation. I expected to go to college the next fall. Now, I can't see how on earth I could have expected to. I knew that there was no money for it. But somehow or other it just seemed to me that a way would turn up.

Mother felt the same about it. She'd say, "If you want a college education badly enough you will get it. Any boy who is determined can work his way through."

That summer we had a scare. There was some sort of strike at Travis and Son. Seems that after the NRA blew up, Old Dave put the girls in the sewing room on piecework and some of them just couldn't make a living. They protested but it didn't do no good. . . . Then some organizer came and got them to go out on a strike. The men went out too, and they ganged around the entrance blocking off part of the street.

Dad didn't know what to do. He walked the floor at home. He said that the girls were right, but he didn't believe they could win out because the mayor had said he'd back Old Dave to the limit. I remember Mama telling Dad, "Oh, Bob, please don't do anything foolish! We've been through such a hard time. What on earth would we do if we had to face it again? I couldn't bear it!"

So Dad went to work the next morning. I had some errands to do for Mama so I went to town with him. Old Dave had called up and said he'd have policemen to carry Dad through the strikers. When we got there the policemen were ready all right. They told Dad they'd rush him through. He started out, with me tagging behind. Then he made me go back to the corner and started again. The strikers were bunched up at the door of the factory. They weren't saying a thing or making a move. Just men and women standing there watching.

I saw Dad stop again. He had an argument with the police. I heard him say pretty loud, "No, I'll go by myself or I won't go at all." He said it two or three times.

The policemen were mad. "Okay, Cap," I heard one of them say, "It's your look-after, not mine."

Dad walked on without them, but they sort of edged along some way behind.

All at once the strikers began yelling and meeowing. Dad walked on. When he was right at them, about a dozen men and women grabbed at him and started tearing his coat and shirt.

I started running down there and so did the police. . . . But right then the strikers got into a free-for-all fight among themselves. Dad had a lot of good friends among them and these friends jumped on the ones who'd grabbed him. They pulled them off and Dad walked on through and went into the factory. He never was bothered again. Old Dave and the others had to have the police to get in and out. Dad came and went without anybody trying to stop him.

So the strike petered out and the strikers were out of jobs. Some of them came to Dad and he tried to get them back on. But Old Dave said he wouldn't touch a one of them with a ten-foot pole.

One night late in July Dad didn't come home at his usual time.
. . . The doctors never did know what was wrong with Dad. He was
sixty, but there wasn't anything like cancer or tuberculosis. One of the
doctors at the hospital told me he was really just worn out completely.
I guess he was right.

56. THE LORD WILL TAKE CARE OF YOU

I like my work. I like working for Christian people. Mr. Pugh owns
the shoe plant here in Hancock and he sure is a Christian man. Do
you know why he's made such a big success in life? It's the Christian
way he lives. They tell me he gives a tenth of all he makes to the church
and the Lord made him successful. It makes you feel good to work for a
Christian man like that.

My work is hard all right. It's hard on me because I ain't but only
seventeen and ain't got my full growth yet. It's work down in the
steam room which they call it that because it's always full of steam
which sometimes when you go in it you can't hardly see. You steam
leather down there and that steam soaks you clean to the skin. It
makes me keep a cold most of the time because when I go outdoors
I'm sopping wet. Another thing that's hard about it is having so much
standing up to do. My hours is from seven o'clock in the morning till
four in the evening. And it's stand on my feet the whole time. When
noon time comes and I'm off an hour, why I just find me somewheres
to set and I sure set there. You couldn't pay me to stand up during
lunch time.

I'm on piecework now and I can't seem to get my production up to
where I make just a whole lot. You get paid by the production hour
and it takes fifty pair of shoes to make that hour. You get 42 cents for
the hour. Highest I ever made in one week was $11 and the lowest was
$7.42. I usually hit in between and make $8 or $9.

Now and then somebody will say, "We ought to have us a union
here of some sort." That kind of talk just makes me mad all over. Mr.
Pugh is a Christian man. He brought his factory here to give us some
work which we didn't have any before. We do pretty well, I think, to
just stay away from that kind of talk. All but the soreheads and trouble-
makers is satisfied and glad to have work.

I don't blame Mr. Pugh a bit the way he feels about the unions. The
plant manager knows Mr. Pugh mighty well and he told my foreman
what Mr. Pugh said. Mr. Pugh said, "If the union ever comes in here
and I have to operate my plant under a union, why I'll just close the

plant down and move it away from Hancock so quick it'll make your head swim." That's his word on it and I don't blame him none. I'd hate to see a union try here. No plant and no jobs for anybody. They just operate these unions out of Wall Street, anyhow, trying to ruin people like Mr. Pugh. Man told me that and he knows. He worked in Detroit during the war. Wall Street set some unions on Henry Ford and tried to put his back to the wall. But did they do it? Don't make me laugh!

Next to the unions, this new wages and hours business of the government's is bad, too. Some people that had been getting as high as $35 a week was cut to only $25 which is about $10 a week less than they'd been getting before. They didn't like it because it meant their salary wasn't as much as it had been. Then some that hadn't got but $5 or $6 got to getting as much as I get. They liked that, but it don't seem fair to me. Why should a man that's not worth as much to the plant as me get as much money as me?

My money has to go a long way. I've got to pay $8 a month rent and I have to buy coal and stove wood. I got to buy clothes for the family and something to eat for them. Then twice a month there's that $5 ambulance bill which it's to take my brother that's got the T.B. to the City Hospital in Memphis where they take and drain his lungs. Sure charge you for an ambulance, don't they? Now, some people say if you just take one trip in an ambulance, the undertaker won't ask a cent for it. Figures he'll get your custom if you pass on. But they sure charge me for my brother.

Well, I'm always glad when it's quitting time. I like to work there, but can't help getting tired. I go on home. I walk four blocks and I'm there. Usually I have to wait a while for supper so I just set at the window. I like to watch and see if maybe something will come along the street and I can watch it. Sometimes there's a new funny paper there and I will look it over—specially if it's Tarzan. That's the best thing in a funny paper, the Tarzan part. Nobody ever gets it over old Tarzan, do they? Most times, though, I like to just set there and watch.

I work steady but I'm most always financially in need of money. It takes a lot to keep a family going. My little sister needs glasses but they cost too much. All of my family has weak eyes but we can't afford to wear glasses.

So I haven't the money for running around. I wouldn't if I had the money, either. The Bible is against running around and playing cards and seeing the moving pictures. . . . So me and a young lady I know of go to church and Sunday School instead of running around. . . .

You know, when you're blue and down at the mouth and don't see any use anyhow, a good sermon just lifts you up. You haven't got a thing to lose by living a Christian life. Take Mr. Pugh. He lives it and look where he is now. And if you don't make out that way, if you're poor all your life, then you get a high place in the Kingdom. Just do the best you know how and the Lord will take care of you either here or hereafter. It sure is a comfort.

57. THE CLEANING WOMAN

The everyday problems of housekeeping when projected into a modern industrial city, crowding itself together tier on tier, take on curious and sometimes menacing characteristics. The business of cleaning the home is comparatively simple. It can be dovetailed in between other routine tasks and gotten through in the limits of a working day. But the cleaning of the buildings in which business and commerce and industry house themselves is set in different limits, and these limits do not conduce to a good life for those who do the work.

The Consumers League has just published a digest of the records of 308 office cleaners in New York City's financial district which was furnished them by Father Moore of the Church of St. Peter in Barclay Street. The report shows the inability of the majority of the husbands and other men in these families to earn wages in any sense adequate to support themselves and their families. The men work on the docks, in the restaurants, and in the buildings of the neighborhood as porters, window cleaners, or elevator operators or starters. In many cases they are totally unskilled and receive meager pay: in the rest, their work is so irregular that although their hourly rate of wages is on the whole fairly good, their yearly incomes are very low.

Of the 308 office cleaners, 270 have been in this country over five years, but only 76 are citizens and 37 have their first papers. Literacy data are unreliable but a conservative estimate places the illiteracy at not over 50 per cent. The majority of the women speak a broken English, although, for the most part, they cannot read or write it.

Most of these women live in the tenements along the lower west tip of Manhattan Island, the shabbiest, most dilapidated dwellings in the city of New York. . . . The flats usually consist of one room and an alcove which has no window, but is sufficiently large to hold a double bed. At night this is made to hold as many members of the family as necessary—and the rest sleep on mattresses spread on the floor, or possibly on a couch in the dining-living-cooking-sleeping room. Families of from two to ten members live in a flat. . . .

As far as hours are concerned, the life of the woman who "works in the buildings," as it is called in Washington Street, is often a complete reversal of the schedule of the rest of the community. The governing factor of their work is not their own strength or the needs of their families but the fact that offices and factories must be cleaned when they are not in use—that is at night. The women come, in some instances, from five or six to eight or nine o'clock at night and again from four or five to eight o'clock in the morning. The sweeping and cleaning of baskets is done at night, and the dusting in the morning. In this way the dust raised in sweeping is allowed to settle before dusting, and the offices used at night may be cleaned before 9 A.M. In one building the work is done in one three-hour-and-fifty-minute shift from 4 to 7:50 A.M. The superintendent states that he made the change from the double to the single schedule of hours during the war when labor was scarce, in order to attract married women. Other buildings have the work all done between the cold middle hours of the night and dawn.

The children must learn to adjust themselves to irregular hours. Many of them help along the family income by "minding" the babies in homes where the mother and father work during the same hours, or where there is no father. School children from eight to twelve years of age thus creep into bed with the babies whom they watch, at four or six o'clock in the morning, and stay until eight or eight-thirty when they leave for school. Two dollars per week is the standard wage for "minding."

As if serving what is usually a large family of children and holding one cleaning job were not sufficient, many of these women do two office-cleaning jobs of four hours each, one in the morning and one in the evening, or a shift in a restaurant in the middle of the day, from 10 to 4 P.M. Many of them, especially among the unmarried girls, do all three. It is difficult to understand how some of them have the strength to endure the strain put upon them.

The superintendent of one building told of a woman whom he had employed for eight years, and had finally discharged because her work became unsatisfactory. She had been working seven hours in the morning cleaning his building; had been assistant cook in a restaurant from 10 A.M. to 3 P.M.—five hours; and had cleaned another office building for eight hours at night. This left her four hours a day, presumably for sleep.

It is not difficult to see why these women look old, although the majority are in their best working years. The following figures, while not absolutely accurate because, in many instances, the women can only approximate their own ages, will give an idea of the range of the 308 women considered:

Under 20 years	9
20 to 29 years	91
30 to 39 years	109
40 to 49 years	45
50 or over	21
No date	26

Ten dollars a week is the standard wage, and in no case did a woman receive more than $12 for the usual shift of four or five hours. This is a decided improvement over the rate of $5 current ten years ago, and $8 generally paid at the beginning of the war.

The amount of floor space which each woman is required to cover varies from . . . twelve to twenty-three rooms with the desks and chairs, and in some cases, a flight of stairs and a lavatory. . . .

In no cases do they receive increased wages with length of service. New employes receive the same amount as a woman who has been at it for twenty years.

58.   HOW THE E. FAMILY LIVES

Mr. E., age thirty-six, is a mechanic in a large factory on the "west side" of Chicago. He is married to a childhood playmate now aged thirty-three, and has three children—Helen, aged seven, Robert, aged five, and Julia, aged 15 months. Mr. E. and his wife have had a common school education and are commonplace people who have no particular abilities or disabilities, but are fairly energetic and thrifty. Until recently they have managed to make a fairly comfortable living. About two years ago they had a fund of several hundred dollars saved up and were hoping to make a first payment on a home in one of the outlying neighborhoods. At that time Mr. E.'s health began to fail, and in a short time he was compelled to quit work. A local physician told him he had "consumption," and Mr. E. began to treat his cough with home remedies and patent medicines. Meantime there was no income, and in about five months every resource was exhausted; savings were spent, cheaper quarters found, superfluous furniture sold, credit at neighborhood stores exhausted, sick benefits from the lodge were withdrawn, and expenses trimmed at every point, even to dropping payments on life insurance. In short there was nothing to do but follow the suggestions of an interested neighbor and "appeal to the charities." They were then about $250 in debt. . . .

. . . An estimate of the family's original average of expenditures follows:

Rent (four rooms, stove heat)	$35.00
Fuel and light (coal and gas)	7.50
Food	62.25
Clothing	24.00
Household expenses (including upkeep on furniture)	8.20
Carfare	5.00
Health	5.00
Insurance	1.15
Spending money and recreation	4.00
Savings	8.50
Average monthly total expense	$160.60

Mr. E.'s earnings at 72 cents an hour, including a little extra money he earned at overtime work, had enabled him to meet this budget very easily. During his illness, of course, the standard of living rapidly fell and no organized scheme of expenditures could be found from the household account book. During the last month before they appealed to the charities, the E.'s had pared their expenses down to absolute necessities: "We barely lived," as Mrs. E. expressed it.

Their expenditures, when classified as above, were as follows:

Rent	$23.00
Fuel and light	4.50
Food	47.88
Clothing	8.00
Household expenses	3.16
Carfare	.85
Health	12.00
Insurance	0.00
Spending money and recreation	.36
Savings	0.00
Total	$99.75

Value of articles given by neighbors, friends, relatives:

Food	$10.00
Clothing	3.00
Fuel	2.00
Total	$114.75

When Mr. E. came home from the sanitarium some eight months later and went back to his work, the worker made a similar estimate to determine whether the family would be fully self-supporting, or would need further assistance. Her figures were approximately those shown in the table, but when the social worker talked over the budget

Item	Total	General Family Expense	Mr. E.	Mrs. E.	Helen	Robert	Julia
Housing	$ 35.00	$35.00					
Food	59.81		$17.77	$14.30	$10.40	$ 8.67	$8.67
Clothing	29.00		9.00	7.50	5.00	3.75	3.75
Fuel and light	8.50	8.50					
Household expenses	5.00	5.00					
Carfare	5.04		3.64	1.40			
Spending money and recreation	2.50		1.00	1.00	.25	.25	
Health	7.00	7.00					
Education	.90	.75			.15		
Insurance	6.25		5.00	1.25			
Savings	10.00	10.00					
Total	$169.00	$66.25	$36.41	$25.45	$15.80	$12.67	$12.42

problem in a friendly way with Mrs. E., the worker pointed out several changes that she proposed should be made. Among these were:

(1) A better grade of food could be secured with perhaps a slight decrease in cost by purchasing in larger quantities rather than from day to day, and by patronizing "cash-and-carry" shops; (2) household expenses could be materially reduced by the same plan and by purchasing furniture, when needed, for cash rather than on installments; (3) the worker believed that the family should have a daily and Sunday paper or some good popular magazine; (4) the expenditures for health had been too low previously, dental care in particular being badly needed; (5) the family had too little insurance for safety; (6) some economies should be effected in spending money; and (7) it ought to be possible to increase the savings item a little. The total budget was a little larger than formerly, but Mr. E. had had a slight increase in wages and could meet it easily. . . .

Mrs. E. confided to the worker that their income had never been large enough to meet their real needs though they had succeeded in living within it and saving a little. Neither she nor Mr. E. had "aspirations beyond their station in life," but they both thought that their present living quarters were inadequate, that they needed several new pieces of parlor furniture and some really nice clothing. They would like to go to church more often and to make friends and also to join one or two neighborhood organizations. Mr. E. in particular was anxious to join a popular fraternal order to which many of the men at the shop belonged. They felt debarred from these relations now because they could not afford suitable clothing and proper home furnishings. For her part she had always wanted to go to the opera and see what it was like, and she wanted to send her washing to the "wet wash." Mr. E. had had the promise of a foreman's job before he became ill, with an increase of pay. He and his wife had thought then that they would be able to have everything they wished. In fact they had worked out a tentative monthly budget. Mrs. E. was reluctant to show this "ideal" budget since they "weren't in the habit of counting too much on the future." The estimate was:

Rent (5 rooms, steam heat)	$ 60.00
Fuel and light (gas and electricity)	5.00
Food	65.00
Clothing	32.00
Household expenses	12.00
Carfare	6.00
Health	5.00
Insurance	3.00
Organization and church dues	5.00
Spending money and recreation	15.00
Savings (including $30 monthly to buy a home)	42.00
Total	$250.00

59. THE FORGOTTEN INDUSTRY

For five years I have been a hotel worker in New York, Illinois, Indiana, and Wisconsin. When I am asked if I have ever worked in a good hotel I have to say "No." But I know that there could be good hotels, because for every bad feature in any hotel I ever worked in I have met a fine and feasible remedy operating in some other place. The law could bring all these good things together in the same hotel.

The hotel in Cleveland, where I worked as chambermaid, had a pleasant cafeteria for its employees on the thirteenth floor, fitted out with small tables and chairs—a big improvement over the common type of Help's Hall, located somewhere in the sub-basement with long wooden tables and backless benches.

Adjustments in hours are spasmodically made by the management. The vegetable and glass pantry girls in the Felton Hotel in Milwaukee work a straight eight-hour day. But the usual broken shift of eleven hours stretched over fourteen, which this replaced, is still required of the help's cook and help's waitresses at the Felton. And in an equally large hotel across the street, the help's waitresses work but eight hours a day and the vegetable girls work over eleven hours.

. . . The laws of twenty states still read like that of New York:

No employee shall be employed, permitted or suffered to work more than six days in any one week. *Exceptions:* Employees in, or in connection with, kitchens of hotels.

In Wisconsin, where I have been working this last year, the law which limits the hours a woman may work applies to: "factories, workshops . . . mercantile establishments, confectionery stores and restaurants," with no mention of hotels at all.

It isn't that hotels haven't a difficult problem with regard to hours—they have. Most hotel departments must give service from six in the morning until midnight, with three times a day when work is heaviest; so it is hard to arrange reasonable hours. But in most hotel departments hours are not arranged at all. The measure of a job is how much work there is, not how much time a girl can be reasonably expected to work.

Margaret Murphy, head cook at the Elk Inn, started the fire at 5:15 every morning, hurriedly served order after order of eggs in different styles, rushed to her preparations for dinner. At about eleven she would say, "I haven't had a drink of water yet; I feel faint." At three she would be through with dinner, only to begin again before five on supper, which would be over about eight. For many years she had worked this thirteen-hour day stretched over fifteen hours.

The two waitresses, the dishwasher, and I as kitchen helper worked an eleven-hour day stretched over fifteen hours. These were not emergency hours, but the regular thing. During the Labor Day weekend, we handled one hundred additional guests. At the end of the week every one was dead tired. The boss had given every girl a dollar tip for her extra hard work, but the day after the rush we were called at five-thirty as usual and put to help can fruit.

The work in the housekeeping department usually is from seven to four o'clock. But some one is needed to clean the rooms after late guests have checked out, and where there are no standardized hours, the day maids come back on a regular night watch. In the Mauriec each day maid had a watch from five to ten at night every tenth night or oftener.

It isn't as though the work in hotels stopped on Sundays and holidays as it does in factories. It keeps right along. The cashier at the Lake Hotel worked for three years without a day off. "I work every day, Thanksgiving, Christmas, all holidays," she told me, "so I never get a chance to see my friends or family. I can't even get off to go to a funeral when my relatives die. I took two weeks off, though I couldn't afford it . . . and I didn't get out of bed for the first four days. I thought I'd get a real rest. I kept wanting to apply somewhere for a job, but you know it took me the whole two weeks to get civil. . . . I felt that ugly and tired after working a whole year from morning to night without a day off."

But among the younger girls who find it easy to get new jobs, the seven-day week is the direct cause of an irresponsible, migratory type of worker. Girl after girl would come to the employment agency and tell of giving up a job she had liked. "Never getting a day off like that, there got to be so many things I had to attend to, I just quit my job and took a few days off and got them done with. Now I need another job."

When I "lived in" in a hotel my room wasn't usually much better than the kitchen. In the Raymond Hotel it was on the ground floor. The windows opened out on the alley where trucks of supplies for the hotel were unloaded. The noise started early in the morning and kept up all day. The room was so dark that lights had to be on even at noon. Two large double beds took up most of the space. Four girls called that home. No place anywhere in that hotel but half a bed to call our own, no place where we could read, sew or receive friends.

The measure of wages in Wisconsin for a woman hotel employee is $30 to $45 a month. Some chambermaids and help's waitresses get $25 and some cooks and pantry girls get $50 and even $60 a month, but they are exceptions. My own wages never went below $30 or above $45. Often they were higher than the wages of the old employees because I happened to be hired when I was badly needed. Girls know they get more that way. The phrase around hotels is, "It's no use sticking; the more you quit the more you'll get."

The whole unfairness of tips is shown by the discrimination against the older, but more experienced workers. It is well known that the older a girl grows the less tips she gets, and the less chance she has to get a new job. An employment agent will say to a girl who looks over twenty-seven or so, "I've got a job with good money in it, but they asked for 'chicken.'"

60.   CHILD WORKERS

Tom is a sharecropper's child, black, in Alabama. His family (father, mother, and four children old enough to make "hands") all work for the landowner, are all collectively continually in debt to him (they get $75 worth of supplies for the growing season and he keeps the books), and all live in a two-room cabin furnished by the land-owner. . . .

Tom . . . is now twelve and old enough to be counted by the Census. (The Census enumeration begins at age ten.) But even six years ago in the year of the last Census Tom was at work, though officially nonexistent, along with the thousands of his little fellow laborers, at age six, beginning to pick cotton.

Tom gets up, or is pulled out of bed, at four o'clock in summer, by his older brother, who is quicker than he to hear the landlord's bell. Work for the entire plantation force is "from can see to can't see" (i.e., from daylight to dark), and the bell is their commanding time-piece. The "riding boss"—what a foreman is to a doffer in a textile mill—sees to that. Little Jenny, aged five, is being left at home today to care for the baby, because it is so hot; on cooler days the baby is carried along to the field and laid on a pallet under the tree, and Jenny can play among the cotton rows with the other children who are too young to work. (There are plantations where mothers of young infants are given fifteen minutes nursing time, no more, morning and afternoon. Then they must take the baby along: there is not enough time to go home.)

Tom is a good, steady chopper and can do over half a man's work. At picking he can do two-thirds. Peter, aged nine, does considerably less than that. In fact when his father asked to stay on at the beginning of the growing season, the landlord told him he didn't see how he could keep him on another year raising a crop on so many acres and living in such a good house, with his family so "no-account."

Tom has been to school part of three grades. The Negro school in his district runs four months "normally" (the white school runs six); but in the year 1932–33 it closed altogether, and since then it has been averaging less than three months. Besides, cotton-picking season in Alabama runs well into November, and after that it is often too cold to go to school without shoes. So from January on Tom and Peter have been taking turns in one pair.

The older brother did a little better. He was a "prosperity" child, and during several of the 1925–29 seasons he got the full four-months school term. By the time he was thirteen, however, he had stopped going altogether, having finished the fifth grade (twenty months of education for a lifetime of work) and being, in the view of the riding boss, "plenty big for a man's work and likely to get uppity soon if he don't quit school."

In picking cotton Tom is not so much "smarter" than some of the younger children. At age twelve he can keep going longer, of course, at the end of a twelve-hour day with the thermometer still close to 100 degrees, than he could when he was seven, but he can hardly pick faster. All the children pick with both hands, and by the end of the first season the lifetime rhythm of pluck, pluck, drop-in-the-bag is long since established. But now that Tom is taller he has to stoop so much, or move along on his knees, while the littlest fellows scramble by with "hardly a bend to them." The cotton plants often grow shoulder-high, to be sure, but the cotton bolls on them grow nearly all the way to the ground; so, for all but a tiny child, this means "stooping, stooping all day." But Tom can manage the big sack that he drags after him by a shoulder strap better now than when he was a little fellow. It grows so heavy dragging along after the smallest pickers all day that it nearly makes up for the "bends" of the older ones.

Chopping cotton is much harder and is done under greater pressure for time, for the growing season will not wait. The six- and seven-year-old children do not engage in this, but Tom has long since become experienced. He handles the heavy hoe with a ready swing, cutting out the superfluous plants with a steady chop, chop, from sunrise to dark.

The ordinary hand hoeing after this is easier (Tom began with that as a little fellow, next after the picking), but still it is heavier than picking. It too requires a stooping position all day long, and the weight of the hoe and the earth are not inconsiderable.

What is Tom—and what are all the hundreds of thousands of his fellows in the cotton belt of the South—getting for this investment of his childhood? An outlook for the future, a foundation for something better for him later on, an immediate financial return even in his own pocket for his present wretched and stultifying toil? On the contrary, Tom is not only burying his own childhood in this cotton patch, he is drawing in return not a dollar of pay, from year's end to year's end. The landlord's account simply chalks up so many acres cultivated against the family's debts for the coming year, and if Tom or his brothers did not work, their father would not get his farm for the next season. Tom's and his family's reward is that he continue shoeless and abominably fed, oppressed and half-illiterate from those first months in the fields when he was six until he shall be an old man. . . .

* * *

Has the reader ever sat in a restaurant at eight-thirty or nine o'clock for a belated evening meal, and heard the familiar voice at his elbow, "Paper, Mister?" (Of course on the street or in the subway would do as well and the hour might be later. This particular lad came into the restaurant, and his hours were better than many.) A boy selling papers and "almost through" for the night. (This was a winter night.) He appeared to be well known by the manager, and apparently often ended up his rounds there. He was ten, he said, but he looked not over eight and his whole development was very juvenile. In the third grade in school and apparently not doing too well. Four brothers and sisters. . . . He has been selling for two years. He begins after school about four-thirty and gets through about eight or eight-thirty. His mother saves some supper for him and he eats about nine and goes right to bed. Sometimes if it has been cold and he gets home late, he sleeps in the kitchen by the stove. His father is a tailor (unemployed) and has made him this cap ("it's awful warm"), also this coat (less so). Yes, he generally has milk for breakfast; "coffee makes you skinny." . . .

What do such little boys earn from their broken rest and neglected schooling? In 1934 when the NRA was at its height and child labor supposedly abolished, the "little merchants" swarming over the streets of our cities were averaging less than 9 cents an hour for those over twelve years of age, about 4½ cents for those under twelve. The youngest children sold the longest hours and earned the least; the average child under twelve all over this country was working eighteen hours a week and earning 82 cents.

In the eyes of the Census of course none of these little workers exist so long as they are of school age and do not play truant altogether; they are counted as "attending school and having no occupation."

Some children naturally earn more, by working impossibly long hours: for instance, a twelve-year-old boy who in 1934 was on the street regularly from eight o'clock in the morning on Saturday to 2 A.M. Sunday morning without interruption, except for one hour off for meals (seventeen hours at a stretch). The same child sold papers on school days from 4 P.M. until midnight . . . and on Sundays from 9 P.M. until midnight. . . . For this mind- and body-destroying routine the child had the previous week earned $2.75—about 5 cents an hour. . . .

* * *

Mary is eight, and lives in Newark, and so do her mother and her four brothers and sisters, and her grandmother, and her father when he is not away from home looking for work. . . . They occupy a four-room flat in a two-family house, and the kitchen where they do their industrial homework is also where they live and eat.

Mary's mother has tried all kinds of homework for her family. Finishing men's clothing paid the best for a while, but the bundles were so terribly heavy for John (the oldest, aged eleven), and he had to cross the track to get them, and the boss was awfully mean and would just as soon keep him waiting two or three hours for the next bundle. So lately they have been working on powder puffs and stringing tags and finally making doll clothes. "Powder puffs make me sick. I had to have a change," says Mary. . . . Tags lasted for a while, until the market became overcrowded and the only kind of knots they wanted you to make were the meanest ones. Mother and Grandma tried bead work for a time and found plenty to do on it, but the children not so much. Finally for a number of months it has been doll clothes. Here all the family can work, though the rates are terribly low. Mary would not mind it so much if she could do all the four different processes that the children do: cutting the threads, clipping apart the trimming from one dress to the next (Mother stitches them on the machine in batches, to save time), turning the finished garments right side out, and packing them in a box. But Mother finds it goes faster if each child does just one thing. And there is a big pile in front of each of them. Also, the hours on this have to run extra long, to make up for the low pay. Mary works from three-thirty to five in the afternoon and again from six to nine o'clock after supper. So do her sister and brother of ten and eleven. Even little Jackie, aged four, does a little off and on in the afternoon and after supper. . . . Mother works on, as late as she may have to, under pressure, to finish the lot. "Sometimes I think I will go crazy," she says, "the work is so tedious."

*   *   *

Young Henry Dickinson at fourteen goes to work in the same mill as his father, to become a doffer instead of a schoolboy. True, it was a slightly worse form of labor when his father began in a cotton mill as battery boy at twelve, and his mother too. They had only two or three years of schooling, and Henry has had eight. They worked eleven hours a day, and until he is sixteen Henry must work eight. . . .

Henry is awakened at three o'clock every morning, along with all his family, because his father, instead of earning $17 as formerly, has been cut twice and now earns only $14 except when he does overtime. So Henry's father goes to work at five in the morning as soon as the mill doors open, and stays until they close at night: he is on piecework and tries to do all the overtime he can to bring up his earnings. "Of course in a few years we will have plenty of help, if we can just make it that long," Henry's mother is wont to remark: there are four younger than Henry, who has reached working age now, and he has a sister who has but two years to go. . . . Dried peas and other dried vegetables now take the place of any fresh vegetables they may have had, before his father's pay cut and the new baby came. He craves meat, but they get it rarely, except pork now and then; and sweets, except molasses, are virtually unknown.

Henry has plenty of time to think his own thoughts now he is a doffer, not a schoolboy, as he pushes his long heavy box mounted on small wheels up and down the great rows of spinning frames, up one alley and down another. He must keep the spinners supplied with full spools, and stoop to pick up the empty ones dropped by the spinners. When his box is emptied of its last few spools, he must hurry to the twister room for a new supply, leaving there his "empties" to be filled. Some of the doffers are boys, some are girls. All of them usually begin work in this village at fourteen.

Strife and Unemployment

61.   DONE IN OIL

Elk Basin was literally a "hole in the ground," gouged out of the naked clay and sandstone, a mile wide, three miles long, and perhaps three hundred feet deep. Huddled in the bottom were the gray mass of the gasoline plant buildings, and a motley assortment of tents, tar-paper shacks, and slate-colored company bungalows, while the gaunt skeletons of the oil derricks and the bleak little corrugated iron pump houses cluttered the fringes. No water, no trees, no grass—not a living growing thing in sight save the straggling sagebrush. Scattered over the desolate floor of the Basin between four and five hundred people were living the long 6½- and 7-day week of the oil fields.

The Elk Basin production is controlled wellnigh lock, stock, and barrel by the Standard Oil interests. . . .

I tackled the boss of the Midwest outfit for a job and he passed me on to the "general office" in front of the company warehouse where my history was taken down and I was signed on as a roustabout at $4 a day —less $1.35 a day deducted for board. My job entitled me to free quarters in one of the one-story bunkhouses and to a seat at one of the long oilcloth tables in the mess shack. There was no ceremony about getting settled: one just dumped one's plunder into one of the unoccupied rooms and took possession without the formality of a key. . . .

Married men who bring their families into the Basin occupy separate "houses"—the tents and tar-paper shacks built by the companies for their employees. . . .

I was awakened at six o'clock my first morning by "Old John," the bunkhouse "crum boss," coming down the line literally blasting the occupant of each room out of bed with the most adequate assortment of profanity I have even heard. . . . Yet I found him in the wash-house ten minutes later lending $10 to a still sleepy roustabout whom he had only the minute before been threatening with death and dire destruction. Later on, when one of the boys in the Ohio camp was rushed to the hospital twenty miles away with appendicitis and a hundred dollars was needed for an operation, it was "Old John" who put up the needed money.

I washed in the hard alkali water in the wash-house, breakfasted with the taciturn double row of men feeding methodically in the mess shack, and shortly before seven checked in at the blacksmith shop and took my seat on the floor with the other men. . . . With one exception . . . they were all American born, mostly the substantial type from the Middle West, and their easy raillery bespoke an open-air life free from the grosser fatigues of the machine operative. The unmarried men had many of them drifted in from other oil fields, all the way from Pennsylvania to California and Mexico, or from the soft coal centers of the Middle West, while many of the married men had originally given up fenced farms in Wisconsin, Iowa, and Missouri and ventured west in that most precarious of all gambles, proving up on a dry land quarter section.

I checked out as one of a gang of eight roustabouts and a "straw boss" assigned to pick and shovel work—and the long grind of those weeks in the Basin was begun. I say "grind" not because the work itself was unbearably hard. Slogging away with pick and shovel at hard-pan soil is punishing business at best, as is also rod-wrenching in the slimy oil ooze about the mouth of a well. But after all, a job's a job, and one worked at pretty much one's own gait, without the constant speeding up to keep pace with a machine that wears out the machine operative. But it was the drab, blistering monotony of seven days a week of it that bludgeoned all the fight out of a fellow. "When you finish a week's work out here," remarked the man next me as he leaned on his pick one Sunday morning, "you ain't good for nothin' but John D." Jobs like these make one realize how fatuous it is to say that the casual laborer *ought* to be "interested in his job." . . .

The drinking water was a constant source of protest among the men and their families in the Midwest camp. The only water in the Basin was alkali water pumped from wells two miles away and condensed for drinking. . . .

The only shower bath in operation in the Basin during the past spring and early summer was the one down in the Ohio wash-house —which was not open to Midwest men. . . .

Least defensible of all the sources of protest in the Basin, however, is the long week that includes Sunday work. . . . In Elk Basin all pumpers, drillers, and tool dressers of all companies—roughly one man in three—work a twelve-hour day seven days a week. . . .

The President's Mediation Commission in 1920 in the California oil fields provided that, "Eight hours actual work at the plant or place of employment shall constitute the work day in the oil industry. . . ."

The vacation policy of the Midwest Company in Elk Basin is to be commended—one week with pay after a year's service and two weeks with pay after two years. The Midwest also provides free company insurance up to $2000 and a compulsory sick benefit plan. Another noteworthy evidence of Midwest welfare policy is the small but clean two-bed infirmary and the doctor sent into the Basin at the company's expense. The Midwest Company also keeps a traveling library of fifty books in the Basin.

Hard as the long day and the seven-day week are on the men, however, I sympathized even more with the women and children of the Basin. Elk Basin is not only over a dozen miles from the railroad, but twenty miles over rutted trails to even the nearest "movie" show. And while the men have the rough pool hall where they while away the evenings gambling mildly, for the women the days crawl endlessly by. In winter they are snowed in for weeks at a time. "Last winter," one mother of a family of five told me, "the snow was so deep that I didn't get out of our front door for six weeks." While, during the brief summers they kept indoors while the sun blazes down as it only can in a treeless country where cloudy days are almost unknown. It seemed always three o'clock in the afternoon in those sun-burned little shacks of the Basin. I used to wonder when I was new in the Basin at the extravagance of the mother of a family of six living on a salary of less than $5 a day who paid $2 for a watermelon, or at the expensive-looking victrolas in one- and two-room shacks. But these things are literally more necessary than bread and potatoes and shoes—they afforded the same imperative relief that the boy next to me in the bunkhouse, a fine, clean fellow of nineteen grinding along twelve hours on and twelve off seven days a week, got at night.

Many of the families of the Basin are substantial American folk whose children might go to college in a more favored community. And it was to the problem of their children that these earnest, patient people of the West recurred most often. For the girls, unless they left home after finishing the eight grades of schooling available in the Basin, there was nothing ahead except work as a "hasher" for the rude crew in the mess shack or marriage to one of the unmarried men in the bunkhouse and—the oil fields throughout all *their* lives too. For the boys the future was less problematical: they hung around the pool hall learning to grow up fast and eventually signed on as roustabouts.

Day followed day in the Basin in glaring procession: up at six, breakfast, on the job at seven, dinner at twelve-fifteen, on the job again at one, supper at five-fifteen, sit about a while, sleep, up at six, breakfast, on the job,—and so on and on and on, hemmed in forever by that grey circle of rimrock. Occasionally the monotony would be varied, as when Frank Du Fran was blown up by a defective boiler, or one of the tar-paper houses went up in flames while the neighbors stood helplessly by without water or fire-fighting apparatus.

These things caused a slight commotion, which immediately flattened out, however, into the dead calm of "all work and no play." . . .

62. TEAMSTERS' STRIKE

A story of the Monday battle as seen from the viewpoint of a union leader follows:

"We built up our reserves in this way. At short time intervals during an entire day we sent fifteen or twenty pickets pulled in from all over the city into the Central Labor Union headquarters. . . . So that although nobody knew it, we had a detachment of six hundred men there, each armed with clubs, by Monday morning. Another nine hundred or so we held in reserve at strike headquarters. In the market itself, pickets without union buttons were placed in key positions. There remained scattered through the city, at their regular posts, only a skeleton picket line. The men in the market were in constant communication through motorcycles and telephone with headquarters. The special deputies [citizens' army] were gradually pushed by our pickets to one side and isolated from the cops. When that was accomplished the signal was given and the six hundred men poured out of Central Labor Union headquarters. They marched in military formation, four abreast, each with their club, to the market. They kept on coming. When the socialites . . . and the rest who had expected a little picnic with a mad rabble, saw this bunch, they began to get some idea what the score was. Then we called on the pickets from strike headquarters who marched into the center of the market and encircled the police. They [the police] were put right in the center with no way out. At intervals we made sallies on them to separate a few. This kept up for a couple of hours, till finally they drew their guns. We had anticipated this would happen, and that then the pickets would be unable to fight them. You can't lick a gun with a club. . . . So we picked out a striker, a big man and utterly fearless, and sent him in a truck with twenty-five pickets. He was instructed to drive right into the formation of cops and stop for nothing. We knew he'd do it. Down the street he came like a bat out of hell, with his horn honking and into the market arena. The cops held up their hands for him to stop, but he kept on; they gave way and he was in the middle of them. The pickets jumped out on the cops. We figured by intermixing with the cops in hand-to-hand fighting, they would not use their guns because they would have to shoot cops as well as strikers. Cops don't like to do that.

"Casualties for the day included for the strikers a broken collar bone, the cut-open skull of a picket who swung on a cop and hit a striker by mistake as the cop dodged, and a couple of broken ribs. On the other side, roughly thirty cops were taken to the hospital."

The battle with the deputies and police in retreat spread to all corners of the city. As late as ten o'clock that night the pickets continued to mop up, or to settle individual accounts in alleys and bars. . . .

One of the leaders and organizers of the citizens' army records his side of it as follows: "There came news that there was going to be trouble in the market district, and Colonel Watson (the military leader of the special deputies) agreed to help with these men. . . . Everyone was divided into sections and it was agreed there would be a uniformed policemen with each section.

"Once in the market we were in touch with our headquarters constantly, with the sheriff and the chief of police. Our men, you understand, were not armed except with a small stick. Colonel Watson had refused to arm them, a good many having no military experience whatever. He was undoubtedly wise. Well, the police did not hold the crowd back. They simply held up their hands to their shoulders and allowed themselves to be pushed till the crowd entered the market. Then unexpectedly the police on duty were relieved and a new detail appeared, which as far as we can discover had no instructions whatever regarding our outfit. . . .

"The strikers were armed with lead pipes, baseball bats with barbed wire around them, and every other goddam thing. Arthur Lyman was killed and there were a great many serious injuries. . . . They were ready to murder us. We armed ourselves with shotguns and side-arms, and went out and stood there facing 'em. Well, when they saw the guns they stopped, and jeered at us. Finally we managed to push our way out. . . .

"After the trouble in the market, I carried side-arms and arranged for special protection for my wife and children. I carried a gun in the office or anywhere I went for three months.

"When the battle was over we tried to keep the men together for a while, but they fell away. *They refused to be exposed to the slaughter when the police offered them absolutely no protection.* And besides there was no more need for them; the strike was settled shortly after."

63. FRUIT OF THE LOOM

A woman comes out through the gate and empties her pan of water into the open gutter of the main street. She is large-boned and stout and her face is sallow. More than thirty-five years ago her husband came from Belgium to work in the mills, and she, his sweetheart, followed. She had come from a "good" family—school teachers and not mill workers. But she could not speak English, so she, too, went to the mill. Now the husband is dead. A daughter and a son, both weavers who average $21 each for a full week's work, support the mother and a younger sister in school. For their five rooms they pay $1 a week rent taken out of the pay envelopes at the mill. Crocheted rugs cover the oilcloth on the kitchen floor. "We need them," the daughter explains; "the floor is so damp." The dirt cellar below is, indeed, constantly damp for the hill behind is of rock and drains off to the uncemented cellars below. . . .

Rhode Island has virtually no mandatory factory-inspection law. Sanitary conditions are left to the discretion of the inspector, at present a political appointee who has held office for twenty-four years.

A former health officer of the Valley says that mill floors in some cases are not washed more than once a year. The law is very lenient about heating, ventilation, lighting, fire requirement, and dangerous machinery.

In the cotton mill a certain amount of humidity must be created artificially by humidifiers, that the cotton may be in proper condition to work up. In Rhode Island there is no law to regulate the humidity in the workrooms nor the source or purity of water used for humidifying purposes.

"It's too hot for any person to work in those mills fifty-four hours," said a town physician who has always lived in the villages. "It's not warm, it's *hot*. Many a time I've seen a girl come out of the mill from an atmosphere of 92, 96, or 98 degrees, her hair wet from the sprinklers, and then stand and wait in the cold outside for the car that runs only every half hour. Yes there's lots of tuberculosis and asthma. We don't know how much. We've no statistics."

The Valley takes advantage of the fifty-four hours which the state allows women to work. I asked a Portuguese, out making his garden, who cooked the meals, for he had told me he had two children in school and that he and his wife both worked in the mill. "Oh, he," pointing to the wife who stood on the door step with the broom. "He get up five o'clock. He get breakfast and go mill ten minute 'fore seven. He get home twenty minute 'fore six. He cook meal."

"And you help I suppose?"

"Me? No! Who want do somethin' after get out that damn jail?"

But Rhode Island, which, because of her textile industry, has at work the highest percentage of girls between the ages of sixteen and twenty-one of any state in the union (67 per cent of the girls of this age in the state are at work), not only allows them to work fifty-four hours but also permits them to work at night. Consequently more than 2000 women are employed on night shifts in the textile industry. These conditions continue in the face of the facts that, according to the draft board, the state is the most illiterate of any of the northern states and is but fourth from the bottom for the union, and that it had the highest percentage of boys physically unfit for service of any state—the result, it is not unlikely, of her indifference to the conditions under which her mothers and future mothers work.

When the children reach the age of fourteen they too start for the mill. It makes no difference what grade they are in. If they can read and write a simple English sentence they are passed as ready to enter the industrial world. And they sweep up the dust and help around the machinery in the heat and noise for eight hours a day until they are sixteen, when the federal law releases them to work Rhode Island's ten-hour day. . . .

A conservative estimate would place the percentage of children fourteen and fifteen years old at work at 50 or 60 per cent. . . . Records in Woonsocket, a cotton mill town in the Blackstone Valley, show 69.9 per cent of children at work left school before the sixth grade.

With the women and children at work, the family budget—under which no single wage earner supports the household but even the mothers and children contribute to it—comes into existence. And there are many styles of family budget in the Valley. There is the outside man or common laborer, whose daughter after a year or two in the mill makes more as an operator than he makes as the head of a family, and who likewise contributes more to the household. There is the typical family in which the father, after the children are released for work, is no longer the responsible financial head but becomes a boarder in his own household. There is the family in which the son, after he becomes financially independent, boards in the village or in the next town and thus escapes family responsibility. With an average wage of $800 in the textile mills of the Valley there is no question even in the minds of the employers that the family wage is a necessity even for the smallest families living in the worst tenements.

The people who shift back and forth from these houses to these mills look like people anywhere. There are no sunbonnets or shawls. The girls, their hair bobbed, wear plaid skirts and sweaters and scarfs —at least while they are new to the mill. The church is the center of the recreation as well as the devotion of the Valley. The school has no place in its recreational life. When the children leave in the afternoon it is closed except for the citizenship classes for foreigners— evening classes in certain of the villages, which may be attended by people from the other villages, their carfare paid by the school board. "It's cheaper than to keep the school here open," a superintendent explained efficiently. If they are not at the movies the boys may be found evenings gambling on the edge of town, and the girls walking with their "fellows" or at home sewing until they turn in at nine o'clock. In recent years a girls' club with units in different villages has been organized and affiliated with the National League of Girls' Clubs. . . .

* * *

Thus they live and thus they work. Theirs the inheritance of a labor policy which aimed to bring in lowest grade labor, and use it as uncomplaining machinery. . . . Stephen A. Knight, one of the Knight brothers whose enterprise built up for the family the great Knight interests, speaking before a club in Providence in 1906, when he was over seventy years of age, drew a picture of the old days. Said Mr. Knight:

". . . The running time for that mill, on an average, was about fourteen hours per day. In the summer time we went in as early as we could see, worked about an hour and a half and then had a half hour for breakfast. At twelve o'clock we had another half hour for dinner and then we worked until the stars were out.

"From September twentieth until March twentieth, we went to work at five o'clock in the morning and came out at eight o'clock at night, having the same hours for meals as in the summer time.

"For my services I was allowed 42 cents per week, which, being analyzed, was 7 cents per day, or ½ cent per hour.

"The proprietor of that mill was accustomed to make a contract with his help on the first day of April, for the coming year. The contract was supposed to be sacred and it was looked upon as a disgrace to ignore the contracts thus made. On one of these anniversaries, a mother with several children suggested to the proprietor that the pay seemed small. The proprietor replied, 'You get enough to eat, don't you?' The mother said. 'Just enough to keep the wolf from the door.' He then remarked, 'You get enough clothes to wear, don't you?' To which she answered, 'Barely enough to cover our nakedness.' 'Well,' said the proprietor, 'We want the rest.' And that proprietor, on the whole, was as kind and considerate to his help as was any other manufacturer at that time. . . ."

64.   I'M SAD AND WEARY

1

I'm sad and weary; I've got the hungry ragged blues;
Not a penny in my pocket to buy the thing I need to use.

2

I woke up this morning with the worst blues I ever had in my life;
Not a bite to cook for breakfast, a poor coal miner's wife.

3

When my husband works in the coal mines, he loads a car on every trip,
Then he goes to the office that evening and gits denied of scrip.

4

Just because it took all he had made that day to pay his mine expense,
A man that'll work for coal-light and carbide, he ain't got a speck of sense.

5

All the women in the coal camps are a-sitting with bowed-down heads,
Ragged and barefooted, the children a-crying for bread.

6

No food, no clothes for our children, I'm sure this ain't no lie,
If we can't git more for our labor, we will starve to death and die.

7

Listen, friends and comrades, please take a friend's advice,
Don't load no more that dirty coal till you git a living price.

8

Don't go under the mountains with the slate a-hanging over your heads,
And work for just coal-light and carbide and your children a-crying for
  bread.

9

This mining town I live in is a sad and lonely place,
Where pity and starvation is pictured on every face.

10

Ragged and hungry, no slippers on our feet,
We're bumming around from place to place to get a little bite to eat.

11

All a-going round from place to place bumming for a little food to eat.
Listen, my friends and comrades, please take a friend's advice,
Don't put out no more of your labor, till you get a living price.

12

Some coal operators might tell you the hungry blues are not bad;
They are the worst blues this poor woman ever had.

* * *

Debs Moreland, being duly sworn, says:

I am a resident of the town of Panzy, Harlan County, Kentucky.
I was born in Birmingham, Alabama, and lived there until 1925 when
I came to Panzy where I have since resided, being employed during
such time by the Perkin Harlan Coal Company, in the capacity of
miner.

On April 7, 1931, the employees of the Perkin Harlan Coal Company went out on strike. I was among them. From that date until
the present time, although the mine has resumed periodic operation
I have not been reemployed there, or elsewhere.

I was arrested on or about August 24th and placed in jail where I was held on a trumped-up charge of Criminal Syndicalism until September 26th, when I was released without having been brought to trial. Judge D. C. Jones called me into his office that night about 6 P.M. and asked me to leave the State of Kentucky. He said, "I will release you on condition you do not go back and resume work which you have been doing." He asked me whether I belonged to the National Miners Union. I replied in the affirmative. He said he proposed to do away with the National Miners Union on the ground that it was a Communist organization and inquired whether I was aware of the fact that the National Miners Union was a branch of the Communist Party's affiliated bodies. I replied that I had not been aware of it, but that if conditions in Harlan County would be improved by the Communists or anyone else, I would throw my lot in with them. During this conversation, Judge Jones stated there would not be a chance of my getting work in Harlan County, intimating that I was to be blacklisted.

On October 15th, at about 11 P.M., four of John Henry Blair's imported deputy sheriffs knocked on my door, called me by my name, and when I opened the door rushed by me into the house. I recognized these as the same men who had come to my house time and again and searched it, claiming to have search warrants. These were a part of a group who were working hand in hand with the officials and the mine owners. They said, "We have a warrant against you for banding and confederating." I asked to see the warrant. One of them said, "You don't have to see this. You are the man we want." I said, "It's mighty funny you have a warrant for me for banding and confederating. I have not been in any trouble." They said, "You know how it is. We have to do our duty. We have the warrant and we have to take you in. You can tell that to the judge."

I was hustled into their auto. They drove through Harlan into Virginia, up at the top of Big Black Mountain, altogether a distance of about sixty miles. When we reached a section uninhabited for miles about, in the midst of a thick forest, the car stopped. On one side of the road was a steep embankment, almost perpendicular, which fell to a depth of about forty feet; on the other side was a sheer precipice at the top of which was an impenetrable forest. It was then about one-thirty in the morning, and a dark, moonless night. Three of these hired thugs got out of the car. The fourth sought to obtain information from me as to the number of organizers there were for the National Miners Union in the county, how many guns we had, and where our guns were. I said I had no knowledge of these matters. He said, "You are nothing but a thoroughbred red, and we haven't any use for you.

And we intend to break it up." At that point he said, "Unload." And followed me out of the car.

I emerged from the car and they formed a circle about me. I asked what they intended to do, beat me up? One answered, "No, you son of a bitch, we are not going to beat you up. We are going to kill you. We are damned tired of being bothered with you reds." At that time I was given a terrific blow from behind on the back of my neck which felled me. When I arose, another one hit me on the cheek and knocked me down again. They pulled me to my feet, tearing at my clothes. I saw that my only hope was to make a dash, so I tore loose and made a lunge over the embankment. I slid and rolled down the embankment about thirty feet . . . until I was stopped by a large rock. I lay there half stunned, just conscious of their flashlights playing about and the whiz of bullets flying all around me. About twenty-five shots were fired. Then I heard them say, "That's one red son of a bitch we are rid of." I saw the reflection of the headlights of their car rounding the curve as they drove away.

I was unable to move and lay there until about 5:30 A.M. Then after numerous attempts I succeeded in reaching the top of the bank. At about six o'clock a car came along and at my request consented to take me along to Big Stone Gap, a town about ten miles further into Virginia.

From there, I made my way to Chattanooga, Tennessee, then to Lexington, Kentucky, then to New York.

It was not until a week after I had been kidnaped from my home for the purpose of murder that I was able to communicate with my wife and child in Panzy. I received a letter from my wife thereafter that Blair denies having issued any warrant for me at any time.

(signed) DEBS MORELAND

Sworn to before me this fourth day
  of November, 1931
(signed) HERMAN CERBERT

*   *   *

Q. Are you a native of Kentucky?

A. I have been here about ten years, I reckon. I came here from the North. My husband is a native Kentuckian and was born and raised in this State.

Q. Is he a miner?

A. Yes, sir.

Q. Has he always been?

A. Yes, sir.

Q. Have you any children?

A. I have got two.

Q. Are they young?

A. Yes, sir.

Q. They don't contribute to your support?

A. No.

Q. Do you live in a Company town?

A. Yes, sir.

Q. How much rent do you pay for this house you occupy?

A. Eight dollars a month, without lights.

Q. How much does your husband average a month?

A. He has been working about three weeks but he hasn't averaged a dollar a day since he started there.

Q. When did he start there.

A. I reckon about three weeks ago. . . .

Q. Is he a strong man?

A. Yes, indeed, my man is a big, strong man and a good coal man. Anybody around any of the mines where he has been will tell you that he is a good coal man.

Q. Since 1927, would you say that you have had as much as $50 a month to live on?

A. No, sir, I wouldn't.

Q. You say he is working now?

A. Yes, but he had to go to work in order to get a house, a Company house. He didn't have no money to rent an outside house and he had to take a job at the mine to get a house.

Q. Has he received any money since he went there two or three weeks ago?

A. Just scrip.

Q. How do you manage to live?

A. We have just managed to exist. I will tell you that I have had one dollar in the last three days to live on, my husband and myself and two children.

Q. I wonder how you distribute that money around?

A. We live on beans and bread. We don't get no dinner. There don't none of you know how hard a man works that works in the mines, and I'll tell you what I had to put in his bucket this morning for him to eat and work hard all day, there was a little cooked pumpkin and what you folks call white meat, just fat white bacon, and that's what he took in the mines to eat and work on and he had water gravy for breakfast and black coffee.

Q. Water gravy—what is that?

A. Water and grease and little flour in it, and he had black coffee.

Q. What do you give to the children?

A. They had the same breakfast and they don't get no dinner.

Q. Where do you get clothes?

A. We don't get none.

Q. Where did you get those you have on?

A. This dress was give to me and the shoes I have on was give to me—and this coat I have on I bought six years ago and my children is naked.

Q. They probably don't go to school?

A. They are not in any situation to go to school because they have no shoes on their feet and no underwear on them and the few clothes they have they are through them.

* * *

You go to bed in a bag of rags but the hellbound Criminal Syndicalist law forbids you to speak.

Hoover says he is unable to handle the situation.

The thing I say is the National Miners Union is ready to handle it, to give you the same livin' conditions you had before the government put in these laws that were unjust. The National Miners stand for the principles that our forefathers fought for us.

The United Mine Workers in their day was a success but we got traitors in and they sold us out. I was a delegate here that was of the Convention. In 1927–28 I was not a member of any union but I was sent to vote the Lewis issue, and they gave me $75. I took the money. That's what they take the money for, and they have the money and you have the bread and beans.

I know some time men will have to make a complete sacrifice; hundreds of men's lives will be sacrificed; but nothing good ever came without somebody making a sacrifice. I love my children but this is the only reason that I would leave my children and make the great sacrifice.

I may be victimized for this but if Judge Jones thinks I am better in jail, then let it be so because I will get better food there than at home. The company for which I now work refuses to reduce my rent one dollar because they say they cannot do it. Yet that man has been able to pay a gun thug (I know because he is my own brother-in-law) to patrol the street.

I am going to feed my children. I am going to kill, murder, rob for my children because I won't let my children starve.

The National Miners Union is the only thing that has not failed us. We don't have to pay $12,000 a year for a man to sell us out and to send us back to scab. In that 1928 convention we voted a raise for Lewis from $8,000 to $10,000 and then we came back home and told the men that they would have to take a cut in wages. Is that fair?

Whatever you get you have to take from the capitalist. We beg and beg and tell them our starving conditions but it don't do no good.

I just made up my mind that I won't work and go hungry any more. Last winter was a cold winter and I want to say to you that during the winter I worked every day at such poor wages and could hardly buy food for my children, who had to go out without a bit of underwear.

And then you say that this is a good country. I say that it is not a good country that denies a man a good fair wage.

We don't want to get rich. We want to eat. If you put a man into poverty then you send him down to Hell and sin. Believe me it would not take much for me to go down and steal a good square meal.

65. TIREBUILDERS IN AKRON

Just before noon a heavy-shouldered man with a thatch of bright red hair strolled up to the main factory gates at Goodyear.

As the factory hands shuffled in a silent mass past the brick walls, the red-haired man stepped forward and held out a flimsy sheet of paper. "The NRA," a bold headline across the page said, "gives workers the right to organize." "Take 'em, boys," the man said, and the workers held out their hands and walked slowly away reading: "The speedup is killing you. Your wages have been cut. President Roosevelt has given you the chance to organize a union without interference from the rubber bosses. Take it."

The red-haired man was Wilmer Tate, president of the Akron local of the Machinists' Union, or at least what there was of it, and secretary of the Central Labor Union, what there was of *that*. He was one of the five men in Akron who, in the last days of May, decided the time had come to organize a rubberworkers' union. These five set the match to the tinder already dried and laid neatly for the firemakers. The rubberworkers soon believed, blindly, passionately, fiercely, that the union would cure all their troubles, end the speedup, make them rich with wages. They had no clear idea, and nobody told them, just how the union would accomplish these aims. Vaguely, they thought President Roosevelt might just order the rubber bosses to raise wages and quit the speedup. Some of them talked strike, but when they spoke about a strike, it was always something gay, like a picnic, a contest that you won right away without any trouble.

Going on strike is rather a formal way of putting what really happened. Tirebuilders simply stopped work and began yelling, "The hell with the speedup! We're through."

The plant manager appeared in the yard, his face red and outraged. "Go back to work," he bellowed from the steps of the office building.

"Boo-o-o-o!" yelled the tirebuilders and after them the pitmen and the moldworkers.

"Listen," the plant superintendent said earnestly, his voice betraying panic. "Listen, we'll raise your wages. I absolutely guarantee that any injustices in pay will be adjusted. I guarantee it."

"Boo-o-o-o!" replied the crowd jovially. Some of the men laughed. It was rather funny, seeing the plant manager so red in the face, promising pay raises, begging.

Now a man leaped up on a truck-engine hood. "Let's have a meeting tomorrow and take a strike vote. What do you say, boys?"

The plant manager broke in, "You can't talk like that on company property. You get out of this yard. You're fired, whoever you are."

"Fired?" said the speaker. "Fired? Hell, I'm on strike. How about it, boys?"

"You said it!" screamed the crowd. "You said it."

That was the way it began. A man in the truck tire department said he wouldn't stand for it any more, and out of that came the strike. The crowd marched out of the gates singing and booing the plant manager and laughing. The rubberworkers went home confident and easy in their minds. . . .

That was the kind of strike it was. The president of the company came down on the picket line and bawled out the strikers. The superintendent turned up not once but half a dozen times and got red in the face yelling at his ex-workers. He kept thinking that the next time he yelled at them they'd surely stop all this nonsense and go back to work. On the surface it looked like a friendly, good-natured strike. The police hung around the picket line and ate the strikers' sandwiches. The strikers cracked jokes with the maintenance engineers allowed in and out of the plant. . . .

Old cars roared through the streets of East Akron long after midnight. Young fellows hung on the running boards screaming, "We won! Boy, we won! The strike's over! We won!"

Saloons kept open until dawn. Men danced in the streets and sang on street corners. It was like Armistice Day, it was like the day Lindbergh landed in France. The kids stayed up and hopped around first on one foot then on another shrieking, "Daddy, let me blow the horn now."

The men on the night shift at Goodyear just quit work and came on out into the happy night to help celebrate. East Akron was wild with joy. The strike was over. The strike was won. Now things would be better. From this day forward things would be new and different.

Next day, in the heat, the valley was quiet while exhausted men slept off the celebration. In the new stillness a few men carefully re-read the strike settlement. In the light of day it seemed very different. . . . The union had not won recognition. . . .

The company agreed not to support the company union financially. That was something.

The company agreed not to reduce wage rates. That also was something.

Finally, the company agreed not to discriminate against strikers.

Not bad, the careful men said to themselves, not good. A beginning, but only a beginning. . . .

Nevertheless, the strike ended in a wave of good feeling. The valley people were satisfied for the moment. The newspapers said proudly that no heads had been broken, no arrests had been made. In Akron, both employers and employees knew how to conduct themselves in a labor dispute.

That's what the papers said.

The prelude was over.

* * *

Promptly at midnight the truck-tire department started work. Under pools of light, the big men stood at their machines. A wheel slowly revolved, as they wound on strips of heavy rubber and fabric. Their hands flashed. Helpers came in quietly and laid piles of carefully folded material beside their machines. Just over their heads, a conveyor belt clattered slowly by. Suspended from the belt were huge thick hooks. Every few minutes, one of the darting hands ripped the finished tire from the machine, slammed it on a hook, and went back to the re-volving wheel. Foremen walked slowly up and down the long lines of tirebuilders, checking material, glancing at the finished tires, sending machine repairmen to a faltering wheel.

No human sound came from this vast room. The clatter and shriek and roar of the conveyor belt and the revolving wheels, the drone of motors, the broken rush and squeaking halt of electric factory trucks, drowned out even a brief salute of one worker to another.

But as a flashing hand reached up to slam a tire on the hook, the worker had half a second when his body came near to the tirebuilder on the next machine.

"Two o'clock," a man muttered as he swung up his tire. The tire-builder next to him did not look up from the revolving wheel. His hands never stopped their expert, rapid motions. He hardly nodded. But when his tire went up to the conveyor belt he said, his face a blank, with such a tight mouth that he might merely have been shifting his wad of chewing tobacco, "Two o'clock."

The man at the next machine never even looked his way. But, a moment later, and this was strange, for he was such an expert workman, he dropped his heavy tire tool. It clattered to the floor quite near the fourth machine. The foreman looked up, his ears trained to pick out of the constant uproar a different, unexpected noise. But he only saw a tirebuilder picking up his tool, brushing against a friend.

"Two o'clock," the clumsy tirebuilder murmured.

After the first hour, the foremen on the truck-tire floor were considerably annoyed when it appeared that two of their best workmen were apparently suffering from kidney trouble. At least they left the floor to go to the washroom; this was nearly unheard of the first hour. A tirebuilder could hardly afford to go to the washroom so early on the shift, because if he went more than once, his pay for the night would take a bad cut.

When they came back, one of them nodded, the barest kind of jerk of the head. Downstairs, in the auto tires, a man on the top machine was saying, as he reached over to grab material, "Two o'clock." And next to him, an auto tirebuilder was dropping his tool and picking it up, saying, through hardly moving lips, "Two o'clock."

A little after one-thirty, a foreman on the truck-tire floor went downstairs to talk to the super on the auto floor. "Everything O.K.?" he asked, shouting in his friend's ear, to be heard.

"I guess so," the foreman from auto tires replied. The two men stood together watching the rows of flashing hands, the rhythmically moving backs. The noise sounded in their ears as familiar music. They knew every variation and could separate the proper drone of the motors from a sudden brief whine of a machine gone sour. Tonight the noise sounded all right.

"I got the jitters, I guess," the super from upstairs said, shaking his big shocky head like a puzzled hunting dog.

"Me, too," the head from the auto tires answered. "I keep feeling there's something phony going on here. But I don't know. The fellows ain't talking any. They're making fast time tonight."

"It's goddamned funny they ain't talking," the upstairs foreman growled. "The last two nights they've been howling. . . . Tonight they're as quiet as a bunch of ghosts."

"Yeah," the auto super replied. "I got a feeling somethin's wrong. Them guys is watching us right now."

The two foremen stared at the tirebuilders. Their hands wove the usual quick .pattern. Their heads were bent over their plies. To a stranger's eye, they were lost in their work, each man a picture of useful concentration. But to the two foremen, there was something wrong. They felt the side-glances of these men. They felt the impact of a quick flash of eyes. They sensed hostility.

"Listen," the foreman from upstairs said, "if anything goes wrong, I'll close up the fire doors right away. You do the same."

"What's going to go wrong?" the auto super said.

"Nothing," the truck head growled, "but if it should, we don't want nothing to spread."

"Yeah." The auto foreman stood unhappily in the doorway as the upstairs super left. His eyes wandered from one hefty tirebuilder to another. Nothing wrong, he could see. But he felt queer. In his bones, he knew something was coming off. Jesus, it gave a man the creeps watching those guys at their machines and knowing they were watching you back, and hating you, and planning some goddamned trick to upset the shift and maybe lose you your job. He walked down the line, brushing past a dozen tirebuilders. They didn't even look up, but he could feel their backs stiffen as he passed. The sons-of-bitches, they were up to something. But what? What?

It was 1:45 A.M. on January 29, 1936.

Upstairs the foreman passed down the lines, his ears cocked for a murmur, for the barest whisper. . . . He was sure getting the jitters lately. But, my God, the company didn't realize how sore these boys were at the rate cut, and you couldn't tell them thickheaded guys in the front office. No, all they'd say was "We hold you accountable for unbroken production in your department." Jesus, was that the way to treat a good loyal company man, threaten to can him if anything went wrong?

The foreman paced slowly past his workmen, his eyes darting in and out of the machines, eager for any betraying gesture. He heard no word, and he saw no gesture. The hands flashed, the backs bent, the arms reached out in monotonous perfection. The foreman went back to his little desk and sat squirming on the smooth-seated swivel chair. He felt profoundly disturbed. Something, he knew, was coming off. But what? For God's sake, what?

It was 1:57 A.M. January 29, 1936.

The tirebuilders worked in smooth frenzy, sweat around their necks, under their arms. The belt clattered, the insufferable racket and din and monotonous clash and uproar went on in steady rhythm. The clock on the south wall, a big plain clock, hesitated, its minute hand jumped to two. A tirebuilder at the end of the line looked up, saw the hand jump. The foreman was sitting quietly staring at the lines of men working under the vast pools of light. . . .

The tirebuilder at the end of the line gulped. His hands stopped their quick weaving motions. Every man on the line stiffened. All over the vast room, hands hesitated. The foreman saw the falter, felt it instantly. He jumped up, but he stood beside his desk, his eyes darting quickly from one line to another.

This was it, then. But what was happening? Where was it starting? He stood perfectly still, his heart beating furiously, his throat feeling dry, watching the hesitating hands, watching the broken rhythm.

Then the tirebuilder at the end of the line walked three steps to the master safety switch and, drawing a deep breath, he pulled up the heavy wooden handle. With this signal, in perfect synchronization, with the rhythm they had learned in a great mass-production industry, the tirebuilders stepped back from their machines.

Instantly, the noise stopped. The whole room lay in perfect silence. The tirebuilders stood in long lines, touching each other, perfectly motionless, deafened by the silence. A moment ago there had been the weaving hands, the revolving wheels, the clanking belt, the moving hooks, the flashing tire tools. Now there was absolute stillness, no motion anywhere, no sound.

Out of the terrifying quiet came the wondering voice of a big tirebuilder near the windows: "Jesus Christ, it's like the end of the world."

He broke the spell, the magic moment of stillness. For now his awed words said the same thing to every man, "We done it! We stopped the belt! By God, we done it!" And men began to cheer hysterically, to shout and howl in the fresh silence. Men wrapped long sinewy arms around their neighbors' shoulders, screaming, "We done it! We done it!"

For the first time in history, American mass-production workers had stopped a conveyor belt and halted the inexorable movement of factory machinery.

The foremen . . . retreated. They locked the fire doors and, five minutes later, opened them on demand. They were amazed by the organization of these revolting workmen. After the first hysteria had died down, the confusion disappeared at once. The ringleader, the man who switched the current off, climbed on the foreman's desk and shouted, "O.K., fellows. Now any of you guys here who ain't with us can get the hell out right now. Go home and stay home and don't let's see your yellow-livered face around here again. Anybody want to leave?"

Nobody did. "O.K.," the speaker went on. "Now we got a lot of things to do. First, we got to have a committee to visit other departments, and let's have some volunteers who aint' chicken-livered." The whole truck-tire department wanted to go. The leader picked half a dozen. "You go downstairs and combine with the auto boys' committee and, listen, it's up to you guys to shut this whole goddamned plant down, see?"

"O.K.," the speaker continued quickly. "Now we got to have a committee to police the floor. We don't want no machinery broken we can get blamed for, and we got to keep the place clean. No gamblin' for money either, and absolutely no drinking. We frisk everybody who comes in, for bottles. We don't take nobody's word for it. A couple of drunks would make this sitdown strike look punk."

"Sitdown strike," the crowd repeated. It was a good phrase. The tirebuilders had never heard it before. They liked it. . . .

The factory superintendent's office was a glum place. Every few minutes a new foreman came in, his eyes blazing, his mouth twitching with rage. "I don't know how they found out," the new ones would say. "My God, I had the fire door locked, but all of a sudden, one of them was up there pulling the switch and right away they open the door and this goddamned roving committee comes in and starts to appoint a police committee and pass out union cards, and get them to elect somebody to this here negotiation committee."

Firestone Plant One gradually shut down completely. The departments that didn't actually sitdown and strike were paralyzed by lack of work or materials. The delicate mechanism of mass production was dealt a brutal fatal blow. Engineers had worked for years to synchronize every labor process in the great factory. The most remote departments were dependent on the flow of materials from some other faraway corner of the great plant. But once the line was broken, factory operations came to an uneven, jerking halt.

As dawn came, the day-shift workers lined up at the time-house, punching in their cards. Still dazed with sleep, they stumbled off streetcars, not knowing what had happened inside the walls of the great yellow brick factory. Yet they found out instantly. . . . The new shift came on, and joined the old sitdowners, the veterans, and listened jealously to their bragging tales of how *they* started it, *they* turned off the current. By noon the men who had come to work at dawn were also veterans, able to lord it over the newcomers. . . .

The strikers themselves were surprised and jubilant when they found so little resistance. They owned the factory. Nobody dared say them nay. So they used power carefully. Clean-up squads kept the factory floors shining. The police committee looked darkly at a man who so much as swore. A tirebuilder, leaning on his machine to watch a tong game was warned by every other man on strike, "Watch out. Don't bust nothin'." Abashed sitdowners apologized to the union committee for suggesting poker at a penny limit. By a little after noon, the tire floors were so crowded a man could hardly find a place to sit down. Three shifts were on sitdown duty and men from the fourth shift illicitly sneaked past the gates and came up to get in on the excitement. Runners carried news between the sitdowners and the union hall. So-and-so's wife had called up to say more power to you, stick it out.

The valleys seethed with the story. Women ran, bundled up in old coats, across their front yards, to call on their neighbors and tell them what was going on at Firestone. Little boys boasted in school recess that their Pops were sitting down in the truck-tire department, and other small boys all but burst with envy and rushed home screaming, "Pa, why can't you sit down?" . . .

The Firestone management for twenty-four hours refused even to discuss settlement with the negotiation committee. . . . The second twenty-four hours they began to change their minds.

Still they hesitated. But at the beginning of the third full day of the sitdown, after fifty-three hours, foremen brought terrible news. All of Plant Two was ready to sitdown in sympathy unless there was an immediate settlement. . . .

Murphy sent for the negotiating committee and consigned to hell the opinions of his fellow factory superintendents. It was all very well to talk about a solid employer front, but in the face of something like this, a man had to act quickly or the whole situation would simply blow up in his face. The settlement promised immediate negotiation on the base rate. It offered three hours' pay per day to all workers who had lost time during the sitdown.

When the committee, breathless and excited, brought the news to the men up in the truck-tire department for a vote, they could hardly talk, they were so jubilant. And the strikers were quite beside themselves. They were getting paid, paid, mind you, for sitting down! And the rate would be negotiated. Glory Hallelujah! . . .

The sitdowners marched out singing, and the sound of their voices went everywhere in the valley. The Firestone sitdowners had won! They won! This sitdown business worked.

66.   TUNNEL WORKERS

FEDERAL EMERGENCY RELIEF ADMINISTRATION
DIVISION OF RESEARCH AND STATISTICS—RESEARCH SECTION
July 10, 1934

Subject: 15 wage earners, 14 of whom are dying of silicosis, provide sustenance for entire community of 91 persons at Vanetta, West Virginia.

Source: Report of Leon Brower, statistician for West Virginia. National Recovery Administration.

In the early months of 1930 large numbers of able-bodied Negroes were brought to Vanetta, West Virginia, an abandoned coal-mining settlement which was prosperous as late as 1925, to engage in the drilling of a three-mile tunnel required by an electric-power development. The mountain to be pierced was found to consist of pure silicate. In spite of the warnings of the West Virginia Department of Mines the contractors took no precautions against the consequences of the workers' breathing the dust, which causes silicosis, a disease which destroys lung tissues and ultimately causes suffocation. As early as the fall of 1930 thousands of workers died, allegedly of pneumonia, but exact figures are not available as many of the sick were allowed to wander away. The labor turnover on the job was estimated at more than 300 per cent.

On the completion of the project in September 1932, Vanetta reverted to the status of an abandoned village. In 1932 there were 91 persons in residence, occupying 61 tumble-down hovels: 14 children, 44 adult females, and 43 adult males. Of the latter all but 10 have silicosis. Support for the community comes from the earnings of 15 of the males, 14 of whom suffer from silicosis. Thirteen are engaged on a road-construction project eighteen miles away and are forced to walk to and from work, leaving them but five hours a day for labor. Moreover many, because of their illness, must lay off work every other day and are frequently too weak to lift a sledge hammer.

Quoting Mr. Brower:

"Coupled with all these hardships is starvation. Relief has always been spasmodic and irregular, and more irregular than is warranted. Every family related the lack of food, and for days at a time during the last winter they had nothing to eat. . . .

". . . Clothing was always inadequate, and there were numerous cases of slightly frozen limbs; also several families were evicted during winter, and nearly every family was served with eviction notices.

"Several men, gathered in a group, related how at first the older folks would economize on food so that the children could have more. And then the men cut their allowances to practically nothing so that the women could eat.

"Direct relief was seldom given. Many families received commodities, but very irregularly. Just three men were given CWA work and these three worked a few weeks only.

"The relief office is fourteen miles from the community. These people would get up at four o'clock and trudge through the heavy snow to the office inadequately clothed and hungry. Too often they found that the relief agency was in no position to give assistance." . . .

Statement of George Robison

Mr. Griswold: Please give your name and residence to the reporter.

Mr. Robison: George Robison, Vanetta, West Virginia.

Mr. Griswold: Tell the committee what you know about the work in that tunnel and the conditions under which it was performed.

Mr. Robison: I went to work there on September 1, 1931, as a driller. . . . They didn't allow any water on the bench drills. The drilling there had to be dry drilling otherwise they couldn't drill fast enough. . . .

. . . A fellow could drill three holes dry to one wet; that is, it's about three times faster when a fellow drills dry. In shooting at the head they rushed so that they did not even square at the top. The boss was always telling us to hurry, hurry, hurry. When the rocks were in danger of falling at any time the foreman kept telling us that everything was all right and that we should keep right on.

Mr. Griswold: Did they kill any men by falling rock?

Mr. Robison: Yes. Me and my buddy drilled only four feet from two other fellows drilling, and those two fellows got killed by falling rock. . . .

When they would bring in water to drink the dust would settle on top of it and one would have to drink that dust too. When drilling, the hole would go straight down and the air would then force the air back into one's face.

As dark as I am, when I came out of that tunnel in the mornings, if you had been in the tunnel too and had come out at my side, nobody could have told which was the white man. The white man was just as black as the colored man.

The groves near the camps had trees that were all colored with this dust. We all tried to clear our clothes somewhat in the parks or groves so as not to have the dust around the shacks. There was so much dust around those groves or parks that it looked like somebody had sprinkled flour around the place. . . .

The camps of the colored men were not close to the camps for the white men. If a colored man was sick and really couldn't go to work in the morning, he had to hide out before the shack rouster came around. That fellow had two pistols and a blackjack to force the men to go to work. He was a fat man and we called him what we called most of the other white men around there, "Cap." . . .

I worked on the night shift a while. We had to pay shack rent amounting to 75 cents a week; doctor bill amounted to 25 cents a week; hospital bill was 25 cents a week; the light bill was 25 cents a week. . . . I didn't get very much, I tell you. I always owed the company at the end of the week. . . . By the time one paid for three meals and got a pint of moonshine, everything was gone.

Mr. Randolph: Did the commissary sell moonshine?

Mr. Robison: No. When we began to cough we thought we had gotten a cold, and we thought it would be well to take some whisky for it. Then, too, we took the moonshine to cut the cold from the lungs. We got the moonshine every day; and I don't believe we could have stayed there without it.

When it got so a worker couldn't make it at all, when he got sick and simply couldn't go longer, the sheriff would come around and run him off the place, off the works. I have seen the sheriff and his men run the workers off their places when they were sick and weak, so sick and weak that they could hardly walk. Some of them would have to stand up at the sides of trees to hold themselves up. And the sheriff and his men could plainly see that the men were sick and unable to go, yet they kept making them keep on the move.

The workers were there from North Carolina, South Carolina, Georgia, Alabama, Florida. . . .

. . . They didn't have any private houses. Everybody on the job had to live on the company's property. One had to keep going on his job, because many hundreds of men were coming in by the trainload and hoboing it. . . .

. . . Many of the men died in the tunnel camps; they died in hospitals, under rocks, and every place else. A man named Finch, who was known to me, died under a rock from silicosis. I can go right now and point to many graves only two blocks from where I live there now. . . . I helped to bury about 35, I would say. . . .

Mr. Dunn of Pennsylvania: Have you silicosis?

Mr. Robison: Yes, sir. . . . For seven or eight months after I quit the tunnel work during which time I took medicine, I felt as good as I ever did; but after that I commenced to notice a slowing down. When I walked fast or up a hill I could notice that it cut down my breathing.

I talked to the different ones that were suing on account of their condition in 1932 and they told me I had better go to the doctor for examination. I went to Dr. Harless and he said, "Haven't you been working in that tunnel?" I told him, "Yes," and he said, "You have that tunnel dust on your lungs." . . . Dr. Harless stated on the witness stand during the trial that any man who had worked in that dust for only 24 hours was afflicted and he could not be cured. He had a list of men there that he said he could show had died from silicosis. He attended all these 35 men I helped to bury. He wasn't the company doctor at that time that I know of.

Mr. Dunn of Pennsylvania: . . . Did you take your case to court?

Mr. Robison: No. A little after that they got a settlement and they came around in cars with releases and said if we don't sign this we would not get anything. I wanted to get something at once because I wanted to leave right away. If one signed the release he was given a dollar. He gave me the pencil, and I signed, and he took the pencil back, and I didn't get anything at all, sir. . . .

Then I went to work in the mines. I tried to get a job in the mine, but the doctor turned me down. Then I thought up an idea of getting another fellow who could pass the doctor's examination to pass the examination for me, to stand the examination for me. He did that, it worked, and I got a job in the mine. . . . I worked there three months, when I took sick and had to go to the doctor myself. . . .

I went to mine in Montgomery and when they examined me the doctor asked, "Haven't you been working in the tunnel?" I said, "No," and he told me, "Now don't lie to me like that, I know you have." Then I said back at him, "Yes; I have worked a little there." Then he told me, "You are not strong enough to work in the mine."

Then I went to Fayetteville to the relief people for help. . . . They put me on relief at $3.50 a week. They cut that down to $1.50 a week and it stayed there until about last Christmas week, when they raised it back to $3.50 a week. I have five in my family.

Mr. Dunn of Pennsylvania: You are supposed to support your family on $3.50 a week?

Mr. Robison: That's what they allowed me; but the family would starve to death on that.

Mr. Dunn of Pennsylvania: What did you do when they reduced your relief allotment to $1.50 a week?

Mr. Robison: It so happens that there are some pretty good white people around that place. . . . I have lived mostly from the help good people have given to me. . . . I have two grown children, a son and a daughter. . . . My daughter cooks at the bus station and my son works in the mine. . . .

Mr. Randolph: How were you first approached . . . about this work being carried on in West Virginia?

Mr. Robison: I had not had a job for two years when I heard about this work in West Virginia. One couldn't get a job anywhere else then. A friend of mine had been up to West Virginia and he found this job. . . .

Mr. Randolph: Did you know what the wages would be before you left the South?

Mr. Robison: Yes. I had to have some work and I couldn't get anything there in the South. . . .

Mr. Marcantonio: How many hours a day did you put in?

Mr. Robison: Twelve hours.

Mr. Marcantonio: And during those twelve hours you worked persistently and there was no let-up?

Mr. Robison: If one let up the boss at once wanted to know what was the matter. A fellow simply had to keep on the move all the time.

Mr. Marcantonio: That is what I would call a speed-up system underneath the silica rock.

67. ON THE STREET

Falling mist, mixed with smudgy flakes of rubber smoke, made the streets damp and slippery. . . . Even at high noon the sky was quite dark and gusts of raw wind bit deeply into thin-covered chests and gloveless hands.

The deputy sheriffs who came to move the furniture out of the little frame house on Moon Street wore thick lumberjackets and warm knit caps with eartabs. Still they flapped their arms across their big chests and shuddered in the clammy cold.

The Miachiaroli kids, all eight of them, followed the deputy sheriffs silently in and out, back and forth, from the front door to the curbstone, watching with eight pairs of round black quiet eyes while the strange men carried out the stove, and the parlor best chair and the two bedsteads, and all the other familiar things of the household.

Just as the deputy sheriffs trundled the last big sofa down the porch steps, Mr. O'Lari, the man from the Unemployed Council, came running down the street. The Miachiaroli kids, huddled around the pile of furniture, shivering in the wet and cold, were glad to see him. He was such a pleasant jolly man. He called the oldest Miachiaroli boy, who was nine, "Old Man."

"Hello, Old Man," he said now. "I see they got a head start on us. Well, keep your chin up, fellow. It ain't all over yet."

The Miachiaroli boy grinned. Mr. O'Lari was funny and nice, and he cheered Pa up too. It was terrible to see Pa cry just like a baby. It made you ashamed. So it was good Mr. O'Lari came, because Pa sort of brightened up and that look on his face that scared you so, went away.

The Miachiarolis built a little bright fire on the curb and put their hands near its warmth and that made the long afternoon easier. Mr. O'Lari kept going away and coming back and every time he said to wait a little longer, everything would be all right in the end.

The sky began to get darker at four o'clock, and the mist turned into a fine rain that was almost sleet. Most of the Miachiaroli kids began to cry. The little bright fire could only warm your hands and feet, and the wind and rain made your back ache with cold.

Then just when Pa began to look all broken in the face again, Mr. O'Lari came back, and this time he brought with him a lot of big cheerful fellows in sort of ragged clothes. Two wheezing old Fords rattled down Moon Street and a lot more men clambered out. The neighbor boys came running and for a few minutes Moon Street was filled with the sound of big men rushing and running and marching down to the Miachiaroli house.

The rain was so cold, but these fellows from the Unemployed Council didn't seem to mind it. They were cheerful, and their voices were loud and sort of happy. Mr. O'Lari and a short little man climbed up on the front porch.

"Here's Scotty," Mr. O'Lari said, and all the big fellows standing around in the yard began to cheer.

Scotty didn't say much. It was getting dark and the rain was growing heavier. He just said, "Is this what we are coming to? Children, poorly clothed, being snatched out of bed and thrown into the streets? Are we goin' to stand it?"

After Scotty's speech, the big fellows picked up the furniture, the bedsteads, and the good chair, and the stove, and all the rest, and carried them back in the house. The crowd hurried, to get out of the rain, but they were careful of the furniture too; they didn't bang it up. The Miachiaroli kids danced around clapping their hands and saying, "Are you goin' to move us back in, mister? Are you?"

Finally their mother called them into the kitchen and told them to stay put; they would all catch colds. One of the big strangers made a nice fire and Mrs. Miachiaroli began to strip the wet coats off her kids and stand them up close to the stove to get warm. The lady next door brought over a kettle of soup, but the Miachiaroli kid Mr. O'Lari called "Old Man" was too excited to eat. He kept running out of the kitchen to watch Pa and the men from the Unemployed Council finish up the moving job.

Now it was nearly pitch-dark outside. Scotty called out to the crowd, "O.K., fellows, let's go. O'Lari, keep a dozen or so to see nothin' happens, and stay around for an hour or so."

Slowly the crowd trickled away. Mr. Miachiaroli stood on the front porch shaking hands. Scotty climbed into a ramshackle Ford and started down the street. A few young boys milled around in the front yard. O'Lari and a gang of workers were shoveling the coal back into the coal bin. In the rainy night a police cruiser turned into Moon Street, passed slowly by the house, disappeared, and then returned.

The rumble of the coal drowned out the first yell. On the second call for help O'Lari raced through the Miachiaroli house, stumbled over one of the smaller kids, burst through the front door to the porch. In the shadows he saw a policeman, night stick raised, aiming a blow at a gangling boy who stood arguing with him. O'Lari caught the night stick, crying, "Hey, what's the idea?"

Patrolman Emery Davis turned sharply. The shouting angry crowd pressed on his heels. He was alone. His cruiser partner had gone to call the station house for reinforcements, leaving him with a final warning. "Don't start no trouble. Just stand by until we get some help."

"What's the idea?" O'Lari repeated. "We ain't doin' nothin'. You can't hit a kid like that."

"You tell him, Alex," somebody in the crowd roared.

"You're under arrest!" Patrolman Davis shouted.

"What for?" O'Lari countered boldly. "Where's your warrant? What are you arresting me for?"

The crowd, muttering, closed in tightly around the cop and O'Lari. In the darkness the faces of the intent weary men seemed frightening to the policeman. He struck out wildly at O'Lari, hit him a glancing blow with the night stick.

"Hey!" O'Lari grunted, surprised. He swung out with his fist at the cop and missed. The policeman struck again with his night stick. O'Lari ducked. The cop, put off balance by his wild lunge, slipped and missed his footing. Kneeling, he drew his gun and fired.

The shot deafened the crowd. In the wild stampede to escape from this cop with the gun, men fell over each other, women screamed. O'Lari crumpled up silently and, spitting blood, fell to the porch.

O'Lari took four days to die. During those days the police and the city authorities made a desperate attempt to cover up the killing. First they said Patrolman Davis was critically injured too, but when Davis went home from the emergency ward next day, that fell through. Then they said O'Lari had attacked the policeman and egged on the crowd to beat him up, but in the end they had no witnesses to prove that.

Finally even the newspapers, which, the first day, carried savage stories blaming the riot on O'Lari, backed down. "Hunger cannot be clubbed down," the *Beacon Journal* wrote three days later; "neither can a destitute family's right to shelter be denied."

68. WHAT ONE CARPENTER FOUND

In the time when the jobs were scarce and lots of men were walking the streets in search for employment there were several large apartment houses in the process of construction in Long Island City, not far from where I lived. Several times I went over and asked the foreman whether they needed any carpenters and every time I received an answer something like this.

"Not just now. Perhaps next week. We hired men yesterday, the day before," and so on.

I noticed that all the men working there were Italians. They talked Italian among themselves and received their orders in Italian.

Then a letter came to me from a friend of mine, a member of my own race, telling me of a job in Far Rockaway. So I took a ride down there and got a job. It took me about twenty minutes to walk to the railway station and then about three-quarters of an hour with the train. So I traveled for about three months from Long Island City to Far Rockaway. In the meantime another bunch of carpenters came from Brooklyn via Manhattan to work in Long Island City.

The reason the carpenters took to traveling this way was that the foreman on the job felt lonesome without the people of his own race around him. The men also liked the boss of their own race better than a stranger and they didn't mind the traveling in order to be associated with their own.

In another slack season during the cold weeks in the end of January I had in mind a big hotel in the neighborhood of Grand Central. There was much carpenter work in sight there, on trim, a good gang working already and with many chances that a score of men might be hired perhaps tomorrow, the next day, or next Monday. So I kept my eye on the job and visited it regularly.

The foreman on the job seemed to be a very decent fellow. He wasn't stuck up because he was a foreman and had the power to hire and fire the men. Every time I talked to him he had a friendly face and was willing to answer queries and at no time showed any signs of being tired of new men and their questions. So I thought there may be something doing. And I came again. But unfortunately I was told every time that they had all the help they needed. It also happened that whenever I missed one single day, then that was the day the foreman hired new men. And I was informed of the sad fact next time I came round.

A young carpenter passed me in the hallway. His face looked familiar to me because I had seen him every time I came over.

"Looking for a job again?" he asked me.

"Yes," said I. "The foreman told me to come around today; he said he might need new men."

"Can you talk Yiddish?"

"No."

"Well, you wouldn't get the job. That's the game here." The cover fell off my eyes. I saw immediately what I could have noticed on the first day, but to which I had paid no particular attention. All the men working there were Jews. . . .

It is useless to enumerate all the races. Because all are equally guilty. And I haven't anything especially against those I have named. All the building trades men realize this. But their attitude is that of getting work. Every foreman feels that his race has been discriminated against and he wants them to come back, when he sees the opportunity. As a result the men suffer. And they know it. Most employers usually also understand this, but they don't take the matter seriously. The rent payers also suffer but they don't know it. Whenever an inexperienced man does work, there is always a unusual waste of material, things that have to be done over, and the whole bill will be paid by the tenant.

We don't ask ourselves why the building trades must travel so much where there is lots of work near by. But people are civilized here and they use civilized methods in their race conflicts. It merely hurts our pocketbooks, but since that is a very common occurrence we pay very little attention to it.

VIII

Workers in a
Managerial Economy

THE two preceding chapters have presented a wide array of materials, statistical and autobiographical, which illuminate the major transformations which occurred during the quarter-century between the entrance of the United States into World War I and the outbreak of World War II. In order to consider the period historically, we will, as previously suggested, divide it into two parts—the years of prosperity up to 1929 and the years of depression thereafter.

The facts, figures, and descriptive materials provide a vivid account of the fluctuating fortunes of the American working man during this dynamic quarter-century, with its promise of a brave new world followed by a nadir of despondency and despair. We will introduce now another dimension to the story by calling attention to a series of forces operating within the ranks of labor itself, in industry, in government, and in the larger society which significantly affected what transpired both in the good years up to 1929 and the bad years that followed.

Rising Standards

One of the most important of these forces was the impact of the reduction in the flow of immigrants on the welfare of the working man. His vulnerability to the whims of the employer was greatly reduced where the employer no longer found before his plant gate a large number of strong young men recently arrived from abroad who were willing to work for very little, no questions asked. In fact, early in the century the competition for jobs had been so intense that many men seeking work simply inquired whether a job was available; they did not even dare to ask about the salary. The improved relationship between demand and supply in the market place helped labor to gain in self-assurance.

Labor made other gains incident to the change in the pattern of immigration. For a long time the American public, both the leadership ranks and the majority of the population, had operated on the assumption that a significant distinction had to be made between an immigrant recently arrived and workers who were native born or who had been here for decades or even generations. It was expected that recent arrivals, unable to speak the language, without much skill, and frequently practicing customs and traditions sharply at variance with those characteristic of the established population—that such greenhorns, as they were called, could not expect adequate wages and working conditions. Playing off one group of workers against another had long been practiced by employers. In addition, however, a high proportion of the native-born group made sharp distinctions between themselves and the foreigners, and these distinctions often interfered with the capacity of labor to mount joint action for better conditions. As the flow of immigrants was reduced a greater sense of unity and identity among the working population developed.

The steady rise in the quantity and quality of urban schooling which had characterized the years about the time of World War I also contributed to raising the aspirations of the American worker. Many children from working class homes learned about the promise of the American dream. John Dewey's theory that the school could serve as a major instrument of social change had an anchorage in the facts. Many a school teacher opened the eyes and minds of his pupils to the vision of a better day. Labor's expectations were on the rise and the school played a significant role in the process.

The economic scene was also a potent teacher and stimulator. The free market, which enables employers and employees to reach separate bargains, always results in a range of situations in which some workers are notably better off than others. Hence those who earn less or work more always have before them unequivocal evidence that they are not doing as well as some other workers. Much has been made of late of the role of the labor leader in taking the initiative to institute drives for better conditions for his members; the assumption is that no labor leader can afford to let another score a large success without undertaking a similar campaign. While this is undoubtedly a factor, it overstates the importance of the leader and minimizes the extent to which he is pushed by the workers, who are likely to be very sensitive to the fact that they are not as well off as some others.

The period of World War I provided a favorable background for labor to push its claims. With orders coming in faster than they could be handled, with many contracts on a cost plus basis, with the dollar decreasing in value, employers were willing to agree to many changes in wages and working conditions. Some of them were concerned about the long-run effects of the large gains that labor was scoring but the majority, while not happy about the trend, saw mainly their short-run profits. In any case there was little that they could do to stem the advances.

There was a new factor in the situation. Government, by virtue of the war emergency, was playing an ever more important role in directing the economy, and government was primarily concerned with output, and only secondarily with the costs of securing it. The heightened importance of government also gave added sanction to the standards which it had established for its own employees which, as in the case of standard hours of work, tended to be better than in the private economy. And, as noted previously, the federal government helped to legitimize trade union activity by placing key labor leaders on various public bodies. This greater public acceptability helped to strengthen labor's hand in its negotiations with employers.

Government, particularly state government, made still another contribution. Woodrow Wilson had helped to crystallize a growing sentiment to use the power of government to protect labor from some of the more serious inequities to which it was exposed. The years immediately preceding and following World War I saw a considerable amount of protective legislation passed by the states, including limitations on hours and conditions of work for women and children, safety legislation and, most importantly, workmen's compensation.

With the election of Harding the role of the federal government in the operation of the economy was strikingly reduced. During the New Era, the federal government took little or no leadership in matters affecting the welfare of the working man. In the opinion of the Republicans the very best that the federal government could do was to do nothing and to leave the initiative where it properly belonged, in the hands of the leaders of the business community. This was the policy of Harding, Coolidge, and to a considerable degree also of Hoover.

It has been observed that the efforts of leading American corporations to improve the working environment, to introduce various benefit schemes for their workers, to encourage joint discussions about problems in the work arena, all of which have been subsumed under the heading of welfare capitalism, were directed, first and foremost, against the growth of trade unions. While there is undoubtedly considerable merit in this view it overlooks an important contributing factor.

After the war it was not possible to return to the conditions prevailing before its outbreak, no matter how much people yearned to. Thus the disengagement of the federal government from its function of leadership in the economy was difficult and could be effected only if this function were filled by others. The farsighted leaders of the business community recognized and acted upon this fact. They understood that the war had brought important changes in social attitudes and values not only at home but abroad and that the best way to protect and strengthen private enterprise was for business itself to eliminate some of the more serious defects of the system.

The fact that many of those who were rising to power had served in the war with the men who now worked for them; that many executives had attended or graduated from college where they had been exposed to views that challenged the rights of property; and that they were living in a period of ferment—witness the passage of the several constitutional amendments—all operated in varying degrees to affect their outlook and behavior.

Two further factors encouraged various large organizations as well as some smaller ones to attempt to improve the conditions under which work was carried out. The war years and, even more, the postwar years had seen a rapid increase in investment in plant and equipment with the result that many corporations found that they had vastly increased their capacity to produce and that their labor requirements had conspicuously declined in relative importance. It was possible therefore for many of these technologically advanced companies to establish liberal conditions of employment. The New Era also saw the increasing penetration of psychology into business; one assumption of this new approach was that employers who "treated their workers right" would be repaid by higher productivity. Psychologists contended that favorable conditions result in high morale, which in turn is reflected in high productivity.

We have seen that the increased demand for productivity during the war period facilitated labor's achieving higher rates of pay and improved conditions of work. In like manner, the great potentials of the automobile industry, as perceived by Henry Ford in the early twenties, gave impetus to the establishment of better circumstances for the worker. Facing a large market and increasing demand, Ford was willing to pay much more than the conventional wage. Ford was among the first to recognize the advantage of organizing factory work on an assembly line basis, among other reasons because of the control which he could exercise over the pace of the worker. The need of the automotive, construction, and certain other industries to increase their work forces substantially provided a good opportunity for labor to improve its bargaining position.

A series of developments on the demographic and social fronts warrant brief mention. First, the war boom accelerated the mobility of labor, especially out of the industrially backward South. Many white and Negro workers came North in search of employment, found it and remained. For the most part, they achieved a vast improvement in their circumstances as a result of relocation. A few Mexican Americans from the Southwest also were able to obtain industrial employment in the Midwest, primarily in hard labor in the steel mills and the meat-packing plants. And many tens of thousands from backward areas who served in the Armed Forces did not return home after demobilization, but settled in expanding localities.

The rapid expansion of Detroit in the 1920's led to the relocation of many additional workers from the South. Companies in search of labor sent recruiters to the border and Southern states. Automobile manufacturing was able to absorb large numbers of unskilled workers who were willing and able to submit to the dictates of the assembly line. Some of the Negroes who came North were recruited by employers, or their agents, as strikebreakers—a role in which they had been used earlier and which served to intensify the hostility already entrenched in the Northern communities.

The impact of increasing use of automobiles would be hard to exaggerate. Many isolated areas, in mountain regions and in the deep South, started to open up. It was possible for people to move about without making permanent commitments. While the mining town and the mill village survived the New Era, they became more accessible to outside influences as a result of the many new roads and the fact that many in the working population finally found the money necessary to own and operate an old jalopy. The extent of the automobile's accomplishment with regard to the relocation of the population was dramatically underscored in the westward migration of the millions who were victimized by the drought in the mid-thirties.

The twenties witnessed the continued growth of urban areas and their suburban satellites. As more and more of the nation's population became city dwellers the birth rate declined, with the result that the money available to working class families was divided among fewer children. Although fewer families had adolescent children as supplemental wage earners, a growing proportion of women were entering the labor force.

The decline of the work day and the work week coinciding with continued gains in real earnings helped to change the whole complexion of the lives of the industrial working population. No longer were men so tired at the end of the day that all they wanted was to drink, eat, and fall into bed. The automobile, which could be purchased on the installment plan, provided a new activity for the family. More and more people took to the road during their free hours in the evening and on holidays.

Higher incomes and shorter hours of work also made it possible for them to enjoy new recreational opportunities, of which the movie was one of the most important.

As the automobile became available to more and more of the working population, it exerted an important psychological influence on their aspirations and their view of themselves and the world in which they were living. In American society there had never been sharp lines to clearly differentiate one class from another. While the well-to-do lived quite differently from the poor there were subtle gradations all along the income range. The important point about the automobile is that it presented an opportunity for broadened consumption for all classes at about the same time. The only difference was that the rich drove a more expensive car. Before the end of the New Era another important breakthrough was made—the radio. This, too, became available before long to all except the very poor.

It may well be that the diffuse sense of well-being that permeated such a large proportion of the American population, including its working men and women, during the New Era reflected these important gains in consumption which followed shortly after workers had achieved substantially better standards of work. The expansion and deepening of public services, especially education, also contributed to a belief in rapid progress.

Another important social force which took place in the aftermath of World War I was the accelerated emancipation of women. They were able both to throw off old shackles and gain new access to work opportunities. So basic a development, coinciding with a marked alleviation of the burdens of homemaking, also helped to create for the worker a sense of very rapid progress.

Brief mention should be made of the participation of many working class families in one old and one new American game: the old one was speculation in real estate; the new one, speculation in the stock market. In every generation many hard working men and women took their savings and bought land or houses as an investment in the hope that they could realize a large gain. The twenties formed no exception and many did very well. The new development in the twenties, especially toward the end of the New Era, was the participation in the stock market of many people of modest means. While only a small percentage of the working population ever bought a share of stock, the fact that every working man knew of relatives and neighbors who were speculating successfully helped to create an aura of unparalleled prosperity.

Toward the end of the New Era, the president of the American Federation of Labor, William Green, delivered a series of talks on the radio about the worker and his money, sponsored by a leading brokerage firm.

The combined impact of these several economic and social trends raised expectations and at the same time fulfilled many of them. This is what gave the New Era its distinctiveness. Most people came to believe that the nation had found the key to perpetual prosperity.

Disorganization and Despair

The collapse of the stock market in the fall of 1929 was much more dramatic than the reversal in other economic trends. After such a long period of general economic expansion since 1915, interrupted only once by the postwar readjustment of 1920–21, the public could not accurately estimate the future. Since for several years leaders of opinion had been talking about the New Era, it is not surprising that President Hoover as well as many prominent businessmen anticipated that the stock market reversal, together with the much more moderate declines in output and employment, would be quickly stemmed and that prosperity would once again be "just around the corner."

While most of the country was optimistic about the future because of the substantial improvements which it had achieved in the preceding decade and a half, there were pockets of economic distress where by early 1930 the outlook was bleak indeed. Many communities in the bituminous coal mining regions, in the textile belt of New England, and in cut-over lumbering areas had been depressed even before the general economic decline had set in. But as long as the rest of the economy had been operating at a high level, many who could no longer find employment at home left to find work in more prosperous areas. So it had always been in the United States. No man was ever assured that he could make a living in the community into which he had been born. But it was part of the American scene that men who were willing to go where there was work could find a job. But by early 1930 this was no longer so: the unemployed and under-employed from distressed areas could not find work elsewhere. It was in these already weakened communities that the more severe manifestations of a deep depression could first be observed.

While a few large corporations, as part of their welfare program, had sought during the 1920's to moderate the ill effects of seasonal employment through modifying their production and distribution schedules, none had even contemplated providing jobs for the bulk of their work force in the face of a major reversal in business. No single employer could even attempt to pursue such a policy in the face of a steeply downward trend in the economy at large. In fact the leaders of the American community had not even considered such an eventuality.

A major depression was not anticipated. It crept up on the country. There had been, in fact, repeated signs that gave some small support to the hope of business and government leaders that the economy was about to turn itself round. Their consequent tenacious hold of the optimistic premise and their inability to read the future correctly proved a major deterrent to corrective action at every level—individual, corporate, governmental. This false assumption did more. It lifted people's hopes repeatedly only to dash them more severely each time the forecast was proved false. The objective battering was bad; the psychological trauma incident to expectations proven wrong made it worse.

By the end of 1930, some fifteen months after the collapse of the stock market, many among the working population were in dire circumstances. The most distressed, as we have seen, were those in communities which had become depressed even while the general economy had been expanding. There were no resources left. Only one step away were the one industry towns where the major plant was involved in the manufacture of capital goods. Since this sector of the economy declined very rapidly and very far, the employment base in these communities all but vanished. While some more socially minded industrialists attempted to keep a few people at work by instituting plant rehabilitation programs, it was not long before their financial situation coupled with the darkening business outlook put an end to their efforts. Others sought to keep the maximum number of people at work by spreading the little work available as far as possible, with the result that by late 1932 many workers had only twelve to fifteen hours of employment per week. In this situation, more families were able to buy food, but fewer families were able to buy anything else, and this turned out to play havoc with the rest of the community's dwindling economy.

Workers attached to such consumer goods industries as food and clothing had a somewhat different experience. Here the demand for the industry's products was reduced but it did not disappear. There was a great intensification of the omnipresent competitive pressures on prices. Employers could stay in business only if they cut prices drastically; they could cut prices drastically only if they cut wages drastically, for wages often accounted for from between half to three-quarters of their total costs. The major consequence of this struggle for survival was the speedy disintegration of labor standards, with respect not only to wage levels but also to hours, vacations, and many of the other emoluments that workers had achieved over the preceding fifteen years.

Where unions had never been established or where they were inherently weak, there were no effective barriers against this erosion. But conditions were only slightly better in many areas where relatively strong unions had long been established. Faced with the alternative of working for a small wage or not working at all, most workers, including staunch union members, were forced to agree to repeated wage reductions, stretch-outs, and other devices which required them to work more for less pay. To some extent, but only to some extent, this situation was relieved because of the substantial decline in the prices of commodities.

Unemployed workers who lived in the large cities were able occasionally to obtain a day's work simply because there remained a sufficiently large number of economically viable companies in these larger communities. With the numbers of unemployed vastly in excess of the amount of casual work available the wages that a man or woman was able to earn were very low, but the prospect did exist of earning an odd dollar now and then.

At the depth of the depression, in 1932 and early 1933, there were many workers who still had jobs, but they no longer received wages in currency; they were paid in scrip. This was true for many who worked for private employers as well as for government. Usually the employing unit made an arrangement with local merchants to honor the scrip, but frequently it was accepted only at a substantial discount.

The impact of the depression on the working population was over-whelming. It threw large numbers on the scrap heap of unemployment; it made them use up their life savings, and forced many to sell their homes. Millions existed on such short rations that their health and the health of their children was seriously undermined. The depression resulted in the severance of social and religious ties for millions of families who could not face the prospect of letting their neighbors know how far they had fallen. Worst of all, it destroyed for large num-bers their dream that America was a land of opportunity in which the working man could look forward to a better future for himself and his family. Working men and women also suffered because of impotent national leadership, which in its floundering underscored the bleakness not only of the present but of the future.

It is against this background of disorganization and despair that one must set Franklin Delano Roosevelt and the changes he brought about after his assumption of office on March 4, 1933.

The first important contribution made by the new President was to commit the prestige of his office to stemming the disintegration of the economy and to instill once again in the hearts of men the hope of a better future. His exhortation to the public that "we have nothing to fear but fear itself" was indicative of his conviction that energetic leadership could successfully reverse the downward trend. And the vast majority caught this change in national leadership and responded.

Labor, organized and unorganized alike, had voted overwhelmingly for Roosevelt. The working people of the country sincerely believed that since a man sympathetic and concerned with their special prob-lems was in the White House, their fortunes would begin to improve. At the time of Roosevelt's inauguration the power of labor in the market place had reached a low ebb. The unions had suffered tremen-dous losses in membership during the preceding three years and many who were still carried as active on the rolls were no longer paying dues. Most unions were bankrupt or close to it.

Just as Roosevelt had injected a new note in the national scene, so he provided the background for a sudden and dramatic change in the attitude and activities of the working man and his organizations. The National Industrial Recovery Act provided an umbrella for trade union organization and representation and a small but aggressive group of labor leaders quickly seized the opportunity to revivify the movement which only a few months before had been close to extinction.

Vast organizing campaigns were initiated. Many groups of workers were ready to respond. Organizers were quick to exploit the friendly attitude of the new administration. In many communities workers were told that the President wanted them to join up. And since many employers did not know how friendly to labor the administration actually was, they hesitated to fight the new organizing efforts. Moreover, in view of the prospect of making a profit for the first time in three years, many preferred to make concessions to their workers rather than enter upon sanguinary battles. Others decided, however, to fight labor's bid for power and the stage was set for major conflicts. Many such conflicts occurred in many parts of the country. For the most part, labor won. A union frequently failed initially to secure more than a small part of its total demands, but it often succeeded in laying the foundation for a permanent structure which would enable it to come back again in a year or two and put forward its demands.

The turmoil that swept the land on the employer-labor front was but one aspect of a major revolutionary change. These years saw a vast acceleration of the power struggle between property and human rights that had long characterized American society. Under Roosevelt's leadership the federal government moved energetically to introduce, through legislation, vast new mechanisms for aiding the most vulnerable groups in the society whose economic foundations had been eroded by the depression. Among the more spectacular of these developments was the initiation of various large-scale relief programs financed by the federal government. Eventually the administration, convinced that work relief was much superior to the dole, provided direct employment for millions of unemployed persons. The wages and other conditions of work on WPA were in many parts of the country as good as or better than those a man was able to secure in the private economy. In addition, under the new programs, commodities were made available to those on relief, such as surplus food, clothing, and other perquisites.

The most revolutionary changes occurred in the South where the several governmental programs—agricultural support programs, Tennessee Valley Authority, Public Works Authority, WPA, Rural Electrification, and many others—pumped large sums of money into an economy which had long survived with very little, since such a large part of the population earned its livelihood by share-cropping. Among the longer-term consequences of this large-scale governmental intervention in the economy of the South was the stirring on the racial front. The New Deal loosened many firm moorings.

Despite these strenuous efforts of the federal government, after six years the major problem of concern to the working population—employment—had not been solved. When World War II broke out, there were still almost ten million unemployed persons in this country.

Part
FOUR

Part
FOUR

IX

World War II and After

ONE of the outstanding characteristics of the American economy during the present century has been the number of quick reversals in the trend of economic activity: the boom incident to the mobilization for World War I, the recovery in 1922 from the postwar depression, and the changes that came about with the New Deal after three years of deepening depression. The most striking of all was the quick upward shift in 1940–41 as the American economy and society became more deeply involved in the second World War.

In the years immediately preceding Hitler's invasion of Poland, an increasing number of economists both in the United States and abroad were concluding that the capitalistic system had undergone a fundamental alteration. It seemed that the system no longer contained the type of expanding forces which in the past had always assured that depression would be followed by recovery, a sufficiently strong recovery which would make available jobs for the unemployed and for new entrants into the labor force. The persistence of such a high level of unemployment as was described in Chapter VI—a level of between 15 and 25 per cent for the entire decade following 1929—led many students to conclude that the economy was actually stagnating and that no ordinary remedies would ever again be able to bring back a condition of full employment. The leading exponent of this view in the United States was Alvin Hansen of Harvard University, whose mentor and guide was John Maynard Keynes.

There is no point in speculating at this late date about what would have happened had there been no World War II—whether the American economy would have remained in the doldrums until an aggressive political leader instituted a second New Deal; or whether, in a little more time, the recuperative powers of the economy would have made possible a new period of expansion. But with respect to what actually did happen the record is unequivocal. The American economy underwent the most startling transformation in its history from chronic industrial unemployment to acute manpower shortages.

Full Employment

At the height of the boom in 1929 the civilian labor force totalled 49.1 million, distributed as follows: 10.5 in agriculture, 37.1 in the non-agricultural sector, and 1.5 unemployed. Eleven years later, the comparable figures were: a civilian labor force of 55.6 million, with 9.5 in agriculture, 37.9 in the non-agricultural sector, and 8.2 unemployed. Thus, there had been a decline of about 1 million jobs in agriculture; substantial stability in the non-agricultural sector; and between a five- and six-fold increase in the number of unemployed. Never before in American history had there been such a long period during which the non-agricultural sector had failed to show substantial growth.[1]

The years immediately following 1940 saw striking changes: employment in agriculture during the next three years declined by about half a million, but employment in the non-agricultural sector increased spectacularly—from 37.9 to 45.3 million, or almost 20 per cent. Unemployment dropped from slightly over 8 million to slightly over 1 million—a decline of about 87 per cent.[2]

But we must add to these striking changes in the civilian labor force a brief description of the changes in the numbers attached to the Armed Forces in order to understand the changes in the total labor force. In 1940 the combined strength of the Armed Forces was about 450,000; by 1943 there were over 9 million on active duty; and at the peak, in 1945, their total combined strength exceeded 12.1 million.[3]

In the three years 1940–43 there was an expansion of roughly 16 million jobs in the non-agricultural sector of the economy and in the Armed Forces combined—or an increase of 42 per cent over the employment proffered by those two sectors only three years previously.

The manpower to supply this phenomenal demand came from many sources: half a million had previously been employed in agriculture; almost 7 million had previously been unemployed; some were those who just reached working age; many more would normally have remained in school; and many others would have retired. Other sources of this manpower were the large group who returned to employment from retirement and the group who had never worked or who had thought of themselves as outside of the labor market—particularly married women.

The events on the front of female employment are particularly illuminating for they cast a shadow ahead. In 1940 there were approximately 14 million women in the total labor force; by 1943, the figure was 18.8 and by 1944 it had reached about 19.4 million. Thus, there was a gain of more than 38 per cent in the female labor force in the first four years of the decade. Of the 5.4 million increase, only about 1.6 million included those who were still in their teens or early twenties. The number of working women between the ages of twenty-four and forty-four, most of whom were married, increased by 2 million; and those between forty-five and sixty-five increased by about 1.5 million. We see then that war industry drew very heavily for its female labor supply on married women.[4]

The phenomenal growth of the total labor force during World War II was recognized as making a major contribution to the winning of the war. But as the day of victory drew near, students became concerned about the future of the economy and of the labor force. They feared that the greatly expanded war economy, together with the very large Armed Services, could not be quickly contracted without ushering in a major depression. The expansion that had accompanied World War I had been followed by a sharp, if short depression. Pessimists were quick to point out that the scale of our mobilization effort in World War II had been much greater, both absolutely and relatively. Many anticipated, therefore, with increasing apprehension a major postwar collapse.

But the collapse did not occur. Many who had stayed past retirement in order to participate in the defense effort left the labor force when the war was ended. Many others who had interrupted their schooling voluntarily or because they had been drafted returned to school. Many married women willingly gave up their jobs either because their position was eliminated or they preferred to withdraw from the labor market.

Some indication of the scale of readjustment which took place is suggested by the fact that the Armed Forces dropped in strength from over 12 million to less than 1.6 million in less than two years. The really remarkable achievement was the expansion of the non-agricultural sector of the economy, from about 44.2 million persons employed in 1945 to 49.7 million two years later; this sector actually sustained a gain of over 12 per cent.[5] This gain, together with the larger number back in school, the larger number of women at home keeping house, and larger number of older persons who retired was not sufficient to keep the number unemployed from rising, but the rolls moved up only moderately—from about 1 to 2.1 million within the two-year period. In percentage terms this represented an increase of from just under 2 per cent to 3.6 per cent of the labor force.[6]

Having accomplished the task of conversion from war to peace with a minimum of difficulty, the economy continued to perform well in the following years, although 1949–50 saw a weakening in some areas of economic activity which resulted in an increase in unemployment to 3.4 million, 5.5 per cent of the labor force. But with the outbreak of hostilities in Korea in June of 1950 the forces of expansion set in once again with corresponding improvements in job opportunities and corresponding declines in unemployment, which by 1953 dropped to 1.6 million, only 2.5 per cent of the civilian labor force.[7] When the economy turned down in 1959 with a level of unemployment higher than at the peaks of the two preceding points of expansion in 1953 and 1956, concern developed about the ability of the federal government to devise policies in accordance with the revolutionary edict of the Employment Act of 1946. For in that year, through that Act, it became the declared intent of the federal government to pursue policies that would contribute to the maintenance of a continuing high level of employment.

Between 1940 and 1960 the United States experienced the longest sustained period of economic expansion in its history. The student of business cycles can find years in this period during which expansion slowed and even was reversed. But these were only modest and brief interruptions of a trend that carried the economy to constantly higher levels of physical output and employment. The sustained nature of this expansion permitted certain forces that had got under way during World War II to gain momentum in the postwar years.

Two trends are particularly worthy of note. In sharp contradiction to what many analysts anticipated, the active participation of married women did not come to an end with the termination of World War II; it has in fact further increased in recent years. In 1940 about half of the 14 million women in the labor force who worked were single; only 30 per cent were married; the remainder were widowed or divorced. In 1960, with 27.5 million in the labor force, the number of single women had actually declined from 6.7 to 5.4 million, while the number of married women had increased almost three-fold from 4.2 to 12.2 million. In 1940 only slightly more than one-third of the women who worked were married; in 1960 it was three-fifths.[8]

The insatiable need for manpower during World War II had led our society and economy to reassess its attitudes or, more correctly, its prejudices against the employment of married women. This, together with the relatively slow growth of the male labor force in the postwar years and the continuation of a restrictive immigration policy created favorable conditions for the increasing employment of women.

Much the same circumstances that operated during the war and postwar years to improve employment opportunities for women also operated in favor of Negro workers. As we sought to demonstrate in *The Negro Potential*,[9] 1940 marked the beginning of a sustained period of economic gains for Negroes. World War II created a great many new jobs in the South and, despite continuing discrimination against the Negro, he gained access to many of them, particularly as operative or service worker. The tight labor market throughout the nation enabled ever larger numbers to leave the rural South where they could barely make ends meet and where there was little or no prospect of future improvement. They moved to the North and West where they found a host of new opportunities. Since discrimination in industrial employment was much less intense in the North and West, some of the new migrants eventually were able through upgrading and on-the-job training to acquire competence which qualified them as skilled workers.

As happened with women workers, the relative tightness of the labor market throughout most of the postwar years helped the Negro to consolidate and enhance the gains which he had made during the war. The flow out of the rural and urban South continued. Most of the migrants were able to improve their positions and, even more, their future prospects by securing a place in the economy of the North or West.

Rising Levels of Income

It was long the proud boast of the American economy, and one that could be substantiated by unequivocal evidence, that this country was the land of opportunity for the common man. But the decade of the 1930's negated this claim. Life was bleak and dismal for the millions who were unemployed and underemployed; those who were fortunate enough to have held their jobs had little opportunity to improve their earnings or their standard of living. Although the thirties cast a deep shadow over the promise of progress, the sun came out

again during the 1940's and 1950's and these decades witnessed spectacular advances in the welfare of the working population.

In 1920, at the height of the boom, the average gross weekly earnings
of workers in manufacturing was about $24.75. A decade later, at the
onset of World War II, the figure stood at approximately the same
level. Since the consumer index had declined by about 15 per cent the
stability in money earnings understates to that degree the real increase in their earnings.[10]

It was a combination of circumstances that made the 1940's and
1950's one of the most spectacular periods of advance in the welfare
and well-being of the working population. At the outbreak of World
War II average money earnings in manufacturing stood at 65 cents per
hour. A decade later they had risen to $1.38 per hour, and by the end
of 1961 they were $2.37 per hour.[11] While the prices that consumers
had to pay for goods and services had risen appreciably during this
period, and taxes had also increased, the fact remains that a worker in
manufacturing with three dependents who had available for spending,
in 1961 dollars, about $50 in 1939 had about $85 in 1961. In slightly
more than two decades the manufacturing worker had made a gain of
70 per cent in the dollars which he had available to spend.[12] But this
gain, substantial as it was, understates by a great deal the extent to
which the working man has been able to improve his economic position since the outbreak of World War II.

In 1935, just prior to the establishment of the Social Security System,
wage supplements consisting of employer contributions to private or
public unemployment insurance, old age, and other types of welfare
plans accounted for only ½ cent per hour for manufacturing employees. By 1957 this figure had risen to 16 cents, or roughly 8 per cent
of average money earnings.[13] Since then it has risen even further. A
somewhat more inclusive estimate suggests that it reached about 25
cents in 1961.[14]

While the wages earned by the head of the household is the major
factor determining the standard of living of a working man's family,
other factors may play a significant role. The most important of these
is the number of wage earners in the family. The substantial gain in
the living standards of American families in the last two decades has
been in large measure a reflection of the increasing number of households in which both husband and wife contribute to the total earned
income.

The median wage and salary incomes of families in current dollars
increased between 1939 and 1960 from about $1300 to $5600, or more
than four-fold. Even if account is taken of the depreciation in the
value of the dollar, the gain is substantial, for during these two decades

median real income doubled. This represents a rise of about 3.5 per cent per annum throughout the period.[15]

An easy way to summarize the trend in family income since 1947—the beginning of collection of comprehensive statistical information—is to note that in terms of constant dollars the number of families with less than $5000 income declined from approximately 25 million to slightly under 20 million in 1960; while those in the $5000 to $10,000 level increased from about 10 million to about 20 million; and those with more than $10,000 increased from about 2 million to over 5 million.[16]

In 1960 there were just as many families with two earners as with one earner. The important point to note, however, is that among the families which earned over $7000 a year, which included about two out of every five, there were twice as many with two earners as there were with one, where the head of the household was under 65 years of age.[17] In families where the head of the household was a full-time male worker, the family income in 1960 averaged slightly less than $6300. But if his wife also worked for wages it rose to over $7800.[18] Thus much of the gain in the income of the working population during the last two decades reflected the substantially improved opportunities for married women to work.

The foregoing data relate to all families, but the center of our interest is on those where the head of the household is a laboring man or woman.

In 1939 the median income of fully employed male operatives and kindred workers was approximately $1270; in 1960 it was $4980. The income of craftsmen had increased from about $1500 to $5870, and that of sales workers from $1450 to $5760. Even more spectacular were the gains of service workers, whose median income rose from about $1020 to $4090; laborers' income went from $990 to $3870. While all of these figures represent current dollars and must be adjusted for the steep rise in the cost of living during this period, they nevertheless indicate that the circumstances of regularly employed workers were greatly improved during the past two decades.[19]

The gains made by women workers who were regularly employed were perhaps even more spectacular; the income of service workers rose from $600 to $2420, that of operatives from $740 to $2970, and that of saleswomen from $1070 to $3580.[20]

The foregoing data reflect the changes in the income of individual working men and women in particular occupational groups during the past two decades. An even more revealing figure is the median income of families in terms of the longest job held by the head of the household in 1960, for such a figure reflects the total income of these workers' families. The families of foremen had a median income of $7940; draftsmen, $6310; clerical and skilled workers, $5950; operatives, $5620; service workers, $4730; and laborers, $4320.[21] All these are median incomes, which means that a significant proportion of the families in each occupational group earned much more. This is suggested by the following: About one out of every seven families which had a foreman or craftsman as head of the household had an income in excess of $10,000; and about one in three had more than $8000. In the case of sales workers, one in five families had more than $10,000; two in five over $8000.

Slightly less than one in five families of operatives had incomes in excess of $8000; and about one in three had incomes of more than $7000. About one in four families of service workers had incomes in excess of $7000 as did almost one in five families of laborers.[22]

While there were as many families earning less than the median as there were earning more, many of those with smaller incomes had but one earner in the family.

The position of the average working man's family in 1960 is indicated by the fact that if the head of the household was regularly employed and if his wife held even a part-time job, the family was likely to have an income of at least $7000 annually; it could live at a middle class level.

The Better Life

While the money a worker earns holds the key to his economic position, his over-all situation is influenced by considerations that transcend the amount of his real income. One important dimension is how much he must work and under what conditions in order to earn his income. Another important consideration is what happens to him and his family in the event that he is unable to keep on working. Finally, the worker is deeply concerned with the opportunities available to his children, and whether he must provide for these opportunities out of his earnings or whether they are made available for little or no cost by other agencies of society, particularly by government. An estimate of how the working population has fared during the past two decades must consider, at least briefly, these further dimensions.

Toward the end of the New Era in 1928, the average work week for production workers in manufacturing was approximately 45 hours. There was a marked drop during the depressed 1930's reflecting more a weakness in the demand for labor than a long-term adjustment to a shorter work week. During World War II average weekly hours were 45, equal to the level of the late 1920's, but in many instances the normal work week, before overtime, was set at 40 hours a week. A decade after the end of World War II the standard work week was at about the same level, only a modest reduction (one to two hours) having occurred in selected industries.[23]

In the service sector of the economy—in trade, finance, transportation—there were significant declines in the average work week over the two decades; by 1960 a work week of around 37 hours was increasingly common, where 40 to 44 hours had been the earlier standard.[24]

In the Spring of 1962 there were 61.5 million persons employed in non-agricultural industries. Of this total about 18.9 million worked 41 hours or more, and 29.5 million worked between 35 and 40 hours; the rest worked less than 35 hours weekly. Clearly the average work week was no longer 40 hours; it was somewhat lower.[25]

The gains that the American working man has been able to achieve since the outbreak of World War II includes the large-scale development of fringe benefits largely financed by employers. The range of these benefits includes paid holidays, paid vacations, various types of health insurance, and pensions. Some benefit plans include supplemental unemployment benefits, savings or profit sharing plans, and other emoluments that go beyond direct wage payments.

Some of these "fringes" first became popular in the 1920's, only to be swept away in a great many instances during the blistering depression of the 1930's, and emerged again during World War II when government encouraged them in lieu of wage increases, since they were less inflationary. In 1960 three out of every four office workers had seven or more paid holidays during the course of the year as did two out of three plant workers. Under varying conditions of service, five out of six office workers and three out of four plant workers could earn three weeks of paid vacation—some after ten years of service, most after fifteen. In fact, four weeks of paid vacation was increasingly common for employees with 20 to 25 years of service: two out of every five office workers and one out of four plant workers enjoyed this benefit.[26]

With the exception of only about 10 per cent, employees were covered by some type of life insurance through employer-contributory plans. About five out of every six employees were covered by health insurance that provided at least for hospitalization and surgical fees. A somewhat smaller percentage, three out of five also had coverage for medical fees, and insurance for catastrophic illness was becoming more popular. About two out of five office workers and one out of five plant workers had this type of coverage. While many of these plans did not provide for paying the full costs of hospitalization and professional services the quality of the contracts was constantly improved as employers and labor alike tried to find policies that provided real rather than purely nominal protection.[27]

A considerable proportion of all workers—about two-fifths of all office employees and two-thirds of all plant employees—also were covered by some type of sickness and accident insurance as part of a contractual relationship governing supplementary wage benefits.[28]

Finally it should be noted that about three out of every four office workers and two out of three plant workers were covered by some scheme which provided them with retirement pensions at the end of their working life if they had spent a large part of it with one employer or, occasionally, if they were members of an industry-wide plan.[29]

Among the more important developments of the last twenty years has been the striking expansion of government's involvement in the field of social welfare. The standard of living of the American worker and the opportunities available to his children are greatly affected by what government does or does not do. Hence we will set out, at least briefly, developments on this front in order to have a more comprehensive picture of the total forces affecting the well-being of the working population whose members are among the chief beneficiaries of governmental appropriations in this field.

In 1940 the federal government spent about $3.3 billion and state and local governments, almost $5.7 billion, for a total expenditure for public programs for social welfare of $9 billion. Of this total the three largest categories were, in order—public aid, education, and social insurance.[30]

Two decades later the $9 billion total had risen to $50 billion, with the federal government's share amounting to about $23 billion, or only slightly less than the combined total for state and local governments. Passage of time had resulted not only in a rapid increase in the scale of expenditures, but also in a shift among the principal programs. Social insurance was now in the lead with total expenditures of over $18 billion, followed by education with expenditures of almost the same amount ($16.6 billion). Two programs which had been relatively small in 1940 expanded substantially during the intervening years— health and medical services increased from about $700 million to almost $4.4 billion; and programs for veterans had increased from about $500 million to $5 billion.[31]

On a per capita basis the foregoing expansion represented an increase in annual outlay from about $67 to $277, or an increase of more than 200 per cent. When account is taken of the inflationary rise of prices that characterized this period, however, we see that the "real" per capita outlay on the basis of 1959 prices increased from $139 to $277, or almost double. When consideration is taken of the fact that real personal consumption expenditures more than doubled over the twenty years, the expansion in public programs appears somewhat less striking.[32]

One further dimension of the changing condition of the American worker warrants at least brief attention. That relates to the dangers incident to working as reflected in death and injury rates. The increments in wage rates, annual earnings, and availability of public services, important as they are, do not have the same compelling significance as risks to life and limb. The key asset of the worker is his health; without it his earning potential is impaired or destroyed. Deaths from injuries sustained at work totalled 13,300 in 1958, the lowest on record. The number of deaths from motor vehicle accidents in that same year totalled 37,000. The probability that a working man would be killed in connection with his job had been cut in half since the end of the New Era, when the rate had been 42 per 100,000.

Another important index is the injury-frequency rate. In 1958 American workers suffered a total of about 1,820,000 disabling work injuries. In 1940 the rate in manufacturing had been 15.3 per million employee hours worked, in 1958 it had declined to 10.9. There remained, however, great variations in safety in different working environments. Certain major manufacturing sectors had rates of between 2 and 3 while logging had a rate of 64 and sawmills of 40 per million employee hours.[33]

The burden of the evidence is unequivocal. The years between 1940 and 1960 saw marked advances made by the American working man on almost every front—in the ease of finding jobs, in real earnings, in supplementary benefits, in less risk of accident or death. But as the 1950's drew to an end an old specter again loomed on the horizon. The balance between the workers seeking work and jobs available was shifting. There had been small groups of workers in distressed areas who had gained little from the prosperity of the 1950's, but as the decade came to a close the number of areas in trouble was on the increase. The trend in the national unemployment rate had crept up. Only a prophet could foretell what the morrow would bring. But the country had reason to be uneasy.

X

High-Level Employment:
Life Histories

Heavy Industry in Transformation

69. *SKILLED FOUNDRYMEN*

THOUGH he was too young to take part in the 1919 strike, Joe Vitagliano grew up with it in his memory. "I went to school in Ellwood City, then got a job in the tube mill in the summer of 1929 as an apprentice patternmaker. I earned 39 cents an hour for a ten-hour day, five and a half days a week. Pretty soon I was earning more money, but during the depression things got tough. For a while, there was only about two days' work a week; then I was laid off. I worked on a PWA project for five months or so, then went to see my old foreman and was rehired. After that, I worked on practically every job, as a chake-out, as a sandmixer, on the Herman core-machine, then finally stayed in the core room.

"I had married after my first big raise, and I've always been pretty much of a family man. I was twenty-four when Fred was born. . . . I want him to have a college education. He's fairly good at school and, something you learn in this business, that diploma is pretty important.

276

It's worth saving for. As for the girls, well, I don't know. They'll probably just get married and then it would be a waste. My brother's daughter, after he'd spent a lot of money sending her through nursing school, married and now isn't even going to help her parents. I don't think that's fair."

A registered Republican, Vitagliano voted for Al Smith and for Roosevelt. "I wish he were alive now," he says, looking at the giant photograph of the latter on the wall of the union hall. "We wouldn't have all this trouble."

"I believe in unions because the working man was mistreated in the past. There's been a lot of favoritism; I know, because I got some of it. There wasn't a fair distribution of jobs. Now the men are represented. They get a chance to speak their piece up here where they feel they belong."

* * *

Dave Williams had worked in the tube mill for forty years. He had come to Ellwood City in 1908 from Greenville, Pennsylvania, about forty-five miles to the north. "I'd started to work at fourteen," he said. "I'd worked in a guide mill that made steel peeling, nut iron, and wrought iron. I remember there just wasn't enough work to do; everybody did a lot of loafing and finally there was a strike. When the mill was closed down my boss, Jim Barton, was transferred to Ellwood City and he wanted me to come down.

"I thought Ellwood City was terrible. . . . I didn't like this town, didn't know the people, didn't like the mill.

"One thing I did notice, though, was that everybody was so friendly . . . nobody's a stranger. You soon get acquainted with everybody in town.

"When I started working at the mill, they had only three hot mills. Often, after finishing twelve hours work I'd be told to go home, get supper, come back and fire up the mill that hadn't been working for the next day. That meant twelve hours plus four or five more, and we weren't paid for any mill changes. All we got paid for was the tonnage we got out. I was the highest paid man in the crew, except the foreman, but there was one twelve hours there when I made only 72 cents. It was really pretty good pay if I made $60 in two weeks. I guess I'm old-fashioned, but I can't understand the attitude of labor today. We used to work an average working week of seventy-two hours. Now it's forty hours, and there's more absenteeism than there ever was. I never thought I'd see the day when labor would get the consideration it does today. In 1915–16 I worked sixteen hours straight, four or five times every two weeks. If I wasn't relieved, I just stayed another eight hours. This was when they had the eight-hour day, but were still working on a tonnage basis."

70. A BOMBER AN HOUR

I am called in and assigned to a job as a stockhandler at 85 cents an hour. Where are those plush wages I've heard about? I start through "channels" to a Mr. Vanderloft in the waiting room to make my declaration—since I was born long ago in a state that didn't bother about registering births in those days.

Medical examination: weight 189; height 5 feet, 10½; blood pressure 144. Two girls X-ray my chest as impersonally as freight-handlers on the Michigan Central. Back in a private booth, I strip for the medical assistant.

"Operations?"

"Yes—appendix out."

"Hold out your hands. Turn them over. Up! Out! Touch the floor! Stoop! O.K. Wait as you are for the doctor."

I wait 20 minutes.

The doctor listens to my heart, tests for rupture.

"O.K. Get your clothes on."

Then on to fingerprinting. But first:

"Get your social security card."

I am back at the badge desk.

"Where do I arrange for a room at Willow Lodge?"

"Right here. One single? That's simple."

I explain that a slight touch of bronchitis requires a single.

"That's easy. Now wait in the big room. I'll have a car take you over and bring you back."

Gee! Is an ordinary stockhandler that important?

A dozen others are also waiting.

My fellow passengers beef about having had to sign their names so often during the hiring-in ritual. It has taken two and a half hours to become war workers.

At the Lodge registration desk I sign a contract in triplicate with the United States Government, agreeing to abide by the rules of Willow Lodge—which I have not yet seen—to take decent care of my room, and to leave all U. S. property in good condition.

Singles are $5 a week. I pay the cashier for a week in advance, and get a key, a few oral directions on how to find B-160, and a leaflet of directions and rules.

(This, incidentally, was a problem for many Lodge newcomers—

how to bridge the gap between arrival and the first payday which in some cases might not arrive for nineteen days. The company paid every two weeks, but started counting only with the first *full* week. Those arriving on a Monday of one week, for example, might have to wait almost three weeks for their first pay check. This required each worker to have at least $35 to $50 in cash at the start in order to see him through to payday. A small matter from company and government points of view, but highly important for many new workers. It should be noted that the plant management in many cases advanced enough cash for the worker to live on until his first pay. This loan was to be repaid through time.)

I find B No. 160—a clean, bare cubicle in brown beaverboard, approximately eight by ten, equipped with an open clothes-nook without hangers, a four-drawer bureau, a wall mirror, one chair, one single bed, one wastebasket, and an outside view through the lone window of the bare "campus."

I arranged with a man from New Jersey to have dinner together. First I invest in two cakes of soap for 26 cents. Then, soup, wieners, potato salad, peas, fresh onions, two slices of rye, one patty of butter, coffee, fruit salad, cherry pie—75 cents. As well cooked and about the same price as a similar meal in Ann Arbor.

(Throughout our tenancy at the Lodge the cafeterias offered a wider variety of foods and especially more meat than did restaurants in Ann Arbor. Prices were about the same, or slightly lower.)

First-day impressions: (1) Plenty of women in cafeteria and recreation room. (2) Mostly young and mostly with men. (3) One family—2 children—in cafeteria. (4) Everybody friendly and helpful. (5) Second floor terribly overheated—80 or 90 degrees.

Friday, December 3: Spent a noisy night. Guests who seem surprisingly courteous face-to-face show no consideration whatsoever for others behind the doors. They come and go all night—heavily, loudly. At 5:30 the day shift tramped to the bathroom.

Eventually I find Department 981 on the balcony near C-18 at 4:45. The man in charge sends me back about half a mile to the employment office for my time card, and when I return am dispatched to find the time clock and punch in, which I do at 5:20. Then I wait for the night superintendent in the materials department. He is very agreeable and we settle on where I am to work. From that point on I am just another dumb stockpusher.

We go down to C-22 where a straw boss leads me to a pile of boxes and metal parts lying on the floor. Without further explanation he tells me to load the stuff on a four-wheeled cart, move it a "couple of bays over," and make "a nice pile."

Can do. The boxes apparently contain nuts of various sizes. I put like boxes together and carefully keep them from projecting beyond the edge of the cart. I load the green metal pieces beside the boxes.

Then the straw boss comes back and stops me. The green metal pieces, it seems, are not to be moved. I unload them. He sets me to emptying the shelves of some metal stockracks and loading those boxes on my truck. I pile them up.

Then it comes out—the *purpose* of the whole thing. The stock is to be moved over to a new location and the green metal pieces are for new racks to be assembled right here to replace the old ones. Why couldn't he have said so in the first place?

Saturday, December 4: Breakfast at noon with a little old guy who comments on the red tape required to get a job with the Government: "Took me two weeks." . . .

One girl resident of Willow Lodge to another: "I thought they'd notify you when your rent runs out. I just owed 'em a week, but they took my clothes right out. I had two weeks' pay coming on Monday."

I walk a mile across empty spaces to the plant. Check in at 4:36.

Tonight I help move stock on "the line," i.e., the long line of rollers that stretches two or three hundred feet, the length of this stock department.

Rumors are flying. One young man, to the slim, bespectacled girl in charge of routing the packages: "I hear they're going to let 2000 men go. Too much loafing."

"I suppose they'll let the last ones go first," she says. "Well, it's nothing to me. I'll just go back to the 5 and 10."

Later the young man asks what I'm getting.

"Eighty-five cents an hour."

It develops he had been moved from a machine job and is getting $1.20, but expects to be cut.

Sunday, December 5: Worked with Bill and a thin chap from Hazard, Kentucky, tonight moving stock on a hand truck from one bay about thirty feet to another. Bill started the evening as a sort of straw boss by calling us into a huddle.

"Let's not kill ourselves tonight. If we move all this stuff here, we'll have to work outside."

So we spent quite a time during the evening "verifying" stock numbers.

Friday, December 10: . . . Struck up conversation with a middle-aged, light-haired chap who runs the movie projector in the Lodge theatre for three shows, three days a week. He lives in Ann Arbor. The theatre draws good crowds and is usually full from 6 to 8 P.M. The 2:45 A.M. show usually draws from 100 to 150. . . . Supper near lunch wagon consisted of a "bomber box"—three sandwiches (two meat, one cheese), a jelly roll, one orange, a plate of macaroni, one frostbite, and a piece of pie, all for 40 cents. Not bad. Reached bus stop—but no bus. Stood in cold wind with a tall chap in a lightweight coat, both of us wondering whether bus had gone or not. The tall chap is a blueprint inspector—recently promoted with an increase of 15 cents an hour from heavy die-cutting. He had just arrived on the Detroit bus. Lives at the Lodge, but went to Detroit with a busload from the day shift to join the crap game that always goes on during that trip. Half the bus riders lop around in the front end and shoot craps. The bus is a special, of course: nobody gets on or off between the plant and Detroit. My friend started with $2.70, lost $2.60, and finished with $2.65.

Saturday, December 11: As I came out of the plant, through the factory gate at 9:30, a guard volunteered the observation that they had to check upon folks going out and write the time of passing the inner gate on their passes.

"Why?"

"Sex pass-outs. We've got to watch so these guys don't go out one door and some girl friend slip out another and meet 'em in the parking lot."

Tuesday, December 21: Back at work yesterday after having been absent since December 11, with influenza. Reported at Employment. Sent to Medical where I stood in a crowd of fifteen or twenty in front of a counter where from one to three languid girls and one young man—mostly one girl—questioned us, sent some to the doctor and others back to work with pink slips. They filled out white, blue, pink forms in triplicate and the applicants signed. A question to me: "Why were you off?"

"Flu."

"Sure you're able to go back to work?"

"Sure, no fever for three days."

"All right. Take this"—the pink slip.

Wednesday, December 22: Moved stock *to* the bins and moved stock *in* the bins back to the upper line, for dispatch to Magnaflux.

The return of the regular foreman seemed to steady things down a bit. Tuesday night both Foreman Lang and his assistant were off on the foreman's strike which had started on the day shift. The result was that a crop of Big Shots appeared from the Material Control office upstairs intent on proving that we could do *more* work *without* regular foremen that we usually did *with* them. With a tall young man who rather forced the pace, I helped box instrument board lamps for about three hours. There was, nevertheless, an air of uncertainty and not-sure-what-to-do-next about all the evening's work, although otherwise things seemed to go on pretty much as usual. The pay-off came, of course, Wednesday when we began to discover the boneheads pulled during the strike—the stuff piled in the wrong bins, and so on. . . .

Tuesday, December 28: Walked to the extreme eastern entrance where the finished bombers go out. Stuck my head into the lower front opening of a nearly-completed ship. Overwhelming array of pipes, wires, instruments, gadgets, control rods, etc. Nobody bothered me or asked questions. No Auxiliary Military Police in sight. Went on to find the pay wagon. Promptly learned one or two things. The cashier raised a new question which the stooge outside translated.

"You have less than eight hours on this time-slip. Get it okayed at the time office. The other one you get at the office."

So—I'm out of line again—no pay. Just a suggestion of some pressures used to cut down absenteeism. Unless a man has eight hours on his current time card he can't collect on his preceding card without an OK.

Wednesday, January 5: Quitting was a complicated process. They gave me the card, which outlines the rigamarole. I took my time card, and then went back to wait ten minutes for my foreman. He had to get a co-signature from an assistant. He gave me a #1 rating on ability, diligence, etc., but #2 on attendance! Rating runs 1-2-3-4 and "unsatisfactory." Told me he'd be glad to have me back. Then I went to the key crib to return the locker key and get my tool clearance: it's about a short quarter of a mile. Then back a nice long quarter of a mile, to get my time card cleared. Then on clear across the factory to the gas rationing board. I did not have any gas tickets from this board any more than I had had any tools from the tool crib. But the clearance is routine to prevent fraud. Got there at 5:30 —closing time! Two girl clerks walked out, ignoring me. I waited beside a troubled chap in his early forties who had used up three months' gas allowance in one and wasn't going to get any more—so the gentleman behind the counter assured him. When the worried gent left, I got my gas clearance in two minutes. If I had been a minute or two later I would have had to look up the Plant Protection office where such clearances are issued at odd hours.

On to the Badge Crib where I turned in my various clearances and my badge.

I was promptly turned over to a big plant protection man who escorted me to the door.

71. ASSEMBLY LINE WORKER

This worker . . . is a graduate of a public vocational school. . . .
He is thirty-seven years old and married; he has a couple of children,
is buying his own home, and "takes home" just under $80 a week. . . .

"In 1940 I heard that they were hiring people for the assembly
plant. Must have been thousands of fellows lined up for the job. The
word got around that they were paying real good money. It was a big
outfit, too. No fly-by-night affair.

"Figured I'd get any job and then, with a little electrician experience I had in vocational school, I could work my way up to a good
job. And the idea of making automobiles sounded like something.
Lucky for me, I got a job and was made a spot welder. . . . There
wasn't much to the job itself. Picked it up in about a week. Later I
was drafted into the Army, and then in 1946 I came back. I tried to
get into the Maintenance Department as an electrician, but there was
no opening, so I went back to the line—we call it the iron horse. They
made me a welder again, and that's what I have been doing ever since.

"My job is to weld the cowl to the metal underbody. I take a jog
off the bench, put it in place, and weld the parts together. The jig is
all made up and the welds are made in set places along the metal.
Exactly twenty-five spots. The line runs according to schedule. Takes
me one minute and fifty-two seconds for each job. I walk along the
line as it moves. Then I snap the jog off, walk back down the line,
throw it on the bench, grab another just in time to start on the next
car. The cars differ, but it's practically the same thing. Finish one—
then have another one staring me in the face.

"I don't like to work on the line—no man likes to work on a moving line. You can't beat the machine. Sure, maybe I can keep it up
for an hour, but it's rugged doing it eight hours a day, every day in
the week all year long.

"During each day I get a chance for a breather ten minutes in the
morning, then a half-hour for lunch, then a few minutes in the afternoon. When I'm working there is not much chance to get a breather.
Sometimes the line breaks down. When it does we all yell 'Whoopee!'
As long as the line keeps moving I've got to keep up with it. On a
few jobs I know, some fellows can work like hell up the line, then
coast. Most jobs you can't do that. If I get ahead maybe ten seconds,
the next model has more welds to it, so it takes ten seconds extra. You
hardly break even. You're always behind. When you get too far be-

hind, you get in a hole—that's what we call it. All hell breaks loose. I get in the next guy's way. The foreman gets sore and they have to rush in a relief man to bail you out.

"It's easy for them time study fellows to come down there with a stop watch and figure out just how much you can do in a minute and fifty-two seconds. There are some things they can see and record with their stop watch. But they can't clock how a man feels from one day to the next. These guys ought to work on the line for a few weeks and maybe they'll feel some things that they never pick up on the stop watch.

"I like a job where you feel like you're accomplishing something and doing it right. When everything's laid out for you and the parts are all alike, there's not much you feel you accomplish. The big thing is that steady push of the conveyer—a gigantic machine which I can't control.

"You know it's hard to feel that you are doing a good quality job. There is that constant push at high speed. You may improve after you've done a thing over and over again, but you never reach a point where you can stand back and say, 'Boy, I done that one good. That's one car that got built right.' If I could do my best I'd get some satisfaction out of working, but I can't do as good work as I know I can do.

"My job is all engineered out. The jigs and fixtures are all designed and set out according to specifications. There are a lot of little things you could tell them, but they never ask you. You go by the bible. They have a suggestion system, but the fellows don't use it too much because they're scared that a new way to do it may do one of your buddies out of a job. . . .

"There's only three guys close by—me and my partner and a couple of fellows up the line a bit. I talk to my partner quite a lot. We gripe about the job 90 per cent of the time. You don't have time for any real conversation. The guys get along okay—you know the old saying, 'misery loves company.'

"I think our foreman is an all right guy. I see him once in a while outside, and he's 100 per cent. But in the shop he can't be. If I was a foreman nobody would like me either. As a foreman, he has to push you all the time to get production out so that somebody above won't push him. But the average guy on the line has no one to push—you can't fight the line. The line pushes you. We sometimes kid about it and say we don't need no foreman. That line is the foreman. Some joke."

The worker then discussed the general working conditions in the plant—the lighting, ventilation, safety conditions, housekeeping, cafeteria facilities, and the plant hospital. He thought these conditions were all good, and that in this respect at least the company had done all it could to make work as pleasant as possible for the workers. Then he added:

"But you know, it's a funny thing. These things are all good, but they don't make the job good. It's what you spend most of the time doing that counts. . . . My chances for promotion aren't so hot. You see, almost everybody makes the same rate. The jobs have been made so simple that there is not much room to move up from one skill to another. In other places where the jobs aren't broken down this way, the average fellow has something to look forward to. He can go from one step to another right up the ladder. Here, it's possible to make foreman. But none of the guys on the line think there's much chance to go higher than that. To manage a complicated machine like that, you need a college degree. They bring in smart college boys and train them for the better jobs."

At this point his wife spoke up:

"I often wish he'd get another job. He comes home at night, plops down in a chair, and just sits for about fifteen minutes. I don't know much about what he does at the plant, but it does something to him. Of course, I shouldn't complain. He gets good pay. We've been able to buy a refrigerator and a TV set—a lot of things we couldn't have had otherwise. But sometimes I wonder whether these are more important to us than having Joe get all nervous and tensed up. He snaps at the kids and snaps at me—but he doesn't mean it."

The worker was then asked if he had considered working elsewhere:

"I'll tell you honest. I'm scared to leave. I'm afraid to take the gamble on the outside. I'm not staying because I want to. You see, I'm getting good pay. We live according to the pay I get. It would be tough to change the way we live. With the cost of living what it is, it's too much of a gamble. Then there's another thing. I got good senority. I take another job and I start from scratch. Comes a depression or something and I'm the first to get knocked off. Also they got a pension plan. I'm thirty-seven and I'd lose that. Course the joker in that pension plan is that most guys out there chasing the line probably won't live 'til they're sixty-five. Sorta trapped—you get what I mean? . . .

"The union has helped somewhat. Before they organized, it was pretty brutal. The bosses played favorites—they kept jacking up the speed of the line every time after they had a breakdown. But the union can't do much about the schedule and the way a job is set up. Management is responsible for that.

"We had a walk-out last year. They called it an unauthorized strike. Somebody got bounced because he wouldn't keep up his job on the line. The union lost the case because it should have gone through the grievance procedure. The company was dead right to insist that the union file a grievance.

"But it was one of those things it's hard to explain. When word got around that the guy was bounced—we all sort of looked at each other, dropped our tools, and walked. Somehow that guy was every one of us. The tension on the line had been building up for a long time. We had to blow our top—so we did. We were wrong—the union knew it and so did the company. We stayed out a few hours and back we came. We all felt better, like we got something off our chests.

"Some of these strikes you read about may be over wages. Or they may just be unions trying to play politics. But I sometimes think that the thing that will drive a man to lose all that pay is deeper than wages. Maybe others guys feel like we did the day we walked out."

Toward the end of the interview, the worker spoke of the company he worked for:

"They are doing what they can—like the hospital, the safety, the pay, and all like that. And the people who run the plant I guess are pretty good guys themselves. But sometimes I think that the company doesn't think much of the individual. If they did they wouldn't have a production line like that one. You're just a number to them. They number the stock and they number you. There's a different feeling in this kind of a plant. It's like a kid who goes up to a grown man and starts talking to him. There doesn't seem to be a friendly feeling. Here a man is just so much horsepower. You're just a cog in the wheel."

72. GOLD STARS BUT NO EXTRA MONEY

I am thirty-four years old and married. I had one year of college and eight months of torpedoman training in the Navy. I got about twelve years seniority this October. My wife is working and I am my sole dependent. I work on the first shift as an internal grinder. I have been on this particular job for eight years.

Seems like I am at a standstill now. It has been like that for the last six years. . . . It is my opinion that a new fellow has a better chance of getting a better job than an older fellow who has been here for quite a while. . . . By better job, I mean one with a higher rate of pay and a higher bracket. The production workers have top money and I have been making top money for six years. In order to make more money in production, I would have to run two machines. . . . I set my own pace. Too, the machine I run is an automatic machine and it sets the pace also. You can only work so fast as the machine will run. . . .

The company is all out for production, but the union says a full eight hours work, that is written in the contract, and if the man reaches production that is all right. If not, that is okay too. . . . Now, they got something new on our line. The man who gets the highest production for a month gets a gold star opposite his station. In other words, if you run about 115 or 125 per cent, you probably will get the gold star. . . . They wouldn't put a dollar in a man's paycheck. They give him a gold star. Now, there are other places in town where when a man puts out more than his share of work, they get more for it. Now, the majority of fellows, if they can make production, they do, but they don't do any more. I know they spread the work out. I do the same thing myself. Of course, the company doesn't know much about this.

I imagine most of the fellows would say 85 or 90 per cent of quota is fair. I think 92 per cent is the highest I have ever seen on the line for monthly average. . . . On mine, you get a job and you can run 100 or 110 per cent. Next week you get the same job and due to the heat-treat wrappage or defects you can work a lot harder and a lot faster and you wouldn't make 100 per cent. . . .

I would say I work about average. . . . I work pretty hard to get my work out. When I work, I work hard, and then I take it easy. Some fellows have a certain rate of speed, but I don't. . . . I don't get paid for turning out more than 100 per cent so I don't turn it out. Now, you younger fellows come in here at a lower rate of pay, lower rated job, truckers, sweepers, and the next raise is 3 cents or so. They do go up the ladder but it always depends on the opening. The younger fellows always work harder than the older, as a general majority that is, but there are definite exceptions. . . . The younger fellows figure they are going to advance. They got to get their production in order to get the high rate. If they don't have 85 per cent or over, the company won't even think about giving you a raise. . . .

Most of the older fellows are getting top rate at the job they're on. One older man I know of on the same machine, he is getting top rate but he has got low production. Now there is another one doing the same thing and he has high production at the same rate of pay. . . . There is no compensation for working hard. That is it. A man gets paid and he turns out the best he can. If you run 90 to 100 per cent, the boss won't bother you at all.

It is a general policy for the bosses not to associate with the men. Like we have stag parties, crap games, or something like that on Saturday night. If you are under a foreman's jurisdiction, they don't want him to associate with you. Now, . . . if a foreman comes out whose jurisdiction you are not under, they don't mind his playing with you, that is, if he is not your boss.

I think if you are doing good work and the foreman comes around and gives you a little credit for it, he will benefit more from his standpoint. . . . I believe the company allows him something like a minute a man per day, and that isn't too much time at all. If everything runs smooth, you probably would have more time, but it is not his fault. I say good morning to him when I first see him in the morning.

. . . I've had other foremen who would associate with you and talk to you, but maybe they had more time, and if you wanted to know something, they would inquire around among the men and tell you, not beat around the bush. . . . This foreman works just for the company, and I never had no falling with him but it seems like with him it takes more time to get things done at all. It seems like all the foremen sort of hang toward the company.

I think unions are all right. . . . This union we got now . . . have had the contract two years and they haven't got a general raise yet, a pension, or a paid insurance. I would rather see this union bring the price of living down than give us a raise. It seems like every time they give us a raise, they raise the cost of everything all over town.

The first jobs they give a man here are simple. Once you do one, that is all there is to it. In other words, all it takes is a strong back and a weak mind. We have quite a few farmer boys here. Plow jockeys we call them. They will work second shift and farm in the day time. They are not really dependent upon the company for a living. That is why I think the union doesn't have much power. In other words, they are not worried about losing two weeks' work. . . .

I think we should be getting more money. I make $1.51 an hour now. I should get about $1.80 or $1.90. I'm probably at the top now. I might get another 6 cents an hour but I could only do that by running two machines instead of one.

I would say R. is a good place. . . . You get five days work and you work eight hours a day, and they pay about as much as anybody in this vicinity.

73. WELDING INSPECTOR

I have been working here since 1923. Fifteen years. I am a group steward and I work as a welding inspector. I am sixty-six years old. I graduated from high school. I am married and have four children, but I have only one dependent now. I make $72 a week gross.

I think this is the best company in the United States—that is since Mr. H. took over. The top management here at S. can't be beat. . . . They consider the men in every way that is possible. I think our wages are higher than any factory in the United States. . . .

Right now they have cut our manpower and I don't like that. It is only natural that the company would want to do that if they could. However, right now we just don't have enough manpower for the inspection that we are supposed to do. . . . The boss listens, but I never get the men that I want. Another thing that I don't like is this incentive business. The boys didn't do much thinking when they voted for that. I had thirteen inspectors when they put that in—now we are down to about seven. The men thought that with that incentive plan they would get more money; the only thing that they got was more work. That is, the company paid each of the men a little bit more money, but they cut off a lot of the other men and saved about four or five times what they are paying extra. . . .

This is my second year as steward. Being a steward is all right. Somebody has to do some straight thinking for the men. The way I work it, when I see that the men are wrong, I go in and tell them so. When I see that they are right, I go to bat for them and do everything that I can for them. . . .

I am fair to the company, too. There are some disagreeable situations coming up all the time. . . . The men want things that they shouldn't have. Some of the men just don't want to work at all. All they are interested in is the pay check. . . . A steward is supposed to listen to their complaints and get them straightened out, if possible. Right now, I think that the men are definitely right in wanting more manpower. . . .

I don't think anybody wants the job of steward. It is just a lot of grief. You have to listen to everybody's troubles. Most men have enough troubles of their own without listening to another's. I suppose some of them go into it for political reasons—they want to go up in the union and be a big union official. Of course, the divisional steward gets the highest rating in his department—so many privileges that sometimes he doesn't even ring his card in. He can take time off any time that he wants and make out like he is on union business and get away with it. I suppose some of the men want it to protect their jobs. The stewards can't be bumped you know. Then, as I said, some wanted to get out of work. . . .

Most of us are making a good living right now. The men want to be able to pay their bills with cash and save a little over besides. . . .

I think the most important thing that a foreman has to have is personality. He has to be able to get along with the men. There are some foremen over there who can come up to a man and tell him something and make him mad just by saying nothing. On the other hand, my foreman comes up to the man and maybe he will argue with him a little bit but he will give in when he sees that the man is right. He doesn't come up to a man and say things in a nasty tone like some of the foremen do. . . .

74. ANY JOB I WANT

I have been working here about forty years steady. I'm a gun welder. I'll probably go on the line because it's lighter work.

I like it very good. I've got plenty of seniority. I could pick any job I want. They told me I could have a riveting job. It's the easiest job in the plant, but I like to do a little work.

I like group work. The wages are as good as any in the country. . . . Always I've never had any complaint. If a man is sick and wants to lay off awhile they never grumble. And they have a hospital where you can take your injuries, your cuts, and your hurts and have them treated there. If you can't work you can lay off for awhile.

One job is the same as the other. . . . One likes one better and the other likes the other better. If a man gets good at his job he likes to do it. . . .

We've been working on day rate now. The company made an agreement that for every twenty trucks we would get piecework. The other hours we would be getting day rate. . . . You can earn more a day that way. If you get only straight time you don't make so much. This way you get an incentive. This way the more you put out the more you get. Piecework makes a difference. On piecework we would be getting $1.88 an hour. The day rate is $1.53 an hour. . . .

My wages have been running from $4000 to $4500. . . . At one time I had six people to support. I was making within $3000.

I have thirty-one years seniority.

You spend most of your life where you work. I remember when they used to kick out the old men. Now they can't do that with the union here. It protects the old men. Probably the old men can do some kind of work better than the young men. The old men got the experience. . . .

. . . We've got a good foreman—he cooperates with the men. I think everybody likes him. . . . The foreman should take the part of the company and at the same time be fair and just to the men. . . . If the foreman is too easy with the men the men start trouble.

We never had labor trouble. We've always negotiated everything. The foreman always talks with the men first before making any decision.

They have a nice record. There have been no strikes as long as the union has been here, and this union was one of the first to be organized. Of course there are a lot of little squabbles. They are only department squabbles—here and there. Sometimes there are some soreheads who stop work, but those are just wildcats. . . .

We want fair wages and steady employment and security—to make a living. . . . That we are sure we got the jobs. . . . We don't want to work ten or twelve or fourteen hours a day. We want eight hours a day, forty hours a week of steady work. We don't want to work fourteen hours a day and then shut down. The union is here to see that that doesn't happen. They cooperate together it turns out good. The company profits and the men get their wages. . . .

The fellows in my department are easy to get along with. You're doing individual work. If you don't want to get along you don't have to.

Everyone has got his job to do. It may be on the line but each one has his own job to do. . . . On a moving line it is different. Each does his definite job. But they all work together. . . . It's all teamwork. If I don't do my part everyone will be waiting for me. You're like a cog in the machine. If the cog stops the machine stops. The man got to work just like a machine. If anything goes wrong you stop the line and everyone stands still. As soon as you find the trouble you can start up again. . . .

I guess I don't feel superior or inferior. I'm as good as anybody else. . . . I do my best.

Trouble Spots

75. CONFUSION IN A TYPEWRITER PLANT

That plant is just a mess. It's the most wasteful inefficient place I've ever been at. And then the way they time jobs is a crime. . . . They time only one cycle, and then set a rate on the job. They time you on that job when the die is new and things are easy. Then you might make the rate easy the first few hours, but when the die begins to get dull the burrs get heavier and harder to get off. Then you won't be making your rate at all. Now if they timed you for the whole job and got the average, then they would set the right rate on the job. . . . And when it comes to putting in this retiming, they've really got the boys. A man earning $1.285 under the old system is now making about $1.03. That's some cut to take in your wages when you're depending on that money to get along. You just don't change your way of living overnight. My wife was making $55 before. Now she's making $43. That's some cut to take in your earnings. But they really got that one by. They said the change was needed so they started by instituting it in isolated jobs. They did it all through the plant, but scattered it so no one group would get hurt at any one time, and no one would make too big a squawk. There was no group hurt at once. They went through the plant doing that, and when they were ready they gave it to the rest of the bunch. Now when they gave it to groups, it didn't matter. The rest of the people who had been cut sat back and said "Good" when the others squawked. "We got cut so why shouldn't you?" So they got it all through.

The whole town is in a bad state now. It's bad when you depend as much on one industry as this town does on *A*. Oh, they say that there aren't so many people walking the streets, but even those working aren't making much. And then the merchants feel it too. When things were good they used to get 2000 people in the cafeteria at lunch time— one third of the plant. Today you don't get more than a couple of hundred. When the people start carrying lunch boxes then things are beginning to get bad. You can always tell.

I was amazed when I was working out my seniority lists to find that most of the people with high seniority were not M_____ people. Now most of the people laid off today walking the streets are people from M_____. I wondered at the time what the reason was for this, and I tried to find out. In the first place, when *A*. came in, this area didn't have anyone living here so he hired people from the outlying districts. Not necessarily farmers, but the fellows who lived in the farming towns around the area. They were looking for an extra way of making some money, and were willing to work for less. They were easily satisfied, too. Give them a high-sounding title, and they'll accept less money, or give them a pat on the back and they won't ask you for anything. They don't depend on the job either. They can always find enough to do around the town. If they're not farmers, there are always chores to be done for the farmers around them. So they came to work around here first. Now they're the ones that are still working, and all the M_____ people are walking the streets.

That plant was always full of stooges. They put great stock in loyalty to the company. There are always people reporting to headquarters in New York. Then we get a policy directive up here based on one of those reports. One of the guys who never has seen this plant hears that something is wrong, and sets up a new plan for it, and sends it on to us to put into operation. I remember one time they must have gotten a report that all work wasn't being reported in, and men were making more money that way. An order came in that the foremen had to weigh in all parts and assign all jobs. That was really a beaut. There were 270 men in our department, and there were only three foremen. So they lined up at 6:30 in the morning waiting for the foremen to give them their jobs. By the time the jobs were handed out it was 9:30, and these guys were all being paid waiting time. They started to check out at 3:45 and weren't through till 6:00. They all got time and one-half for this, because it was overtime. How that cost the company money. They were always pulling boners like that.

Most of the grievances you'll find are because of the foremen. The more ignorant they are, the worse they are. It seems that if you take one of those guys who never got an education, or left school early, and elevate him over some other mortals, he really takes it out on them. The company will take men from the ranks for foremen. They take a sweeper and make him foreman of the sweepers. Brother, then you ought to look out! And if there's a guy with a little education under him, he'll lord it over them all the more. That's what causes a lot of grievances.

76. A YOUNG MAN HAS
A GOOD CHANCE—TODAY

I was a janitor. I retired last September because my wife is sick. She has high blood pressure.

I don't want to work anyway. You see, I cannot stand up very long anymore. My legs and back hurt. I've got lumbago in my back. They would not want me. When I was a janitor, I cleaned out the locker rooms, cleaned out the toilets. It was not good work, but it was a living. I started at *D.* in 1933. I worked there as a janitor for eighteen years, until last September. Before that . . . I had many jobs. I've always done hard work, labor work mostly, heavy hard work. I came over to this country in 1906. I landed in New Orleans. I went to work in a sugarcane field there. They paid me 65 cents a day for fourteen hours' work. I had a Spanish and a Negro foreman. We were just foreigners to them, and they treated us like that mostly. The work was hard, and they would swear at us. All the time, my foreman would call me a son of a bitch. He would say, "Come here, you son of a bitch." So I quit. Then, I went to work for the railroad up in Mississippi. I carried ties. It was heavy work, but it was a much better job. They paid me $1.25 for twelve hours' work. Then, from there I went up to Detroit. But everywhere I went, I was just a foreigner. I went to work at the stockyards. Then, I went to work for the Atlas Cement Company. I stayed there for eleven years, up until 1932. I operated a crane there.

In 1932 they shut down the section in which I was working. I could not find a job for 1½ years, and I went on relief. Then, in 1933, when Roosevelt came in and they had the NRA, *D.* opened a plant. They called for men, and I went over there, and they gave me a janitor job.

If I were a young man and could do anything that I wanted to, I think I'd want to be a crane man, like I was at Atlas Cement Company.

When you are a crane man, you push the levers, you operate the crane; you make the crane go. When you're a laborer or a janitor, they push you around, they tell you what to do.

A young man has a good chance today. He should stop complaining and try to protect what he has got. You see them loafing around the locker room, complaining about the boss.

If they don't like the way the boss speaks to them, they tell him to go to hell. Yet the ones you always see complain are never the ones you see at the union meetings. When the other men went out on strike, they worked at the plant. When the contract was signed, they got the benefits of the contract too. I joined the union when the union first started. Many a time, I went out on the picket line in the snow, in the winter, in the cold. Now, don't get me wrong. I'm not saying that all Democrats are good and all Republicans are bad. I'm not saying there are not some rotten eggs in the union, too. There are, there are lots of them. In 1948, when I went out on the picket line in winter time, I ate that slop that you called soup. And walked out in the snow and cold. You said that was for all men in the union. Yet, when the contract was signed, who got the back pay? The foremen, they got the back pay. The skilled workers, they got back pay. But the janitors, the laborers, what did they get? They got nothing.

I've only cried for one man in my life, and that was when Franklin Roosevelt died. He was the only man who has ever done anything for me. He saved my home.

He got me a job. He made it possible for unions to protect the rights of the working man.

77. WE ARE THE LAW HERE

STATEMENT OF MRS. EDNA MARTIN CONCERNING HER ABDUCTION
FROM MRS. POUNDS' ROOMING HOUSE IN TALLAPOOSA, GA., ON
MONDAY, NOVEMBER 17, 1947

I have worked in cotton mills all my life and have been a member of
the Textile Workers Union of America, CIO, for four years.

Because I know what the union can do for cotton-mill people, I
have been putting in all the time I could in the last three months as a
volunteer CIO organizer.

One of the places I have been helping on has been the American
Thread Mill at Tallapoosa. . . . There are about 300 workers in the
mill and about half of them were on a list of those interested in a
union.

One of the union members at the mill found a room for me in the
rooming house of Mrs. George Pounds. I paid Mrs. Pounds a week's
rent in advance and told her that I was a CIO representative.

While I was taking my things into the room, Mr. McGill, American
Thread Mill superintendent, drove by the house, went down to the
corner of the block, turned around and came back the second time,
and eyed me very closely.

At four o'clock I went down to Cliff's place to meet a group of our
union people, because I had an appointment with them there.

When I went out the door, there was a 1939 Ford sitting down below the house, and it turned around when I walked out on the porch,
and when I got on the sidewalk it passed on. I walked on about half
a block and the car passed me again. A man was driving the car. He
went down about half a block and turned and came back and passed
me the third time right at Cliff's place where I met the people.

After this visit, the people I was with drove me back to the rooming
house. . . . About midnight there was a knock on my door and a
woman's voice called out: "Mrs. Martin," and I answered. She said:
"I would like to talk to you." I got out of bed, turned on my flashlight
and turned on the light in the middle of the room.

I said to the woman: "Are you by yourself?" She said: "No, I am
not." I asked her: "Who are you?" And she did not answer. Then I
said: "Well, you will have to excuse me." At this time, while I was talking to the woman outside the door, four men came in at the windows

as I was facing the door expecting somebody to turn the knob and come in, as there was no lock on the door.

One of the men crossed the room and opened the door and pushed the table in front of it back, and five women came in—three of them came on in the room and the other two stood in the door.

Each of the four men had a long shotgun. I remember I was looking in the hole in a single-barrel gun as it was pointed at me. At this moment I said: "I would like to put on a dress." The man who seemed to be the leader of the mob said: "You don't need no God damn dress where you are going." . . .

Then an outspoken woman in the mob began talking. She said: "Mrs. Martin you represent the CIO." I said: "Yes." She said: "Well, we don't want no God damn CIO here, and we don't want no CIO representative here." She said: "In fact we are not going to have a union here and you have got to leave."

I said: "It is your privilege if you don't want a union, but I am not going anywhere. My son went across the water to fight for freedom that I go where I want and stay where I please. I am not going to bother you."

The woman said: "Well you are not going to say here in Tallapoosa." I said: "Well if you want me to leave why don't you give me a fighting chance and go get a policeman and tell him I say come down here and carry me to Atlanta. I have no way out of here except walking."

Then the old man who was the mob leader said: "We are not bringing the God damn law in this—we are the law here." . . .

About this time the old man said: "There has been enough damn arguing. Go get the hemp rope from the truck." A man in the mob who had a crooked mouth went and got the rope.

Meantime they were going through my clothes and my other things, including my pocketbook. . . .

I asked them again to let me put on my dress; I did not have on anything but my gown, and the old man turned around and said: "Put on her God damn dress." I asked the men to get out while I put on my dress and they refused to get out. The woman put my dress on before all those that were present. I did not have on any underclothes.

Then one of the men tied my hands in front of me with the rope. One of the women that had on men's pants took a knife out of her pocket and cut the rope. They left the unused part in the room.

As we left the room one of the men stuffed a piece of cloth in my mouth. I took it to be a man's dirty handkerchief. It made me gag and nauseated me.

All the time the argument in my room was going on, Mrs. Pounds' living-room door was open and the light was on. As they took me out the outspoken woman said: "Thank you, Mrs. Pounds." . . .

They took me out to the truck and pulled me into the back. It was an old truck with a built-on body of wood which brought the sides up to shoulder height. They kept the lights off when they started and the truck did not turn around. I don't know which way we went out of Tallapoosa. The whole mob went along, with most of them in back with me. One of the women was half sitting on me.

Before we left the room, the people went through all my things and then pitched them together, carried them out and put them in the back of the truck. They threw my shoes in the truck, too, and I went out barefoot. They pulled me up into the truck. I was half lying down and could not see anything. . . .

The driver, who was the watery-eyed old man, said: "This is about as good a place as any." Then I was pulled out of the truck and my things pitched out, including my radio.

Only one man got out with me. He took the thing that was in my mouth and the hemp rope off my hands and took them with him. . . .

The truck started rolling and the man on the road had to run after it. Before he left he said: "Don't come back to Tallapoosa or you will be shot on sight." The truck moved off without its lights on.

78. FATHER OF FIFTEEN

My name is Cledis Turner. I am a former employee of the Elk Horn Coal Corp.; I am the father of fifteen children, all living. Five years ago this mine was employing approxiamtely 700 men; it was closed down permanently July 17, 1954.

I am wondering if you gentlemen can comprehend the effect of this catastrophe upon our community. We have made the best of a bad situation. Our women are in some instances working gratis in order that the school-lunch program will not be abandoned. Our local union officers have assisted the certifying agent in signing up and disbursing the free commodities sent in by the Government; however, these commodities are entirely inadequate and actual hunger is stalking our mining communities.

In one of our neighboring schools, one of the grade pupils was caught foraging in empty cans for food by the high school pupils. I made a personal investigation of this case and was told by the mother that they did not have the 25 cents for the lunch at school and saw no way of getting it. At last reports, other children were cheerfully dividing their lunch with this kid.

My oldest son, who teaches school, recently loaned one of his buddies, who is unemployed, a suit of clothes to wear to the funeral of a relative.

Our family doctor has told me that many of his cases are undernourished to the extent that they have to be hospitalized.

Recently, a father carried his baby into the office of an undertaker to ask if he would bury the child. The undertaker told him he would and asked, "Where is the child?" The father handed the man the dead baby that he had carried several miles on foot, because he had no money for transportation.

I also wish to point out that within five minutes' walk of any courthouse in eastern Kentucky, this one here included, you can find hunger. It is not the hunger of lazy or indolent people, but hunger of people who would gladly line up for work at the toot of any industrial whistle. In fact, our chief item of export for the last several years has been the flowers of our State's manhood and womanhood, our young people who have gone North. Our land is not a farmland; in fact, in my county of Floyd, with 53,000 population, there is not a half-dozen farms where one could make a living on farming alone.

We have traveled far and wide seeking employment, only to be rebuffed on account of age, forty or over. Our hills are denuded of all timber big enough to make a mine prop, trees as large as a man's leg.

Gentlemen, unless we get some relief in the form of jobs, not commodities, our society, as we have always known it, is in danger of breaking down completely. We cannot maintain our PTA's in our schools, our churches, and lodges when the economic bloodstream of our community is dried up. I mean that our mine payrolls have vanished.

We look to the future with fervent prayers and hope that something can be done in our seat of government to alleviate these conditions, and this is my humble petition as a citizen, exercising my constitutional rights, to help us in our troubles. It's jobs we want gentlemen, and not charity.

79. A JOB ON A SHIP

Along about 1928 I went into the Marine Service Bureau in San Francisco. . . . I will refer to it as a "fink" hall, because that is seamen's language for the place. . . .

I went up to the window, . . . asked if I could get a job on a ship. I was told, "There is no work here."

I went around the hall there asking different men, "How do you go about getting fixed up for a job on a ship?" Some of them told me that, "If you have got five bucks, you can get a job pretty quick. If you have ten bucks, you can get out today." . . .

It developed also that if you got a letter from somebody, you could go in the back door or through the office and you could present the letter and you would be given a job.

I proceeded then to get a letter, and I got a job.

I made several trips. My job was that of a scullion on the steamship *Malolo* for the Matson Navigation Co. I made several trips on the ship, and then quit and went back up to the hall again to get another job. I just couldn't crack through. I was on the beach about five months trying to get a job through the "fink" hall. This was in 1929.

Then it developed that I could get a job by piecing off the shipping masters on the waterfront or the port steward if I got out on a ship. I could bring them back a case of whisky. It was during prohibition days. I could get a job going to Australia and bring back a case of whisky, and I would be guaranteed a job almost any time I wanted to, because when I came back I had to bring a case of whisky.

Or I could get a job going to the Orient, but I would have to bring back some perfume for somebody.

I didn't care for a lot of these things, and I found it very difficult to get work.

These "fink" halls were always filthy. The sanitary facilities were broken down, and the places smelled quite badly. There was no place to sit. They had a few benches there. You couldn't sit down at a table or enjoy a game of cards. There were no facilities whatsoever. You just came into a big barn. Either you played the game the way it was supposed to be played, or you were just out of luck.

In talking around to a lot of the fellows hanging around the place, I learned about the union. I was told how they were trying to overcome these things. I became interested and joined the union in 1934.

This was how men were hired before the hiring hall. And on the ships the food was unimaginably bad, the living conditions intolerable, the speed-up on the job inhuman. It was a common experience to find canned food in the galley stamped: "Unfit to be sold on the market but fit for human consumption." And one shipping company boasted that it could feed its men on 30 cents a day. . . . I worked on the steamship *Sonoma,* which was operated by the Oceanic Steamship Co. on the Australian run. The bunks were three high. In order to take a bath, you had to get an ordinary bucket and fill it with some water, some fresh water, and sponge yourself off; and then when you got through, you dumped the bucket over you, and that is how you got your bath. . . . The system of hiring men at that time was controlled by the shipowners, who also controlled the conditions aboard the ships. . . .

We also had to work fifteen, sixteen, and eighteen hours a day, and with no such thing as overtime. If you opened up about having to work so many hours, the gangplank was greased for you and you got the skids. . . .

There is no need to comment on the morale and efficiency of a crew hired under these circumstances and living under such conditions aboard ship.

In 1934 I was assigned to the motorship *Potter*. . . . The radio officers had to buy their equipment out of their own funds. It was a part of what each man paid for his job.

Sometime during the year, this company had reduced the wages of its radio officers from around $85 per month to $60 per month. There were two radio officers on each ship, and each stood a twelve-hour-per-day radio watch. As each man relieved the other for meals, close to two additional hours were added to the twelve hours, with the result that each man put in about fourteen hours per day, seven days per week. When the wages were reduced, the men called a strike, and the strike was lost. It was lost because of their inexperience in union activities, and lack of support from any outside source. The men who went on strike were fired. They didn't get their jobs back.

One day in June 1935, newspapers of the United States blazoned forth on their front pages a story about three radio officers going on strike and delaying the departure of S. S. *Manhattan,* one of this company's class-A passenger liners. It seems that the three radio officers had gone to the captain's office at exactly 11:55 A.M.—the ship was due to sail at twelve noon—and made certain demands, among which was a big increase in wages, and the hiring of two additional radio officers to help handle the radio traffic. The captain ordered the three men back to their posts; but, instead of complying with the captain's orders, they walked off the ship instead. The ship was loaded with 1150 passengers bound for a European holiday. It was Saturday, and a hot June day. Few men showed up at the hiring room that day, and those who did went home or to the beaches promptly at noon. The hiring room was closing at the moment the men walked off the ship and would not be reopened until Monday morning. It was a great day for such a strike.

The steamship company held the ship at its pier until 7 P.M. and then signed the men's demand. The ship sailed seven hours late with five radio officers on board instead of three, plus a greatly increased wage scale, $210 for the chief.

If I am not in error, each of the five men was fired upon the vessel's return. Men more amenable to the spirit of 1890 were assigned to the big ship. Wages were reduced by about $25 per month for each man, and only four assigned to the ship in place of the five who had sailed her.

The chief, who was the ringleader, was blacklisted by both radio-service companies and the steamship companies; and, unable to follow his radio-operating career further, he got a job selling vacuum cleaners.

There were no vacations. Vacations for seamen at that time were unheard-of anywhere, and were a huge joke even among sailors themselves. There were no overtime provisions for anything. Not a single man on any American-flag ship was paid overtime in 1935 for any kind of work. The agreement contained no transportation provisions. A ship could leave New York and tie up in Houston, Texas, where the crew would be paid off, with the pleasure of walking back for all anyone cared.

But, most important of all, there was no provision in this early agreement to protect the union itself from destruction at the hands of the steamship company and the radio-service company. In their hiring and firing tactics, they could wreck any union. Let us see.

The men who made sacrifices to win these early and very meager demands saw themselves defeated and driven from the field, even though they had won tremendous victories for radio officers. They were dismissed from employment, and blacklisted for their pains. The men who benefited by what the union had done were the finks, scabs, chiselers, and fair-haired boys who took the places of the strikers. The tactics of the employers in hiring and firing, which invariably resulted in the union members losing not only their jobs but also losing all possibilities of obtaining further employment, drove the radio officers into the arms of the unlicensed personnel. . . .

The unions learned the hard way that they must control hiring in order to preserve their organizations. . . .

The current situation: Out of the maritime strikes of the second half of the thirties, new collective-bargaining agreements were agreed to, new conditions developed on the ships, and new crews with a new outlook and morale gradually took over the industry. These were men with pride in their work and pride in their union.

Decades of experience had convinced the seamen that, without union control over the hiring of its members, stabilization of employee-employer relationship was impossible; and union responsibility for the performance of its members while on the job was equally impossible to maintain.

The established, tested, and accepted method of hiring in the industry has been through the union hall. It is, for the seamen, the only guaranty against discrimination, against blacklisting, and against the destruction of his trade-union. . . .

The length of time of work is covered by union contract. The unions had to win that. We were awarded under the longshore board in 1934 a ten-hour day and a spread of fifteen hours. We gradually reduced it to where now we have an eight-hour day on ships, and a forty-hour week while the ship is in port, a forty-eight-hour week when the ship is at sea. . . .

STATEMENT BY CHARLES KASWAN, SECRETARY, BROOKLYN LONGSHOREMEN'S RANK AND FILE COMMITTEE

We are appearing before this subcommittee as representatives of several thousand longshoremen in Brooklyn, New York, who are concerned with the hiring-hall issue. The hiring-hall principle is basic to maritime trade-union interests. Without hiring through a union hall, the maritime workers are subject to the most evil of hiring practices, resulting from the "casual" nature of the trade.

The history of the maritime workers' struggles is filled with the fight against crimp joints, shanghaing of sailors, rotten conditions aboard ship, and the degradation of the slave-market shape-up. . . .

The longshoremen today in the port of New York are in the midst of depression conditions. Commissioner Murtagh (formerly Commissioner of Investigation, New York City) reported last year (1948–49) that, of 46,000 men in the port, only 2500 men made more than 2000 hours, or about $4000 a year. Over 31,000 men made less than 1120 hours, or about $2200 a year; 10,000 men made 200 hours or less, or about $500 to $600 a year. This is true for all longshoremen, and more true for the Negro longshoremen, who are especially discriminated against and, as a result, are today fighting for an equal share of the work.

As unemployment continues to mount, thousands of men drift to the waterfront to pick up a day's work. As a result, there is not only a reserve of labor but a tremendous surplus of men on the waterfront.

As a result of the "shape-up" system, men look for work every day without any knowledge of what the day will bring. From 5:30 A.M. to 7:30 A.M. men "shape" at Columbia Street in Brooklyn. From there they go to the different piers to "shape" on the odd chance that they will be hired. Most of the time they do not make it. Each pier has its steady men who report for work when a ship is in. If it rains, they are sent home to report back and "shape" again at one o'clock. If the ship must get out in a hurry, they work all night to meet the schedule. Thousands of men are riveted to individual piers while other companies may be searching for men. But the set-up is such that even men who are in so-called regular gangs do not make a living. The figures prove that. On the waterfront, it is either feast or famine.

The whole system is rotten with corruption and bribery. Men must be lackeys to hold onto the job and servile to get one. It is an inhuman, indecent method of hiring.

The speed-up follows the "shape-up" and the accident rate for longshoremen is higher than in any industry in the country. This does not stop these people from keeping a brutal hiring system alive. . . .

Just what do we mean by a hiring hall? Very simply, it means this. When ships arrive any place in the port, the union hall is called to supply the gangs, gangs are then dispatched from the hall, and they work the ship until it finishes.

This system has proved to be efficient not only on the West Coast but in every major part of the world. Such a union hiring-hall system would, of course, be honest only if it was run by a committee of men elected from the rank and file and responsible to them. The earnings of all gangs, regular and extra, would be published each month in the hall. On the West Coast, experience has shown that over the years the regular and extra men have made about the same amount of money. The average for San Francisco in 1947–48 was $3500 to $3700 a year, which is about $1200 to $1300 more than we made here.

We must also remember that this method makes it possible to cut down the speed-up, control the sling load, and enforce safety conditions. For the Negro longshoremen, it is the only guaranty of a fair share of the work without discrimination because of race.

Negroes and Discrimination

80.   *METAL FINISHER*

I have been working here just five years now. I'm a metal finisher on the convertible. I get the metal ready for the paint shop. I sand and rub the metal down so the paint shop can go ahead with the prime and painting. I like it swell. . . . Most of the time it is pretty easy. They are reasonable in what they expect of a man. Of course, they expect a full day's work, but they are not unreasonable about it. . . . The job you are doing, being satisfied with the work, and being able to get along with your associates makes it easier.

In time, I want to take up welding. . . . I want to learn as many different jobs as I can. I want to advance myself as much as possible. I think I can get a welding job when I am ready to take one. The company will give you a chance on any job just as long as you have the seniority and can qualify for the job. . . .

I am paid on group piece and I am satisfied with this way. . . .

My seniority is low, because a lot of the men have been in the department since 1918 and 1920. I think the seniority system is fine. . . . A person has some protection in his job. Otherwise anyone who wanted it could take it. . . . It gives a person with seniority protection on his job.

My boss is head foreman. He has to get out his production in order to satisfy the company. He has to see that the quality of the work is the best. He has to keep harmony in his group and see that most of the men are satisfied with working conditions. . . . I like him very well so far. I have no complaints and neither do the other men in my group. . . . A man who has the right personality for the job makes the best foreman. One who can get along with all types of individuals. One who has patience with his men, especially the new men who come on a job and when they are still learning some of the job. . . . So far, in my department, I would say the foremen have been rather neutral. They take the side of the company when it comes to getting out production, but I don't feel that they are unreasonable about it. After all, that is their job.

If I felt I knew everything about the job and were capable of handling it, I would want to be a foreman. I feel that I could handle men and get along with them. My chances for becoming a foreman are not too good, but I suppose if there was an opening and I could qualify for the job, the company would take me into consideration.

On my line, we have a chief steward and a steward. The steward should look after his men. He should carry out all their complaints to the end. He should keep them informed about company-union relations. He should give the men an answer on the complaints they make to him and the questions they ask him. . . . I like my steward very well.

The union wants to see that the men make a living and that they are treated right, and not like years ago before the unions when the working man had to do anything the company said, reasonable or otherwise. They want to see that the men are not pushed or crowded in their work. . . . We are better off with a union—we have better working conditions and we earn better wages. . . .

The union co-op is swell. Prices are a little cheaper. Regardless of race, they welcome you just the same. I buy there about once a week.

I guess I go to union meetings as often as the rest of the men. There is no discrimination at the meetings regardless of color. I can get up and argue a point as well as anyone else. All of the members are very congenial. There has been no discrimination shown toward me because I am colored. I feel good about that. As for my case and my race, I think that depends on the individual man. It depends on how he acts. If he is okay with the other men, they will treat him well in return. We all get along swell. . . .

81. NEGRO MEATPACKER

Compared to previous years, my take-home pay has been most enormous this past year because we have had a tremendous influx of business. My pay hasn't increased so much but the hours that I'm working have increased. . . . From last August right on through now we've been just steady-going—in that department we haven't had a week under forty hours this past year. The men who made less than forty hours a week there are laying off for sickness or something like that at home. But the one who works the required amount of hours has averaged more than fifty hours a week for the past year. We get time and a half for overtime and double time for Sunday.

. . . I've got two children, a girl fifteen and a boy twelve. They're deciding now on their careers—they're both studying music. . . .

I'm a veteran—I've been in two wars. I was in World War II for four years and went back into the Service in '50 and went to Korea in '51. . . . The Army has the policy of utilizing manpower to the point where whatever you can do, the field is open for you. . . . The branch of the Army that I followed . . . The Service Air Corps, there's a field open for whatever talents you can follow. . . . When a Negro comes to *T.* the ceiling is very low, that is, he has to give manual labor from the time he gets here to the time he dies. Or to the time he quits or leaves. . . . If you have a strong back and a weak mind, there's always a place for a Negro at *T.*'s; but not if you're looking for promotion, . . . not if you want to feel as though you are a part of the big movement at *T.* . . . A man who's been here for forty years will probably be drawing within 15 cents of the same wage. . . . But, it adds up to something else, too. You have to live and we've spent too much time in one place . . . to start migrating or start shopping around for something different. When you can't bring your job earnings up to your way of thinking, you have to bring your way of thinking down to your income. So, that's the size of it. . . .

It is assumed when a Negro comes to this place seeking employment that he has no qualifications other than to partially . . . follow instructions. What he knows is not important, they're more or less not concerned with it. It's *Can you pull this truck?* or *Can you lift this?* or *Can you drive that tractor?* or something like that. . . .

I read in the papers that our President, for instance, says that he doesn't believe in a second-class citizen! Well, I'd be the last one to say that *T.* is a second-class industry but why should they have second-class employees? . . .

In the past ten years . . . the ceiling for Mexicans has been lifted. There's a little more fraternization between the Mexicans and the Caucasions . . . for the Negro I'd say that the ones who have gone out when they were sixty-five were doing some type of physical labor. I'm thirty-eight years of age and if I have to stay here . . . until I get sixty-five, then I have to do physical labor for the next probably twenty-seven or thirty years. . . . I don't think there's any place here in *T.* for a Negro technician of any type. Not so long ago we had a colored kid, . . . a college kid—been in the service for a couple of years, he's a lieutenant in the Air Force, and he came here seeking employment. . . . I doubt seriously that they even know . . . the qualifications that he has for adapting himself or qualifying for any type of position. . . . He left here in disgust. . . . I think in time maybe, the distant future—won't be in my lifetime, I'm sure—that there will be more or less a basis of equality in all industry to operate efficiently and whether you're blue or black they'll more or less have to utilize their manpower—get the best out of every individual regardless of his race, color or creed. . . .

I've been in my department since the first of 1940 . . . I am a sealer. . . . The top job in there is a back-breaking job—that's lugging beefs. . . . The top job, excluding lugging beef is ribbing. It's cutting the carcass. . . . They have two gang leaders. . . . That is, with pay for a gang leader. We have a night gang and a day gang. I definitely would not have a chance at that. I venture the chance would be about ten thousand to one.

. . . The foreman that I have knows his job as well as anyone could know it, because that's all he *knows.* I'd say that you couldn't find a better man anywhere, but I do find (this is my personal opinion, not the opinion of the gang) that he's a little less efficient in placing a man on the job. Right now you take the loaders up there. The loaders are the backbone of the department because they carry the heaviest load. The only way they can get it in the department is to carry it. Now, there's nothing in the world that's any more demoralizing to them than to have a gang of five or six men carrying one load and then without any warning the foreman will come by and take three of them away and leave three men to do the same job that six men were doing. . . . I always said a cheerful word out of the foreman the first thing in the morning to all the employees sets them about their task in such a happy mood and before you know it you'd have 25 per cent more production coming out.

In that department . . . or in all related industry right now—there are certain jobs in there that are Negro jobs, there are certain jobs that are white jobs. In the past couple of weeks you could say there is a white fellow lugging beef out there—that's true, he is—but he's not lugging beef for a living, he's lugging beef to make some money to go back to school on.

A Negro, he's a funny fellow . . . if he's given no consideration, given no representation, well, in a lot of cases he'll act the jester. He has no sense of responsibility—he's just as carefree as he wants to be. . . . A man'll come to the Army just as trifling as he can be—he don't care whether he goes to the guardhouse . . . and just as soon as you give him a little responsibility you'll see him change just like day and night; it was true in my case; I went to the Army and first thing I had one thing in mind—getting out. . . . Well, first they gave me a job as clerk-typist and I . . . didn't have to get out and march with the other guys and I felt like a little more or less a privileged character. I did that for a little while and then they promoted me and I went to the Supply Station but had I not been given a job of responsibility, then I probably would have been just a potential—what you might say—a guardhouse threat. It's the same way here at *T*. You find men who don't give a darn—all they do is walk around there and shoot the bull all day long—they don't care; if you tell me what to do then I'll do it—why accept the responsibility and get gray hairs like you're doing if I'm not going to get the money—I'll use my strength and you use your head; you know, that's as far as I'm going. You know, they develop that attitude quickly, but in the same way with a little orientation or a little more or less psychoanalysis of the individual you could put them in a position of responsibility and you could get the maximum I would say.

82. PORK CUTTERS

My job is ham pumping, vein pumping. In the first place, it's a very disagreeable work. . . . We have to work in a department where the temperature is down to thirty degrees, that's only about six degrees above freezing. And all around our heads and all around us is ice coils. This cold . . . will penetrate your clothes, and get inside and you become chilled. . . . You don't do hardly any work with your feet. . . . All your work is done around the shoulders. And it tires you out all through there, and all through the neck, and you've got to be lookin' down. . . . And at the tremendous speed that you got to go at there, to make the standard.

There are other jobs but because of the condition that exists there in the plant, the colored people don't have the opportunity to move into those jobs regardless of qualifications. . . . I, myself, . . . have, in the employment office out there, . . . a record of where . . . I'm capable of being a ham boner, or beef boner, or a sheep boner. Now that's a hard department for Negroes to get into. That is, the boning departments, where they make the larger salaries. . . . And also, I don't have it on this record, but some of the foremen know it right in my own particular department—on the outside of the plant, I'm a cabinetmaker. I build cabinets and I also do carpenter work. And on top of that, see . . . I'm an upholsterer. . . .

But it's hard to get in the carpenter gang. It's hard to get into those skilled jobs . . . because of the favoritism that is played there because of discrimination. And also because of the union there that don't favor people that don't belong in their organization. Now it would probably be a way for me to get in there. . . . If I would go and rejoin the Independent union, and play along with the foreman and do whatever the representation desires, why maybe I might have a better chance of getting in there than if I stood my ground and was a man.

When I wanted to go bone hams, I was in the Independent union, and they hired men from the gate. They sent down to Texas, where they could get ham boners and brought them in there from the gate. . . . And I didn't have the opportunity to go over there. . . . It wasn't only . . . racial prejudice in this case because people working right in the trimming room . . . wanted to go over in the boning room where the vice president of the union, H. I., is employed as a ham boner. He told Rudy to his face that "we don't want you over here . . . you're a Hunk and you cause too much trouble and we don't want you over here and you're not coming over here." Now the man'll tell you that hisself if you talk to him and ask him that. And he hasn't gotten over that today. So it only doesn't apply to just us as a whole—it's who they want to work with. That's the situation, there; if I have a dislike for the way you look, or the way you act, something like that, I'll tell the boy, "Well, I don't want to work with you."

I'm in pork cut . . . I've done practically everything in the cutting. Started as a hog pusher. That was in 1919. During the strike there in 1921, that's when the AFL was there . . . I had a chance to advance to the cutting room . . . and I trimmed loins for a while. I trimmed bellies for a while. And then as far as seniority was concerned in those days, it didn't mean anything. It's just who the foreman wanted to work on certain jobs, well . . . it's according to the color of your skin. Now, loin pulling, scribing, and those hard jobs, we, as Negroes, could get those jobs. But when it comes to trimming bellies, and sawing shoulders, and trimming hams and skinning hams, they had all white men on the job at that particular time. But as the war came along we advanced to those jobs. But it still remains a fact that the foreman can still work you where he wants to. Now I've pulled loins as I stated before, I scribed, and I trimmed loin, I trimmed bellies, and finally I graduated to the ham table, which is the highest priced job in the cutting room. They've reduced the ham trimmers down to one man. . . . And that's me, of course, because I've got thirty-two years service there, and I'm next to the oldest man in the department.

The only reason I do the job is because I'm just like every other poor person, trying to make a living. I have a family, I have a home, I'm trying to live up to the best living standards that I can get out of life. . . . I like a decent living, I like to wear a few decent clothes, I like to have a decent home to live in, I like to have a decent car to ride in, if I want to get out of here and go someplace on the weekend, I like to feel that I can do that, after working thirty-two years. . . . And that's one of the reasons that I take the job. It's not because I want to work that hard. Now I did have in mind at one time transferring to the police department. But I got to figuring there that I would come up at least $25 or $30 less on the week. And I just figures that I couldn't stand that much of a cut. . . . Naturally, since I went into that department from wanting to make more money, worked in there all through my younger days, why I'm just like the average packing house worker, I'll stay there until I drop, if I don't reach the retirement age before I drop out.

I guess you know about the screening process of women when they are hired in there. They get put on the roughest job in there.

I have two stepdaughters, and we have spent quite a bit of money on trying to get those kids an education. Of course, they have been through college. . . . They are capable of running those dictaphones and . . . teletype machines. . . . If they had the opportunity to get such jobs, or even if they had the opportunity to go into a plant and work on a job until they had an opening to get an advancement, or go into the departmental offices as clerks, like the other people has the chance to advance, under those conditions, I wouldn't hesitate to let them come to *T.*

T. uses . . . pretty elaborate policy as far as the personnel they employ. They know how to press the employees without causing a reversal in their attitude towards working. . . . They're pressing almost to the breaking point, . . . and yet . . . they're still patting them on the back and saying this and that and . . . offering them . . . incentives and all the other concessions, fixing up the dressing rooms a little better than . . . *R.*'s or *S.*'s plant. . . . *T.* has a more diplomatic policy in handling its employees. But on the whole . . . *T.* is exacting more work per man out of the employees through this policy that they use than they are in . . . *R.*'s or *S.*'s.

83. CAFETERIA WORKER

I'm up at four o'clock every morning, and I leave home at five o'clock. It's always five-thirty when I get down. I first go out to the Chief's office and pick up the keys and the money.

I start up the plant: turns on the grill. Then I turns the water in the can and makes twenty-four gallons of coffee to start with. Then I starts wrapping the rolls, after I get the coffee made, and we make about twenty or twenty-five loaves of toast, and we fry around nine dozen eggs; that's just the *start* of it. Then the bucket line then starts at seven o'clock. I like this job . . . because it's a part of me. When I first started to working here though I started up in the kitchen as a cook—I was the third cook. I made all the bread and the pies: well, as the years passed after wartime then the work got lighter than it was when we first started: they was *three* of us girls then, now it's down to one. The work isn't bad—I find that it isn't so much the boss, it's our fellow-man we work with.

We get along pretty good, I guess. . . . The same crew been on the job ever since I been here. . . . All that's here now is been here around ten, eleven years: they just been working right together and they bound to have some little jealousy sometimes, but I'm just one of those that take it that way, just go along with it. I have no objection to the pay, because Uncle Sam takes all of it now. We are rated the same as the girls are in the plant. The only difference is we're on a straight forty hours basis. And they on a thirty-six hour basis. *We* gets our uniforms and get our meals. We draw down our regular paycheck, $54 a week—well, that isn't bad, you know. We don't work on Saturday—and they allow you $26 a year for uniforms and they pay that in installments, 50 cents a week, it comes on your check, each and every week, and of course if you order your uniforms they take it out of your check that particular time that you order it. Then they allow you fifteen minutes at breakfast time, they pay you for that.

If I had a son and if he were old enough I'd bring him down to get him a job. You see, this place is going to be like a *family* like—I think everybody in here is sorta relations.

I worked in private families for years an' years an' *years,* you know that's difficult as hell.

84.   THE WAITER

This restaurant is said to be one of the biggest in the world. There is seating for 2800 at capacity, with a turnover of 25,000 daily during the summer season. Approximately two hundred forty waiters are employed; cashiers, cooks, processors, dishwashers, utility men account for another one hundred employees.

The waiters, dishwashers, food processors, supply room men, cooks, and bakers are all Negroes. The bartender, salad, clam and oyster openers, checkers, cashiers, and utility men are Caucasians of German descent usually, or of other Nordic background. The jobs that Negroes have are applied for by coming in off the street. The other employees are usually friends of present employees who recommend them. In the case of cashiers and checkers formal recommendations and some school background or experience is required.

The wage of waiters is one dollar per hour. There is a very tentative schedule of regular waiters and their stations. However, waiters may informally take off any day, except Sunday, the one compulsory work day for everyone except the Boss. If a waiter or any other employee does not work on Sunday, he cannot return to work until the following Sunday. In the case of waiters not working on Sunday, there is a reduction in the wage to 75 cents per hour for all hours worked preceding that Sunday. . . .

Waiters who do work on Sunday must turn in six checks, or be penalized to the 75 cents an hour rate. Each waiter is given a book of checks on which he writes the customers' orders. . . .

The waiters have difficulty getting six checks out. The answer to this problem is for the waiter to give several of his checks to waiters in the Clam Bar or First Section, who make out many checks in excess of the minimum. One has to be careful to give his check to a friend, because the checks are numbered, the head cashier and the checker make hourly counts of the checks coming in. . . . If a waiter is discovered doing this, the waiter will be fired. . . . If the head cashier is in a good mood, then both waiters concerned will be given only a week "in the street."

The waiters may not eat anything on the menus but tea, coffee, soups, and biscuits.

There are special cotton uniforms supplied to waiters. The bow ties that must be worn, the waiters must purchase outside. The uniforms are given out twice weekly. Often the supply is exhausted before half of the waiters have had a chance to exchange.

An alternative is to take shirts and pants, the most easily dirtied item, off of the laundry hamper, when the truck delivers the linen. These extra items are hoarded in the lockers.

There are two sizes of tray, small and large. The large size is by far the more popular and practical. However, there are not enough of the large trays to meet the demand. Consequently, on the eve of weekends or holidays, most waiters hide a tray somewhere in the kitchen upstairs, or in the locker room. Some waiters even put their trays in the refrigerator room where no waiters are allowed.

All breakages are the responsibility of the waiter. If a waiter accidentally bumps into you and upsets your tray, you are responsible. If a waiter slips and falls on a wet spot or some spilled food, he has to pay. The price can be quite high. Thus when a waiter drops something out of sight of the cashier or checker, he will keep on moving as if it never happened. When this happens in the kitchen, the checker chooses whoever is standing near the damage that he thinks is guilty. Since the checker never says who he thinks is to blame, waiters never know who was charged until one comes up short on payday.

When customers accidentally knock over a waiter's tray, the waiter must pay. If a customer complains that he was soiled by the accident, then the waiter must pay for the cleaning job.

Walkouts are the constant fear of every waiter, especially when he is in the Clam Bar, where the lower class of patrons eat. The waiter is responsible for the check being paid at all times. If there is a walkout, he must pay or else be fired.

There are many reasons why a customer will register a formal complaint. Most of the complaints are due to impatience and non-consideration by the customer. Many such complaints result in the waiter being permanently "put into the street."

The causes of complaints generally fall into three categories—verbal insults, poor service, and refusal to take a customer's order.

Verbal insults usually result from a patron "running" a waiter to the kitchen for one item at a time, and concludes by leaving a miserable tip. This type of character is known as a "snake." The waiter, after several snakes, has had his patience peeled thin. When a waiter has more than one party, a snake can put him "up a tree." Thus a remark may slip out, and the customer complains. Some waiters have thrown miserable tips on the floor or else told the customer to keep his money. Often for an $18.98 check, a party of six will give a waiter a twenty and tell him to keep the change. If the waiter says, "What change?" the customer is insulted.

Another type of customer who pressures the waiters are the "wheels." Each Friday afternoon and often during the dinner rush, a group of well-dressed Armed Forces officers or businessmen enter. The waiters without experience think this is a good party, since men tip much better than women or mixed groups. This party usually orders lots of drinks, stressing speed, and how good the waiter is, while they loudly discuss their interests. When the bill is presented they get the menu and sit for fifteen minutes figuring to the penny what each man had, and taking up a collection. In such cases the waiter rarely gets even 10 per cent of the check.

Another type waiters avoid is a couple with small children. The table is usually a mess, and no other party wants to sit near a party with children, if any other table is available. Besides this, there is the running for extra plates, high chairs, the porter for spilled food, and clean silverware to replace what drops on the floor.

A further annoyonce is also the silver situation and the kitchen system that causes many delays which precipitate complaints of inattention. There is not enough silverware to have a complete setting when the restaurant has all sections open, which is the case on weekends, and summer evenings. The waiters that come in early have first pick and they hide an extra set so when the rush is on they will have silver available for resetting the table. The waiters who come in late wait by the dirty silver drop and pick up pieces that come in and wash them themselves. When waiters come into the kitchen with dirty silver they do not drop it, but keep it and wash it so they can have another setting. Teaspoons and knives and cocktail forks are especially low in supply but high in demand. Waiters will steal from another waiter's set-up table and thus that waiter has to find more silverware at the silver drop or steal from someone when he gets customers. This eats up time.

Another source of delay besides long lines at each of the particular points in the kitchen is the stealing of orders. All food except drinks, soups, steamed clams, and vegetables must be ordered, then picked up when they are ready. Often a waiter who has forgotten to order will pretend he has, and pick up some other waiter's order. When the original waiter returns to pick up, there is nothing there and he must reorder and wait. With a tray of hot food this can put a waiter "up a tree," and make the patrons think his service is poor.

Waiters often pay off the lobster, steak, chops, and broiled fish cooks, usually weekly, to insure fast and favored treatment in the filling of orders. This proves very beneficial in the rush when the waiter has more than one party. He can order and pick up somebody else's order immediately, rather than having to wait as long as fifteen minutes for his own order to be cooked. All fish and meat is cooked to order as are "gratins" and newbergs.

Another source of waiter irritation and delay are the personality conflicts one has with the cooks and the men behind the counters in the kitchen. The cooks have more authority than waiters do, but yet they must take orders from the waiters. Often waiters are misunderstood, and their orders are not filled, so they speak harshly to the cook concerned. This means the cook will take his time about getting the order out to show the waiter who is really boss. These kitchen men, except dishwashers and porters, eat whatever they like except steak. The checkers and cashiers also may have whatever they care to eat and may sit in the dining area at some waiter's table and be served their meals. They leave no tip, and the waiter does not expect one. They represent lost money. Some cashiers and checkers will sit in unopened areas and be served.

The cashiers are not annoying to the waiter, but it is obvious in the situation, that they have much more status than waiters. The head cashier, who might better be called the floor manager, is the exception. In almost every complaint or ambiguous situation, he will side against the waiter. When a customer says his food was not cooked as he requested, the waiter has to pay for the unsatisfactory food, if the head cashier gets into the situation.

Skill and Satisfaction

85. A DIE DESIGNER

I'm a die designer. We draw up the prints when somebody has a bright idea for a new die. They come around to the planner and ask him whether or not we should work on it. They then give it to us and we have to design a die that will compete with one that they might have designed outside.

I used to make dies, that's how I got started. I came to *E.* for my apprenticeship. I had never done anything else. Right out of high school. I had a friend whose father was a supervisor and this fellow started in. In those days jobs were tight and it wasn't too easy. I came in after he did. He told me about it and managed to get me in. But I wasn't doing tool and die work then. They started me on the line. I worked on the line nights. But after I was in the plant for a while I looked around and I thought that I'd like to go into die work.

You'd walk into the die shop and it was always so neat and clean. They clean the machines up every weekend. The floors were always clean. Maybe the day superintendent was just tired of seeing me around or maybe he thought I could do the work, but he took me on as an apprentice. I had to take a cut in pay but it was worthwhile.

In die-making I could always see that there was something ahead. On the line you can only go so far and then maybe you could earn more money if you worked harder but there was never any chance for advancement. Here, you could go right up to the top. Most of the biggest men come from die-making you know.

I talked to my wife about this move, only we weren't married yet. She thought it was a good idea, too. So I started at the bottom. That was about two years before the beginning of the war. Along with this you were supposed to go to school at night. We started there by taking what they called a five-year course. I finished it up in 2800 hours. That meant some going. They taught us all that an engineer learns but with a practical standpoint. All this time I was moving up.

Things always seemed to break right. My bosses have always been great guys. I guess I must be lucky about things like that. Because I've seen a great many fellows doing the same work as me drop or just not move up. But this is the way I look at it.

I'm always going to do the best job I can. *E.* is my company. I'm going to stick with them until they cross me up. Until now they've been very good to me. If what I want doesn't satisfy them, well, that's just too bad. I can't do any better and they're just going to have to take it.

When I got back from the Army I thought I should be in a higher position. I never said anything about it but one day the superintendent called me into his office and he asked me if I wanted to be a designer. I had never been any great shakes at drawing in school but I figured I'd have a go at it. Well, that's what I'm doing today and I'm one of eight in the whole *E.* plant. You see what I draw and design in eight hours can keep men busy for fifty or sixty.

I never thought about college. College had nothing for me. Besides, my father never had much and he couldn't have afforded to send me. He had great plans.

I have a brother and he expected that we would all go into business together. He sent my brother to the State Trade School for drafting and would you believe it he hasn't drawn a line since he left. He's a foreman outside of town. He has a good job, so I guess it wasn't wasted.

My father wanted me to be a sheet metal worker. A tin-knocker. But I could never see it. I think I'm better off the way I am. But, did you ever notice how each generation the father wants something better for his sons than he had for himself. Now my father worked on the line. Oh, he called himself a position setter but actually he was only a production worker. He always wanted me to have a trade. Now with my son I want him to have a profession.

But not engineering. That's not a profession.

The engineers have to come to me to ask questions. I won't take anything away from them, they're smart. They know all about stresses and strains but when they want something done they have to come to me. That's something I'm very proud of. No, what I mean by a profession is something like a doctor, or a dentist. A dentist; you know someday I'm going to sell the house, get a trailer, quit my job, and take up Uncle Sam's offer to go to school and become a dentist. I guess that sounds silly to you. But really, I've thought very seriously about it. I'll probably never do it, but still it's a possibility. If I wasn't married there'd be no doubt, that's what I'd do. I think my son, well I don't know, those things never work out. Just look at my father. What he wanted for me never panned out so probably what I plan for my son won't pan out either.

I'm not a money man. I always will have enough but I guess I'll always want a little more. That's the way Americans are. I always want to give whoever I work for my very best. I figure if they go out on a limb and hire me the least I can do is to work. There are some fellows who will work only when the boss is watching them. On my job we have to keep working. No one watches us but we have a certain, I guess you might call it pride in our work. You see, we're just not line workers. We're doing a highly skilled job and it wouldn't be fair unless we turned out the work. Lately the shop hasn't been working as efficiently as it could, that's why they are making this change. Things are tightening up. Before, if it said 150 hours on a job and it took 200 hours nobody said anything but now if it isn't done in the proper time somebody will have to answer up.

I always thought that if somebody had his own business he was all set. But it's pretty dangerous, one false move and you're all through, and when you've got a wife and kids you can't take chances like that.

The smart ones become foremen. The ones who keep their mouth shut and don't give trouble. *E.* alumni are usually given preference. *E.* breaks us in the way they like and most of the time these guys come up. But that doesn't mean another man hasn't a chance. Although it's only fair to say that just the other day I saw a fellow who was much the better of a couple of men get dealt out of a good job because there was an *E.* man ahead of him.

There'll always be something ahead for me. There always has been and there's no reason why it should stop now. I'm pretty good and they know it.

86.   I RUN A ROTATOR

I came here when I was twenty years old. I really never worked anywhere else. . . . The worst thing that I ever had against this place was those standards checkers. Those fellows, in my estimation . . . they're the type of person that's going to tell somebody what they should do when they've never done anything their self.

They're getting their food pretty free in my way of thinking. They're living off somebody's sweat and toil.

Of course, they're not bad now because you can get help, but in hard times . . . a great big, fat lummox came around . . . telling you you're not doing enough. And that time I was weighing about . . . 135 pounds, and there I was taking a big old truck down to the pickle cellar and . . . pulling eleven or twelve hundred pounds of meat around, and then some of them jokers telling you you're not doing enough and here he's on his fanny, living off me—that's what gets me.

It's set up so that you can do so much work in an hour and if you do more you're supposed to get paid more. The funny thing about it is the harder you work the less you make. . . . It don't take you long to get wise to that: if you get in too big of a hurry then you don't make anything. . . . You should just keep busy and stir around. . . . Right now it's better with the bonus system, because they can't push men around—they'll quit and go to work somewhere else. But in hard times, when you can't get a job nowhere, like it was when I came here, I'd rather be without it 'cause it's a hard way to go.

Now, you get to makin' too much money, they'll come down there and have their stopwatch out and start looking all around and, whenever business falls off and the expenses start running a little high in the department, here they come. . . . The first they do is to cut labor.

I run a rotator. The rotator's used to do several things. They run mayonnaise through it and they use it for ice cream and for margarine. I watch the rotator and pack the butter. It's very nice—it's not a bad job—it isn't bad at all.

I got no kick about the pay—it's pretty good. . . . I don't have any trouble, unless I have sickness or something. I generally take a month or six weeks off during the year.

The boss down there is a pretty good fellow. . . . He's like me, he wants to stay around here, see? He kind of says: "I like it because my boss likes it." He knows that if he don't do what they want him to do then they're goin' to get rid of him. That's the way I got him figured out.

I think this new superintendent is a pretty square man. The reason I think he's a good man's because all the bosses are scared of him. . . . I want you to leave your Lodges and churches at home, he told me. He says, I don't care what church you belong to.

I'm from the old school. When I came here we really worked. It looks like play now to me. . . . These guys that's younger acts like they're being abused, but I can't see it. . . . I came here in '33, right at the bottom of the depression. It was pretty rough. You don't work that way any more.

You'd be surprised at the people around here that live from hand to mouth. And on payday, their wives is comin' down there to meet them to take them home. If *my old lady and my kid* ever came down here to take me home, I'd be so ashamed of myself, I'd go stick my head in that door. They got to come down here and take the old man home on payday to be sure they'll get something to eat.

87.   *I'M A FITTER*

I'm a fitter. I'm on the floor three days and two days I'm upstairs. We make appointments to fit regular customers then. I like it. You have to like our line of work because if you don't like it you'd have to give it up because you need so much patience.

I've worked hard since I was fourteen years old and I've had responsibility. I think when I get to be sixty-five I would like to have a few years left to do just as I felt like. I'd like to do charity work and work for orphans and then I'd work a few days out by the day. Money, you know. You have to have a terrible lot of money to get along without it. I do think I would miss the work when I retire, because you get used to the girls just like one big family, you know.

I cut and fit that Princess Margaret dress we had in the window. This was wonderful. I got a big thrill out of it. It's a very beautiful dress. The responsibility was it, I guess. Thinking you could do it. I cut and fit that dress, made a pattern and copied the picture. After all you do have to have something to know how to do that. You have to have a gift to do that kind of work. I started doing it when . . . my mother just said I would have to sew. That was all. There were eight of us. I was the one that was picked to do the sewing. I was fourteen. Past fourteen when I started out. I started out just because she said I had to work. I had to work for one and a half dollars a week. Fifty cents car fare and did part of the housework after I came home besides. I worked from eight to six, six days a week. From that I jumped to about three-fifty and thought I was brilliant. Then I worked at the _____ building two and a half years and got up to seven dollars and then twelve dollars and from there I came here and I had charge of the lining table. We made fitted linings at that time and later went out again myself. We don't have that now. That was regular custom dressmaking. It's much harder than ready-to-wear because when you cut and fit you only have one dress. You don't see any other like it.

I was younger then. I liked it then. But I wouldn't want it anymore. Now I like to alter. I don't want to be responsible in that way and there's not enough money. I haven't got that much patience any more. Age makes a difference.

I used to take off July and August. Always two months and for six or seven years maybe longer, I went to New York and I would work in the highest class factory. I was getting then, for five days a week, forty dollars. That was big money. The reason I went to New York was I got my ideas at high-class shops.

I just went as an ordinary machine operator. I didn't tell them about my experience. I didn't want that kind of job. I wanted easy work. I studied the big shops and how they did things. And for nineteen years I taught night school. I taught four nights a week, twenty weeks a year besides my day work. I love to teach. Yes, I really should have went into that because I got some pupils who couldn't sew . . . a button on and I turned out some mighty fine pupils. It's really nice to see results. Nothing makes you feel happier. And I met a lot of friends . . . people who are still friends.

I'm just ambitious, that's all. And when the day is over I want to know what I done. I want to accomplish something. I couldn't sit down and read a book and just do nothing. I also want to get something done besides taking care of my house and doing shopping and everything else. I think people that work and keep themselves busy are happiest. Other people get in a rut. Some people say, "an idle mind is the devil's home," and I think it is.

88. FURNACE MAN

I work on the open hearth, on the molds. . . . I work on any furnace that's ready to pour. I get the ladle in place and make sure the mold is ready. I do it on all the furnaces in the open hearth. . . . It is a dangerous job, but I've never been hurt. You have to use your head and be careful. Some men have been killed out there when they weren't careful. I don't believe in taking chances—I use my head.
. . . . It's the best job I ever had. I sure do like it. At least it's the best job for me. It's easy work. When I'm through one furnace, I can go rest for a while until they're ready to tap another. And I can work by myself. I don't have a boss telling me to keep busy all the time.
. . . The only thing is, it's a little hot and dangerous. In the summer it gets pretty hot—but not like on the other hearth where I used to work—the chargers and helpers have to stand right by the furnace and work. My job gets a little hot sometimes, but not like by the furnace.

I have had this job for nine years. I've worked with the same men all that time, too. They call me "uncle" because I know them so well. I've been in the open hearth seventeen years altogether, since I first came to D. I used to work in a labor gang on the furnaces. Then I got to be helper. I quit that job, though, because it was too hot and hard.

. . . I came to *T.* first in 1929. I worked at the rolling mill over here in East Chicago for a few years, till 1933. Then, you know how it was—I couldn't find any job till 1935. The rolling mill shut down, and I heard *D.* was hiring men. I came over at least once a week and they'd let me work for a day. Then, in 1935, they hired me at the open hearth.

I came up to this country from Mexico in 1907. I worked on a farm first—then got a job on the railroads. I worked on the railroads a long time, as labor. Then I quit and came to the rolling mill in East Chicago. . . . If I could be a young man again . . . I'd go right to *D.!* I'd want my job—I'd have gotten it a lot younger if I'd known about it, but I was there a long time before I knew about it and I was pretty old then. It's the best job I've ever had, like I said.

I don't get a lot of money on this job, but I can take it easy, do my work, and still feel healthy. Some people all they want is money—they think they'll do anything for money. So they get jobs that pay well and they leave their lives at their jobs—they kill a man before he's thirty. I knew a young fellow who got a job as helper when he was twenty or twenty-five. Inside of ten years, he was half dead—he was dragging his arms, couldn't see—he was killing himself just for the money. I wouldn't want more money that bad. When I was working as helper, I was getting the same way, feeling half dead, dragging my arms, not hungry, couldn't sleep—so I quit and got my other job. A man feels healthy if he's got a good job, but he can kill himself if he's just working for money. I don't care about money that much.

I'd rather have friends than be a foreman. The best friends you have are the men you work with, and if you're a foreman, you have to be boss and tell your friends what to do. . . . I used to be foreman. Pretty soon, I didn't have any friends anymore; everyone stayed away from me. So, after six months, I quit. I didn't want the job anymore.

A man dies if he doesn't have a job—a lot of men retire, then die as soon as they receive their first pension check. When I was sixty-five, I left for two weeks. Then I came back and said I wanted to go back to work. They said the law was I had to retire when I was sixty-five, but I could go on working if the superintendent said so. I asked my superintendent and he let me have my job back.

89. LEARN A TRADE

Oh, I like my work—it's a good class of tool and die work. It's a nice clean place. And they're more lenient there than in most places.

There's a lot of things I dislike, but I know there's nothing I can do about it. If you want a job you got to go get your own job, especially on the night shift. I think the job should be given to you. Actually, I think the supervisor should give you the type of job that he thinks that you can handle. And he don't do that. You just go out and pick out a die, and then after you get into it you find out that it's over your head—and then you're stuck with it, you can't stop then, you got to go ahead with it. Which is sometimes good, but I would say it's bad for the company. After a die-maker has been in the game for quite some years, all dies are alike. I don't have any trouble with any of them. You just pick one out and start to work on it; if it's a hard one, it's just a hard one, that's all there is to it. Have to put a little more effort behind it to get the thing done.

I believe that they could stand a newer type of machine than what they have to do the job. Some of the machinery that they're using there has been used for twenty-five or thirty years, and to do the job, it's difficult. You just work and work, and when you get done you don't know whether it's going to be good or bad.

Them bench lathes that they have are just about thirty years behind times. We call them a perforator, that's what you perforate holes with; I've seen fellows grind perforators, takes them six or eight hours to grind a perforator—where the job could be done in less than twenty or thirty minutes if they had the right machinery. And the company doesn't seem like that they care—they see it going on every day. The bosses know it, and they don't care, so why should the fellows care? You can't do much suggestive work out there.

I like the job real well, but I'm in a little different category than most of the fellows out there—I've got my own business that I'm operating, I've got my mind on it, I have more of a tendency to not even care as much as the rest of them.

I do like supervision work.

It gives me a chance to use my ingenuity, my ability. Out here, I don't think that I've ever used my ability.

I think my immediate supervisor at the plant, the man I'm working for now, is below average. His personality for one thing, is just rotten. I know what I think of the man—of all the men that I've ever worked for, I've worked for quite a few, he's just about the most hateful, disrespectful, conceited person that a man would ever meet—I don't know how he ever got that job. He has no judgment whatsoever. And he's lazy. The day boss can come out and offer me a job, I don't care what it is, and I'll just break my neck to help the man out, I just can't wait to get started on it, and this other fellow comes out and gives me a job, and I can't wait to put the brakes on. That's just the difference in the two.

It's a nice plant. By the way, most of the people I've met there, I'd say 90 per cent of them are pretty good people all the way around. They're nice people—course you've always got a few rotten eggs in the basket, but the majority of them are pretty nice guys, and if you're stuck they'll just drop whatever they are doing and help you. And the factory goes out of their way to keep the employees contented. And I believe the company gives them about every break that they can afford to give them. And I think they pay about as good money as you could get anywhere. And it's just a good general all-around company, that's all.

As a tool and die maker, I feel that I have ability that the average man don't have. I can look at almost anything even in this room and tell you how it was made, and if I had to turn around and make the dies to duplicate it, I believe I could. And anything that I do in my normal course of life, the die-making helps me. I know how to put things up real quick to make them work, and I believe that it was one of the best steps I ever took. I think it's got all other skill trades beat a hundred miles. In the apprenticeship training—you had to spend 9000 hours in the shop, 9000 hours to become a journeyman tool and die maker—8000 hours for a machinist.

It takes a lot of thinking sometimes, it'll bring the good and the bad out of you. You get a job sometimes where it requires a lot of thinking, a lot of time, you've got to measure twice and cut once, and when you get a job say like on a big molding die, where you've already put say four or five hundred dollars in it, just one slip and it's wrecked, it's no good, you got to stop and think. Got to make sure you know what you're doing, and you don't want nobody bothering you when you're doing it. You got to be in a good frame of mind, and I believe that when a man does that when you get the job all done, why, you've gotta pat yourself on the back and start on something else.

I talked to all the young fellows that I know—I mean I tell everyone of them to learn a trade of some kind, get a skilled trade underneath your belt, and then after you've learned it, then you can go anywhere and do anything.

I have my sights set on some things that might be selfish in a way. I got my sights set on a new home, a nice home for my family. I've been up and down the ladder twice. I had a nice beautiful home once, and I sold it and spent the money, and I had nice cars and everything; I've had beautiful furniture before, but I'm getting a little older now, not quite so wild. I'm willing to work hard for it; I want my boys to have a good education, I want to be able to provide for them, I want them to have things that I never had, and in order to strive for that goal, I believe you got to really get out and hustle. And I want my wife to have things that she never had before, and in order to achieve all that, I can never do it working at *H*. I could do it, but it would take me all my life. All my life I would work out there, and I would have to save and scrape, and save and scrape, and maybe by the time I was fifty or sixty, I might have it. I don't want to wait that long.

I wouldn't quit my job at $150 a week to take a job less. Never have, always take a job for more money. And I believe that I can make two or three times that amount. I have did it, I have been doing it right along, I make about two or three times the amount I make at *H*. And so, I decided that my business is a good one and I better stick right with it. Better drop the tool and dies. . . . Most people will want something, and they stand and talk about it, and they tell their friends what they would like to do, but they never do nothing about it. They just want somebody to come along and give it to em. I've always been under the assumption that if you want something real bad, all you've got to do is start looking and hustling and sooner or latter, you'll find somebody who will help you, and all you got to do is just get out and start pushing.

I spend forty hours in my shop a week. My primary activity is getting this shop going. I try to tell my wife, have patience with me, because when you work so many hours, it's hard to stay in a good humor; when you get out of bed in the morning it's hard to be in a good humor, and I try desperate to smile all the time.

Oh, it doesn't take all my time. I try to work around the house, and I allow a certain amount of time for recreation for my kids, and take them places, and come Sunday that's their day, wherever they want to go, whatever they want to do, and the weekend's for my wife and I.

90. *JUST OUT OF SCHOOL*

I do clerical work. I work on lapsing and reinstating policies. I am called a clerk. I won't say I *like* this sort of a job, but I don't mind it too much. I haven't been here too long, so I don't have a chance to judge. I was just out of school in June. I like the parts which have a lot of figuring on them—I like figuring.

But I don't like getting up early in the morning, or the filing and picking, as we call it. I get little nicks in my fingers and I guess that's why I don't like it. I don't like the bickering the girls do once in a while, either. Also, I don't like the monotony of the work I do. Every week your work is set up for you and you do the same thing at the same time every week. Usually the time passes quickly—if there is enough to do. But the days when we're not busy, like Friday afternoons, it passes very slowly.

In my job I make decisions that are so small you really can hardly consider them decisions. I'd like a job in which I could make decisions. I like the feeling of responsibility. I like to do things on my own. If I make mistakes, they're just my own. So I wouldn't want to supervise many people. I don't like to be responsible for people. It's all right to have them ask you questions, but I don't want to have to tell them what to do and watch them do it.

I get a feeling of accomplishment from the work I am doing. I take a pile of transfers and get them done. I especially like to get them done ahead of time—it makes me feel very good. My job is considered unimportant around here, though; there are so many people doing the same thing and they don't require special qualifications for it . . . and I don't think it's important at all. They could do without me and anybody else could take my place. They hired me to do a job —any job. . . . They didn't hire me for what I am able to do. I didn't need special training to do this work.

Before I started working I wanted to go to the interior decorating school. Now, I'm going to a modeling school. If I'm still ambitious when I finish there, I'll go into interior decorating.

91. CALCULATOR

I do calculating and mathematical work. The job is called calculator. At one time I liked it but am at the stage now where I am disgusted with it—too many petty policies, no chance for promotion. I like particularly the freedom given to you on the job, and it pays well but could pay better. . . . I dislike too much working under pressure; hard work is not recognized in making promotions. Time passes quickly. The work, I must admit, is interesting. I make few decisions, if any at all. It is simply in reference to procedure or interpretation of rules. I definitely would like to have a job in which to make decisions because of my knowledge.

In the Army, I made decisions and good ones. It gives one a feeling of prestige to be able to make decisions and to know that one has that ability. I definitely would like a job where I supervise people, because

I have done supervisory work. In the Army, I always managed to get put in charge of something or other.

I get a feeling of accomplishment from the work I am doing. I get it because I know that the tremendous amount of work piles up and I can do the work and do it properly. There is a sense of gratification there. Of course, the work goes on and on, and if there is an extra bulk of it and you get that done—there is satisfaction. Although, I always know at the end of the day I have done a good day's work, there is really no feeling of accomplishment. Only once in a very great while I have that feeling.

I presume my job rates as an important job, since one must have a good deal of knowledge of department procedure and company practices.

No, I don't think it's a job for me because I think I could do a better job somewhere else. They never give you a chance around here to find out where you can fit in best. After all, 12,000 people working for S., there are all sorts of interesting jobs but they put you in one place and unless you are tops or very poor, you stay right where you are. Just doesn't seem any chance in this company to get ahead. Keep asking more and more from you and giving nothing in return.

Naturally, my future lies here. You can't throw away twenty-two years, but the future looks dull and dim. I was in the Army from 1940 to 1943 and there might have been some future there, but I can't take the chance.

When you first start, you're inexperienced. You stay on hoping for a promotion, then a depression comes; by that time you have been here ten years, afraid to change—that's the picture.

I like the hours; lenient about time off; vacations are good. I'll give the devil its due, working conditions aren't too bad.

I expect to be working at S. indefinitely. Anyway, until the age of sixty when I can retire.

The most important thing in getting ahead around here is knowing the right person and being able to say yes when required, and knowing when it is required. Ability is secondary.

92. *FIREBALL IN THE OFFICE*

I'm secretary to the divisional merchandise manager. It embraces everything in an office from housekeeping to all the stenographic work and the telephones. The office had two girls in it but, a year ago, the girl left for a better position, and they have never put in another girl.

Oh, yes, I expect more money. I never intend to stand still, regardless of age. If the job warrants, if I'm producing results that you want, if I'm capable, I expect to be remunerated. I told them that. They call me "fireball" in the office because I talk like this to all of them. I don't keep it just to myself or only tell it to you.

I came from the Davis store. I went into that store after my husband was killed and—I was then thirty-eight years old—and I was immediately put into a very fine job in the executive office. I had charge of that office, and I was there about ten years. Then they sold the store and everybody in it, but my employer asked me to stay.

My biggest contention here has been that they remove the incentive after you reach a certain point. Maybe they have a right to do that, but I don't think so.

I went to Mr. M. and I said, "Mr. M., I'm making my living here and I feel that I'm entitled to more money." He said, "I know, and you know that I feel that you are and Mr. C. feels that you are, but there's no way to get more money for the job that you have now."

He said the only way to get more was to get into one of the executive offices and that's ridiculous. I won't get into one of the executive offices. And compare what I do here with what they do up there—we handle style items here. Style items aren't like rugs. They change, things happen fast, there's always something new and it involves a lot of work, it makes a big difference in the amount of activity in an office and what you have to be able to do. There's always something new happening, and I have to absorb all that tension. I ought to be paid for that and for my experience.

It's the salary that happens to be what I'm most interested in, and I think everybody else is too. But that's the policy and that's the way it'll be, and there isn't much that you can do about it after you reach a certain age, because as the saying goes, they've got you coming and going.

I like the work though. I love people and I like merchandise. I've always been enthusiastic about it. Oh, we have our scraps, just like everybody else. But I love to work. But of course, it's gotten to a point now where you have to watch every penny. I've had to do that anyway. I support my mother, and I've had to do outside work to support my mother. I feel that I'm entitled to certain things—some pleasures along with my work.

I love it, and I like the store you know. I don't think anything can hold a candle to the store itself.

I'd never have a daughter of mine work in *L.*'s for the simple reason that there's too much politics. You have to know somebody.

I'll be retired in three years. I've always contended that a person should be permitted to work as long as he could produce. I feel that if the store felt that he wasn't capable of carrying on the duties, he should be given some duties in a lighter vein rather than put away.

I want to work. I want to earn it. And I want to have fun while I'm doing it and I want people to appreciate what I do, and to tell me they appreciate it.

93.　I LIKE SELLING

I like to deal with people. I like to give people what they want. "The customer is always right," they say, and that's so. He's right and it's up to us to see that he gets what he wants. And some of them come in so out of sorts. You know, I almost get more fun out of waiting on the ones that are hard to please than out of the others. I like to take them on. It's more of a challenge. . . . I can hardly wait to get down here in the morning. I start to live when I hit the floor.

Some days just go good from start to finish. A good customer first thing in the morning always starts it off right. Maybe you get several, and everything goes well. You make a good hard sale—like today. I started out with a "personal." Someone asked for me, and then after I had taken care of him and was waiting on someone else, another came in and wanted me. That's the way you like to start the day. And you like it to keep up. Sometimes you have a good hard fight. I had a sale of an overcoat to a man and his wife. I had him sold right away, but she thought of this and thought of that, and it was forty-five minutes before I sold her. But finally I did, and I know they both went away satisfied. I was able to answer her questions satisfactorily and to convince her that it was a good buy, and I know they both like it now. And that makes you feel good. I like that best—when I can carry through and win my point. I think that's one of the best things about selling.

You need to keep doing something to stay young and keep active. . . . I'll be retired here in three years. I'm sixty-two now. But I'll keep working. Even if I had plenty of money I wouldn't quit work; work is too important. It keeps you going. You need to work.

You know there are so many things the younger fellows don't do. Nothing's too much for a customer in my opinion. I've always been willing to take time to help a customer. Once I took several hours to get a pair of trousers to the principal of the Pullman School. He was a friend of mine, and it was important for him to get those trousers. There wasn't anybody that could take them though. It took a lot of time to go out there and take his trousers to him so he'd get them on time, and it wasn't my job, but no one could do it right away, and that's the kind of thing that's important. These young fellows don't feel that way. They seem to think there's something wrong with putting themselves out any.

These young fellows don't like to take time to do anything that isn't a part of their job. Some customer has an exchange or something—they say, "Why should I take care of it? They've got a staff here in the store to take care of things like that. It's not my job." They don't want to take the time or the trouble. They're afraid they'll lose a sale maybe.

If I had it to do over again I'd do exactly what I did do. That's what I want to do and I know it, but I don't know about a young man today. Some of them make good certainly. We have them in the store all the time, but somehow it doesn't seem as though young people today generally fit into this. I couldn't say why I feel that way though. . . .

XI

Workers in a
Mixed Economy

THE attitudes and expectations of workers toward their work and toward the larger economy and society of which they are a part are usually determined by the cumulation of their experiences. In shaping their attitudes, their present circumstances are always a dominant factor. In view of this, it is interesting to note that more than half of all persons currently in the labor force were too young to have had any direct experience with the job market during the depressed 1930's.

This means that their frame of reference and their basis for comparison is in terms of the exceptionally high levels of employment that characterized the years of World War II and the somewhat less active labor market that has prevailed for most of the other years during the last two decades.

But there are still in the labor force, or there were until only recently, men and women whose experience has been much broader. Many of them retain a sharp recollection of the disastrous thirties and even recall the relatively good years that were typical of the period between World War I and the end of the New Era.

Marked differences in experiences and exposures in the labor market will be clearly reflected in differences in the ways in which workers appraise their present circumstances and their future prospects. There is another important determinant of differences in appraisals. Men and women change with age and with changing family circumstances. Their picture of themselves and their future is likely to be one thing at twenty, when they begin to work; another at forty, when their family is growing up; and still another at sixty, when they are approaching retirement.

In light of these two interacting axes which influence attitudes and expectations—the environmental and the life cycle—it may be helpful to consider some of the more interesting developments of the last twenty years in terms of significant changes in the labor market and in the life experiences of different groups of workers.

Dynamic Trends. It has been contended that Americans are no longer as mobile as they used to be and that the plight of the depressed areas is a reflection of the unwillingness of people to relocate to communities in which jobs are available. But this contention is not supported by an appeal to the facts. During World War II great numbers poured into the centers of defense industries; and in the postwar period large numbers of people continued to migrate from areas where jobs were relatively scarce to others where work was more readily available. The substantial growth of such manufacturing areas as Detroit up to 1953, and the even more spectacular growth of California, the Southwest, and Florida throughout the entire two decades, are indicative that Americans have not lost their interest in moving or their willingness to move to areas where jobs are plentiful and wages high. Not only are they willing to move but they are willing to live under very straitened circumstances while they seek to establish themselves more firmly in the new environs. The westward migration during the 1950's exceeded that of any previous period in the country's history.

One factor that had considerable influence on reducing the migration of people out of agricultural areas where work is scarce has been the increasing frequency with which many corporations have decided to locate new plants right in such areas. Iowa, for example, is today more of an industrial than an agricultural state. This pattern of establishing plants in farming areas has appeared throughout much of the Midwest and increasingly in many regions of the South.

From the worker's point of view this development has had some striking implications. Many farmers are now regularly employed in industry. But they continue to run their farms—by getting up early in the morning; by working late at night; and by occasionally taking a couple of days of leave from the plant. Sometimes both husband and wife hold jobs in industry and continue to operate their farm on the side; sometimes one works the farm while the other works in the plant. While the employer may find some difficulties in integrating these moonlighting farmers into his work force, he gains an advantage from the fact that they are less likely to insist on higher wages since they have multiple sources of income. Thus, many families, especially in the South, where both husband and wife have been able to obtain jobs in industry, have leaped from poverty into a comfortable middle class status.

Among those who profited most from the recent expansion of employment opportunities in the manufacturing centers of the North and West were Negroes. Long concentrated in the South, they had been forced to eke out a living as tenant farmers, or in low paying service trades. Only a few had been able to live well—those who provided professional or business services for their own people. The war and postwar boom opened the door for many Southern Negroes to leave restricted communities and obtain jobs which enabled them to enjoy some measure of economic ease. The Northern Negro, who had also been restricted for a long time to the bottom of the occupational ladder, likewise was able to improve substantially his job and living circumstances. The trend, once started, continued. In recent years many Negroes have succeeded in getting production jobs and some have even found an opportunity to acquire skill and to move up into higher categories of work and pay.

Nevertheless, overt pressures of wide job discrimination or subtle pressures of the existence of impediments to skill acquisition and promotion continued to operate against the Negro, even in the less prejudiced North and West. Frequently the Negro was blocked for no reason other than the color of his skin; at other times he was simply one of a group of unwelcome outsiders. The number of preferred jobs is always fewer than the number of applicants and those who control the better jobs will be inclined to share them in the first instance with their relatives or friends. On both scores, the Negro is severely handicapped.

The prejudices of white workers and white management are likely to reinforce each other so that the barriers to Negro advancement are indeed strong. In many sectors of the labor market the union determines in large measure who shall be hired and who promoted, and while the employer may resent in general the union's power he is not likely to precipitate a struggle over greater equality for the Negro.

Although prejudiced unions, prejudiced white workers, and prejudiced employers have certainly retarded the occupational progress of the Negro, many industrial unions have contributed substantially to opening opportunities to him. By insisting in their contracts on objective criteria for assignment, training, and promotion, these unions have acted as a battering ram in enabling the Negro to gain equality of opportunity. Many of these same unions have contributed to an alleviation of prejudice off the job by making a place for all members in their ogranizational, educational, and social activities.

The union operated on many other fronts to improve the circumstances of other members. It helped to put an end to the fear which for so long stalked older workers that the day would come when they would be fired because they would no longer have the strength and stamina to cope with demanding jobs. One of the major achievements of union activity has been to influence the distribution of work so that older men are assigned to the less onerous duties.

Another important contribution of union activity was its establishment of a check to the exploitation and reprisals so frequently engaged in by management. There were, of course, many employers who did not attempt to squeeze wages down to the minimum, and many others did not resort to hiring thugs or engaging in illegal activities in order to prevent their workers from organizing; but many others have remained unreconstructed. They look forward to a return to conditions prevailing before Franklin Delano Roosevelt initiated the New Deal.

As late as 1946 a group of workers were shot in the back and killed, not in an isolated mill town in the South where many employers remain very anti-union, but in the largest city in the state of Ohio.

Many workers were conscious of the heavy hand of their employer even when he took pains to keep the pressure on them from reaching the breaking point. In many corporations the scientifically oriented management attempted to set and maintain a work pace which insured a high level of productivity at the same time that it introduced a series of supports and benefits for the workers to moderate and mitigate the more negative aspects of the working environment.

For the most part workers appreciated these benefits and they responded in much the way that management hoped they would—by a willingness to accept the bad with the good. On balance they were willing to keep up a fast pace even though they resented many of the conditions under which they were forced to work. Periodically the subtle balance that management had sought to maintain was dissipated by a rank-and-file explosion. Wildcat strikes have long been characteristic of those sectors of the economy where assembly lines exist. Assembly line workers eventually rebel against the fact that the machine so largely controls their work. The conditions under which the line moves are subject to union approval, and changes on the part of management are subject to union check. Although the union can mitigate the sense of helplessness of the men, it cannot do more than draw off a small part of their resentment. From time to time after small annoyances have accumulated men are likely to demonstrate spontaneously by walking off the job and thereby proving to themselves, and to management, that they are men and not robots.

We might ask why, if so many men find assembly line conditions to be particularly onerous, they continue to do such work, especially in a period when alternative employment opportunities are available. The answer must be sought in the way in which the men themselves see the benefits and the losses involved in making a change. Many do change employers and many others move to a different job with the same employer where their work is less tightly controlled. But many, despite their negative reactions, stay on the line. They do so for the same reason that many other workers who do not like their jobs stay with them. The longer a man has been with one employer the higher his wages and the greater his seniority are likely to be. After a man has remained with an employer for a considerable number of years, he will hesitate to seek another job because of the substantial reduction in income that he is likely to suffer and, equally important, his increased vulnerability in the event that the job market should slacken and lay-offs become necessary.

Many workers, once they acquire considerable seniority, feel that they are locked in their jobs and cannot afford to move. The fact that they usually acquire substantial seniority at a time of life when their family responsibilities are reaching a peak puts additional pressure on them to tolerate known discomfort or unpleasantness rather than seek a more satisfactory job. Their cautious approach is likely to be reinforced by a view of the job market which holds that most jobs inevitably leave much to be desired and, if they do not have a specialized education or skill which will give them a competitive advantage over other job seekers, that their prospects of finding a more satisfactory job are not good.

One of the more pervasive developments of recent decades, and one that has impressed almost all workers who have given the matter any thought, is that large-scale business enterprises in particular have established a moat between the workers and their foremen and all other supervisory personnel. It is increasingly rare for a working man to advance more than one step up the managerial ladder. He can become a foreman, but that is all. The other members of management are selected, not from among men who have worked in the plant, but from among college graduates who have been taken into the business explicitly to join the ranks of management.

This widening gap between workers and management indicates in the first instance the need for managerial personnel to have a broad educational and technological background—that is, to have much more formal knowledge and to be capable of higher orders of theoretical and analytical thinking than is characteristic of the production worker. But the very fact that management relies on two different sources of supply for its manpower has broadened the gap beyond what functional necessity demands. There is an important element of social and class snobbery in thus keeping separate the less- and the better-educated groups, the men with more and those with less social polish.

This pattern, whose roots are deep, has come to characterize all sectors of the economy. It is more dominant in large organizational structures with highly formal personnel systems and methods of recruitment, assignment, and promotion. It is less prevalent in distribution than in manufacturing, in transportation than in finance. But in every large-scale organization, it is inevitable that subgroups emerge, and that the head of each exercises authority and influence over those who work for him. It is characteristic of every large organization that "political" considerations play a significant role in the promotion process. The worker who is well liked by his superior will get ahead; the man who is less favored, for whatever reasons, is left behind. Many times it is the most competent and the most hard-working man who is promoted. But all too often competence is not the criterion. Personal relations between supervisor and worker become the determining factor. In view of this all too human element, the future of white-collar unionism is likely to be determined in considerable measure by the extent to which large organizations succeed in establishing more objective systems of promotion for their clerical and sales personnel.

We know that the success of a large organization depends in very considerable measure on the effectiveness of its supervisory structure, since the small numbers at the top management level cannot possibly come into contact with all of the many individuals who work throughout the company. The past two decades have witnessed continuing efforts to improve supervision in every sector of the American economy but it is not easy to assess the success of these efforts. For example, in manufacturing plants, the first line supervisors—the foremen—are responsible for seeing that their work group meets a quota. This demand is placed on them by their supervisors. But whether they meet their quotas depends in large measure on the attitudes and behavior of the men whom they direct. Even the quotas which are set are determined largely by past performance; they reflect, therefore, what the immediate work force considers a reasonable day's work.

The past two decades have seen staff personnel experiment with a wide range of policies and procedures to spur worker motivation and performance, but the outcome of their strenuous efforts is still in balance. However, a few tentative conclusions are beginning to emerge.

Workers are always aware of whether their company is following a straightforward policy or whether it is attempting to exploit its personnel. In the first instance they are likely to be tolerant of new proposals; in the second they are likely to balk at any innovation overtly or circumspectly. They are also influenced by their estimates of whether management's proposals hold direct or even indirect threat to their jobs. If they visualize even a minor threat, they will be recalcitrant; and if they consider the proposals a major threat they are likely to fight them even to the point of striking. The preoccupation of workers with the security of their jobs explains why even the most imaginative and ingenious management team is likely to make only limited headway in introducing plans aimed at altering working rules and conditions. Radical proposals are likely to place at least some jobs in jeopardy, and such a threat always acts to unify workers in opposition.

A sizable literature has grown up during the past decade or so aimed at assessing different styles of supervision. Often the argument has been put forward that supervisors who are less authoritarian, those who tend to involve their workers in the decisions which affect them, will in general have a more satisfied work group and one that is more productive. There may be, of course, another cause of this effect: the more autocratic supervisors may have other limitations —they may be less competent technically, less capable instructors, or they may simply be less pleasant persons. The lower output of their groups may reflect any one or a combination of these factors as well as tightness in supervision.

Aside from the question of the most productive type of supervision is the question of how far even the best supervisor can go within the realities of the environment in which he must operate—the limitations placed on him by top management, the ever-present suspicion of the workers that the firm is seeking to exploit them, their anxiety about their jobs, and the ubiquitous union, which insists on its right to be party to even minor changes.

The widespread conception that management has a broad scope for improving its employee relations is not always based on fact. It is not always possible to effect changes, first because of barriers erected by the workers themselves and their union. Equally important are the constraints experienced by the company because of actual or potential competitors. While expenditures on wages today often represent a relatively small proportion of total costs, these expenditures are seldom so small as to be insignificant. Management therefore must carefully weigh any innovation that it is considering to determine whether it promises returns that will at least cover the costs involved.

There are nevertheless two important trends in the present managerial environment that have contributed to accelerated innovations aimed at improving employee loyalty, morale, and productivity. The executives who run most of the country's large enterprises are a hired management. They seldom own any significant part of the business which they manage. Their interest and concern is to keep their operations on an even keel, and toward this end they frequently attempt to balance the conflicting aims of different groups. Today management's primary objective is steady growth rather than maximum profits. As a consequence they are likely to be a little more responsive to the needs and desires of their work force than are owner-managers who see every rise in wages or fringe benefits as a diminution of their own profits.

Another trend that has accelerated rapidly since the onset of World War II is leaving its mark in the arena of employer-employee relationships. Government has become an ever larger force in the economy, and many contracts let by government, especially the federal government, have been on a cost-plus basis. This had led many managements to be less stringent in negotiations with their work force, since they are negotiating with the government's money. Moreover, they frequently stand to gain if they meet their schedules, while they run the dangers of penalties if they are late. Their concern, therefore, is not so much with controlling the size of their wage bill as it is to attract and retain the manpower they need to meet their schedules. To this end they frequently agree to an advance in wages or an improvement in working conditions. This trend has had an impact not only on the companies and industries directly affected but also indirectly on the market for manpower.

Since the onset of World War II labor has experienced other significant gains as a direct result of the larger role of government in the structuring and functioning of both the economy and the society in general. The important social security legislation passed in the middle 1930's became increasingly effective in the 1940's. Through this legislation many of the worst disabilities suffered by working men and women were mitigated, and some were eliminated. Government's expanded role was also reflected in its influence on men in uniform. About 25 million men have served in the Armed Forces since the onset of mobilization in 1940. Military service has had a tremendous impact on the occupational aspirations, educational development, and skill acquisition of a significant proportion of all who served.

Finally, note must be taken of the fact that since 1953 direct employment by government has expanded by about 40 per cent, a rate much higher than the employment increase in any other major sector of the economy.

The striking changes which have occurred in both the private and public economy since the outbreak of World War II have substantially altered the circumstances of workers' lives on and off the job. These changes in turn left their impact on workers' expectations. The major transformations were the reduction of the time that men must work in order to earn a living wage; the substantial shift in the relative power of employers and labor to determine the conditions under which men work; and the much improved prospects for workers' families to enjoy a satisfactory standard of living.

Back of these improvements was the steady broadening of opportunities and options. Young people can go to work and earn a good wage at eighteen, or they can stay in school and become prepared for better jobs; young men can opt for skill training and accept a lower initial wage in favor of learning a skill which will enable them to greatly improve their position later on. Married women can decide to supplement their family's income by working part-time or full time, for part of all of the year. Older people may decide to retire as soon as they reach the age of eligibility or they may prefer to stay at work. In these and many other respects the recent sustained period of high level employment added not only to the wealth but to the welfare of the working population by providing an ever larger number of them with a broader range of significant options.

But the picture is not completely satisfactory. Many workers have not participated in the gains we have described because of personal limitations such as handicaps of age, physical disability, lack of education and skill; or social limitations such as handicaps of location, discrimination, or economic vulnerability. Moreover, in the last several years a new disquietude has appeared. The economy has failed to provide as many new jobs as previously. The number of persons employed has increased, but so has the number of unemployed. Even more significant is the increase in the number in the working age groups who do not belong to the labor force because of lack of jobs, not because of personal preference.

Part of the explanation is demographic: the supply of workers is increasing more rapidly than previously. Part is technological: the new machines are resulting in a net decline in the demand for workers even if employment in industries involved in the manufacture of the machines is added to that in industries which use them. Part is economic: American business is experiencing difficulty in finding profitable opportunities for expansion, at the same time that it is facing much more intense competition.

No nation has ever before been confronted with the task of making a success out of an affluent society. There are no guidelines as to the adjustments required so that all, or at least most, of the men and women able and willing to work will have the opportunity to do so. The success that the United States has in quickly discovering the necessary adjustments will largely determine the future prospects of the American worker.

Part
FIVE

Part

FIVE

The American Worker:
Continuity and Change

THE thesis was advanced at the beginning of this book that even
students who devote a lifetime to the analysis and evaluation of institutions and ideas find it difficult to appreciate and understand the
order of change that takes place in a dynamic society of which they
themselves are a part. It is difficult to see oneself or the environment
in which one lives in perspective. It is even more difficult to assay the
significance of changes which one does recognize. For the essence of
historical change is that no one factor ever changes alone. It is always
influenced by and, in turn, influences others. Therefore the meaning
that attaches to larger orders of change must be sought in the transformation of broad social complexes and not in the alteration of
isolated variables.

These difficulties now become apparent as we face the task of de-
riving some broad generalizations about the American worker in the
twentieth century. While we have been able to accumulate a considerable body of information about each of the distinctive periods into
which this volume is subdivided, we must now in this concluding
chapter attempt to distill the major elements of continuity and
change. Only thus can we extract from history the full measure of
its contribution, which is to show how the past has influenced the

343

present and to suggest how the future in turn may differ from the present.

Transformations. In order to delineate the more important changes that have taken place in the work and lives of American working men and women during this century, we must first provide an assessment of the changes that have occurred in the job arena itself, in employer-employee relations, in the strength of trade unions, in the influence of government, in the standard of living of the average family, and in the position of labor in the larger community. To each, we now turn.

No single factor exercises a more determining influence on the shape of the lives of working people than the number of hours and days that they must labor in order to support themselves and their dependents. And in no aspect of life have recent changes been more spectacular. The last three-quarters of a century has seen the working man's day shortened to a point where he is now able increasingly to add a major new dimension to his daily life: one part he devotes to work; the other is his to do with as he likes—to putter around the house, to engage in a serious hobby, to participate in trade union or political activities, or to spend it on recreational pursuits. In every week, he has two days for himself and in one week in five he is likely to have three days free. During a year, workers with some continuity of employment will have three, or even four, weeks of paid vacation. The time that working men spend at their work had been reduced during these past seventy years by approximately 40 per cent.

Paralleling this substantial quantitative reduction in hours spent at work has been an almost equally important qualitative change in the demands made on workers during the hours that they are on the job. Poor lighting, noxious fumes, dangerous machinery, fire hazards, unsanitary conditions—all too prevalent at the turn of the century—have been almost completely eliminated. While workers are still injured, and some even lose their lives at work, the reduction in the rates of accident and death during employment has been spectacular indeed. Even more striking are the general improvements in the work setting which have contributed so much to the maintenance of the health of the work force as well as to creation of a pleasant environment for them.

We must also mention the changes in the nature of the work performed. Here the record is more equivocal. There is no question but that the amount of actual physical labor required of the worker has been vastly reduced; most men and women today do not end their work day physically spent. On the other hand, improvements in management have led to a vast rationalization of the work process with particular attention to improved scheduling. Less and less working time remains unscheduled. As a consequence many more workers spend their days under the dictation of the clock. Even here the record is confused, for one of the important changes has been a shift from piece to day work. We know that because of low piece wages, many workers used to drive themselves to the very limit of their capacity in order to earn enough for their large families. Today, they must approximate the standard of work for the day but they are constrained from going far above it, even if they wanted to, by pressure imposed by their fellow workers.

On balance, workers today surely expend less physical energy than they and their fathers were required to earlier. Whether or not they expend more emotional energy can be assessed only after the focus is broadened to take account of changes in the relationship of employees to their employers.

Changes in this area were substantial indeed. At the turn of the century the only brake on the power of the employer to set unilaterally the terms of the labor contract was the state of the labor market. And since very large numbers of people were entering the country from abroad and equally large numbers were leaving the farm in search of industrial employment, the labor market exerted great pressure on workers to accept jobs at modest wages. These were the years when the employer had a great many special advantages; he often controlled the entire community—even judges were in his debt. He could fan internecine warfare among competing wage earners so that it would be difficult or impossible for them to combine against him. He was usually assured a friendly press if he had to fight. And the fact that workers had to live off their meager savings or exist on the small help that they might receive from friendly unionists or from charitable sources gave the employer an overwhelming tactical advantage if he engaged in a long strike or lockout.

Because of their markedly superior power, most employers were able to rule with an iron hand. They could be arbitrary, play favorites, cheat, or otherwise exploit those who worked for them. Of course, not all, not even a majority, did in fact engage in this kind of nefarious action, but even those who were scrupulously honest did not by their honesty establish the basis for a satisfactory relationship with their employees. For workers could never overlook the simple reality that if they did anything to displease their foremen, even if it was nothing overt, they might be out of a job just as quickly as they could be paid off. It is worth recalling in this connection the ways in which Henry Ford in his most expansive days saw fit to interfere with and regulate the lives of those who worked for him. He might offer them a loan to build a house, but only if he had first looked into their icebox to be sure that they were not beer drinkers!

Many factors led to the reduction in this early arbitrary power of the employer: the reduction in the flow of immigrants, the rising level of education achieved by new members of the work force who had been imbued in school with knowledge of their democratic rights, the general trends toward more liberal political and social values characteristic of the larger society, the altered views of the judiciary which acted to shift the balance between property and human rights. Of overwhelming importance was the growth of trade unionism, which provided labor with a powerful weapon of its own through which to accomplish a redistribution of costs and benefits between the employer and the employee. Among the primary objectives of unions was to cut back drastically the power of the employer to discharge workers without cause. As the years went by, the unions were able to narrow the grounds for just cause for dismissal. Recently the unions have received a major assist from the courts, which are developing the doctrine that in giving his labor to an employer over a period of years the worker is strengthening his claims to a job in the future, even if the owner relocates his plant at a new site thousands of miles distant.

We are now better able to answer the question of whether on balance the worker today is under more or less emotional stress during his day's work than previously. Even if we were to postulate that the emotional stress connected with the actual performance of one's tasks is greater today than in decades past, which is an assumption that would be hard to defend, we would still conclude that there has been an over-all easing of tension since the worker is today so much less vulnerable to arbitrary action by the employer. And in the worker's hierarchy of values job security is at the top. Moreover it usually is easier to put up with even a high order of stress if the period is not prolonged.

Let us now consider the broader implications of the expansion of trade unionism for the welfare of the working man. Some economists have argued that the union has failed on balance to obtain significant gains for its members. They argue that such gains as union members have achieved would have come to them in any case from the workings of the competitive market.

There is no need to deny the power of the market. But neither is there any reason to question that the distribution of power in our type of democratic society influences the shares of income received by various groups. Another factor is the subtle interactions that occur both in the economy and the larger society as groups take aggressive or defensive action to increase their shares or to protect them. No thoughtful employer has any serious doubts about the efficacy of a strong union to alter his profit position; and many have been willing to make substantial concessions to their work force in the belief that taking the initiative will be better than to recognize an outside union.

Even if the doctrinaire economists were correct about the relative unimportance of the trade union and could adduce proof, this position would be inaccurate because it ignores the substantial contribution that unions have made by providing the working men and women in this country with a formal institutional mechanism through which to voice their needs and desires with regard to the central challenge of their lives—their work and the income that they earn as a result of it.

It can surely be proved that many workers have been injured and exploited by the growth of unions. Members have been exploited by arbitrary or corrupt leaders; non-members have been deprived of opportunities to acquire skill or work; jurisdictional struggles have forced many non-participants to be idle—and the list of negatives could readily be extended. Despite these disadvantages the unions have been able to achieve a great deal. While some employers would be willing to attempt to undermine the unions and many more would attempt to prevent their further growth, the public's mood can best be gauged by the type of labor legislation passed by Congress. Both the Taft-Hartley and Landrum-Griffin Acts were measures aimed at correcting a limited number of specific abuses. While there remain serious differences of opinion as to whether these acts should be amended, they surely did not succeed in undermining the trade union structure, nor were they directed toward this end.

Friends of labor have been concerned about the slow growth of unionism in recent years, about the lack of inspired leadership, about the absence of a dynamic ideology. But this disquietude must be placed in proper perspective. Without question, one of the major determinants of the vast gains achieved by American labor during this century has been the trade union. It has given the working man a greater sense of dignity and self-assurance; it has added to his powers so that he could bargain more successfully with his employer; it has helped to awaken the whole society to the human waste and injustice prevalent in many sectors; it has encouraged the development of constructive public and private policies to cope with these challenges.

The relations between labor and government have been complex during the past seventy years and have undergone important changes during this period. The power of government at every level to influence the welfare of the working man has long been substantial, both when it has been used and when it was withheld. Prior to World War

I, and thereafter with minor exceptions until the election of Franklin Delano Roosevelt, labor had little reason to look to the federal government for help except on very limited fronts. For the most part the men elected to the presidency as well as those elected to Congress were much more sensitive to the rights of property than to the needs of the worker. Nevertheless labor had been able to encourage the federal government to take constructive steps in establishing better working conditions for its own employees. And labor had, in association with groups of employers and other citizens, finally prevailed on Congress to take the major step of reducing the flow of immigrants.

At the level of state government, labor had pushed aggressively for many reform measures aimed at moderating the harshness of the competitive job market, especially with respect to its impact on working women and children. In these efforts, the spearhead of reform had been interested citizens, most of whom belonged to the middle or upper income classes. But the working population and its organizations, which stood to gain most from such legislation, contributed the political momentum which helped to pass constructive measures.

Labor made its greatest gains and suffered its greatest defeats at the local level. Many of its efforts were directed toward moving the local political structure from a position of overt hostility to one of at least neutrality and preferably to a more positive stance; otherwise the working population would continue to face obstacles in any and all efforts to improve its conditions of employment through union action or other means.

Although labor did seek help from the federal government when there was a prospect of receiving it, as in the case of immigration control, the overriding impression of the relation between American labor and the federal government during the first three decades of this century is that of a stand-off. Although the leaders of American labor were not satisfied with the conditions of work offered by private enterprise, they did not see much hope of help from the federal government. During these years Government was not sympathetic to labor, particularly during the twelve years from 1921 to 1933 that the Republicans controlled the White House.

The great depression of the early 1930's led to major changes in the basic assumptions of every interest group. Nowhere was the change more dramatic than in the case of the working population. There was unequivocal evidence that no working man could assure his own future and that of his family in the face of a major business decline. There was equally clear evidence that even the most sympathetic and liberal employer could do little for his workers if his market was cut back or disappeared. There was daily proof that union funds were inadequate to help their members over a prolonged period of unemployment. Philanthropy was unable to fill the breach. American workers were soon forced to realize on the basis of personal experience that there remained but one agency to which they might look for assistance and support. That was government. Many local governments were close to financial insolvency. Many state governments were in the same plight. Consequently all eyes turned to the federal government which alone had the reserve power to cope with a major national emergency such as was sweeping the land.

Conservatives are inclined to blame the major transformations which occurred between government and business on President Roosevelt and his advisors. But this conclusion ignores the more fundamental transformations which took place at that time in attitude and behavior of the major economic interest groups—farmers, businessmen, and workers—which made the New Deal possible. No group made a more complete and quicker turn-around than labor. American workers had come to realize that they had little to lose and much to gain from seeking assistance from the only agency of society still potent enough to help them.

The succeeding years witnessed a continuation and deepening of the new trend. Labor looked more and more to the federal government for help in accomplishing objectives which it could not hope to realize through collective bargaining or through the operations of the market place alone.

Nevertheless, despite this major change in attitude toward the federal government, organized labor continued to share with management a basic ambivalence about governmental power as it impinged on collective bargaining. Powerful labor leaders did not hesitate to seek presidential intervention in their disputes with management when they expected to benefit. This paralleled the behavior of industrial leaders when they saw government as a possible ally. But both groups continued to suspect that they might be forced in the long run to pay too high a price for such government intervention. Henceforth government would be able more easily to inject itself into labor-management negotiations which up to this point had been limited to the two major contestants. But it is a rare leader indeed who will willingly forego the possibility of an immediate victory because the long term costs may be too high. As so frequently happens, the inherent contradictions have not been resolved but have persisted. Labor has wanted to continue to use the offices of a friendly government on its behalf but it has realized the danger of a shift in the attitude of government more friendly to management or more aggressive in determining where the public interest lies. The dilemma persists and there is little likelihood that it will be shortly resolved.

Another dimension of the changing relation of labor and government warrants attention. Among the major advances made by the American working man during the Roosevelt years was the establishment of a social security system which provided a mechanism through which employed persons could contribute, while they were earning, to a system that would protect them and their dependents against the contingencies of unemployment, permanent disability, retirement, and death. During World War II and again during the Korean conflict when the federal government used its powers to keep a control over prices, wages, and profits, unions found that they were permitted leeway to negotiate various types of benefits with employers. Strong unions were able to secure important gains through the instrument of collective bargaining, gains that in many instances would be paid for exclusively by the employer. Many non-union employers gave their workers similar benefits in order to keep them satisfied. The development of these fringe benefits—which were the more attractive because of the power they gave many labor leaders to exercise discretion over the investment of funds accumulated as a result of these new benefits—lessened organized labor's interest in improving the social security system and related government programs. Various programs needed improvement, however, since their benefits were being eroded by inflation; many millions of workers were still not covered by social security, and the types of risk covered were far from comprehensive.

The unmistakable preference of union labor for many years to concentrate more efforts on what it could secure through collective bargaining than through an improvement in social security and other governmental programs has a further explanation. Under governmental programs, workers who receive the highest wages are likely to pay more of the total costs than are workers who earn less. Sometimes this higher cost may be returned in higher benefits but not always and not proportionately. Thus, as more and more of the total population is brought under the social security umbrella, and more and more wage earners pay taxes, the financing of governmental programs is so structured that better paid workers help to defray much of the costs incurred on behalf of lower paid workers. The increasing recognition of this fact has undoubtedly acted as a brake on the improvement of some older governmental programs and the institution of newer ones. The enthusiasm of strong labor groups for governmental programs has not increased substantially since they have found at least a partial answer to their own needs in collective bargaining.

So far we have discussed the continuity and change in the experiences of the American worker primarily in his role as worker, member of a trade union, and citizen who is the beneficiary of governmental programs. There remains the other side of the coin—the changes in the way in which he lives—in his family life and his participation in the community and the larger society. To these we now turn.

Early in the century the typical worker's household had a large number of children, frequently including preschool children, those in school, and those who were already at work but still living at home.

The worker's wife led a very busy life trying to care for her large family. She nursed the children, who were frequently ill, she made their clothes, baked their bread, did the laundry in a washtub, and otherwise coped with the vast array of responsibilities which were considered her normal lot. In these multiple tasks she was frequently assisted by an older daughter or an unmarried female relative who lived with her. But even with such help—if she had it—her work was arduous and her days long.

She did not get much help from her husband, both because the social mores still made a sharp distinction between men's and women's work and because his own work day was so long and exhausting.

Nevertheless, except when work was slack, or on the rare occasions when there was no work because of a depression or a major strike, working class families managed to make a go of it, although many were close to the margin of subsistence. Others were able to live quite well, depending on the number and skill of those who earned money and the number of dependents among whom it had to be divided.

Throughout the years major changes have taken place. Today fewer and fewer families exist at a minimum level, although some still do. The size of the average worker's family has been substantially reduced—from five or six children or more to three or even fewer. No longer are most working class women drudges, although to bring up children on less than $5000 a year, as so many must, is still a challenge to their ingenuity and a drain on their physical and emotional energy.

No longer do children go to work at twelve—or even younger—as many did at the turn of the century. When they do enter the labor market in the seventeenth or eighteenth year, they are likely to contribute little to the household. One of the reasons for this is that so many of them go into the Army or are married within a year or two. Among the major transformations that have occurred, especially since 1940, is the extent to which married women whose children are in school have entered or reentered the labor market. Today it is the wife rather than an older child who is the important supplemental wage earner. It is the $1500 or so that she earns which helps to provide additional margins for her family.

Building on the strong desire for home ownership already manifest early in this century, a high proportion of all workers at the present time own their homes. If they have children still at home, they are more likely than not to live in suburbs and to drive a car. Their pattern of life is often not significantly different from that of other more affluent suburbanites except that they are unlikely to held membership in a country club.

The life of the American working man and his family during the past several decades has been affected by the double impact of the increasing real income which he has available to spend and the substantial increase in the quality and quantity of governmental services to which he has access for nothing or for a relatively small fee. Both of these developments have contributed substantially to raising the standard of living of the American working class family to a level never before approximated by workers in any country. It is worth noting that the average American Negro family, and particularly the Negro family which lives in an urban community, has an annual income above that of the average Britisher. This despite the fact that the United Kingdom stands close to the top of the per capita income scale for European countries.

The last decades have also witnessed important gains obtained by the American worker that go beyond income earned or standard of living achieved. At the turn of the century, and in fact up to World War I, a significant proportion of all industrial workers were either immigrants or the children of immigrants. As such many did not consider themselves to be full-fledged members of the American society and they were not so considered by many of the native-born Americans. There was considerable difference between the pattern of life and aspirations of immigrant workers and those of native-born Americans.

Three wars, the sharp reduction of immigration, and the passage of time itself has vastly reduced this gap to a point where it scarcely exists. There are still marginal groups of workers in American society but they consist primarily of Negroes, Spanish-speaking workers, the Indians, and small groups of others who continue to live in the Appalachian range or in the Ozarks or who have recently relocated in urban communities where they have not yet been fully absorbed. But the vast majority of American workers are now an integral part of American society. Moreover they are a sufficiently large group and have sufficient income, political power, and social status that the future of American society will be in no small measure affected by how they think and what they do.

The Future. At the end of the first decade of this century almost one million immigrants entered the United States annually; a decade later the number had dropped precipitously. In the late 1920's most workers were improving their standard of living in every respect; a decade later about one out of every five was unemployed and many more were underemployed. In the decade between Pearl Harbor and the outbreak of hostilities in Korea the American worker was again able to achieve great gains. The widespread manpower shortages characteristic of the early 1950's were followed by increasing concern with automation and unemployment at the end of the fifties. In view of these sudden and radical shifts, a forecast of the future must be a cautious one. Nevertheless, one of the principal reasons for studying the past is to obtain some sense of the possible direction of the future.

Within the confines of the possibility of error, it may still be helpful to identify some of the major axes along which the future of the American worker will be determined. It is beyond the scope of such an effort to assess the interaction of these several axes, and this in turn makes it impossible to reach a judgment of the outcome. It may nevertheless be helpful to point directions.

Within the work arena we can identify first the likelihood of continued rapid technological change. Whether such change will be of the same or greater order of magnitude than has characterized the American economy since the beginning of this century is hard to say. But there is no reason to anticipate that it will be slower. Technological change carries with it many threats to groups of workers who currently hold good jobs as well as to many who are not yet in the labor market. Earlier in the century technological advances pushed large numbers off the farm. Men who migrated to the city found work in the burgeoning economy. In general, they improved their circumstances. They worked less and earned more. Today, automation is resulting in the displacement of workers whose earnings frequently have been in excess of $100 weekly. There may be jobs for some of these men, but probably at a lower occupational level, at less pay.

Secondly, automation is only now beginning to make headway in the fields of distribution, finance, and service, which for many years have been the fastest-growing sectors of the economy. While few employees actually lose their jobs when radical technological improvements are introduced, it is likely that jobs which otherwise would have been available for young people when they were ready to begin work will not be there. The suspiciously high unemployment rate for young people—about three times that for older age groups—suggests the validity of this hypothesis.

The less than full demand for labor which has characterized the American economy since about 1955, and which threatens to worsen not only because of automation but because of the substantial increases in the number of young people becoming available for work, has inevitably set off a campaign on the part of the leaders of labor for a shorter work week. Although this drive has met opposition from the administration, which fears that such a reduction in the work week will lead to higher labor costs and therefore to a worsening of America's competitive position and a decline in employment, it is likely to gain momentum and to show increasing results in the years ahead. While the dangers envisioned by the administration are surely potential, they are probably exaggerated. Moreover, the administration has failed to suggest any alternative plan for bringing about a better balance between the demand and supply of labor. Since during this century approximately two-fifths of the gains in productivity have been reflected in an equivalent increase in leisure, it is difficult to comprehend why this important mechanism is ignored at the present time. Shortly after World War I, John Maynard Keynes looked forward to a reduction in the work week by the end of the century to around fifteen hours. The margin between the present work week and his forecast leaves ample room for experimentation and adjustment.

An important linkage can be made between accelerating technological change and a shorter work week. There is ample evidence already at hand which suggests that the future will differ from the past particularly with respect to the speed with which the education or training that a man receives early in life becomes obsolescent. In decades past it was reasonably assumed that during the years before one became fourteen, or eighteen, or a little older, a young man or woman would acquire all the knowledge and skill that he or she would need to hold a job and to cope with the other responsibilities of adulthood.

We know now that this no longer obtains. Steps have been taken to fulfill the need for new skill acquisition among older workers. Larger and larger expenditures have been made by corporations, the armed services, trade unions, and communities to provide more and more workers with an opportunity to refurbish and broaden their skills and to add to their knowledge. We can be confident that the decades ahead will witness a need for much more continuing education and retraining, all of which will require more and more of workers' time. For those who are concerned about what people will do with their increased leisure, here is one answer. They will study to insure that they can remain productive.

Unless there is a major collapse of the economy or an outbreak of war—neither of which catastrophes is foreseen—the years ahead should see a substantial increase in the real income available to workers' families to spend or save. The margins between essential and discretionary expenditures should steadily widen. The fact that the practice of birth control will probably soon be adopted by most working class families and the further possibility that the trend toward larger families characteristic of our society since the end of World War II may be reversed suggest the prospect of still more rapid gains in the standard of living. Higher earnings will be divided among fewer dependents. Moreover, as social security and other governmental programs are strengthened to provide for older persons, workers will be less responsible for contributing to the care of indigent parents.

Among the interesting transformations to which attention was called earlier was the fact that during the past several decades the gap between college-trained and professional men and those with less education has widened to a point where it has become increasingly difficult for workers with only a few years of school to move more than one or two rungs up the occupational ladder. Since our society is becoming ever more dependent on men with advanced knowledge and intricate skills this gap is likely to widen. As it does, the rigidities in our social, occupational, and economic structures will probably be increased. This places increasing importance on broadening the availability of the access of educational and training opportunities to children and adults from working class backgrounds. Only as these are available and can be utilized without crippling costs will there be much prospect for the worker to realize the American dream in the years ahead. How far a man can go in our society will increasingly be determined by his education and training. This is largely determined before he starts to work. But his initial preparation need not be the sole determinant. The United States has shown considerable imagination in pioneering in adult education and training within industry. There is scope for much more, including the establishment of broadened opportunities for mature women who want to begin or return to work in their thirties or later.

The years ahead will undoubtedly see a continuity in the ways in which the American worker will seek to realize his aspirations and goals. He will aim to better himself when the job market offers the opportunity; he will look for gains through his trade union; he will press government for benefits that he cannot obtain through his own efforts or from his employer.

But when the income of the working population reaches a level where it represents a very high percentage of the entire national income, the margins for further gains will depend increasingly on a strengthened economy which can continue to grow and compete successfully in the markets of the world.

Even more, the future of the American working man and woman will depend on the extent to which the nation shows judgment and fortitude in meeting the overwhelming challenges which it faces as the leader of the free world. To the extent that the American worker can help the nation meet these challenges successfully—to that extent, and only to that extent, can he look forward to the improvement in his own circumstances and those of his children and his children's children.

Notes

Notes

CHAPTER III. THE TURN OF THE CENTURY

1. *Our Growing Population,* U. S. Census of Population, 1960.
2. *Historical Statistics of the United States,* U. S. Dept. of Commerce, 1960, p. 64.
3. Stanley Lebergott, "Annual Estimates of Unemployment in the United States, 1900–54," in *The Measurement and Behavior of Unemployment,* A Conference of the Universities, National Bureau for Economic Research, Princeton, 1957, p. 215.
4. *Historical Statistics, op. cit.,* p. 62.
5. *Ibid.,* p. 56.
6. *Ibid.,* p. 60.
7. *Ibid.,* pp. 11–12.
8. *Womanpower,* National Manpower Council, Columbia, 1957, Ch. IV.
9. *Historical Statistics, op. cit.,* p. 72.
10. *Ibid.*
11. *Ibid.,* p. 74.
12. *Ibid.,* p. 56.
13. Lebergott, *op. cit.,* p. 215.
14. *Historical Statistics, op. cit.,* p. 409.
15. Henry David, "Labor Protests: The Pullman Strike," in Earl Schench Miers (ed.), *The American Story,* Channel Press, 1956, pp. 224 ff.
16. *Ibid.*
17. *Historical Statistics, op. cit.,* pp. 76 ff.
18. *Ibid.*

19. *Ibid.*
20. Albert Rees, "Patterns of Wages, Prices, Productivity," in *Wages, Prices, Profits and Productivity*, American Assembly, Columbia University, June, 1959, pp. 15–16.
21. *Ibid.*, p. 92.
22. *Ibid.*, p. 91.
23. Robert W. Smuts, "The Living Conditions of the American Worker in 1890," unpublished manuscript, Conservation of Human Resources Project, Columbia University.
24. *Historical Statistics, op. cit.*, p. 98.
25. *Ibid.*
26. *Ibid.*, p. 99.

CHAPTER VI. THE NEW ERA AND THE GREAT DEPRESSION

1. Lebergott, *op. cit.*, p. 215.
2. *Recent Economic Changes in the United States,* Report of the Committee on Recent Economic Changes, Vol. II, p. 450.
3. *Recent Social Trends in the United States,* President's Research Committee on Social Trends, McGraw-Hill, 1933, p. 579.
4. *Womanpower, op. cit.*, p. 114.
5. *Ibid.*, p. 144.
6. Albert Rees, *New Measures of Wage-Earner Compensation in Manufacturing,* Occ. Paper 75, National Bureau of Economic Research, New York, 1960, p. 3.
7. *Historical Statistics, op. cit.*, p. 91.
8. Rees, "Patterns of Wages, Prices, Productivity," *op. cit.*, p. 15.
9. *Historical Statistics, op. cit.*, p. 94.
10. *Ibid.*, p. 98.
11. *Ibid.*, p. 99.
12. Lebergott, *op. cit.*, p. 215.
13. Eli Ginzberg, *The Illusion of Economic Stability*, Harper & Bros., 1939, *passim.*
14. *Historical Statistics, op. cit.*, p. 139.
15. *Ibid.*, p. 73.
16. *Ibid.*
17. Lebergott, *op. cit.*, p. 215.
18. *Recent Economic Changes, op. cit.*, Vol. II, p. 548.
19. *Historical Statistics, op. cit.*, p. 74.
20. *Recent Social Trends, op. cit.*, p. 832.
21. *Ibid.*, p. 834.
22. *Historical Statistics, op. cit.*, p. 573.
23. *Recent Social Trends, op. cit.*, p. 827.
24. *Statistical Abstract of the U.S. 1961*, U. S. Dept. of Commerce, p. 106.
25. *Historical Statistics, op. cit.*, p. 657.
26. Ginzberg, *op. cit.*, p. 146.
27. *Ibid.*, p. 153.
28. *Ibid.*, p. 172.

29. *Historical Statistics, op. cit.,* p. 73.
30. Lebergott, *op. cit.,* p. 215.
31. *Historical Statistics, op. cit.,* p. 92.
32. *Ibid.,* p. 200.
33. *Ibid.,* p. 97.
34. *Ibid.,* p. 98.
35. *Rees, New Measures . . . , op. cit.,* p. 3.
36. *The American Worker's Fact Book,* U. S. Dept. of Labor, 1960.

CHAPTER IX. WORLD WAR II AND AFTER

1. *Historical Statistics, op. cit.,* p. 70.
2. *Ibid.*
3. *Statistical Abstract, op. cit.,* p. 240.
4. *Historical Statistics,* op. cit., p. 71.
5. *Ibid.,* p. 70.
6. Lebergott, *op. cit.,* p. 216.
7. *Ibid.*
8. *Statistical Abstract, op. cit.,* p. 213.
9. Columbia University Press, 1956, *passim.*
10. *Economic Report of the President,* January, 1962, p. 240.
11. *Ibid.,* p. 241.
12. *Ibid.,* p. 242.
13. Rees, "Patterns of Wages, Prices, Productivity," *op. cit.,* pp. 15–16.
14. Based on Studies of the U. S. Dept. of Labor, *Bul. No.* 1308: *Employer Expenditures for Selected Supplementary Remuneration,* 1959, p. 8.
15. *Income of Families and Persons in the United States: 1960,* Current Population Reports, Series P-60, No. 37, January 17, 1962, pp. 1–2.
16. *Ibid.,* pp. 4–5.
17. *Ibid.,* p. 9.
18. *Ibid.,* p. 26.
19. *Ibid.,* p. 54.
20. *Ibid.*
21. *Ibid.,* p. 32.
22. *Ibid.,* p. 30.
23. *Historical Statistics, op. cit.,* p. 96.
24. *Statistical Abstract, op. cit.,* p. 222.
25. *Monthly Report on the Labor Force,* March, 1962, U. S. Dept. of Labor.
26. *Statistical Abstract, op. cit.,* p. 224.
27. *Ibid.*
28. *Ibid.*
29. *Ibid.*
30. *Ibid.,* p. 260.
31. *Ibid.,* p. 261.
32. *Ibid.,* p. 262.
33. *The American Worker's Fact Book: 1960, op. cit.,* pp. 174 ff.

Index
of
Cases

Index of Cases

Mill and Mine

1. Giant Steel Worker. Louis Adamic, *From Many Lands,* Harper, New York, 1940, pp. 147 ff.
2. Life in Homestead. Margaret F. Byington, *Homestead,* "The Pittsburgh Survey," Russell Sage Foundation, New York, 1910, pp. 59 ff.
3. Lithuanian Meat Packer. Anatanas Kaztauskis, "From Lithuania to the Chicago Stockyards," *The Independent,* LVII, 1 (1904), pp. 241 ff.
4. Anthracite Miner. Testimony before *The Industrial Commission* by Benjamin Jones, 1899, XII, pp. 138 ff.
5. Miner's Story. "A Miner's Story," *The Independent,* LIV, 2 (1902).
6. Colorado Miner. Ross B. Mundy, "The Story of a Cripple Creek Miner," *The Independent,* LVII, 1 (1904), pp. 380 ff.

Young Men at Work

7. Pottery Worker. Testimony before *The Industrial Commission* by John W. Morgan, 1901, Vol. XIV, pp. 643 ff.
8. On a Cattleboat. Frances A. Kellor, *Out of Work,* Putnam's, New York, 1915, pp. 174 ff.
9. Hoboken Seaman. Josiah Flynt (pseud.), *My Life,* Willard, Outing, New York, 1908, pp. 120 ff.
10. San Francisco Drayman. *Teamster Life in San Francisco Before World War I* as told by William J. Conboy to Corinne L. Gilb, Oral History Project, Institute of Industrial Relations, University of California, Berkeley, 1957.
11. Alteration Painter. Philip Zausner, *Unvarnished,* Brotherhood, New York, 1941, pp. 28 ff.
12. Kansas Farm Hand. M. A. Barber, "On the Recollections of a Hired Man," in Thomas Nixon Carver (ed.), *Selected Readings in Rural Economics,* Ginn, Boston, 1916, pp. 547 ff.

13. An Italian Bootblack. Rocco Corresco, "Biography of a Bootblack," *The Independent*, LIV, 4 (1902), pp. 2863 ff.

14. Lumberman. Kellor, *op. cit.*, pp. 130 ff.

15. Six Months' Work, Not One Penny. *Ibid.*, pp. 116 ff.

16. Jack-of-All-Trades. Walter A. Wyckoff, *The Workers*, Vol. II of *The West*, Scribner, 1899, *passim*.

Women Workers

17. Shirt Worker. Mrs. John Van Vorst and Marie Van Vorst, *The Woman Who Toils*, Doubleday, Page, New York, 1903, Ch. III.

18. Shoe Presser. *Ibid.*, Ch. VII.

19. Pickle Processor. *Ibid.*, Ch. II.

20. The Last Box Was Done. Dorothy Richardson, *The Long Day*, Century, New York, 1906, Ch. VII.

21. The Star Rose-Maker. *Ibid.*, Ch. XII.

22. From Salesgirl to Stenographer. *Ibid.*, Epilogue.

23. Salesgirl. "A Salesgirl's Story," *The Independent*, LIV, 3 (1902), pp. 1818 ff.

24. Laundry Worker. Richardson, *op. cit.*, Ch. XV.

25. Jobs for Domestics. Kellor, *op. cit.*, Ch. VII.

26. Washerwoman. "A Washerwoman," *The Independent*, LVII, 2 (1904), pp. 1073 ff.

27. Home-work. Kellor, *op. cit.* Ch. II.

Workers in the Slums

28. Sweaters of Jewtown. Jacob A. Riis, *How the Other Half Lives*, Scribner's, New York, 1890, pp. 124 ff.

29. Capmaker. Rose Schneiderman, "A Cap Maker's Story," *The Independent*, LVIII, 2 (1905), pp. 935 ff.

30. Poor Without Work. Rose Cohen, *Out of the Shadow*, Doran, New York, 1918, pp. 83 ff.

31. Sweatshop Girl. Sadie Froune, "The Story of a Sweatship Girl," *The Independent*, LV, 3 (1902), pp. 2279 ff.

32. Children in a Southern Cotton Mill. Van Vorst and Van Vorst, *op. cit.*, Ch. IX.

33. Boys and Girls Should Work. Testimony before *The Industrial Commission* by C. C. Houston, Editor, *Journal of Labor*, Atlanta, Ga., 1901, Vol. VII, pp. 550 ff.

Up the Skill Ladder

34. Hot Blast Man. Charles Rumford Walker, *Steel, The Diary of a Furnace Worker*, Atlantic Monthly Press, Boston, 1922, Ch. III.

35. Fifty-four Years in the Mill. Robert J. Havighurst, Interview.

36. The Air Hammerer. *Ibid.*

37. The Old-Time Roller. *Ibid.*

38. Painter by Trade. *Ibid.*

39. Steel and All That. Whiting Williams, *What's On the Worker's Mind?*, Scribner's, New York, 1920, pp. 13 ff.

The Job Is Satisfactory

40. G.M. Draftsman. *My Job and Why I Like It*, General Motors, 1948, pp. 71 ff.

41. Negro Workers. E. Franklin Frazier, *The Negro Family in the United States*, Dryden Press, 1948, pp. 338 ff.

42. Ex-Electrician. Eli Ginzberg, Interview.